VISUAL QUICKSTART GUIDE

MAYA 7

FOR WINDOWS AND MACINTOSH

Danny Riddell, Morgan Robinson, and Nathaniel Stein

⬤ Peachpit Press

Visual QuickStart Guide
Maya 7 for Windows and Macintosh
Danny Riddell, Morgan Robinson, and Nathaniel Stein

Peachpit Press

1249 Eighth Street
Berkeley, CA 94710
510/524-2178
800/283-9444
510/524-2221 (fax)
Find us on the World Wide Web at: http://www.peachpit.com
To report errors, please send a note to errata@peachpit.com
Peachpit Press is a division of Pearson Education

Project and Development Editor: Kristin Kalning
Associate Project Editor: Alison Kelley
Production Editor: Myrna Vladic
Copyeditor and Proofreader: Tiffany Taylor
Tech Editor: Alexander Kucera
Compositor: Debbie Roberti, Espresso Graphics
Indexer: Joy Dean Lee
Cover design: Peachpit Press

ISBN 0-321-34899-0

9 8 7 6 5 4 3 2 1

Printed and bound in the United States of America

Dedication

To the memory of Steve Anzovin.

Acknowledgements

Nat Stein:
I would like to thank Steve, for giving me this opportunity; Kristin Kalning for being a pleasure to work with and making this easy the first time around; and Tiffany Taylor and Alexander Kucera for their knowledgeable reviews. I would also like to thank Raf Anzovin for his contribution and expertise, and the rest of Anzovin Studio for answering my questions; Danny Riddell and Adrian Dimond for the quality of the previous edition; and my friends for their late night moral support and always asking how the book is going. A big thanks to Morgan, for writing all the chapters I didn't want, and for her meticulous care in doing so.

Morgan Robinson:
Thanks to Kristin, Alexander, and Tiffany, who were a pleasure to work with, and to everyone else at Peachpit Press who made this book happen; to Nat, for keeping track of everything and writing more than half the chapters; and to my family, who didn't get to see much of me during this process. Finally, thanks to Steve Anzovin, for the opportunity to work on this book and for all of his support and encouragement over the years.

TABLE OF CONTENTS

INTRODUCTION

Welcome to *Maya 7 for Windows & Macintosh: Visual QuickStart Guide.*

Maya® is a high-end 3D graphics program. It's widely used in the film and game industries to produce many of the CG movies, special effects, games, and commercials you see daily. From characters to critters to cars, Maya provides a full toolset for each step of your project. Whether your aims are personal or professional, realistic or stylized, Maya's depth can help you bring your vision to life.

Maya has long been the industry standard software for both film and television at studios worldwide. Its myriad toolsets, powerful scripting language, and plentiful rendering options make it a good option for a variety of tasks. Recently, this flexibility, as well as improvements to the polygonal modeling tools, have made Maya the software package of choice for much of the game industry as well.

This book introduces you to Maya's interface and features. You'll soon realize, though, that Maya has enough depth to keep you learning for years. This book covers the different fields in Maya, giving you the concepts and functionality that you'll need on your way to becoming a Maya guru.

Who Is This Book For?

If you want to learn basic 3D concepts, or if you're familiar with other 3D software and want to learn Maya, this book is for you. You should be familiar with computers and other graphics software packages, but you don't need prior 3D knowledge (although it will make Maya easier to learn). This book will guide you through the expansive Maya interface and show you how to animate and render your 3D projects. If you work through this book from cover to cover, you'll end up with a solid Maya foundation—familiarity with the user interface and the capability to model, texture, and animate 3D content.

After exploring Maya's various subject areas—modeling, shading, animation, scripting, and special effects—you may find that you're better at one or the other. As you work through this book, think about which area interests you most. Using Maya could develop into a hobby or even a career in creating 3D content for movies, product ads, and interactive entertainment!

What You Will Need

For starters, of course, you need a license for Maya or the Maya PLE (the free Personal Learning Edition) for Windows or Macintosh installed on your computer. See Maya's documentation for instructions on installing the program.

Maya's documentation will also give you information about the program's hardware requirements, or you can find it on Alias's Web site (www.alias.com). Maya is resource intensive, so you should beef up your machine as much you can manage. We recommend at least 1GB of RAM; and if you plan to do a lot of rendering, we also suggest ample processing power.

Another important aspect is the kind of video display card you use with Maya. The video card affects the speed of your real-time display and can drastically improve response times while you're working. The support section of the Alias Web site contains a current list of qualified display cards. For Windows, Quadro FX or Fire GL cards are recommended. See the Alias Web site for specific models and driver versions.

For Mac, Alias recommends the Quadro FX4500 display card. Always check the card manufacturer's Web site for driver updates, because out-of-date drivers are often shipped with cards.

Also be aware that Maya requires a three-button mouse, because the middle mouse button is used as a Virtual Slider feature for many functions. Using Maya without a three-button mouse is possible but very, very cumbersome: any serious Maya user will want to purchase a three-button mouse.

Check out the Maya documentation for minimum system requirements and additional information, or visit the Alias Web site.

Maya Versions and Flavors

This book covers Maya 7 for Windows and Mac OS X (10.4+). With Maya 7, there's little difference between the Windows and Mac versions, at least in the features covered here. However, whenever a disparity in functionality exists, we'll point it out.

Let's take a closer look at the different flavors of Maya for Windows:

◆ **Maya Complete** comes with a full set of modeling tools for working with NURBS, polygons, and subdivision surfaces. It also includes advanced character animation tools, dynamics (the use of physics to simulate real-world forces), and effects. Maya Complete is everything you need to get started doing production work for games, video, and film.

◆ **Maya Unlimited** includes all of Maya Complete's tools and features, plus Maya Cloth, Maya Fur, Advanced Modeling Tools, Fluid Dynamics, and Maya Live for Matchmoving.

Because this book is for beginning to intermediate users, it covers only those features and tools found in both versions.

What's new in Maya 7?

Maya 7 boasts improvements in almost all areas, including dozens of minor changes to make the workflow smoother, as well as some new major features in modeling, rendering, and rigging.

Changes of note include greatly improved poly modeling and UV tools, enhanced integration with Photoshop and Illustrator, and more robust hair and fur tools.

Also new in Maya 7 are toon rendering features that allow you to create images with outlines and simple, flat shading. These features allow you create the illusion of hand-drawn images and traditional cel-shaded animations.

Maya 7 now comes with full body inverse kinematics (IK) support—a new IK solver that uses the whole skeleton of the character in resolving any adjustments. Full body IK's strength lies in easily poseable characters and integration with Motion Builder technology.

For a full list of all the new improvements in Maya 7, go to www.alias.com/eng/products-services/maya/new/index.shtml.

MAYA VERSIONS AND FLAVORS

Additional Resources

Hundreds of Maya- and 3D-related resources are available on the Web. For general news about the animation industry, visit Animation World Network (AWN; www.awn.com) or Animation Nation (www.animationnation.com). You can find character animation resources and forums on CGtalk (www.cgtalk.com) and CGChar (www.cgchar-animation.com). The 10 Second Club contest (www.10secondclub.com) is a great way to get animation experience and be noticed by industry professionals. Highend3D (www.highend3d.com) and 3D Links (www.3dlinks.com) offer tutorials and forums as well as a nice collection of inspirational images and videos. Other good 3D tutorial and informational sites include 3D Café (www.3dcafe.com) and 3D Ark (www.3dark.com).

Off the Web, Eadweard Muybridge's books of photos (*Animals in Motion* and *The Human Figure in Motion*) provide great modeling and animation references. *The Animator's Survival Kit* by Richard Williams is a great book for aspiring animators to have by their side.

ADDITIONAL RESOURCES

MAYA BASICS

Maya's user interface is complex but powerful, giving you in-depth control over the application's wide range of functions. This chapter introduces you to that interface and then shows you how to set up a project, work with files, and access online help. First, though, it's a good idea to know something about the way Maya works.

About Maya

Maya is a node-based program. A *node* stores and processes related pieces of information (**Figure 1.1**). Everything you create in Maya is represented by a node or several connected nodes (**Figure 1.2**). The nodes themselves are made up of many *attributes*, which contain the information that defines the node, such as an object's position or a material's color. The advantage of this node-based architecture is that it gives you precise control over both a node's attributes and its connections to other nodes (**Figure 1.3**). This allows you to determine the exact appearance and behavior of the objects in your scene.

Maya's coordinate system

Traditional graphics applications, like Adobe Photoshop, are used to create two-dimensional images. As such, they work with two axes, usually *x* and *y* (**Figure 1.4**). An XY coordinate system provides height and width but lacks depth. A skilled artist can create the illusion of three-dimensional objects, but a Photoshop file is still flat, like a painting.

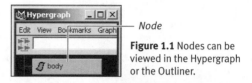

Node

Figure 1.1 Nodes can be viewed in the Hypergraph or the Outliner.

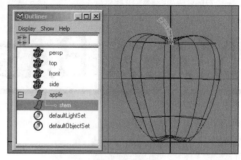

Figure 1.2 Like everything in Maya, this apple is made out of nodes. Here the stem node is selected, so the stem geometry is highlighted.

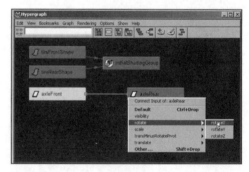

Figure 1.3 You can connect nodes in the Hypergraph. Arrows indicate pre-existing connections.

Y axis   *X axis*

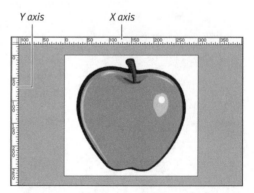

Figure 1.4 Flat, 2D graphics use the *x* and *y* axes but lack three-dimensional definition.

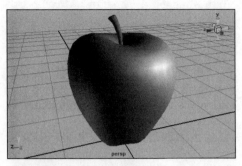

Figure 1.5 Adding another axis allows objects to be created in three-dimensional space rather than on a flat plane.

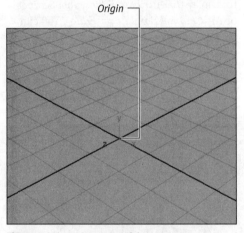

Figure 1.6 The center point of the Maya scene is called the *origin*. All directional values start at 0 from the origin.

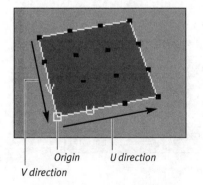

Figure 1.7 Each surface is described with a U direction and a V direction.

3D applications like Maya add a third axis, z (**Figure 1.5**). The addition of this third axis allows you to create objects with depth. Although these objects are still displayed on a 2D screen, they are genuinely three-dimensional. This means that using Maya is more like sculpting than like painting.

In an XYZ coordinate system, every point is defined by three numbers, which represent its x, y, and z values. The point 0, 0, 0 is called the *origin* (**Figure 1.6**). Maya has two systems of coordinates: *world* and *local*. In *world space*, the origin is at the center of the scene. But when you're working in *local space*, the origin is at the center of an object.

Objects also have what's called *UV coordinate space*. A surface has a U direction and a V direction. In the simple example of a plane, the U direction goes from left to right, and the V direction goes from top to bottom (**Figure 1.7**). This system is like latitude and longitude on a world map. Just as you can find a position on earth by its latitude and longitude, you can determine a point on a surface by its U and V coordinates. This becomes especially important when you're positioning textures on a surface.

Maya's Interface

Maya is a powerful application with many tools and features. Because of this, its interface is complex, and can appear daunting at first glance. It may take you some time to learn where everything is; but once you're familiar with the Maya interface, you'll find that it's actually very organized and easy to navigate (**Figure 1.8**).

Along the top of the Maya interface is the main menu bar. Because Maya contains so many menus, they're grouped by task into five menu sets, which you can access from the pull-down menu at the far left of the Status Line. The Status Line is located directly beneath the main menu bar; it includes icons for selection functions and various common commands. Below the Status Line is the *Shelf*, which holds often-used tools, categorized in a set of tabs.

Along the left side of the interface is the *Tool Box*, which holds Maya's manipulation tools. You can use these tools to select, rotate, move, and scale objects or pieces of objects, which are called *components*. Below the Tool Box is a series of Quick Layout icons, which allow you to change what is displayed in the main window.

You can use the right side of the interface to display the *Attribute Editor*, *Tool Settings*, or the *Channel Box / Layer Editor*. You can change which of these is displayed by using the corresponding icons on the far right of the Status Line.

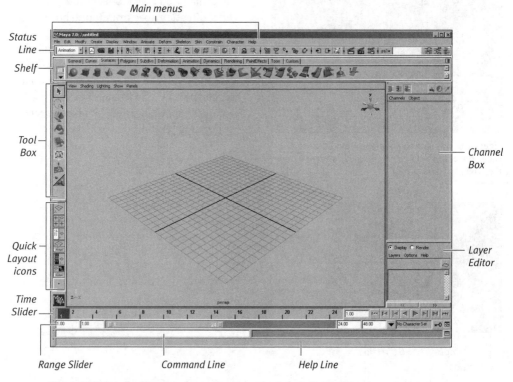

Figure 1.8 This is the Maya interface as it appears by default. Many of the elements shown here can be hidden or customized to suit the task at hand.

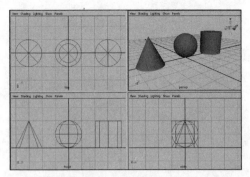

Figure 1.9 A four-panel view lets you see three orthographic views (Top, Front, and Side) at the same time as your Perspective view.

View Compass

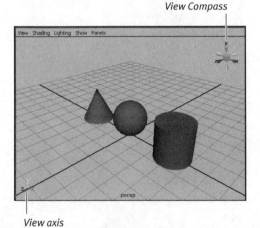

View axis

Figure 1.10 The View Compass lets you switch to a different view by clicking one of its six component cones or the central cube.

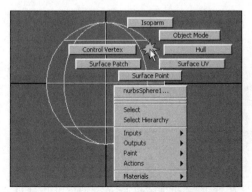

Figure 1.11 A marking menu displays context-based options.

At the bottom of the interface are the *Range Slider* and *Time Slider*, which allow you to control your position in time for animation; the *Command Line*, which you can use to enter text-based commands; and the *Help Line*, which displays useful information.

Framed by all of these interface elements is the *main window*. The main window can display one or more *panels* (**Figure 1.9**), and each panel can show a different *view* of your scene. A view lets you see what your scene looks like from a specific angle, either from a camera you've created or from one of Maya's four standard cameras: *front*, *top*, *side*, and *persp*. Panels can also display non-view windows, like the Outliner or the Hypergraph. The main window defaults to a single panel displaying the "Persp" or Perspective view.

By default, all views in Maya display a *view axis* in the lower-left corner, which indicates the orientation of the *x*, *y*, and *z* axes. In addition to a view axis, the Perspective view includes the *View Compass* in the upper-right corner. The View Compass allows you to quickly switch to any one of six orthographic views (Front, Back, Top, Bottom, Left, and Right) or to the default Perspective view (**Figure 1.10**).

In addition to the main menu bar, you can access menus from within individual panels and through *marking menus* (**Figure 1.11**). Marking menus provide a convenient way to quickly access tools or commands. They appear when you right-click an object or click within one of the regions of the Hotbox (see "About the Hotbox," later in this chapter).

✔ Tip

■ You can use the Spacebar to quickly switch from a single panel view to a multi-panel view or vice versa. Tap it quickly while holding your mouse over a panel.

Using the Shelf

The Shelf gives you a place to store often-used tools and commands. Maya provides an extensive set of preset shelves (**Figure 1.12**), but you can also add items and new shelves to fit your own style of working. For instance, you can create one shelf for all the modeling tools you frequently use and another shelf for your favorite rendering tools.

To create a new shelf:

1. Click and hold the arrow to the left of the Shelf to display the pop-up menu.

2. Select New Shelf.

3. When prompted, enter a name for the shelf.

    A new shelf tab is added to the Shelf.

To add an item to a shelf:

1. Select the shelf tab to which you want to add the item.

2. Select the menu item you want to add while pressing Ctrl/Control and Shift at the same time.

    The object is added to the shelf.

To remove an item from a shelf:

◆ Using the middle mouse button, drag the icon from the shelf to the trash icon on the right side of the shelf.

    The object is removed from the shelf.

Figure 1.12 The Shelf holds tools and commands, categorized by type. If a shelf tab contains more icons than can fit your Maya window, use the scroll bar to the right of the tab to display the rest.

MAYA'S INTERFACE

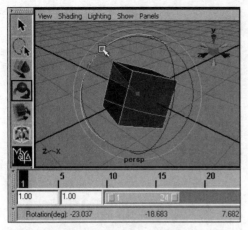

Figure 1.13 The Help Line, at the bottom of Maya's interface, shows helpful information about commands and transformations. Here it shows the rotation of a cube in degrees.

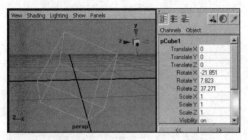

Figure 1.14 The Channel Box, at right, displays information about a selected object, including its position (translate), scale, and rotation.

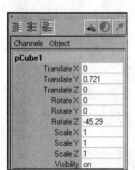

Figure 1.15 By default, the Channel Box shows ten attribute listings for an object.

About the Help Line

The Help Line provides information about menu items or the tool you have selected. And if you use one of the transform tools to move, rotate, or scale an object, the Help Line reflects the change numerically (**Figure 1.13**).

About the Channel Box

The Channel Box lists a selected object's *keyable* attributes (**Figure 1.14**). Keyable attributes are object properties that can be animated. To change an attribute's value in the Channel Box, you can enter values in the attribute's field; or, click the attribute's name, and then click and drag with the middle mouse button in any view panel.

Ten default attributes display in the Channel Box when an object is selected (**Figure 1.15**): Translate X, Translate Y, Translate Z, Rotate X, Rotate Y, Rotate Z, Scale X, Scale Y, Scale Z (known collectively as *transforms*), and Visibility. You can add other attributes to the Channel Box list by using the Channel Control, which can be found in the Window > General Editors menu.

MAYA'S INTERFACE

If more than one object is selected, the Channel Box displays the last object selected; however, any value change to an attribute is applied to all selected objects. You can also click and drag across multiple fields in the Channel Box to select them (**Figure 1.16**). With multiple attributes selected, you can change all the values at once, rather than making the same change to each attribute individually.

Below the attributes list are the Shapes and Inputs sections (**Figure 1.17**). These two sections list the shape and input nodes associated with an object. Input nodes form the object's *construction history*; you can view or modify their attributes by clicking a node name.

✔ Tip

■ If you hold down Ctrl/⌘ while dragging to scale or translate an object, the two *unselected* axes change together.

About the Attribute Editor

The Attribute Editor is similar to the Channel Box in that it allows you to view and change attributes. However, the Attribute Editor provides a much more detailed representation of the object's attributes, including those that aren't keyable (**Figure 1.18**). Attributes are categorized, and you can hide or reveal each category using the small arrow to its left. In addition to working with the object's attributes, you can use the tabs at the top of the Attribute Editor to access the attributes of other associated nodes.

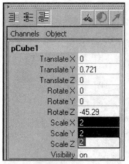

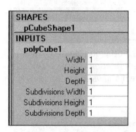

Figure 1.16 If you select multiple attributes in the Channel Box, you can change them simultaneously.

Figure 1.17 Input node attributes can be adjusted to modify an object after it has been created.

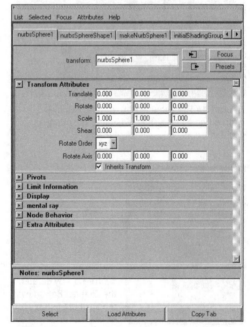

Figure 1.18 The Attribute Editor contains all the information about a selected object.

MAYA'S INTERFACE

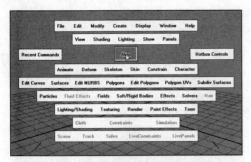

Figure 1.19 The Hotbox appears at the mouse pointer's location when you hold down the [Spacebar]; it disappears when you release the [Spacebar].

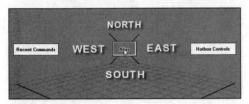

Figure 1.20 Clicking each of the five Hotbox regions— North, South, East, West, and Center—reveals a different marking menu. The Center region is defined by the Alias symbol.

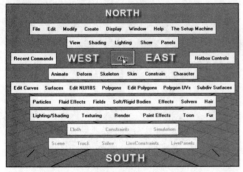

Figure 1.21 The regions of the Hotbox can be accessed even when all menu sets are visible.

About the Hotbox

The Hotbox is a collection of menu sets. You can access it from anywhere your mouse pointer is located by holding down the [Spacebar] (**Figure 1.19**). By default, the Hotbox displays all of Maya's menu sets, but you can hide any or all of them.

To hide all menu sets in the Hotbox:

1. Hold down the [Spacebar].

   The Hotbox appears for as long as you hold down the [Spacebar].

2. Click and hold on Hotbox Controls.

   A marking menu appears at the point where you click.

3. While still holding down the [Spacebar] and the mouse button, select Hide All from the marking menu. Release the mouse button, but continue to hold down the [Spacebar].

   The menus disappear, leaving Recent Commands and Hotbox Controls buttons (see **Figure 1.20**). You can use Hotbox Controls to restore the menu sets at any time.

The advantage of hiding these menu sets is that doing so provides easier access to the marking menus. The Hotbox includes five different marking menus, which you can access by clicking one of the Hotbox's five regions: North, South, East, West, and Center (Figure 1.20). These regions are accessible in the default configuration, but you must click outside of the Hotbox's menu sets (**Figure 1.21**).

The default marking menu for the North region holds shortcuts to different panel layouts (**Figure 1.22**). The Center marking menu changes the current panel to a different view (**Figure 1.23**)—for example, from a Front view to a Perspective view. The South marking menu changes the contents of the selected panel to any of the non-view options (**Figure 1.24**)—for example, the Outliner (see "About the Outliner," later in this chapter). The West marking menu holds preset selection masks (**Figure 1.25**), which filter the object types that can be selected. The East marking menu hides or displays specific user-interface elements (**Figure 1.26**)—for example, allowing you to hide the Shelf to create more screen space.

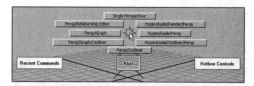

Figure 1.22 In the North marking menu, you can select from different interface layouts.

Figure 1.23 You can change views using the Hotbox's Center marking menu.

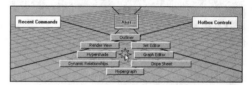

Figure 1.24 The South marking menu allows you to change the contents of panels.

Figure 1.25 You can change selection modes with the West marking menu.

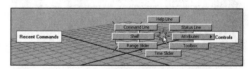

Figure 1.26 You can toggle interface elements on and off with the East marking menu.

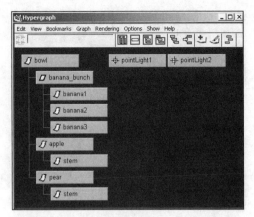

Figure 1.27 Here the Hypergraph is used to display the hierarchy of a simple scene.

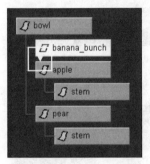

Figure 1.28 You can collapse a branch of the hierarchy to hide its nodes.

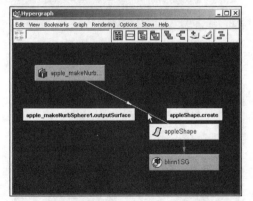

Figure 1.29 Hold your mouse over a line to see what attributes it connects.

About the Hypergraph

The Hypergraph window shows how all the nodes in your Maya scene are organized and connected. The organization of the scene's nodes in parent-child relationships is called the *scene hierarchy*. Nodes in the scene hierarchy can also be connected to each other. You can view and modify the scene hierarchy and the connections between nodes in the Hypergraph (**Figure 1.27**).

To show the Hypergraph:

◆ From the Window menu, choose Hypergraph.

The number of nodes in your scene hierarchy will quickly increase as your scene becomes more complex. If you want to focus on a specific area of the hierarchy, you can collapse any branch you aren't currently working with by double-clicking its topmost node. The nodes below it disappear, and a red arrow indicates that part of the hierarchy has been hidden (**Figure 1.28**). Double-click the branch again to expand it one node at a time, or right-click the top node and select Expand All from the pop-up menu.

The Hypergraph can also display *input and output connections*, which show how the attributes of various nodes are connected. To view these connections, select a node and click the Show Input and Output Connections icon. The arrows on the lines between nodes show the direction of the connections, and you can hold your mouse over any line to see the attributes to which it connects (**Figure 1.29**).

Although most of the nodes and connections in your scene will be generated automatically as you use Maya's other tools, you can also use the Hypergraph to connect nodes directly.

To connect two nodes in the Hypergraph

1. Right-click the right side of the first node.

2. Select the attribute you want to connect (**Figure 1.30**).

3. Right-click anywhere on the second node.

4. Select the attribute you want to connect to (**Figure 1.31**).

    A connection is created between the two nodes (**Figure 1.32**). The attribute you selected from the first node now controls the attribute you selected from the second node.

To delete a connection between two nodes:

1. Click the line representing the connection.

2. Press (Delete).

    The connection is removed.

✔ Tip

- Each Maya object type has an associated icon (**Figure 1.33**). As you get more familiar with Maya, you'll begin to recognize these icons. For example, a CV (Control Vertex) Curve tool's icon is 🖾 and a Spot Light's icon is 🔦. As an additional visual cue, non-animated nodes are rectangular, whereas animated nodes appear slanted (**Figure 1.34**).

Figure 1.30 You can connect any attribute of any node in the Hypergraph.

Figure 1.31 When connecting an attribute to another node, the compatible attributes of that node are displayed for you to choose from.

Figure 1.32 The X rotation of two sets of wheels has been connected. Now, when the front wheels are rotated, the back wheels spin as well.

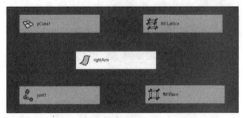

Figure 1.33 A small icon on each node reveals that node's object type. For example, a surface node (center) has a small, blue icon that resembles a simple surface.

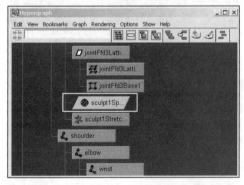

Figure 1.34 Animated nodes appear slanted, making it easy to distinguish them.

Figure 1.35 The Outliner is less powerful but often more convenient than the Hypergraph.

Figure 1.36 The default camera views and sets appear in the Outliner before any objects are created.

Figure 1.37 To see an object's children, click the plus signs to expand the hierarchy.

About the Outliner

The Outliner is similar to the Hypergraph; but it displays the hierarchy in a small, vertical window (**Figure 1.35**), which makes it easier to find and select objects. You can use the Outliner to change an object's position in the hierarchy as well as to quickly select objects.

Before any objects are created, you'll see several icons in the Outliner. These are the standard camera nodes and the defaultLightSet and defaultObjectSet nodes (**Figure 1.36**). As each new object is created, a new node appears. Once objects have been parented or grouped and a hierarchy of nodes has been established, a plus sign appears next to the top node in the hierarchy; you can click it to expand the list of objects within the hierarchy (**Figure 1.37**).

To show the Outliner

◆ From the Window menu, choose Outliner.

Beginning a Project

Because of Maya's complexity and the numerous files that may be produced for each project, an organized file structure is essential. Maya makes building this structure easier by allowing you to create a special folder set called a *project*.

Creating a new project automatically sets it as the working project, so Maya knows which folders to put your newly created files in, and where to start looking when you open pre-existing files. However, if you work on multiple projects, you'll need to set the project whenever you switch back and forth.

To create a new project:

1. Choose File > Project > New (**Figure 1.38**).

2. Enter a name for the project in the Name field at the top of the dialog box that appears.

3. Click Browse (next to the Location field), and select a folder in which to create the project folders (**Figure 1.39**).

4. Click Use Defaults to use preset folder names (**Figure 1.40**).

5. Click Accept.

   A project folder is created at the specified location; it has multiple subfolders created with the default folder names.

Figure 1.38
Creating a new project places a new project folder on your hard drive, with multiple subfolders to organize images, renders, textures, and scene files.

Figure 1.39
Browse to a folder where you want to consistently place new project files.

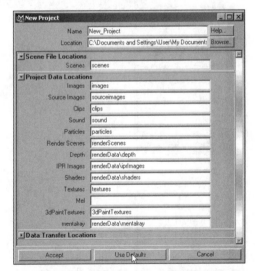

Figure 1.40 Using the default names for the folders helps maintain consistency among projects.

BEGINNING A PROJECT

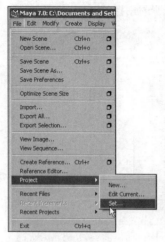

Figure 1.41
The project you set as the working project determines where Maya places saved files.

Figure 1.42 Maya opens with a new scene by default. If you've saved this scene or if you'd like to start over, select File > New Scene.

To set a project:

1. Choose File > Project > Set (**Figure 1.41**).

2. Browse to and select the folder for the project you want to use.

3. Click OK to set the project.

   The working project is set to the selected project. Maya will use the associated sub-folders when saving and opening files.

Using files

A Maya working file is called a *scene file;* it can be saved, opened, and imported into other scene files.

To create a new scene:

◆ Choose File > New Scene (**Figure 1.42**). A blank Maya scene is created.

✔ Tip

■ When you create a new scene, you may want it to have customized settings or content by default. You can set any scene file as your default new scene under New Scene Options. Click the box next to New Scene in the File menu to display this window.

BEGINNING A PROJECT

To save a scene:

1. Choose File > Save Scene.

The Save dialog box appears the first time a file is saved.

2. Click the pop-up menu next to "Look in" to select a folder in which to save the file (**Figure 1.43**).

If you have set the project correctly, the dialog box displays the scenes folder inside the project folder you set.

3. Enter a name for the file in the "File name" field, and click Save.

The scene is now saved in the Scenes folder.

✔ Tip

■ Maya allows you to save your scene as either of two different file types: Maya ASCII (.ma) or Maya Binary (.mb). Maya Binary files are smaller, while Maya ASCII files allow you to view and modify your scene in any text editor. Maya Binary is the default format.

To open a scene:

1. Choose File > Open Scene.

The Open Scene dialog box appears (**Figure 1.44**).

2. Select the file you want to open, and click Open.

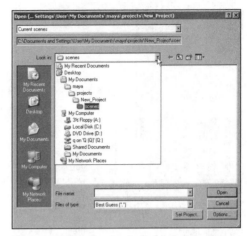

Figure 1.43 If a project has been set, the Save dialog defaults to that project's scenes folder.

Figure 1.44 Like the Save dialog, the Open dialog automatically starts in the current project's scenes folder.

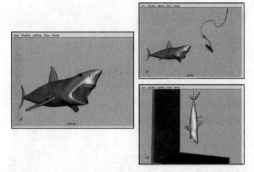

Figure 1.45 Referencing a file into multiple scenes allows the original scene file to be edited; the reference files inherit the changes.

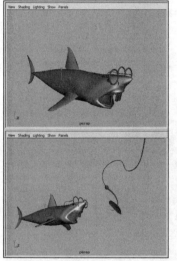

Figure 1.46 Changes made to a referenced file are automatically included in each scene in which the referenced file is used.

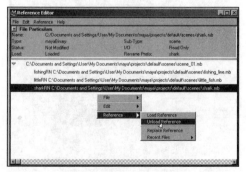

Figure 1.47 Unloading references can greatly improve real-time performance while animating.

Importing, Exporting, and Referencing

There are two ways to bring files and geometry into a Maya scene: importing and referencing. When you *import* a file into Maya, you're merging a copy of the file's contents into the current scene. If you make changes to the original file, they aren't reflected in that scene, and vice versa.

Alternately, you can use the same file in multiple scenes by *referencing* it (**Figure 1.45**). A referenced file isn't copied into a scene; instead, it's loaded into a scene every time you open it. Referencing a file allows you to edit the original file and have those revisions reflected in all the scene files that use the reference. For instance, you can create a character in one file and then reference it into different files for each camera shot in your animation. If you later want to make changes to the character, you can open the original character file, make the changes, and then save the file. When you open your animation files, your character will be updated (**Figure 1.46**).

In addition to importing and referencing, you can also export objects out of a scene.

✔ Tips

■ When you're editing referenced files, the names of nodes and objects become extremely important. If the names change in the original file, then any scene that refers to them will no longer be able to find those objects.

■ You can temporarily unload referenced files in the Reference Editor to make complex scenes more manageable (**Figure 1.47**).

To import a file:

1. Choose File > Import (**Figure 1.48**).
   The Import dialog box opens.

2. Navigate to the folder where the file you want to import is located.

3. Click the file you wish to import, and then click Import.
   The file is imported into the scene.

To reference a file:

1. Choose File > Create Reference (**Figure 1.49**).
   The Reference dialog box opens.

2. Navigate to the folder where the file you want to reference is located.

3. Click the file you want to reference, and then click Reference.
   The file is referenced into the scene.

To export selected objects:

1. Select the objects you want to export.

2. Choose File > Export Selection (**Figure 1.50**).
   The Export window opens.

3. Navigate to the folder where you want to place the exported file, and enter a filename.

4. Click Export.
   The selected objects are exported.

Figure 1.48 Importing a file into another scene combines the imported file with the open file.

Figure 1.49 Select File > Create Reference to reference a file into an existing scene.

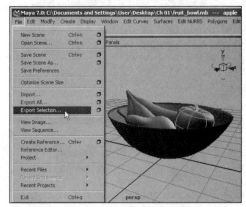

Figure 1.50 This apple has been selected to be exported separately from the rest of the scene.

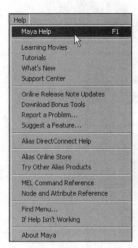

Maya Help

Maya includes a variety of reference materials, which you can find under the Help menu in the upper-right corner of the interface. Here you'll find Maya's manual, learning movies and tutorials, links to the Maya Support Center and other Alias sites, and a Find Menu feature in case you forget where a particular function is located (**Figure 1.51**).

Figure 1.51 The Help menu puts all of Maya's reference and support materials in one place.

When you select Maya Help or Tutorials from the Help menu, a Web browser opens with the appropriate index loaded. You can browse through this index or enter a topic in the search box at the top of the window. You'll be given a list of links for both Information and Tutorial documents (**Figure 1.52**).

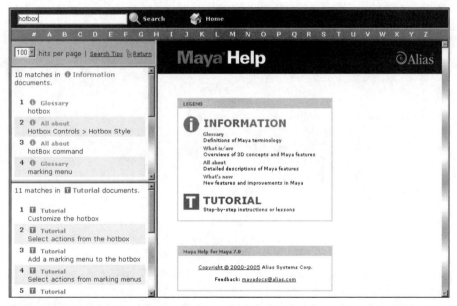

Figure 1.52 Maya Help's search feature displays multiple listings for information and tutorials on a specified topic.

In addition to the primary Help menu, **Maya** includes context-based Help menus in **many** of its sub-windows. These menus provide quick access to the corresponding topics in Maya Help (**Figure 1.53**).

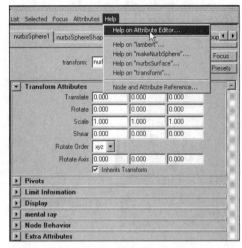

Figure 1.53 Many of Maya's windows have their own context-based Help menu.

Navigating and Changing the Interface

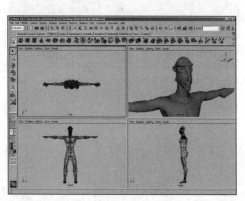

Figure 2.1 You can customize almost every aspect of Maya's interface.

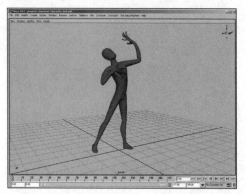

Figure 2.2 By using keyboard shortcuts and the Hotbox, you can work effectively in Maya with a minimal interface.

Maya's interface is highly customizable, so you can alter it to suit your current project and workflow. For example, if you're modeling, you may want to hide the animation controls and use a standard four-view layout (**Figure 2.1**). If you're animating, you can hide everything but the animation controls and use a single Perspective view (**Figure 2.2**). However, even when the menus are hidden, you can access them via the Hotbox by holding down the Spacebar.

You choose how much detail is displayed in any given view by hiding or showing specific object types and by changing display options for shading and lighting. You can also *dolly*, *track*, and *tumble* to see your scene from any angle.

In this chapter, you'll learn how to use these and other commands to navigate the scene. We'll also cover some of the ways you can change Maya's interface.

Dollying, Tracking, and Tumbling

Dollying, *tracking*, and *tumbling* are movie industry terms for the camera movements that let you change your view of a scene. In Maya, virtual cameras provide you with different views of your 3D scene. Because you're always looking through a camera, dollying, tracking, and tumbling provide ways to move that camera around the scene. This movement changes the distance and angle at which you see the objects in a scene, which is very important when working in Maya. Whether you're modeling or animating, you need to be able to see objects from many different perspectives.

Tracking a view moves that view up, down, or sideways. You might track a view to get a look at an object that's currently out of view.

Dollying a view moves its camera "in" or "out," bringing objects closer (zooming in) to make them appear larger, or moving them farther away (zooming out) to make them appear smaller.

Tumbling a view visually rotates it around the center of interest—useful for getting the full 3D effect of the scene. For example, you can tumble around an object to get a view of its front, back, and sides from any angle.

To track a view:

1. Move the mouse over any panel.

2. Hold down [Alt] ([⌘] on a Macintosh), and use the middle mouse button to drag the scene in the desired direction (**Figure 2.3**).

To dolly a view:

1. Move the mouse over any panel.

2. Hold down [Alt]/[⌘] plus the right mouse button, and drag left to shrink the view or right to enlarge the view (**Figure 2.4**).

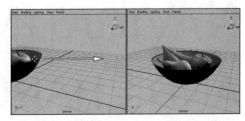

Figure 2.3 Tracking moves a view up, down, or sideways. Here we track right in a scene of a fruit bowl.

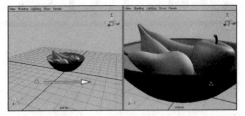

Figure 2.4 Dollying is used to zoom in and out of the scene; moving the mouse right while dollying enlarges the view.

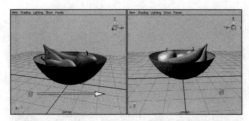

Figure 2.5 Tumbling rotates a view around its center point. Here we tumble 180 degrees around the fruit bowl.

To tumble the view:

1. Move the mouse over the Perspective view.

2. Hold down [Alt]/[⌘], and use the left mouse button to drag and rotate the scene in the direction desired (**Figure 2.5**).

✔ Tips

- You can use the scroll wheel on your mouse to dolly without holding down any other mouse buttons. Scrolling up enlarges the view, and scrolling down shrinks it.

- You can marquee-zoom in by pressing [Ctrl] and [Alt]/[⌘] while dragging a marquee from upper left to lower right with the left mouse button. You can zoom out by dragging from lower right to upper left. The smaller the square, the larger the zoom.

- You can hold [Shift] while tumbling to constrain the tumble along a specific axis.

- You can find additional camera movement tools in the View > Camera Tools menu in any view panel. This menu also includes options for dolly, track, and tumble, accessible by clicking the box to the right of the corresponding menu item.

DOLLYING, TRACKING, AND TUMBLING

Using the View Menu

The View menu offers a number of additional camera tools and settings. In this chapter we'll cover only the options that relate to navigation. We'll go into more depth about the camera settings that are used for rendering in Chapter 16.

The ability to bookmark your current panel's viewpoint can be useful when navigating your scene. This option lets you preserve the specific camera position and angle in your view so that you can return to that precise point later.

Even without creating a bookmark, you can navigate back through recent viewpoints by selecting Previous View from a panel's View menu; you can use the Next View menu option to go forward again. Alternatively, you can use the square bracket keys, ([) and (]).

The View menu also includes the Frame All and Frame Selection options, but you may find it more convenient to use the equivalent keyboard shortcuts. Framing automatically positions the camera to give the user the best view of one or more objects in a scene. The frame option can be particularly useful when you'd like to quickly zoom in on a small or distant object.

To bookmark a view:

1. From the View menu in the panel displaying the view you wish to bookmark, select the Bookmarks > Edit Bookmarks menu item (**Figure 2.6**).

2. In the Bookmark Editor, click the New Bookmark button.

3. In the Name field, type a new name for your bookmark (**Figure 2.7**).

4. Click Apply, and then click Close to complete the bookmark.

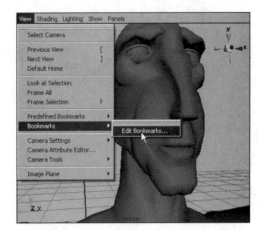

Figure 2.6 The Bookmark Editor lets you create bookmarks of your view.

Figure 2.7 The new bookmark's name changes to the name you enter.

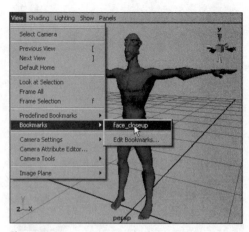

Figure 2.8 You can return to the bookmarked view at any time by selecting it from the View > Bookmarks menu.

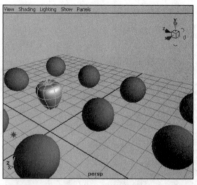

Figure 2.9 Framing an object lets you focus on it. Here we've selected an apple to frame.

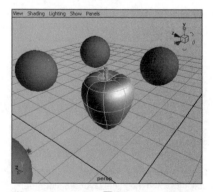

Figure 2.10 Pressing f frames the apple, centering it in the view and zooming in.

To access a bookmarked view:

◆ From the View menu of the panel for which you created the bookmark, select the Bookmarks > (bookmark name) menu item (**Figure 2.8**).

The view returns to the bookmarked viewpoint.

To frame selected objects in a view:

1. Select an object or objects (**Figure 2.9**).

2. Hold your mouse over the view you want to change.

3. Press f.

The view changes to frame your selection (**Figure 2.10**).

To frame all objects in a view:

1. Hold your mouse over the view you want to change.

2. Press a.

The view frames all of the objects in the scene (**Figure 2.11**).

✔ Tip

■ When using a multi-view layout, the commands above will only change the selected view. You can make all of the view panels frame your object or objects by pressing Shift plus f or a.

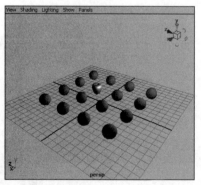

Figure 2.11 Pressing a frames all of the objects in the scene.

Changing the Layout

The main window in Maya can display from one to four panels, with each panel showing a different view of the current scene (**Figure 2.12**). A panel can show a visual display of the objects in your scene, commonly referred to as a *view*, or any one of a number of other Maya windows that allow you to view and modify your scene in various ways.

The number and size of these panels, as well as the views they're set to display, are called the *layout*. You can switch between preset layouts, modify the current layout, and even create and save your own custom layouts. Also, when using a layout with multiple panels, you can temporarily expand one of them to fill the main window.

To change the panel layout:

◆ From the Panels menu in any panel, select Layouts and choose the preset layout name you want—Two Panes Side by Side, for example (**Figure 2.13**).

 or

◆ Select the icon of the layout you want from the toolbar of quick layout buttons on the lower-left side of Maya's interface (**Figure 2.14**).

Figure 2.12 This custom layout consists of a perspective view as well as panels containing the Outliner and the Hypergraph.

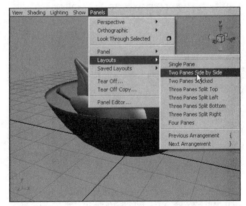

Figure 2.13 You can pick any of the possible panel layouts from the Panels > Layouts menu.

Figure 2.14 The quick layout buttons let you quickly switch the panel layout to a number of different preset options.

Top View
Side View
Front View
Persp View

Outliner
Graph Editor
Dope Sheet

Trax Editor
Hypergraph
Hypershade

Visor
UV Texture Editor
Render View

Blend Shape
Dynamic Relationships
Devices

Relationship Editor
Reference Editor
Component Editor

Paint Effects
Web Browser

Figure 2.15 You can change the contents of each view of your layout by clicking the arrows below the quick layout buttons. This contextual menu allows you to change the contents of the corresponding panel.

✔ Tips

- You can change the contents of your chosen layout by holding down the arrows at the bottom of the layout toolbar. Doing so lets you choose what will be displayed in the corresponding panel. The number of arrows varies with the number of panels in the current layout (**Figure 2.15**).

- You can adjust the relative sizes of the panels in your layout by clicking and dragging the frame that separates them (**Figure 2.16**).

To save a layout:

1. Set up the layout you would like to save and use later.

2. Choose Window > Save Current Layout.

3. Enter a name for the layout, and click OK.
   You can now access the new layout from the Panels > Saved Layouts menu.

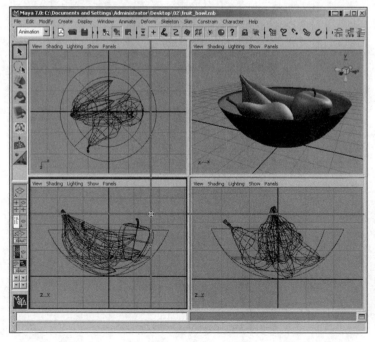

Figure 2.16 It can be helpful to resize your panels to make the size of each one comparable to its use. For instance, you might want to make your Perspective panel larger so that you always have more working area in that view.

CHANGING THE LAYOUT

To access a saved layout:

◆ From the Panels menu in any panel, select Saved Layouts and choose the name of the saved layout you would like to use.

To edit a layout:

1. From the Panels menu in any panel, select Saved Layouts > Edit Layouts.

2. Under the Layouts tab, select the name of the layout you would like to edit (**Figure 2.17**).

3. Under the Edit Layouts tab and the Configurations subtab, select your desired configuration from the pop-up menu.

4. Pull any of the center dividers for the numbered blocks to adjust the panels' relative size (**Figure 2.18**).

5. On the Contents subtab, use the numbered drop-down boxes to specify the contents of your panels (**Figure 2.19**).

6. Click the Close button to close the window.

Figure 2.17 Because the layouts accessible through the quick layouts toolbar are also editable, you need to scroll down to find your saved custom layouts.

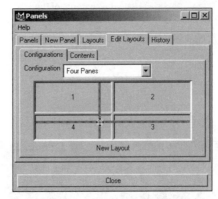

Figure 2.18 Click and drag the divider to adjust the relative size of the numbered blocks.

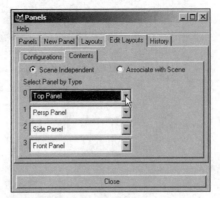

Figure 2.19 Each numbered block in the Configurations tab has a corresponding drop-down box in the Contents tab.

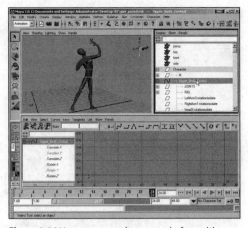

Figure 2.20 You can expand any panel of a multi-panel interface by holding your mouse over it and tapping the Spacebar.

Figure 2.21 You'll get more working space when you expand a panel. To return to your multi-panel view, tap the Spacebar again.

To expand a panel:

1. Move the mouse over the panel you would like to make larger (**Figure 2.20**).

2. Tap the Spacebar once. Be sure to tap it rather than hold it down (which brings up the Hotbox rather than expanding the panel).

   The panel expands to fill the main window, hiding the other panels (**Figure 2.21**).

✔ Tips

- Tap the Spacebar again to reset the panel's size (uncovering the other panes).

- Press Ctrl + Spacebar to hide most of Maya's interface as the panel expands, so that the panel uses the maximum screen space.

CHANGING THE LAYOUT

About the default layouts

By default, Maya displays a single panel set to a Perspective view (**Figure 2.22**). To switch from this view to the default four-view layout, place your cursor over the view and tap the (Spacebar). The Perspective view shrinks to fit in the upper-right corner, making room for the Front, Side, and Top views (**Figure 2.23**).

These views are *orthographic*, which means they present a 2D view of the scene from a fixed angle. The three orthographic views combine to provide an accurate portrayal of the objects' placement relative to the rest of the scene. Users new to 3D often forget to check their objects in multiple views, which can cause placement problems: Objects that look perfectly positioned in one view may be completely off when viewed from another angle (**Figure 2.24**).

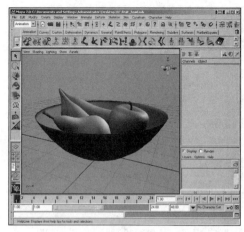

Figure 2.22 The default layout in Maya is a single Perspective view.

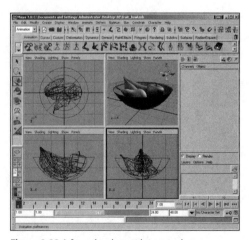

Figure 2.23 A four-view layout lets you view your scene from four different angles at the same time.

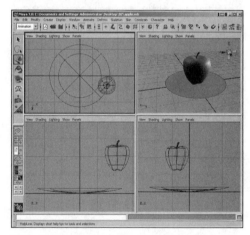

Figure 2.24 In the Perspective view, this apple appears to be in the center of the plate. In the orthographic views, you can see that the apple is actually floating above the edge of the plate.

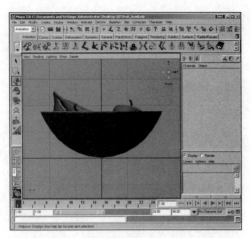

Figure 2.25 Using the view compass, you can switch a Perspective view to any orthographic view (Front, Back, Right, Left, Top, or Bottom).

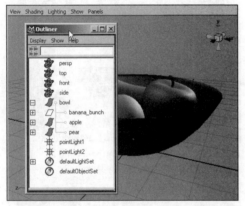

Figure 2.26 The Outliner can be displayed in a panel, or you can view it in a separate window that appears on top of your layout.

Changing individual panels

You can use the View Compass to temporarily switch the Perspective view to any of the six possible orthographic views: Top, Bottom, Left, Right, Front, and Back. Simply click the corresponding point of the View Compass in the Perspective view's upper-right corner. The view will rotate to that angle. (**Figure 2.25**). Click the cube at the center of the View Compass to return to a Perspective view.

Maya also lets you change any panel to display a different view of your scene, whether perspective or orthographic. Panels can also provide convenient access to other tools within Maya. These tools include animation editors, like the Graph Editor, and node-based representations of your scene, like the Outliner.

You can also view all of these tools as separate windows (**Figure 2.26**) by selecting them from the Window menu rather than a Panel menu. As you learn more about Maya, you'll discover how each of these tools fits into your workflow, and you'll develop your own preferences for arranging them in your layout.

To change a panel into a Perspective view:

◆ From the Panels menu at the top of the panel you want to change, select Perspective > persp (**Figure 2.27**).

To change a panel into an orthographic view:

◆ From the Panels menu at the top of the panel you want to change, select Orthographic > front, side, or top (**Figure 2.28**).

To change a panel to display a non-view tool:

◆ From the Panels menu in any panel, select Panel and choose the tool you want—Outliner, for example (**Figure 2.29**).

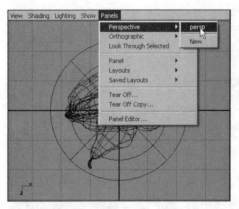

Figure 2.27 You can change any panel into a Perspective view from its Panels menu.

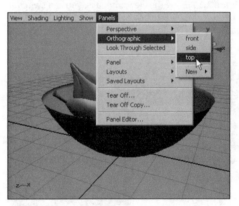

Figure 2.28 You can change any panel into an orthographic view from its Panels menu.

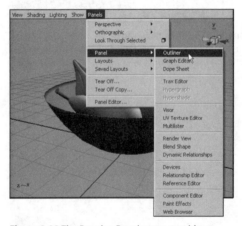

Figure 2.29 The Panels > Panel menu provides access to all of the Maya tools that can be displayed in a panel.

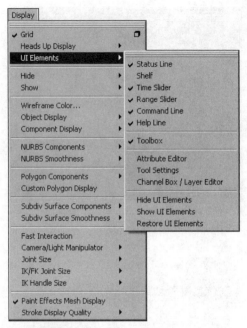

Figure 2.30 You can turn each interface element on and off, allowing you to save screen space when the element isn't needed.

Click here to hide the Channel Box

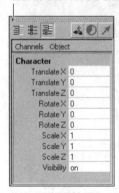

Figure 2.31 Clicking the small bar above or next to each interface element hides that element.

Changing the Interface

Maya gives you a great deal of control over which of its interface elements are displayed. By default, all elements of the interface are displayed, but you may want to hide some or even all of these elements. Doing so can give you more available screen space for your main panel or panels, which may be significant, depending on your monitor size and resolution. It also simplifies Maya's powerful but information-dense default interface, which may be unnecessarily complex for a particular project or for your general work style.

The menu bars at the top of Maya's main window and above each panel provide important access to vital tools and functions, and take up only a small amount of space. Even if you choose to hide all UI elements, these menu bars remain visible. However, you can hide (and restore) them if you wish, via the Hotbox.

The Hotbox is the only interface element that is hidden by default, since it is intended to be displayed only when you are actively using it. Its menu sets are also unaffected by hiding all UI elements, but can be hidden and shown independently.

To hide or show a UI element:

◆ Choose Display > UI Elements, and choose the UI element you would like to hide or show (**Figure 2.30**).

Each UI element name toggles between hidden and shown. If it's hidden, selecting it shows it, and vice versa.

✔ Tip

■ You can also hide any visible UI element by clicking the area just above it (for vertical elements) or to its left (for horizontal elements). These areas are indicated by a small arrow followed by rows or columns of dots (**Figure 2.31**).

To hide all UI elements:

◆ Choose Display > UI Elements > Hide UI Elements.

All elements are hidden except the menu bars and your current panel layout (**Figure 2.32**).

To show all UI elements:

◆ Choose Display > UI Elements > Show UI Elements (**Figure 2.33**).

All UI elements are shown.

To hide or show the main menu bar (Windows only):

◆ Hold down the (Spacebar) anywhere in a panel, and select Hotbox Controls > Window Options > Show Main Menubar (**Figure 2.34**).

This command toggles the visibility of menu bar on and off. If it's on, selecting this option turns it off, and vice versa.

To hide or show the panel menu bars:

◆ From the Hotbox, select Hotbox Controls > Window Options > Show Pane Menubar.

This command toggles the visibility of the menu bars in all of the panels.

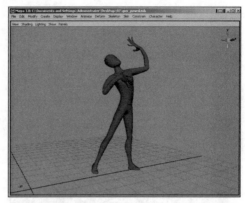

Figure 2.32 Use the Hide UI Elements command to quickly gain more working space.

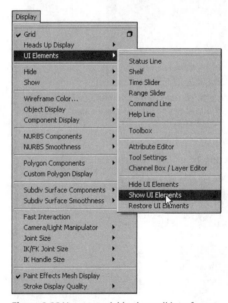

Figure 2.33 You can quickly show all interface elements when needed by using the Show UI Elements command.

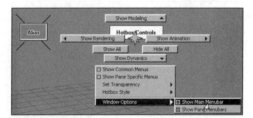

Figure 2.34 You can turn the main menu bar on and off via the Hotbox.

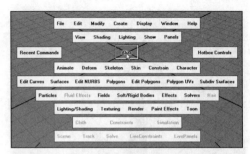

Figure 2.35 Holding down the Spacebar opens the Hotbox.

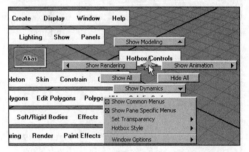

Figure 2.36 You can hide menus you don't want to access via the Hotbox.

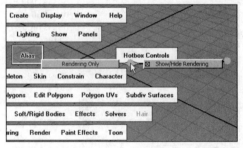

Figure 2.37 You can change the menus that are shown in the Hotbox by using the appropriate marking menu in the Hotbox Controls.

To show and hide the Hotbox:

1. Show the Hotbox by holding down the Spacebar (**Figure 2.35**).

2. Hide the Hotbox by releasing the Spacebar.

To hide and show menu sets in the Hotbox:

1. Show the Hotbox by holding down the Spacebar in any panel.

2. Hold down the left mouse button over Hotbox Controls to show the Hotbox Controls marking menu (**Figure 2.36**).

3. Move the mouse over the menu set name you want to show.

   An additional marking menu opens (**Figure 2.37**).

4. Select Show/Hide (menu set name).

   The menu set is shown if it was hidden, and vice versa.

About the Channel Box, Attribute Editor, and Tool Settings

The Channel Box and the Attribute Editor both allow you to view and adjust a selected object's attributes. The Channel Box provides access to keyable attributes, which can be animated. It's also the most convenient way to access these attributes, even when working on non-animation tasks. The Attribute Editor requires more space, but it displays additional attributes not accessible from the Channel Box. The Tool Settings allows you to view and change the settings for the current tool.

Because the Channel Box, Attribute Editor, and Tool Settings all open on the far right side of the Maya interface, you can view only one of them at a time. The Channel Box and Attribute Editor are both commonly used

continues on next page

tools, so toggling them on and off and switching between them is likely to become part of your workflow. Maya provides several different ways to do this.

To show or hide the Channel Box:

Do any of the following:

- Click the "Show or hide the Channel Box/Layer Editor" icon 🔲 on the right side of the Status Line. (The Status Line is the toolbar below the main menu bar.)

- Choose Display > UI Elements > Channel Box/Layer Editor.

- If the Attribute Editor is visible, press Ctrl+a once. Otherwise, press Ctrl+a twice.

  The Channel Box appears on the right side of the Maya interface (**Figure 2.38**).

To show or hide the Attribute Editor:

Do any of the following:

- Click the "Show or hide the Attribute Editor" icon 🔲 on the right side of the Status Line.

- Choose Display > UI Elements > Attribute Editor.

- Press Ctrl+a.

- Choose Window > Attribute Editor.

  The Attribute Editor appears on the right side of the Maya interface (**Figure 2.39**).

To show or hide the Tool Settings:

- Click the "Show or hide the Tool Settings" icon 🔲 on the right side of the Status Line.

  or

- Choose Display > UI Elements > Tool Settings.

  The Tool Settings appear on the right side of the Maya interface (**Figure 2.40**).

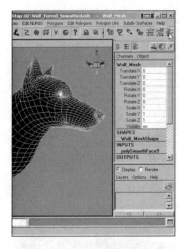

Figure 2.38
The Channel Box displays an object's keyable attributes.

Figure 2.39
If you show the Attribute Editor while the Channel Box is visible, the Channel Box is hidden so the Attribute Editor can be displayed.

Figure 2.40
The Tool Settings allow you to adjust the currently selected tool's settings.

CHANGING THE INTERFACE

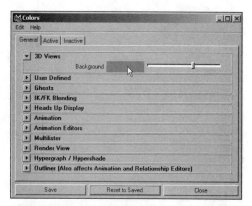

Figure 2.41 You can use the color slider to quickly change the brightness of the color, while clicking the color swatch lets you change the hue, saturation, and value.

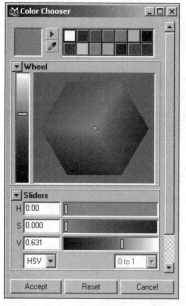

Figure 2.42 The Color Chooser provides several different methods of selecting the color you want.

Changing UI components

In addition to allowing you to hide and show UI elements, Maya gives you various options for some specific components of those elements. You can experiment with these options to find your own personal preferences.

To show and hide the grid:

◆ Choose Display > Grid to toggle the grid displayed in the Perspective view on and off.

✔ Tip

■ You can adjust the size, closeness, and colors of the grid lines in the Grid Options. In the Display menu, click the square to the right of the Grid menu item.

To alter your Maya color scheme:

1. Choose Window > Settings/Preferences > Colors.

   The Colors dialog box opens.

2. Click the 3D Views arrow to view the Background color slider.

3. Click the color swatch next to Background to open the Color Chooser (**Figure 2.41**).

4. In the Wheel, click the color you would like for your Maya background (**Figure 2.42**).

5. Click Accept.

   Your Maya background updates to reflect your chosen color.

✔ Tips

■ You can follow the same steps to change any part of the interface color scheme.

■ Pressing Alt + b toggles the background color in your camera views between several shades of gray.

To change the size of Maya's manipulators:

1. Selected any object. If there are no objects in your scene, choose Create > NURBS Primitive > Sphere.

2. Select the Move tool by pressing [w] or clicking the Move icon in the Tool Box ⬥.

3. Choose Window > Settings/Preferences > Preferences.

4. Select Manipulators in the Categories list (**Figure 2.43**).

   The Manipulator Display Preferences are shown to the right of the Categories list.

5. Move the Preferences dialog box so you can see your selected object and the Move tool manipulator (**Figure 2.44**).

6. In the Manipulator Display Preferences, adjust the Global Scale slider.

   You can see your manipulator change in size as you adjust the slider. Choose the size that works best for you (**Figure 2.45**).

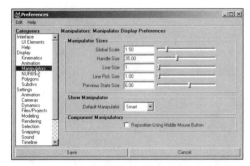

Figure 2.43 The Manipulators section of the Preferences dialog box lets you customize Maya's manipulators.

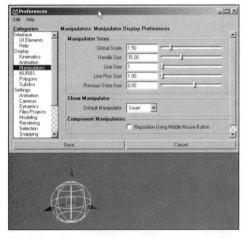

Figure 2.44 You can see the changes to the manipulator as you make them.

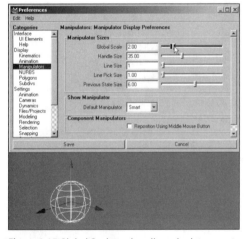

Figure 2.45 Global Scale scales all manipulators, not just the one currently selected.

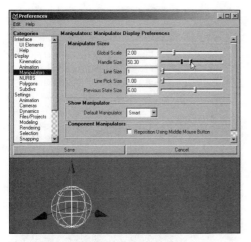

Figure 2.46 Handle Size affects both the Move manipulator (shown here) and the Scale manipulator.

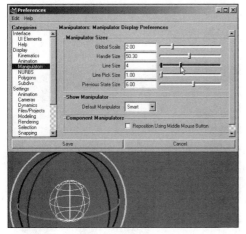

Figure 2.47 Line Size affects the Rotate manipulator.

7. Once you've sized the Move tool manipulator to your satisfaction, adjust the Handle Size slider to change the size of the manipulator's handles (**Figure 2.46**).

8. Without closing the Preferences window, switch to the Rotate tool by pressing the (Spacebar) or clicking the Rotate icon in the Tool Box .

   The Rotate manipulator appears, scaled to a size determined by the new Global Scale.

9. In the Manipulator Display Preferences, adjust the Line Size slider to change the size of the Rotate manipulator's lines (**Figure 2.47**).

About menus

Maya has four main menu sets: Animation, Modeling, Dynamics, and Rendering. Each of these sets displays menus specific to its topic, as well as the common menus File, Edit, Modify, Create, Display, Window, and Help. The common menus are always accessible, regardless of which menu set you're currently using.

Most of Maya's menus can be "torn off" of the interface. These menus then function as separate windows, which will remain visible at all times and can be repositioned freely. This feature can save you time if you're likely to use many commands in a row from a particular menu.

To change the menu set:

◆ On the left side of the status bar, use the pop-up menu to select the appropriate menu set (**Figure 2.48**).

or

◆ In any view panel, hold down ⓗ and the left mouse button to select a menu set from the marking menu (**Figure 2.49**).

To tear off a menu:

1. Open the menu you'd like to tear off.

2. Click the tear-off bar (indicated by two parallel lines) at the top of the menu.

   The menu becomes a separate, free-floating window. (**Figure 2.50**).

Changing undo settings

Maya defaults to allow for 50 undos. Although this is enough in most situations, you may want to increase this limit or even set it to infinite. Keep in mind that each saved undo takes up memory, so if memory is an issue, you may want to lower the undo limit.

To change the number of undos:

1. Choose Window > Settings/Preferences > Preferences.

   The Preferences dialog box opens.

2. Under Categories, click Undo to view the Undo preferences (**Figure 2.51**).

3. Enter your preferred undo limit in the Queue Size field, or change the Queue setting to Infinite, and click Save.

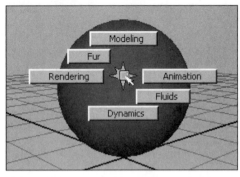

Figure 2.48 Each menu set holds menus specific to the type of process you're working on.

Figure 2.49 You can use this marking menu to change your menu set when you've hidden the Status Line or if you want to speed up your workflow.

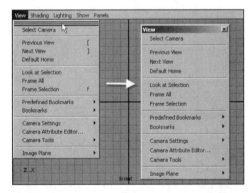

Figure 2.50 You can tear off almost every menu in Maya.

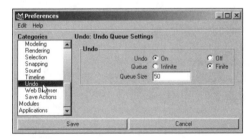

Figure 2.51 You can change the number of undos in the Preferences dialog box.

Figure 2.52 An apple viewed in bounding box, wireframe, flat-shaded, and smooth-shaded modes.

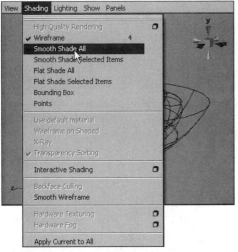

Figure 2.53 The Shading menu controls the display mode for each individual panel.

About Display Options and Smoothness

By using a panel's display options, you can change the way objects are viewed—or whether they're viewed at all. You can find these options in the Shading, Lighting, and Show menus at the top of each panel, and the most commonly used options have associated keyboard shortcuts.

You can view your scene in wireframe, smooth-shaded, flat-shaded, bounding-box, or points mode, depending on your current task (**Figure 2.52**). Bounding-box mode can be used to speed interaction in complex scenes. Wireframe mode is handy for selecting components, because you can see the components through the object. Smooth shading gives you the most accurate picture of your objects, whereas flat shading is a compromise between accuracy and speed.

The hardware texturing and lighting options also increase the accuracy of your scene, allowing you to view an approximation of your objects' textures and the effects of the lights in your scene.

Although it isn't a panel-specific view option, you can also select NURBS and Subdiv objects to change their display to one of three smoothness levels: rough, medium, or fine. Choosing a setting of rough can ease component selection, because fewer surface lines are shown. A fine setting comes closest to matching the final surface.

To change the display options from the Shading menu:

◆ From the Shading menu in any panel, select one of the following shading options: Wireframe, Smooth Shade, Flat Shade, Bounding Box, or Points (**Figure 2.53**).

ABOUT DISPLAY OPTIONS AND SMOOTHNESS

Shading and smoothness shortcuts

1 = Rough smoothness (**Figure 2.54**)

2 = Medium smoothness (Figure 2.54)

3 = Fine smoothness (Figure 2.54)

4 = Wireframe mode (**Figure 2.55**)

5 = Shaded mode (**Figure 2.56**)

6 = Hardware Texturing (**Figure 2.57**)

7 = Hardware Lighting (**Figure 2.58**)

Figure 2.54 From left to right, rough, medium, and fine smoothness.

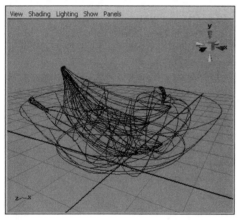

Figure 2.55 Wireframe mode lets you see through objects and view their entire geometry.

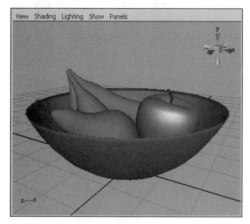

Figure 2.56 Shaded mode presents the surfaces of objects in gray by default, showing their shape but not their texturing or lighting.

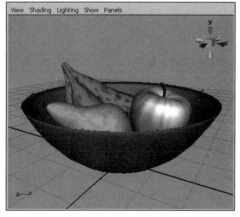

Figure 2.57 Hardware Texturing shows an approximation of the textures that have been applied to objects.

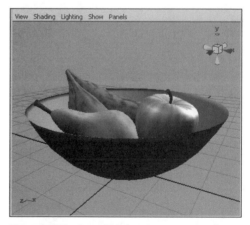

Figure 2.58 Hardware Lighting shows an approximation of the scene's lighting.

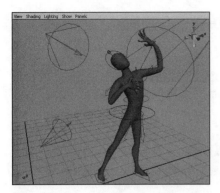

Figure 2.59 Even a simple single-character animation involves various object types, not all of which you need to work with at once.

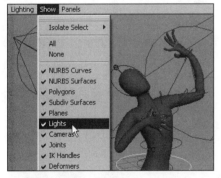

Figure 2.60 The Show menu lets you hide or show all objects of the chosen type. If you choose Lights, all the lights in the view are hidden.

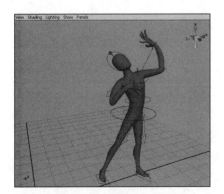

Figure 2.61 Hiding the types of objects you aren't currently working with can make it easier to view and select the objects you want to focus on.

Using the Show menu

The Show menu comes in handy when you want to work with a particular type of object, such as curves or lights. With it, you can quickly hide the object types you don't need to view, allowing you to see the particular objects that you're working with more clearly. This can be very helpful in complex scenes (**Figure 2.59**).

The Show menu lets you turn all types on and off simultaneously, and you can also turn objects on and off individually. You may want to turn off all objects first and then turn on only the object type you want to isolate.

The Show menu only visually hides or shows object types; it doesn't delete the objects. Object types turned off in the Show menu still appear in the final render.

To hide object types with the Show menu:

◆ From the Show menu in any panel, select the object type you want to hide (**Figure 2.60**).

The object type selected is hidden from view (**Figure 2.61**).

To show hidden object types with the Show menu:

◆ From the Show menu in any panel, select the object type you want to show in the panel.

The object type selected becomes visible.

Keyboard Shortcuts

Any function in Maya can have an associated keyboard shortcut, or *hotkey*. Hotkeys can be huge time-savers, because you can use them rather than go to the menu bar to select a function or command. Many of Maya's functions have hotkeys associated with them by default. As you become more familiar with Maya, you may want to add additional hotkeys.

To create a new hotkey:

1. Choose Window > Settings/Preferences > Hotkeys (**Figure 2.62**).

   The Hotkey Editor opens.

2. In the Categories list, click the category name for the command you want to set (**Figure 2.63**).

   The category name is the same as the name of the menu the command is under.

3. In the Commands list, select the command for which you want to create a hotkey.

   If the command already has a hotkey assigned to it, you'll see it under Current Hotkeys. If you still want to create a new hotkey, delete this preexisting hotkey by selecting it and clicking Remove.

4. In the Assign New Hotkey section, choose a Key and an optional Modifier for the command (**Figure 2.64**).

5. Click Assign, and close the Hotkey Editor.

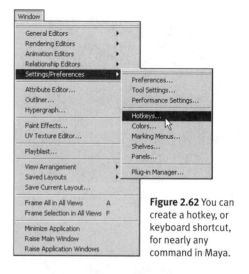

Figure 2.62 You can create a hotkey, or keyboard shortcut, for nearly any command in Maya.

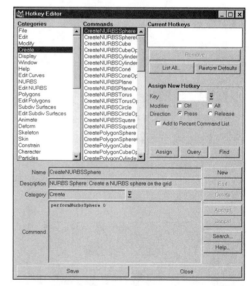

Figure 2.63 Commands are organized by category in the Hotkey Editor.

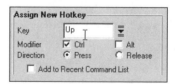

Figure 2.64 If you assign a Modifier as well as a Key, you'll need to press them both to use the hotkey.

CREATING PRIMITIVES AND TEXT

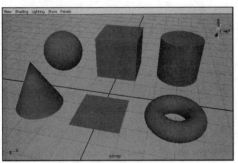

Figure 3.1 The basic primitives (clockwise, from top left): sphere, cube, cylinder, torus, plane, cone.

Primitives are pre-made geometry sets, usually in simple shapes: spheres, cubes, cylinders, planes, cones, and toruses (**Figure 3.1**). New in Maya 7.0, you can also create more unusual polygon primitives: prisms, pyramids, pipes, helixes, soccer balls, and platonic solids (**Figure 3.2**).

Figure 3.2 Maya 7.0's new polygon primitives (clockwise, from top left): prism, pyramid, pipe, platonic solid, soccer ball, helix.

Primitives are the building blocks of 3D modeling, simplifying the creation of more complex objects. Some real-world objects can be constructed out of a single primitive shape: a baseball is a sphere, an unopened book is a scaled cube, and a box of doughnuts is a box of toruses. Other objects combine a number of different primitives. For example, a bicycle wheel combines thin cylinders for the spokes and hub with toruses for the rim and tire (**Figure 3.3**).

Not everything is made out of primitives, but Maya's modeling tools allow you to modify primitives so extensively that you can make nearly any shape by *starting* with primitives. This makes them valuable time-savers for almost any modeling task. If your scene needs text, you can also save time by using Maya's text tool, which automatically generates geometry for the text you enter.

Maya's construction history feature allows you to change the attributes of primitives and other objects after you've created them. You can also rename them to make management of your scene simpler.

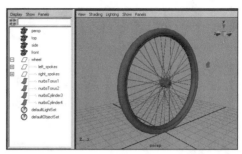

Figure 3.3 This bicycle wheel is made from cylinder and torus primitives.

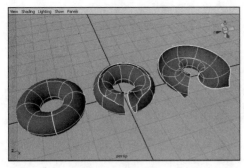

Figure 3.4 A NURBS torus, like all NURBS surfaces, is made from a single sheet of geometry.

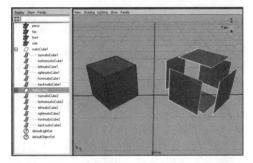

Figure 3.5 Due to the inherent limitations of NURBS surfaces, a NURBS cube primitive is constructed from six surfaces, one for each side.

About Primitive Types

Maya includes three primary types of primitives: *NURBS, polygons,* and *subdivs.* Each of these types has its own strengths and weaknesses, making them appropriate for different types of models.

About NURBS

NURBS stands for *Non-Uniform Rational B-Spline,* which describes the mathematical nature of this type of object. Topologically, a NURBS surface is always a single surface with four edges, like a sheet of paper, which can be curved and stretched into different shapes (**Figure 3.4**).

NURBS can provide smooth surfaces with relatively few control vertices, so you can easily control the general shape of the object. However, your ability to selectively add detail to a NURBS surface is limited, because its control points must always form a grid (even if it's a highly distorted grid). As a result, you can only increase the number of control vertices by increasing them across the surface in one or both directions. Also, because of NURB surfaces' simple topology (**Figure 3.5**), many objects require more than one NURBS surface. This makes NURBS inconvenient to use, if not impossible, for many types of objects. However, for simple objects, they provide a quick and easy way to create smooth surfaces.

NURBS primitives are most useful when you intend to use them as primitives, alone or in combination, rather than modify them to create other shapes. For more information on NURBS objects, see Chapter 7.

About polygons

Polygons are flat surfaces defined by three or more *vertices*, or points (**Figure 3.6**). By using Maya's tools to create many connected polygons, you can produce high-quality, smooth surfaces. Using fewer polygons results in low-resolution, fast-rendering surfaces (**Figure 3.7**).

Unlike NURBS, you can create a shape with any topology as a single polygonal mesh, and you can add detail to the specific areas that need it. However, because the number of vertices increases with the number of polygons in an object, adjusting a polygonal object's general shape can be more time-consuming than doing so for an equivalent NURBS surface (**Figure 3.8**).

Polygon primitives are most useful as a starting point for creating more complex polygonal models, especially relatively low-resolution models. For more information on polygonal modeling, see Chapter 8.

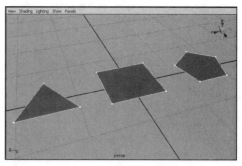

Figure 3.6 Three and four-sided polygons are most common, but polygons can have any number of points.

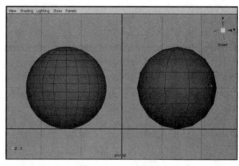

Figure 3.7 The sphere on the left is smoother, but the lower-resolution sphere on the right will render faster.

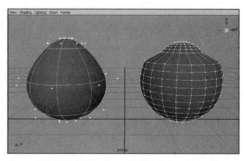

Figure 3.8 A NURBS sphere (left) can be shaped into an egg by scaling the upper control vertices. A polygonal sphere (right) needs more vertices to be smooth, so it can't be reshaped as easily.

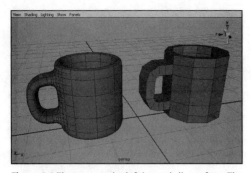

Figure 3.9 The mug on the left is a subdiv surface. The mug on the right is the equivalent polygonal mesh.

About subdiv surfaces

Subdivision surfaces, or *subdivs,* combine the best aspects of both NURBS and polygons. Like a polygonal object, a subdiv surface uses only one mesh to define complex surfaces, and it provides the same smoothness and high-level control as a NURBS surface (**Figure 3.9**).

Although subdivs have been around since 1978, computer hardware has only recently become fast enough to make working with them manageable. Depending on the complexity of your model and the processing power of your computer, subdivision surfaces can be significantly slower to manipulate and render than NURBS or polygons.

Subdiv primitives, like polygons, are most useful as a starting point for creating more complex models. Subdivision surfaces are particularly useful for high-resolution work. For more information on subdiv modeling, see Chapter 9.

About NURBS Primitives

NURBS primitives are useful, predefined curves and surfaces. Maya includes eight NURBS primitives: *sphere, cube, cylinder, cone, plane, torus, circle,* and *square* (**Figure 3.10**). The first six of these primitives are NURBS surfaces; the circle and square primitives are NURBS curves, which can be useful when you want to construct surfaces yourself.

Each primitive has a number of attributes, which you can change in its Options dialog box before you create the object (**Figure 3.11**). If construction history was enabled when the primitive was created, you can also adjust the properties after it's been created. To do so, select the node labeled makeNurb plus the name of the primitive from the Channel Box's Inputs section (**Figure 3.12**).

In this section, we'll show you how to create NURBS primitives and how to change some of their attributes both before and after the object has been created.

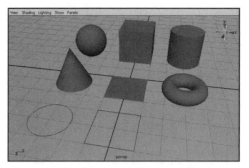

Figure 3.10 The eight NURBS primitives (left to right, from top): sphere, cube, cylinder, cone, plane, torus, circle, and square.

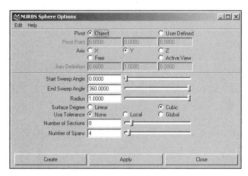

Figure 3.11 A primitive's attributes can be changed in its Options dialog box.

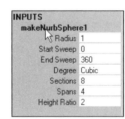

Figure 3.12 The construction history lets you change an existing primitive's attributes.

Figure 3.13 You can create any of the NURBS primitives from the Create > NURBS Primitives submenu.

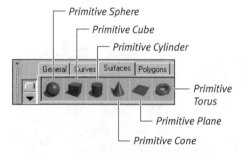

Primitive Sphere
Primitive Cube
Primitive Cylinder
Primitive Torus
Primitive Plane
Primitive Cone

Figure 3.14 You can quickly create NURBS primitives by clicking their icons in the Surfaces Shelf.

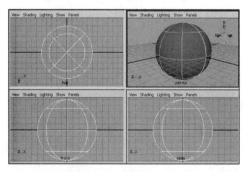

Figure 3.15 When creating primitives, Maya places the center point of the primitive at the origin of the scene.

Creating NURBS primitives

NURBS primitives are found in the Create > NURBS Primitives submenu (**Figure 3.13**). You can create a primitive by selecting its name from this submenu or from the equivalent submenu in the Hotbox. You can also use the Surfaces Shelf to quickly create any of the primitive NURBS surfaces (**Figure 3.14**).

When you create a primitive surface or curve, Maya places the object's center point at the origin of the scene (at the coordinates 0, 0, 0), which puts most objects half above the grid and half below it (**Figure 3.15**). The exception is the cone, whose center point is at its base and which appears to rest on the grid.

To create a NURBS primitive using the main menu:

1. Choose Create > NURBS Primitives.

2. Select the name of the primitive you want to create (for example, a cone) (**Figure 3.16**).

   The NURBS primitive appears at the origin of the scene.

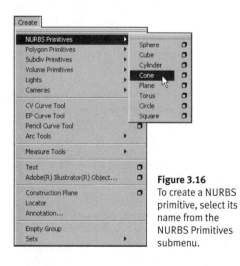

Figure 3.16
To create a NURBS primitive, select its name from the NURBS Primitives submenu.

To create a NURBS primitive using the Hotbox:

1. Hold down [Spacebar] anywhere in the scene to show the Hotbox.

2. From the Create menu in the Hotbox, select the NURBS Primitives submenu.

3. Select the name of the primitive you want to create—in this case, the sphere (**Figure 3.17**).

   The NURBS primitive is created at the origin of the scene.

To create a NURBS primitive using the Surfaces Shelf:

◆ From the Surfaces Shelf, select the NURBS primitive icon for the object you would like to create (the cylinder is shown here) (**Figure 3.18**).

   The primitive is created at the origin of the scene (**Figure 3.19**).

✔ Tip

■ If the Shelf isn't visible, open it by choosing Display > UI Elements > Shelf.

About NURBS primitive attributes

Each NURBS primitive has an associated set of attributes, which you can change to alter its appearance. Some attributes are common to all NURBS primitives, and others are specific to just one or two.

The following are some important NURBS primitive attributes with their definitions. You can set these in the Channel Box or in the object's Options dialog box:

◆ **Radius**—The radius of an object is the distance from the center of the object to its edge—or, in the case of a torus, the distance from the center of its cross-section. Adjusting the radius resizes the object proportionally on all three axes.

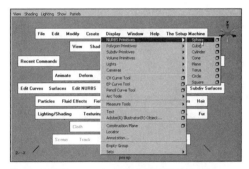

Figure 3.17 You can also create NURBS primitives from the Create menu in the Hotbox.

Figure 3.18 The Surfaces Shelf holds shortcut icons for the NURBS primitives that are surfaces. The circle and square can be found in the Curves Shelf.

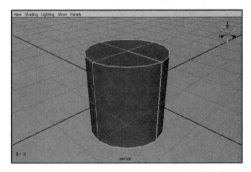

Figure 3.19 When you create a NURBS primitive, it appears at the origin of the scene.

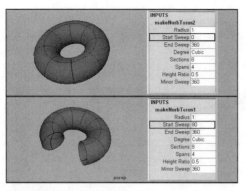

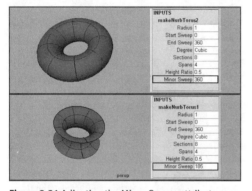

Figure 3.20 Adjusting the Start Sweep attribute causes the beginning and end of the surface to separate.

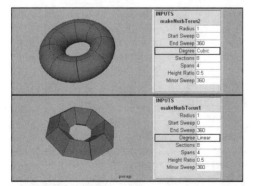

Figure 3.21 Adjusting the Minor Sweep attribute separates a torus's surface along the U direction.

- ◆ **Start Sweep**—Adjusting the Start Sweep causes the surface to separate from its end in a clockwise direction. The result is a slice of the surface, or a surface of less than 360 degrees (**Figure 3.20**).

- ◆ **End Sweep**—Adjusting the End Sweep has a similar effect to adjusting the Start Sweep; however, instead of working clockwise from the end point, it works counterclockwise from the starting point to open the surface.

- ◆ **Minor Sweep**—Adjusting the Minor Sweep attribute, which is specific to the torus primitive, separates the surface along the U direction. This creates a slice of the surface similar to a spool, rather than a full doughnut shape (**Figure 3.21**).

- ◆ **Degree**—A NURBS primitive can be linear or cubic. If the Degree attribute is set to Linear, the surface is planar and faceted. If the Degree attribute is set to Cubic (default), the surface is curved and smooth (**Figure 3.22**).

- ◆ **Sections**—Adjusting the Sections attribute changes the level of detail of the surface in the U direction (**Figure 3.23**).

continues on next page

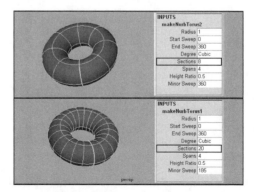

Figure 3.22 If the Degree attribute is set to Cubic, the surface is curved (top). If the Degree attribute is set to Linear, the surface is planar and faceted (bottom).

Figure 3.23 Adjusting the Sections attribute adds more detail to the surface in the U direction.

ABOUT NURBS PRIMITIVES

◆ **Spans**—Adjusting the Spans attribute changes the level of detail of the surface in the V direction (**Figure 3.24**).

◆ **Patches U and Patches V**—Patches U and V are specific to the plane and cube primitives. Adjusting these attributes increases the surface geometry in the U or V direction (**Figure 3.25**).

Changing a NURBS primitive's attributes

You change all of the NURBS primitives' attributes in the same way. This section shows you how to change the Radius attribute, which is common to the NURBS primitive sphere, cone, cylinder, torus, and circle, and affects the size of the object in all dimensions. You can follow the same steps to change other object attributes.

To set the radius of a NURBS primitive from the Create menu:

1. Choose Create > NURBS Primitives.

2. Select the box next to the name of the primitive for which you want to set the radius—in this case, the sphere (**Figure 3.26**).

   The selected primitive's Options dialog box opens.

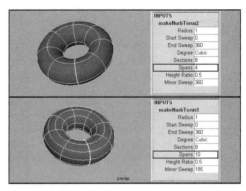

Figure 3.24 Adjusting the Spans attribute adds detail in the V direction.

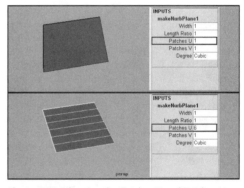

Figure 3.25 Adjusting the Patches U and Patches V attributes increases the surface geometry in the U or V direction.

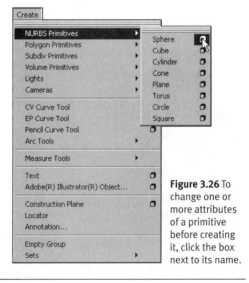

Figure 3.26 To change one or more attributes of a primitive before creating it, click the box next to its name.

ABOUT NURBS PRIMITIVES

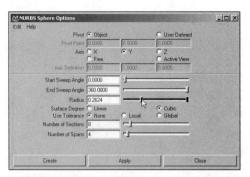

Figure 3.27 Adjust the Radius slider to the desired value.

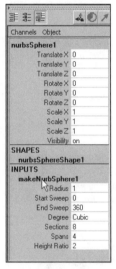

Figure 3.28 To display a NURBS primitive's attributes, click the makeNurb(*Object*) label under Inputs in the Channel Box.

Figure 3.29 You can click in any attribute's field to modify that attribute's value.

Figure 3.30 The sphere on the right has had its radius doubled.

3. Adjust the Radius slider to half the desired diameter of the primitive (**Figure 3.27**).

4. Click Create to make a primitive with the new radius setting.

✔ Tip

■ You can type in a value larger than the slider's highest value.

To change the radius of a NURBS primitive for an existing object:

1. Select a primitive NURBS sphere, cone, cylinder, torus, or circle.

2. Click the makeNurb(*Object*) label under the Inputs heading in the Channel Box.

The selected primitive's attributes are displayed (**Figure 3.28**).

3. Click once in the Radius field to select it (**Figure 3.29**).

4. Change the number to the size you want the object's radius to be.

5. Press (Enter) to complete the radius change (**Figure 3.30**).

✔ Tips

■ You can also click the attribute's name (in this example, Radius) in the Channel Box, and then click and drag the middle mouse button left or right in the View window to interactively change the object's radius.

■ The makeNurb node isn't available for a duplicated object unless you select Duplicate Upstream Graph from the Edit > Duplicate Options dialog box before you duplicate the object.

ABOUT NURBS PRIMITIVES

About Polygon Primitives

Polygon primitives, like NURBS primitives, represent a collection of predefined surfaces. These surfaces can save you time in creating simple objects and give you a head start on creating more detailed shapes.

Maya includes 12 polygon primitives (**Figure 3.31**). Six of these are similar to their NURBS or subdiv equivalents: *sphere, cube, cylinder, cone, plane*, and *torus*. The other six, new in Maya 7.0, are only available in polygonal form: *prism, pyramid, pipe, helix, soccer ball*, and *platonic solids*.

You can change each of these primitives' default attributes in the Options dialog box before you create an object (**Figure 3.32**). Like NURBS and subdiv primitives, polygon primitives have a construction history that lets you adjust the properties of a polygon primitive after it's been created. The attributes associated with the construction history appear in the Inputs section of Channel Box under *poly* plus the primitive's name (**Figure 3.33**).

This section covers creating polygon primitives, some important polygon primitive attributes, and how to change these attributes both before and after creating an object.

Creating polygon primitives

Polygon primitives are found in the Create > Polygon Primitives submenu. As with NURBS primitives, you can create polygon primitives from the main menu, the Hotbox, or the Shelf. Newly created polygon primitives are placed with their center point at the origin of the scene (at the coordinates 0, 0, 0).

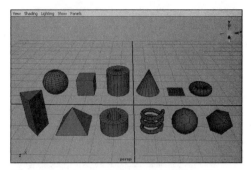

Figure 3.31 There are 12 polygon primitives. Top row: sphere, cube, cylinder, cone, plane, and torus. Bottom row: prism, pyramid, pipe, helix, soccer ball, and platonic solids.

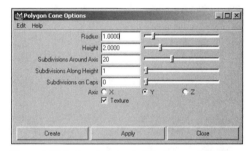

Figure 3.32 Each polygon primitive has attributes that you can set in its Options dialog box before creating the object.

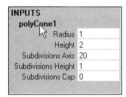

Figure 3.33 Construction history gives you the ability to adjust a polygon primitive's attributes after it's been created.

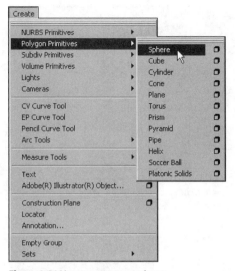

Figure 3.34 You can create a polygon primitive by selecting it from the Create › Polygon Primitives menu.

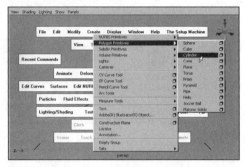

Figure 3.35 You can also create polygon primitives from the Hotbox.

Figure 3.36 The Polygons Shelf lets you quickly create most of the polygon primitives.

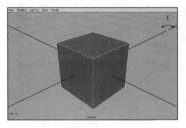

Figure 3.37 Maya places the center point of a newly created primitive at the origin of the scene.

To create a polygon primitive using the main menu:

1. Choose Create > Polygon Primitives.

2. Select the name of the primitive you want to create (the sphere is shown here) (**Figure 3.34**).

   A polygon primitive is created at the origin of the scene.

To create a polygon primitive using the Hotbox:

1. Hold down (Spacebar) anywhere in the scene to display the Hotbox.

2. From the Create menu in the Hotbox, select the Polygon Primitives submenu.

3. Select the name of the primitive you want to create (the cylinder is shown here) (**Figure 3.35**).

   A polygon primitive is created at the origin of the scene.

To create a polygon primitive using the Polygons Shelf:

◆ From the Polygons Shelf, select the icon of the polygon primitive you would like to create—for example, the cube (**Figure 3.36**).

   The primitive is created at the origin of the scene (**Figure 3.37**).

✔ Tips

■ If the Shelf isn't visible, open it by choosing Display > UI Elements > Shelf.

■ By default, not all of the polygonal primitives are displayed in the Polygons Shelf; the prism, soccer ball and platonic solids are missing. To add any of these primitives to the Shelf, hold down (Shift)+(Ctrl)/(Control) and select the primitive from the Create menu.

About polygon primitive attributes

Like NURBS primitives, each polygon primitive has a number of attributes that you can set for the object before or after it's created. Changing these attributes affects various aspects of the object's appearance. The following are some important polygon primitive attributes:

◆ **Radius**—As with NURBS primitives, the radius of an object is the distance from the center of an object to its edge, with two exceptions: With the torus, the radius is the distance from the center of its cross-section; for the helix, it's the radius *of* the cross-section. In all instances but the helix, adjusting the Radius attribute resizes the object proportionally on all three axes.

◆ **Section Radius**—This attribute is only used by the torus polygon primitive. Adjusting the Section Radius changes its cross-section, fattening or slimming the torus's doughnut-like shape (**Figure 3.38**).

◆ **Subdivisions Height, Width, Depth**— These attributes adjust the number of times the height, width, or depth of the surface is divided. Adjusting these attributes adds or subtracts faces in the direction of the corresponding axis (**Figure 3.39**).

◆ **Subdivisions Axis**—For primitives with a circular cross-section, like the sphere or the cylinder, this attribute adjusts the number of times the surface is divided around the center axis. Increasing the Subdivisions Axis adds faces to the object, and decreasing it removes faces (**Figure 3.40**).

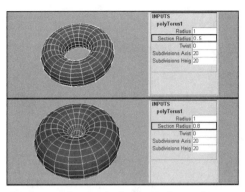

Figure 3.38 Adjusting the Section Radius attribute fattens or slims the torus's shape.

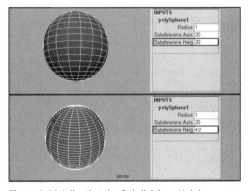

Figure 3.39 Adjusting the Subdivisions Height attribute adds or subtracts polygons along the height of the object.

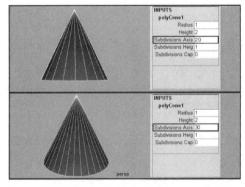

Figure 3.40 Adjusting the Subdivisions Axis attribute adds or subtracts polygons around the center axis of the object.

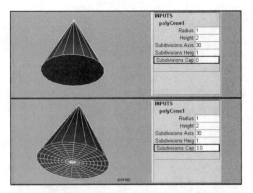

Figure 3.41 Adjusting the Subdivisions Cap(s) attribute adds polygons to or subtracts them from the object's cap(s).

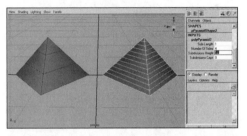

Figure 3.42 The pyramid on the right has had the value of its Subdivisions Height attribute increased to 12.

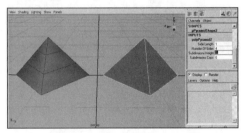

Figure 3.43 The pyramid on the right has had the value of its Subdivisions Height decreased to 1, the minimum value.

◆ **Subdivisions Cap(s)**—Four polygon primitives have caps: the cone, cylinder, pipe, and helix. A *cap* is a piece of geometry that covers the hole at the end of a surface. The Subdivisions Cap(s) attribute adjusts the number of times the surface's cap is divided. Adjusting this attribute adds faces to or subtracts them from the object's cap, radiating out from the center (**Figure 3.41**).

Changing a polygon primitive's attributes

You change all of the polygon primitives' attributes in the same way. This section shows you how to change the Subdivisions Height attribute of a polygon primitive. You can follow the same steps to change other object attributes.

The Subdivisions Height attribute is common to most of the polygon primitives, with the exceptions of the helix, the soccer ball, and the platonic solids. It determines the number of times the surface's height is divided. By raising the number, you increase the number of polygons along the height of the object (**Figure 3.42**). If you lower the number, the number of polygons alone the height of the object is reduced (**Figure 3.43**).

ABOUT POLYGON PRIMITIVES

To set the Subdivisions Height attribute of a polygon primitive from the Create menu:

1. Choose Create > Polygon Primitives.

2. Select the box next to the name of the primitive for which you want to set Subdivisions Height (the pipe is shown here) (**Figure 3.44**).

   The Options dialog box opens.

3. Adjust the Subdivisions Along Height slider to the number of divisions you want along the height of the surface (**Figure 3.45**).

4. Click Create to make a new primitive with the new Subdivisions Height setting.

✔ Tip

■ You can type in a value that's higher than the slider allows.

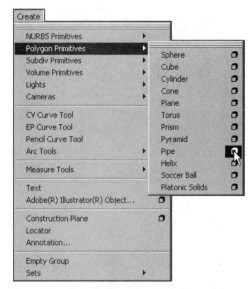

Figure 3.44 Click the box next to a primitive to bring up its Options dialog box.

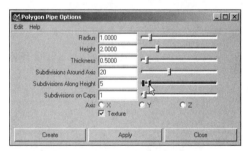

Figure 3.45 You can adjust any of a primitive's attributes from its Options dialog box.

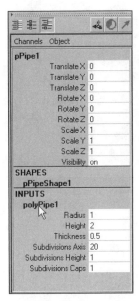

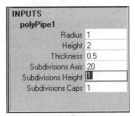

Figure 3.46 Click the poly(*Object*) label in the Inputs section of the Channel Box to display the primitive's attributes.

Figure 3.47 Click an attribute's field to change its value.

To change the Subdivisions Height attribute of a polygon primitive after the object has been created:

1. Select a polygon primitive.

2. Select the poly(*Object*) title under the Inputs heading in the Channel Box (**Figure 3.46**).

3. Click the Subdivisions Height field to select the number there (**Figure 3.47**).

4. Change the number to reflect the number of times you want to divide the height.

5. Press [Enter] to complete the change (**Figure 3.48**).

✔ Tip

■ You can also click the attribute's name (Subdivisions Height in this example) in the Channel Box, and then click and drag the middle mouse button left or right in the view window to interactively change the attribute value.

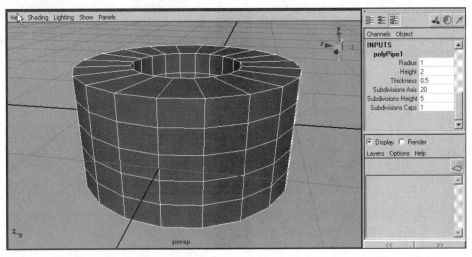

Figure 3.48 The Subdivisions Height attribute of this pipe primitive has been set to 5; this creates five subdivisions along the height of the object.

ABOUT POLYGON PRIMITIVES

About Subdiv Primitives

Subdiv primitives come in the six basic primitive shapes: *sphere, cube, cylinder, cone, plane,* and *torus* (**Figure 3.49**). Like polygon primitives, you can use these six basic shapes as a starting point for more detailed subdiv models. And like NURBS primitives, it's very easy to adjust the overall shape of a subdiv primitive.

However, unlike NURBS and polygon primitives, subdiv primitives have no attributes to adjust. To learn how to adjust the smoothness and level of detail of subdiv surfaces, see Chapter 9.

Creating subdiv primitives

Subdiv primitives are found in the Create menu within the Subdiv Primitives submenu. You can also access this menu via the Hotbox, as described in this section. Alternately, you can quickly create any of the six subdiv primitives by clicking their icons in the Subdivs Shelf.

When you create a subdiv primitive, Maya places the center point of the object at the origin of the scene, just as it does when you create a NURBS or polygon primitive.

To create a subdiv primitive using the main menu:

◆ Choose Create > Subdiv Primitives, and select the primitive you want to create (**Figure 3.50**).

A subdiv primitive is created at the origin of the scene.

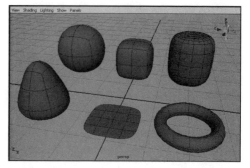

Figure 3.49 The six subdiv primitives (clockwise from top left): sphere, cube, cylinder, torus, plane, and cone.

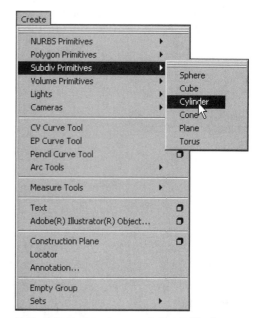

Figure 3.50 You can create a subdiv primitive by selecting it from the Create > Subdiv Primitives menu.

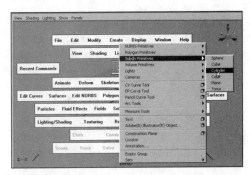

Figure 3.51 You can also use the Hotbox to create a subdiv primitive.

Figure 3.52 Using the Shelf to create a subdiv primitive can save you time.

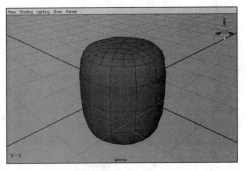

Figure 3.53 Newly created subdiv primitives are positioned at the origin.

To create a subdiv primitive using the Hotbox:

1. Press the Spacebar anywhere in the scene to display the Hotbox.

2. From the Create menu in the Hotbox, select the Subdiv Primitives submenu, and select the name of the primitive you want to create (**Figure 3.51**).

   A subdiv primitive is created at the origin of the scene.

To create a subdiv primitive using the Shelf:

◆ From the Subdivs Shelf, select the icon of the subdiv primitive you would like to create—for example, the cylinder (**Figure 3.52**).

   The primitive is created at the world origin of the scene (**Figure 3.53**).

ABOUT SUBDIV PRIMITIVES

About Text

The text tool in Maya lets you create geometry in the shape of text. You can use any font you have installed and generate one of four different types of geometry: *curves*, *trim*, *poly*, and *bevel* (**Figure 3.54**). You can choose from these options and enter your text in the Create > Text Options dialog box.

To create text:

1. From the Create menu, select the box next to Text (**Figure 3.55**).

   The Options dialog box opens.

2. Click the Text field, and type in your text.

3. Click the arrow next to the Font field, and then click Select to display the font options. Choose your font, and click OK (**Figure 3.56**).

4. Select the type of text you want to create (**Figure 3.57**).

5. Click Create.

   Your text appears in the scene, with the bottom-left corner of the text at the origin (**Figure 3.58**).

Figure 3.54 Maya lets you create four different text types (clockwise, from top left): curves, trim, bevel, and poly.

Figure 3.55 Select the box next to Text in the Create menu to bring up the Text Options dialog box.

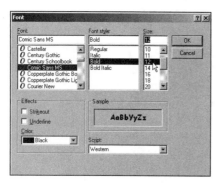

Figure 3.56 You can create text in any font you have installed on your computer.

Figure 3.57 The four text types are described in the next section.

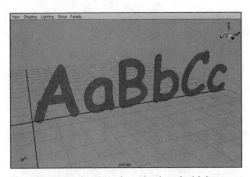

Figure 3.58 Newly created text is placed with its bottom-left corner at the origin.

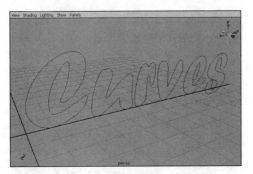

Figure 3.59 The curves text type generates no surfaces, only curves.

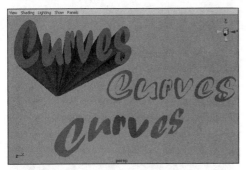

Figure 3.60 You can use the curves generated by the curves text type to create geometry.

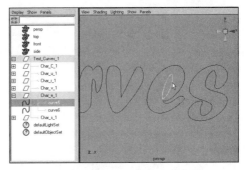

Figure 3.61 You can select and manipulate the individual curves generated by the curves text type.

About text types

The four different text types allow you to generate different types of geometry. Curves, trim and poly are all two-dimensional, whereas the bevel text type, new in Maya 7.0, is three-dimensional. This makes bevel the most immediately useful text type for most purposes, but the other types offer greater control and flexibility for certain tasks.

Curves is the first and default text type option. Using this type results in text defined by curves, with no surfaces (**Figure 3.59**). You might use this curve-based text as a non-rendering label in a model or to generate geometry in a variety of ways (**Figure 3.60**).

Notice that the text is created in separate, selectable pieces. For instance, the letter *e* has a curve for the outside part of the letter and another curve for its center (**Figure 3.61**).

The second text type setting is Trim. Using this text type is equivalent to selecting all the curves generated by the curves type and making them planar (see "Creating Surfaces from Curves" in Chapter 7). It creates the text as a single planar surface trimmed by the text's curves (see Figure 3.58).

You can select and move these curves individually. However, if you move any of them out of alignment with the trim text's plane, the planar surface will no longer be visible within that curve (**Figure 3.62**).

The third text type setting is poly, which generates flat text made out of polygons (**Figure 3.63**). This text type includes numerous options for controlling the number of polygons used on the text, but the default settings provide the best results for most tasks.

The final text type setting is bevel. This text type also generates text made out of polygons, but the text is three-dimensional and beveled (**Figure 3.64**). You can change the size and style of this beveling to create text with a variety of appearances.

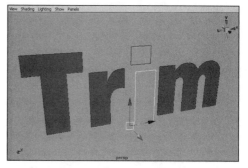

Figure 3.62 This trim text curve has been moved in the z direction, out of alignment with the planar surface displayed within the other curves.

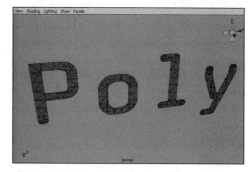

Figure 3.63 Text generated by the poly text type is made out of polygons.

Figure 3.64 The bevel text type, new in Maya 7.0, generates 3D text.

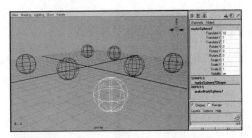

Figure 3.65 By default, the seventh NURBS sphere created in the scene is nurbsSphere7.

Figure 3.66 Click the object's name at the top of the Channel Box to change it.

Figure 3.67 A descriptive name makes the object easier to distinguish from other objects.

Figure 3.68 You can also change the name of an object by double-clicking it in the Outliner and then typing a new name.

Naming Objects

Each time you create an object, Maya gives it a default name. This name is a description of the object, followed by the number of times that object type has been used in the scene. For example, nurbsSphere7 is the default name for the seventh NURBS sphere created in a scene (**Figure 3.65**).

To make an object easy to find later, you can change its default name to something more descriptive. For example, if you create a torus that you intend to use as a tire, you can change its name to *tire* or even *frontLeftTire*. Using descriptive names keeps things organized and clear as you add objects to your scene.

To change an object's name:

1. Create an object, or select an existing one by clicking it.

2. Select the object's default name at the top of the Channel Box (**Figure 3.66**).

3. Replace the default name by typing in a new name—for example, bowlingBall (**Figure 3.67**).

4. Press (Enter) to complete the name change.

✔ Tip

- You can also change an object's name by double-clicking it in the Outliner and then typing a new name (**Figure 3.68**).

NAMING OBJECTS

About Construction History

As you build objects in Maya, the software stores information about the tools, options, and geometry used to create them. This information is referred to as the object's *construction history*, and it can be found under the Inputs heading in the Channel Box (**Figure 3.69**). As you've seen throughout this chapter, you can make changes to the construction history to modify the final object's shape.

Construction history can be very useful when you want to tweak a surface without having to rebuild it. However, using construction history requires some extra processing power, which can become significant for complex objects. If you're certain that you won't need to change an object's construction history, you can delete it. You can also turn off this feature; doing so causes all new objects to be created without construction history but doesn't affect existing objects.

To turn the construction history off or on:

◆ Click the Construction History On/Off icon in the status bar. is on, and is off.

To delete an object's construction history:

1. Select the object whose construction history you want to delete.

   If there are no objects in your scene, you can create one by select Create > NURBS Primitives > Sphere.

2. Choose Edit > Delete by Type > History (**Figure 3.70**).

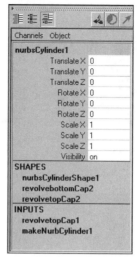

Figure 3.69 An object's construction history can be used to modify the object.

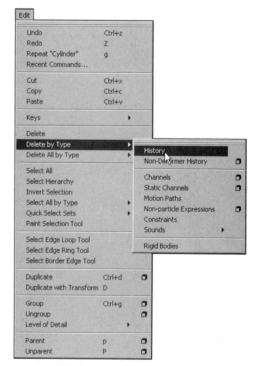

Figure 3.70 For complex objects, deleting the construction history can improve manipulation speed.

TRANSFORMING OBJECTS AND COMPONENTS

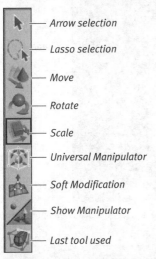

- Arrow selection
- Lasso selection
- Move
- Rotate
- Scale
- Universal Manipulator
- Soft Modification
- Show Manipulator
- Last tool used

Figure 4.1 Maya's manipulation tools.

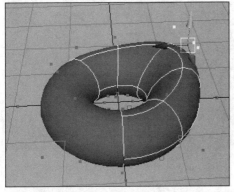

Figure 4.2 The Move tool's Translation manipulator is used to move objects and components around the scene.

Maya gives you many ways to move, rotate, and scale objects around a scene, and many shortcuts for completing these common tasks. These actions, known as *transformations*, can be performed in a couple of different ways: You can type new coordinates or values in the Channel Box or use one of the many manipulation tools (**Figure 4.1**) to drag the object freely around the scene or constrain it to an axis.

Using the same tools you would employ to manipulate objects in the scene, you can also manipulate *parts* of an object, known as *components*. Each object type has its own components that can be translated (**Figure 4.2**), rotated, and/or scaled to change their look and position, in turn changing the appearance of the object.

Most tools include advanced features (shown in the Tool Options) that you can explore as your knowledge base grows. The duplication options provide a good example of this. Once you get used to using them, you can employ a number of advanced options like duplicating an object multiple times throughout your scene, or using them to construct and mirror objects.

Moving, Rotating, and Scaling Objects

Maya provides multiple tools for moving, rotating, and scaling objects and components. The Universal Manipulator tool, new in Maya 7, can perform all of these operations at once, which can be helpful when an object requires all three transformations. We'll discuss the Universal Manipulator tool in more detail later in this chapter.

Each of these tools, including the Universal Manipulator tool, has axes that you can grab and move to transform an object. These axes, called *manipulators* (**Figure 4.3**), let you translate (move), rotate, or scale the object. Manipulators make it easy to constrain objects along a particular axis: You click and drag the colored line for the axis along which you want to constrain the object. The colors remain consistent for each tool. RGB colors coincide with the *x-y-z* axes (**Figure 4.4**): The manipulator's *x* axis is red, the *y* axis is green, and the *z* axis is blue. If you forget an axis's color, check the View axis in the lower left-hand corner of each pane or the View Compass at upper right (**Figure 4.5**). The axis selected on the manipulator is always yellow.

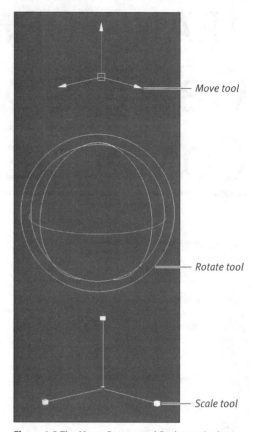

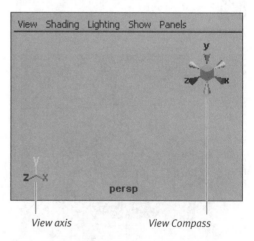

Figure 4.3 The Move, Rotate, and Scale manipulators.

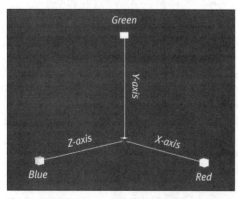

Figure 4.4 RGB colors match the *x-y-z* axes.

Figure 4.5 Check the View axis in the lower-left corner of each pane to remind yourself which color is associated with each axis.

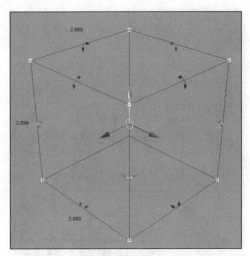

Figure 4.6 The Universal Manipulator combines the common functions of the Move, Scale, and Rotate tools.

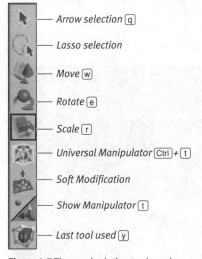

Arrow selection q

Lasso selection

Move w

Rotate e

Scale r

Universal Manipulator Ctrl + t

Soft Modification

Show Manipulator t

Last tool used y

Figure 4.7 The manipulation tools and their shortcut keys.

In addition to constraining an object along an axis, you can freely manipulate the object by clicking and dragging the square in the middle of the Move, Scale, and Universal Manipulator tools (**Figure 4.6**), or by clicking and dragging anywhere inside the Rotate manipulator.

To get precise results, you can also use the Channel Box for numerical entry. The Channel Box allows direct access to any of the attributes (translation axis, rotation axis, and scale values) that the translation tools affect.

Each of the tools in the toolbar—with the exception of the Lasso tool, the Soft Modification tool, and the Universal Manipulator—has an associated shortcut that coincides with qwerty keys on the keyboard. You can press a tool's key (or, in the case of the Universal Manipulator, the key combination) to turn on its manipulator.

The shortcut keys and the manipulators they turn on are as follows (**Figure 4.7**):

q Arrow selection tool

w Move tool

e Rotate tool

r Scale tool

Ctrl + t Universal Manipulator

t Show Manipulator

y Last tool used

✔ Tip

■ Be aware that these keys won't work if the Caps Lock key is on. Maya is case sensitive: Capitals represent different hotkeys with different functions mapped to them. For example, the Move, Rotate, and Scale tools' associated keyboard shortcuts are q, e, and r, respectively. However, when those same keyboard letters are capitalized, they set an animation keyframe on the translation, rotation, or scale channels instead (keyframes are discussed in Chapter 12).

To translate an object or component using the Move tool:

1. Select an object or component by clicking it.

2. Press ⓦ or click the Move tool icon [icon] in the toolbar.

   The Move manipulator becomes visible on the object or component (**Figure 4.8**).

3. Click and drag the manipulator's arrow in the direction you want the object to move (**Figure 4.9**).

   This action translates the object along the selected axis.

   or

   Hold down (Shift), and then, with the middle mouse button, click and drag in the direction you want the object to move (**Figure 4.10**).

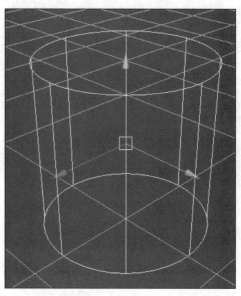

Figure 4.8 The Move manipulator is used to move the object around the scene.

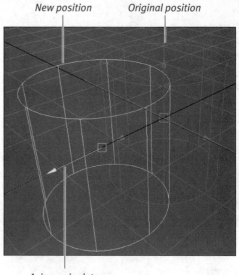

New position   Original position

Axis manipulator

Figure 4.9 Click and drag the axis to which you want the object constrained so that you can maintain precise control over the surface's position. This is particularly useful in the Perspective view.

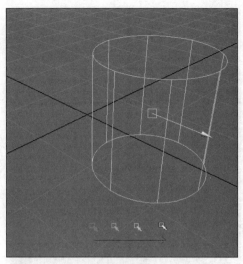

Figure 4.10 By holding down Shift and dragging with the middle mouse button, you can move an object without using the manipulator handles.

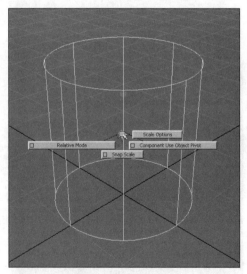

Figure 4.11 The Scale tool's marking menu includes shortcuts for scaling proportionally and changing the pivot options for components.

This action selects the appropriate manipulator axis and translates the object in that direction. This is particularly useful if you've created an object at the origin but moved the camera away from the grid. You can pull the object into your camera view if you know the direction of the origin.

or

To translate the object freely, click and drag the center of the manipulator, and the motion will not be constrained on any axis.

✔ Tips

- You'll usually want to avoid using free translations for large adjustments in the Perspective view. The nature of the view can lead to translations in unwanted directions.

- You can also hold down x to activate grid snap. In addition, if you drag with the middle mouse button anywhere on the grid, the object snaps to that location.

- You can use the + and – keys to enlarge or shrink the manipulators.

- From anywhere in a view pane, you can hold down the keyboard shortcut for the Move (w), Rotate (e), or Scale (r) tool and click to bring up that tool's marking menu (**Figure 4.11**). Maya's Transform marking menus include shortcuts to many of the tools' options.

To scale an object or component using the Scale tool:

1. Select an object or component by clicking it.

2. Press r, or click the Scale tool icon in the toolbar.

   The Scale manipulator becomes visible on the object or component (**Figure 4.12**).

3. Click the small square of the axis on which you want to scale the object or component, and drag in the direction you want the object to scale (**Figure 4.13**).

   or

   While pressing (Shift), click and drag with the middle mouse button anywhere in the pane in the direction in which you want the object to scale (**Figure 4.14**).

   This action selects the appropriate manipulator axis and scales the object in that direction.

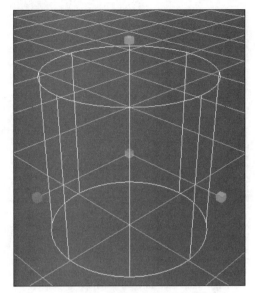

Figure 4.12 You use the Scale tool's manipulator to scale an object proportionally or along a single axis.

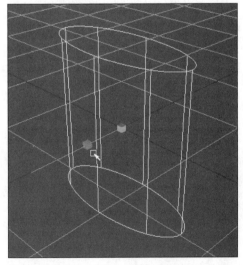

Figure 4.13 Click and drag a Scale tool's axis to scale an object along a particular axis.

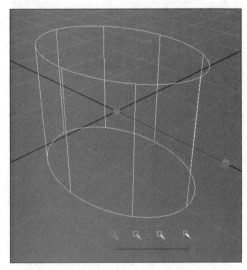

Figure 4.14 This cylinder is being scaled along the *x* axis by shift clicking and dragging with the middle mouse button.

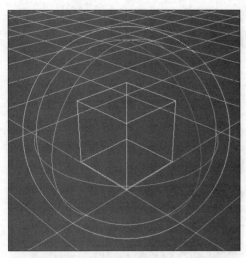

Figure 4.15 The Rotate manipulator is used to rotate the surface on one or more axes.

Figure 4.16 Click and drag the axis circle to which you want the object constrained. A gray pie slice shows you how many degrees you have rotated the object.

To rotate an object or component using the Rotate tool:

1. Select an object or component by clicking it.

2. Press e or click the Rotate tool icon 🔄 in the toolbar.

   The Rotate manipulator becomes visible on the object or component (**Figure 4.15**).

3. Click the circle of the axis around which you want to rotate the object or component, and drag in the direction you want the object to rotate (**Figure 4.16**).

✔ Tips

- You can click anywhere within the Rotate manipulator sphere, and click and drag to rotate the object without being constrained to any axis.

- Once the axis you want to use is yellow on the manipulator, you can click and drag anywhere in the pane with the middle mouse button to rotate the object around that axis without touching the axis or the object.

- The light blue outer ring rotates the object or component around an axis that always faces the camera view (**Figure 4.17**).

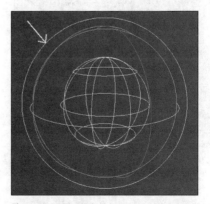

Figure 4.17 The light-blue outer ring rotates the object or component in the view plane.

To translate, rotate, or scale an object or component using the Channel Box:

1. Click an object or component to select it.

2. In the Channel Box, click once in the field next to the attribute you want to change (**Figure 4.18**).

3. Type a new value in the selected field. The object reflects the value change (**Figures 4.19**).

   or

   Click to select the attribute's name, and then move the mouse over a view pane. Hold down the middle mouse button, and drag left or right to interactively change the value of the selected attribute (**Figure 4.20**).

Using the Universal Manipulator

The Universal Manipulator provides easy access to three transformations in one tool (**Figure 4.21**). It can be used to enter in exact values without using the Channel Box, and also enables you to quickly perform these operations around different temporary center points.

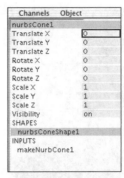

Figure 4.18 Click the field name of the attribute you want to change (in this case, Translate X).

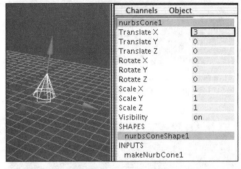

Figure 4.19 Changing the Translate X value to *3* moves the cone three units in the positive *x* direction.

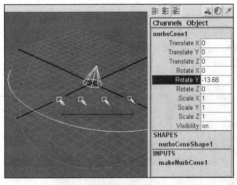

Figure 4.20 You can use the middle mouse button to interactively change values anywhere in a pane.

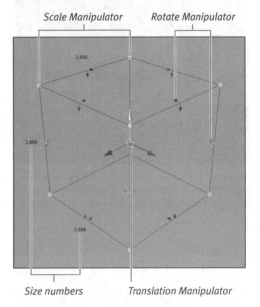

Scale Manipulator   Rotate Manipulator

Size numbers   Translation Manipulator

Figure 4.21 The Universal Manipulator combines many functions for quick manipulation. It's a great time saver for performing common transformations.

MOVING, ROTATING, AND SCALING OBJECTS

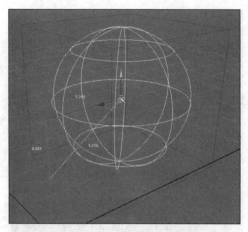

Figure 4.22 Using the translation axis displays a color-coded triangle showing exactly how far you have moved your object along each axis.

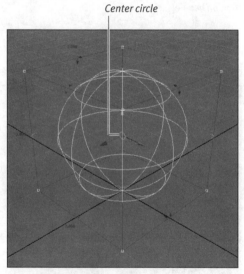

Center circle

Figure 4.23 The Universal Manipulator shows a bounding box around your object.

The Universal Manipulator also provides real-time information about how far you have translated or rotated an object (**Figure 4.22**).

The Universal Manipulator does have its limits. For instance, it can't rotate freely in all directions, and you can't use it to manipulate components, only objects.

To translate an object using the Universal Manipulator:

1. Select an object or component by clicking it.

2. Press Ctrl+t, or click the Universal Manipulator tool icon 🖼.

    The Universal Manipulator becomes visible on the object or component (**Figure 4.23**).

3. Click the axis you want to translate, and drag the mouse to translate in that direction.

    or

    Click the center circle, and drag the mouse to translate the object freely.

    or

    Click once on the tip of the translation axis, and enter a numerical value in the box that appears (**Figure 4.24**).

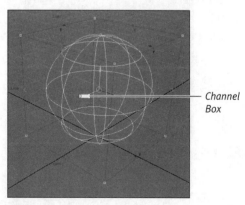

Channel Box

Figure 4.24 Entering in a precise value saves a trip to the Channel Box.

To rotate an object using the Universal Manipulator:

1. Select an object or component by clicking it.

2. Press Ctrl+t, or click the Universal Manipulator tool icon ▩.

3. Click the arrow corresponding to the axis you want to translate, and drag the mouse to rotate on that axis (**Figure 4.25**).

   or

   Click once on a rotation arrow, and enter a numerical value in the box that appears.

To scale an object using the Universal Manipulator:

1. Select an object or component by clicking it.

2. Press Ctrl+t, or click the Universal Manipulator tool icon ▩ in the toolbar.

3. Click a vertex of the bounding box, and drag to scale the object universally (**Figure 4.26**).

   Note that the Universal Manipulator uses the opposite corner from the one you've selected as the center point for the scale. This means that it will scale towards the opposite corner instead of the center of the object

   or

   Click one of the size numbers, and enter a numerical value.

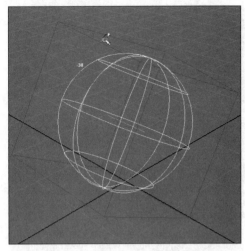

Figure 4.25 When you're rotating an object on an axis using the Universal Manipulator, the length (in degrees) of the rotation will be displayed near the rotation handle.

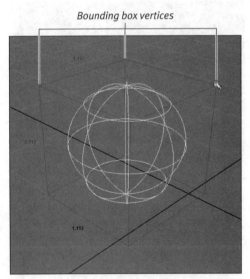

Bounding box vertices

Figure 4.26 Scaling with the bounding box scales to the opposite corner of the one you've selected.

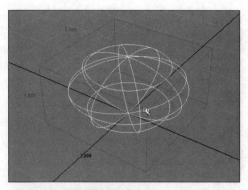

Figure 4.27 Using Ctrl allows scaling on an axis instead of to a corner.

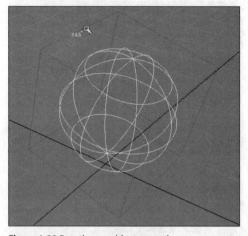

Figure 4.28 Rotating an object around a corner saves you from having to reposition the pivot point every time.

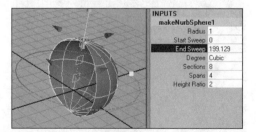

Figure 4.29 The additional manipulator on the Show Manipulator tool controls additional input attributes, saving you from going to the Channel Box. In this example, the end sweep was changed to less than 360 degrees by moving the circular manipulator.

✔ Tips

- To restrict scaling to one axis, hold Ctrl and move the mouse in the direction of that axis (**Figure 4.27**), or click a size number and enter in a value.

- Pressing Shift when performing scale operations performs them from the center of the object rather than a corner or side.

- Pressing Ctrl when rotating the object using the Universal Manipulator rotates the object around the bounding box edges. The edge it will use is the one opposite the rotation arrow you chose (**Figure 4.28**).

Using the Show Manipulator tool

The Show Manipulator tool 🔲 lets you access the Inputs node of an object (known as its *construction history)* to alter a surface or curve. In other words, the Show Manipulator tool gives you access to certain attributes used in the creation or manipulation of an object that are usually only available in the Channel Box or Attribute Editor (**Figure 4.29**).

The Show Manipulator tool is commonly used to adjust a spotlight or camera. When you use it on a spotlight, the light has three manipulators instead of one—one to move the light; one for the light to point at, which makes adjusting lighting easier; and one represented by a circle with a tick mark, which adjusts the attributes to be manipulated.

MOVING, ROTATING, AND SCALING OBJECTS

To aim a spotlight using the Show Manipulator tool:

1. Select Create > Lights > Spotlight.

2. Click the Show Manipulator icon 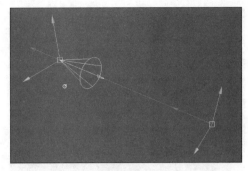 in the toolbar.

   The spotlight now has one manipulator at its base and another in front of the light (**Figure 4.30**).

3. Select and move the manipulator at the base of the spotlight (**Figure 4.31**).

   The spotlight moves with the manipulator but continues to point at the second manipulator.

4. Select and move the manipulator in front of the spotlight.

   The spotlight remains in place but continues to point at the manipulator (**Figure 4.32**).

Figure 4.30 Two manipulators appear, giving you more precise control over what objects the spotlight is pinpointing and the direction in which the light is aimed.

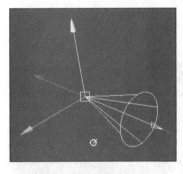

Figure 4.31 Select the manipulator attached to the spotlight to translate the light.

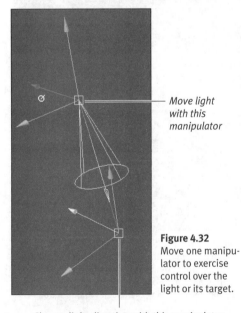

Move light with this manipulator

Figure 4.32 Move one manipulator to exercise control over the light or its target.

Change light direction with this manipulator

Changes which history node is currently viewed   *Adjusts cone angle*

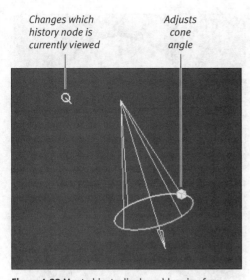

Figure 4.33 Most objects display a blue ring from which you can access that object's input nodes or attributes interactively.

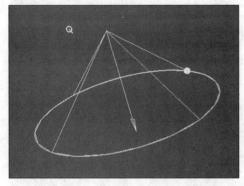

Figure 4.34 The cone angle controls the width of the light beam.

5. Click twice on the ring that hovers near the spotlight.

The manipulators change into a ring around the cone of light. Each time you click the ring, it cycles you through some of the cone's input nodes (**Figure 4.33**).

6. Click and drag on the cube atop the circle that surrounds the cone.

The cone angle changes interactively as you drag the mouse (**Figure 4.34**).

About Pivot Points

Each object in Maya has a pivot point. When you rotate an object, it rotates around its pivot point, and when you scale an object, it scales to and from the pivot point. By default, the object's pivot point is at the center of the object, but Maya lets you move the pivot point according to your needs. For example, if you model a clock, you can position the pivot point of each hand at the center of the clock rather than the middle of the hand. This lets you easily rotate the hands around the face of the clock (**Figure 4.35**).

Figure 4.35 This simple clock has had the pivot points of its hands repositioned to the center of the clock face.

To change an object's pivot point position:

1. Select the object whose pivot point you would like to move.

2. Select the Move tool from the Tool Box, or press ⓦ.

3. Press Insert/Home to go into pivot point mode.

   The pivot point manipulator is now visible (**Figure 4.36**).

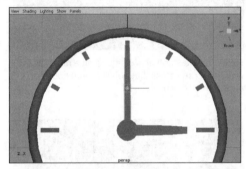

Figure 4.36 By default, an object's pivot point is located at the center of the object.

4. Click and drag one of the pivot point manipulator handles to move the pivot point to a new position (**Figure 4.37**).

   The new position will be the new rotation point for the object.

5. Press Insert/Home to disable pivot point mode.

To position the pivot point in the center of an object:

1. Select the object whose pivot point you would like to center.

2. Choose Modify > Center Pivot.

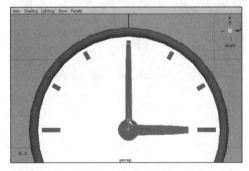

Figure 4.37 You can reposition an object's pivot point by using the pivot point manipulator.

Figure 4.38
This flower was made with two objects and one duplication, which placed the petals around the center.

INPUTS	
makeNurbSphere1	
Radius	0.504
Start Sweep	0
End Sweep	360
Degree	Cubic
Sections	8
Spans	4
Height Ratio	2

Figure 4.39 The sphere's Inputs node holds its editable history attributes.

Figure 4.40
From the Edit menu, select the box next to Duplicate to open the Duplicate Options dialog box.

Duplication Options

Maya provides duplication shortcuts for modeling objects with repetitive geometry—for example, a staircase or flower petals. To model a flower in a minimum number of steps, you could make one petal, and then reproduce it many times around the center (**Figure 4.38**).

You can use the Duplicate tool for simple object duplications as well as for more complex duplications, including ones that apply changes to the rotation, translation, and scale of an object. You can also use the Duplicate tool to mirror and create instances of objects.

You can duplicate objects either with or without their Inputs or History nodes (**Figure 4.39**). (See Chapter 1, "Maya Basics," for more information on construction history.) It's important to note, however, that history duplication is set to *off* by default.

To duplicate an object:

1. Select an object.

2. From the Edit menu, select the box next to Duplicate (**Figure 4.40**).
   The Duplicate Options dialog box opens.

continues on next page

DUPLICATION OPTIONS

3. Enter the number of duplicates desired in the Number of Copies field (**Figure 4.41**.

4. Click Duplicate.

The specified number of copies are duplicated and placed on top of each other.

To duplicate an object with rotation:

1. Select an object.

2. From the Edit menu, select the box next to Duplicate.

The Duplicate Options dialog box opens.

3. Select a rotation amount for each additional copy, and type that amount in the Rotate field of the axis you want to rotate around (**Figure 4.42**). The fields are, left to right, x axis, y axis, and z axis.

If you've used a sphere, you'll only notice a rotation in wireframe mode.

4. Click the Duplicate button to duplicate the object.

✔ Tips

■ You can use the same technique to translate or scale a copy.

■ You can reset the duplication options to their original state by selecting Edit > Reset Settings in the Options window.

The standard duplication tool can be cumbersome because there are so many options to adjust or reset for even a simple duplication. The Duplicate with Translation tool, on the other hand, comes in handy when all you want to do is make a copy and move it down an axis, or if you only want to produce one or two copies.

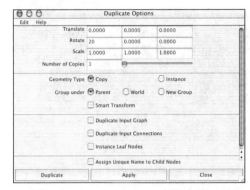

Figure 4.41 Enter the number of duplicates you desire in the Number of Copies field.

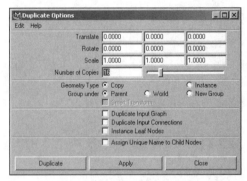

Figure 4.42 Enter the amount of rotation desired in the first field of the Rotate attribute. The first field is the rotate x field.

Figure 4.43 Choose Edit › Duplicate with Transform.

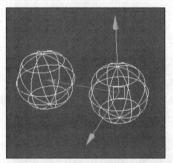

Figure 4.44 Move the sphere the distance you would like your future duplications to copy.

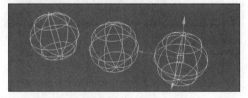

Figure 4.45 Duplicate the object again.

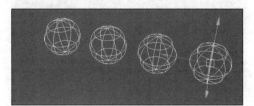

Figure 4.46 Each new copy moves down the axis the same amount as the original copy.

To duplicate an object with simple translation:

1. Create a primitive sphere.

2. Choose Edit > Duplicate with Transform (**Figure 4.43**).

3. Move the duplicated sphere a few units in the z direction (**Figure 4.44**).

4. Choose Edit > Duplicate with Transform.

   A new sphere is created. It's the same distance from the second sphere that the second sphere is from the original (**Figure 4.45**).

5. Press ⌗Shift+⌗d.

   Another duplicate is made, an equal distance from the last (**Figure 4.46**).

✔ Tip

■ Use the Duplicate with Transform tool when you want to make just one copy of an object. This allows you to preserve your duplication settings for more complicated tasks.

DUPLICATION OPTIONS

Constructing with duplication

Now that you have a general idea of how to duplicate an object, let's put the options into action and create a simple staircase. You'll use the same technique you employed to create a copy with rotation, but now you'll use the Translate, Rotate, and Scale options together.

The key to successfully creating a duplicate with translation is placing the pivot point in the correct position for the objects to rotate around (**Figure 4.47**).

To create a simple staircase:

1. Select Create > Poly Primitive > Cube.
   A cube is created at the origin.

2. Type 0.5 in the Translate Y field in the Channel Box, and press Enter (**Figure 4.48**).
   This setting moves the cube up so that its base sits on the grid.

3. Type 6 in the Scale X field in the Channel Box, and press Enter (**Figure 4.49**).
   This widens the cube.

4. Press w or click the Move tool icon in the toolbar.

5. Press Insert on the keyboard to go into pivot-point edit mode.

6. Move the pivot point to the far-left edge of the cube, using the *x*-axis manipulator (**Figure 4.50**).

7. Press Insert again to turn off pivot-point edit mode.

8. From the Edit menu, select the box next to Duplicate to open the Duplicate Options window.

Pivot point

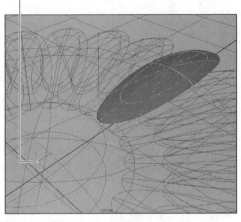

Figure 4.47 The pivot point's placement determines the placement of a duplicated surface.

Figure 4.48 Type 0.5 in the Translate Y field to move the cube's bottom so that it sits on the grid.

Figure 4.49 Type 6 in the Scale X field to scale the *x* axis of the object by six units.

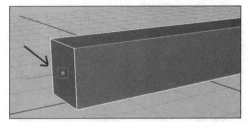

Figure 4.50 The pivot point determines the point in space around which the staircase rotates.

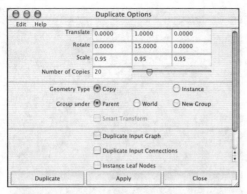

Figure 4.51 Set the duplicate options as shown to properly duplicate the cube.

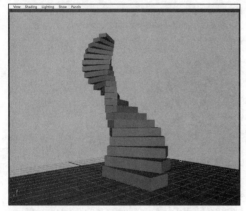

Figure 4.52 You can use the Duplicate tool to quickly construct geometric or repetitive shapes like this staircase.

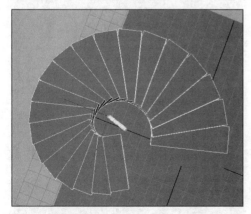

Figure 4.53 The pivot points of the steps are shown here, revealing that they form a straight line up the center of the staircase.

9. Set the duplicate options as follows (**Figure 4.51**).

   ◆ **Translate: 0, 1, 0**—This setting moves each new duplicate up the y axis one unit. The cube is one unit high, so each copy sits on top of the previous one.

   ◆ **Rotate: 0, 15, 0**—This setting rotates each duplicate 15 degrees more than the previous one around the y axis.

   ◆ **Scale: .95, .95, .95**—This setting scales each duplicate proportionately to 95 percent the size of the last. The staircase gets smaller as it goes higher.

10. Enter 20 in the Number of Copies field. This setting will create 20 new steps.

11. Click Duplicate.

    The specified number of copies are made and placed on top of each other after being rotated and scaled (**Figure 4.52**).

✔ Tips

- It's a good idea to check your options before duplicating. The previous settings are retained unless you reset them. To return the options to their default settings, with the Duplicate Options window open, select Edit > Reset Settings.

- Move the pivot point farther down the x axis before duplicating to make room for a pole in the center of the staircase (**Figure 4.53**).

DUPLICATION OPTIONS

Mirroring and Instancing Objects

In addition to translating objects, you can use the Duplication options to create a mirror image of an object (that is, a reversed copy of the original). Body parts or characters make good candidates for mirroring because many characters are nearly symmetrical. This allows you to model one half of a character and mirror it, saving yourself almost half the work (**Figure 4.54**).

Additionally, you can create *instances* of objects—duplicates that retain a connection to the shape of the original (**Figure 4.55**). The beauty of this technique is that you can then edit any of the objects and have each of the rest follow those edits interactively. For example, if you're creating a building with multiple identical pillars, you can create one pillar and then create a number of *instances* of it to get the additional pillars. If you later decide to change the look of the pillars, all you have to do is edit one, and the rest will be updated automatically.

Mirroring

Mirroring an object produces a precise reverse copy of the object. This technique is great for symmetrical objects, such as creating one side of a face and then mirroring the face across an axis to complete it (**Figure 4.56**). The pivot point is used as the mirror axis, which means that the farther the pivot point is from the object, the farther the mirrored copy will be from the original.

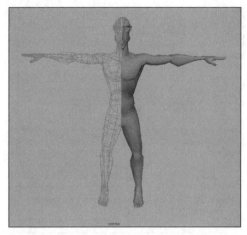

Figure 4.54 By mirroring a character or anything symmetrical, you can save a lot of work.

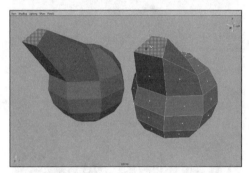

Figure 4.55 Instances of objects mimic the edits of the first object interactively. Here one poly sphere reflects the change to the other.

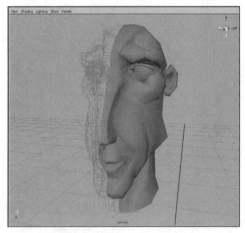

Figure 4.56 You can create half a face and then mirror it to complete the rest of the face.

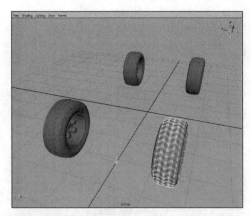

Figure 4.57 Any symmetrical object is ideal for mirroring. Here, a pair of tires is flipped to the other side of the *x* axis.

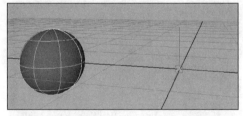

Figure 4.58 Type -2 in the Translate X field of the Channel Box to move the object two units in the negative *x* direction.

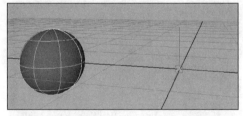

Figure 4.59 Move the pivot point to the origin to send the copy an equal distance away from the origin.

You can also use mirroring to place objects an equal distance away from an axis line, creating a mirrored copy that's perfectly placed (**Figure 4.57**).

In the following task, you'll mirror a sphere across an axis, as if to create two eyes.

To mirror an object:

1. Select Create > NURBS Primitives > Sphere, or select an object to mirror.

2. Type -2 in the Translate X field in the Channel Box (**Figure 4.58**).

   This setting moves the object two units down the negative *x* axis.

3. Press w or click the Move tool icon in the toolbar.

4. Press Insert on the keyboard to go into pivot-point edit mode.

5. Holding down x, move the pivot point to the origin (**Figure 4.59**).

   x snaps to the grid, which ensures that the pivot point is precisely at the origin.

6. Press Insert to get out of pivot-point edit mode.

7. From the Edit menu, select the box beside Duplicate.

   The Duplicate Options window opens.

continues on next page

8. Select Edit > Reset Settings in the Duplicate Options window to reset the settings, and then set the Scale X field to –1.

9. Click Duplicate.

   A mirrored copy is duplicated an equal distance from the pivot point (**Figure 4.60**).

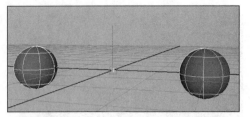

Figure 4.60 A mirrored copy is duplicated an equal distance from the pivot point.

✔ Tip

- Often, mirroring is used in conjunction with instancing so your modifications are automatically reflected across the object (**Figure 4.61**).

Instancing

Instancing is a great way to save time, both in modeling and in rendering. An instanced object follows the edits of the original, making instancing ideal for any object that will have identical copies anywhere else in the scene (**Figure 4.62**). Instanced objects only are loaded into memory once, saving on render time. Very large scenes can be populated by instanced objects and still stay workable. You can still scale, rotate, and move the objects independently once they've been instanced.

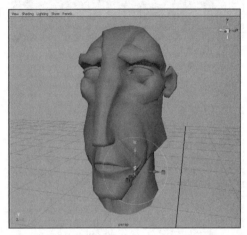

Figure 4.61 Combining mirroring and instancing allows adjustments to one side of this face to be reflected on the other.

To make an instance of an object:

1. Select an object by clicking it.

2. From the Edit menu, select the box next to Duplicate.

   The Duplicate Options window opens.

Figure 4.62 Oil drums are instanced to cut down on the number of edits that need to be made. The objects are rotated to hide their similar attributes.

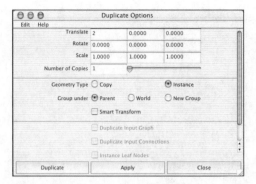

Figure 4.63 Set the Translate X field to 2.

Figure 4.64 Selecting Copy duplicates the object; however, selecting Instance results in an additional connection to the original object.

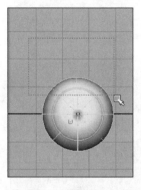

Figure 4.65 Marquee-select across the top third of the object to select control vertexes to manipulate.

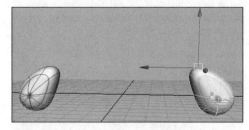

Figure 4.66 The other object follows the translation of the selected surface but in the opposite direction, like an object in a mirror.

3. Set the Translate X field to 2 and the rest of the Translate and Rotate fields to 0 (**Figure 4.63**).

You add a translate here so the copy doesn't sit directly on top of the original.

4. For Geometry Type, select Instance (**Figure 4.64**).

5. Click Duplicate.

The duplicate is now an instance, or virtual copy, of the original.

6. With one of the objects selected, press [F8] to go into component-selection mode.

7. Marquee-select across the top third of the object to select one of its components (**Figure 4.65**).

8. Press [w], and translate the components in any direction.

Note that the other object follows the translation of the selected surface (**Figure 4.66**).

✔ Tip

■ Once you've created an instance of an object, you can't modify its components independently. However, you can translate, rotate, or scale the whole object without affecting the other instances.

MIRRORING AND INSTANCING OBJECTS

Duplicating input connections

Often, you'll want the construction history to remain attached to an object when you create a copy of it. This produces an effect like instancing but allows you to alter the objects independently as well. You can do this by selecting the Duplicate Input Connections check box in the Duplicate Options window. The objects then share the same Inputs node, and both the original and the duplicates are changed by it.

To duplicate an object with its input connections:

1. Select an object that has input connections attached to it—a primitive sphere, for example (**Figure 4.67**).

2. From the Edit menu, select the box next to Duplicate.
   The Duplicate Options window opens.

3. Select the Duplicate Input Connections check box (**Figure 4.68**).

   This option connects the duplicated object to the Inputs node of the original. Now, if you alter the Inputs node of one, the duplicates are also affected.

4. Type the number of duplicates you want to produce in the Number of Copies field.

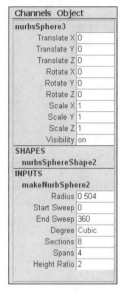

Figure 4.67 A primitive sphere's Inputs node holds the editable history of the sphere.

Figure 4.68 Select the Duplicate Input Connections check box in the Duplicate Options window to copy the input connections to the new object.

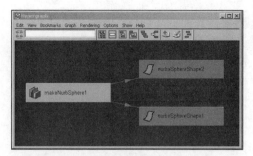

Figure 4.69 The same makeNurbSphere node is connected to both spheres.

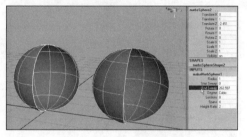

Figure 4.70 Since both spheres share the input node makeNurbSphere1, adjusting the sweep of that node will adjust both spheres.

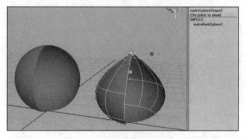

Figure 4.71 When you retain the Inputs node on duplicated objects, you can continue to make individual changes to the surfaces.

5. Click Duplicate.

A copy of the object is made, and its connections are attached to it (**Figure 4.69**). The new object sits directly on top of the original.

6. Select the Move tool, and move the duplicated object away from the original.

7. In the Channel Box, select the End Sweep attribute name, and drag the middle mouse button in the View pane to confirm the connections.

The End Sweep is changed on both objects interactively (**Figure 4.70**).

8. Right-click a sphere, select CV's from the marking menu, and move a few around.

When you duplicate with input connections, you can make changes to the new copies with out affecting the rest. (**Figure 4.71**).

Soft-Modifying Objects

The Soft Modification tool  gives you the ability to *sculpt*, or smoothly modify, dense surfaces (**Figure 4.72**).

You can use this tool for modeling as well as animation, because its parameters can be keyframed as long as the construction history has been enabled (see Chapter 1 for more about construction history). The Soft Modification tool's uses range from adjusting a dense facial mesh, to creating smooth terrain, to animating bulging muscles on a superhero's arm (**Figure 4.73**).

The Soft Modification tool works by tapering the effect of adjusting points on surfaces. This allows smooth adjustments of a surface across several points. This technique is especially useful when you're working with dense surfaces: Without the Soft Modification tool, it would be far too time-consuming to individually move the large number of components required to make smooth changes.

As with the other translation tools, you can activate the Soft Modification tool and then select the area of the object you want to soft-modify. Or, if you select an object first and then choose the Soft Modification tool, the effect is automatically applied to the center of the object. The effect can be moved at any time, unless you delete the construction history.

To soft-modify an object:

1. Create a primitive polygonal plane (Create > Poly Primitives > Plane), give it Subdivisions Height and Width of **100**, and scale it to about 20 times its original size (**Figure 4.74**).

2. Make sure your plane isn't selected, and then click the Soft Modification tool  in the toolbar.

— *Soft Modification tool*

Figure 4.72 Choose the Soft Modification tool from the toolbar.

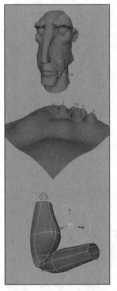

Figure 4.73 Faces, smooth terrain, and muscles are just a few examples of what Soft Modification can do.

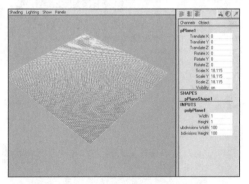

Figure 4.74 In the Channel Box, increase the Subdivisions Width and Height to create a dense polygon plane.

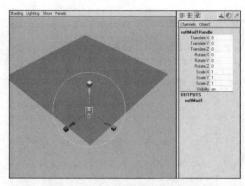

Figure 4.75 Add a softMod to a surface.

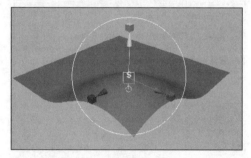

Figure 4.76 Drag the *y* axis of the softMod manipulator.

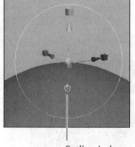

Cycling Index

Figure 4.77 The Cycling Index is a circle with a line through it under the softMod manipulator. Click the Cycling Index to toggle on the Falloff manipulator.

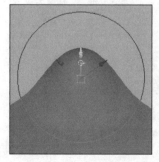

Figure 4.78 Click and drag the red circle around the Falloff manipulator to adjust the drop-off area.

3. Click the part of the object where you want to create the soft modification (softMod).

   A softMod node is added to the surface, and its manipulator becomes active (**Figure 4.75**).

4. Select the *y* translate axis of the manipulator, and drag it up (**Figure 4.76**).

5. Click the Cycling Index to display the Falloff manipulator (**Figure 4.77**).

6. Click and drag the red circle surrounding the Falloff manipulator to increase or decrease the drop-off area (**Figure 4.78**).

7. Click the translation icon on the Falloff manipulator, and drag it from side to side (**Figure 4.79**).

continues on next page

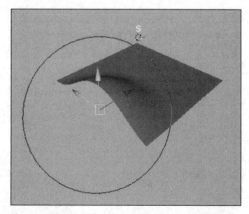

Figure 4.79 Using the Move tool, click and drag the Falloff manipulator.

SOFT-MODIFYING OBJECTS

8. Press Ctrl+a to open the Attribute Editor for the softMod (**Figure 4.80**).

9. In the Falloff Curve section of the Attribute Editor (**Figure 4.81**), click the ramp to create a new edit point (**Figure 4.82**).

10. Click and drag the edit point into the desired position.

or

Click the box with an x in it to delete the edit point.

11. Add two edit points, and position them as they are in (**Figure 4.83**).

You can see the results of editing the falloff curve on the surface of the softMod you created.

✔ Tips

■ Before clicking the Soft Modification tool in the toolbar, be sure you don't have any objects selected on your screen. If you do, a softMod node will be added to any selected objects when you choose the tool.

■ If you deselect the Falloff manipulator, you can click the S icon floating above the surface and then press t to reactivate it.

■ Soft modification can work on selected components as well as the entire object.

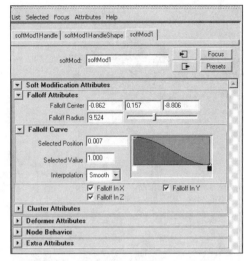

Figure 4.80 Edit the falloff curve in the softMod Attribute Editor.

Figure 4.81 Click the graph in the Falloff Curve section...

Figure 4.82 ...to create edit points.

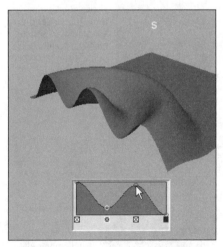

Figure 4.83 The softMod now has a smooth, wavelike shape.

SELECTION MODES, HIDING, AND TEMPLATING

A Maya scene can include hundreds of objects, which can add up to a major headache when you're trying to focus on one specific area (**Figure 5.1**). Fortunately, Maya provides various tools that you can use to hide, template, layer, and select objects, eliminating much of the frustration of dealing with complex scenes.

View Shading Lighting Show Panels

Figure 5.1 A Maya scene can include hundreds of objects.

Selecting a specific object or piece of an object (known as a *component*) can sometimes be tricky. For instance, you might click to select a joint, and accidentally select the surface in front of the joint instead (**Figure 5.2**). Maya's object selection mask makes this situation easier by allowing you to choose which types of objects are selectable (**Figure 5.3**).

You may also find that certain objects block your view of other objects. This is where hiding, templating, and layering come in to play. You can use these functions to make objects invisible, or less obtrusive, making it easier to work with the objects you *are* interested in.

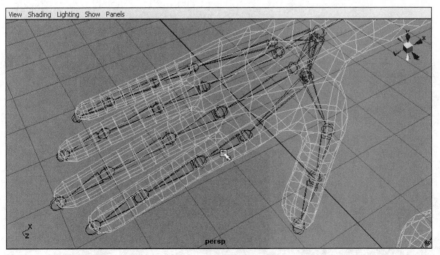

Figure 5.2 Trying to select a joint can sometimes result in selecting a surface in front of the joint instead.

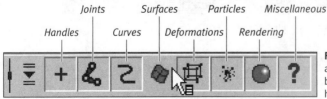

Figure 5.3 These selection mask icons allow you to determine which objects can be selected at any given time. Surfaces have been disabled in this figure.

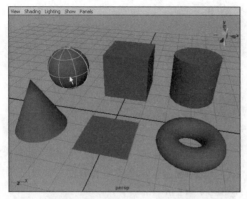

Figure 5.4 Clicking an object is the simplest selection method.

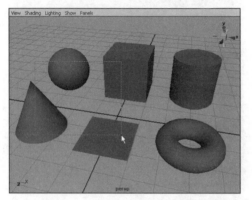

Figure 5.5 By clicking and dragging a marquee that overlaps multiple objects, you can select several objects at once.

Selecting Objects

Most commands in Maya require that you select one or more objects or components to apply the command to. Maya provides several different methods of selecting objects, each of which can be useful, depending on the circumstances. For example, if you can clearly see the object(s) in the view, you can click or click and drag a marquee to select them. If not, it may be easier to make your selection from the Outliner.

Alternately, if you know the exact name of the object, or if you'd like to select all the objects that contain a certain string of characters, you can use the Select Field. And if you want to select all but one or two of the objects in your scene, it may be quicker to select those objects first and then use the Invert Selection command.

To select an object or objects:

◆ Click the object (**Figure 5.4**).

or

◆ Click and drag a marquee that overlaps all the objects you want to select (**Figure 5.5**).

To add objects to a selection:

◆ While holding down (Shift), click each object you want to add to the current selection.

or

◆ While holding down (Shift), draw a marquee that overlaps part of each object you want to add to the selection.

✔ Tip

■ If you drag a marquee around part of an object that's already been selected, you deselect the object. To avoid doing this, hold down both (Ctrl)/(Control) and (Shift) when making your selection.

To subtract objects from a selection:

◆ While holding down [Shift], click each object you want to subtract from the current selection. The objects are subtracted.

or

◆ While holding down [Shift], drag the mouse to draw a marquee that overlaps part of each selected object you want to subtract.

or

◆ While holding down [Ctrl]/[Control], drag the mouse to draw a marquee that overlaps part of the objects you want to subtract. Doing so only removes objects you have selected, whereas using [Shift] adds unselected objects if your marquee overlaps them.

To invert the selection:

1. Select one or more object(s) (**Figure 5.6**).

2. Choose Edit > Invert Selection (**Figure 5.7**).

   Deselected objects become selected; selected objects become deselected (**Figure 5.8**).

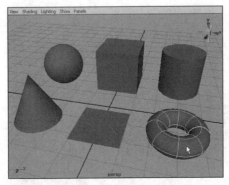

Figure 5.6 After inverting the selection, all objects *except* this selected torus will be selected.

Figure 5.7 Choose Invert Selection from the Edit menu to invert the selection.

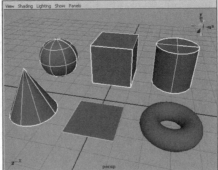

Figure 5.8 When Invert Selection is used, deselected objects become selected, and selected objects become deselected.

Figure 5.9 You can select an object in the Outliner by clicking its name.

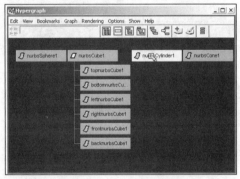

Figure 5.10 You can select an object in the Hypergraph by clicking its name.

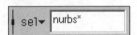

Figure 5.11 You can use the Select Field to select objects by name.

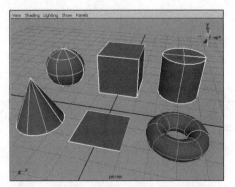

Figure 5.12 Because all the objects in this scene have names that begin with *nurbs*, all of them have been selected.

To select an object using the Outliner:

1. Choose Window > Outliner.

2. Click the name of the object you want to select (**Figure 5.9**).

   The object becomes selected.

To select an object using the Hypergraph:

1. Choose Window > Hypergraph.

2. Click the node of the object you want to select (**Figure 5.10**).

   The object becomes selected.

✔ Tip

■ You can click and drag to select multiple objects in the Outliner and the Hypergraph, or ⟨Shift⟩-click to add to the current selection.

To select an object using the Select Field:

1. Click within the Select Field at the right of the Status Line.

2. Type the name of the object(s) you'd like to select. By using the asterisk wildcard character (*), you can select objects whose names only partially match the text (**Figure 5.11**).

3. Press ⟨Enter⟩ to select the object(s) (**Figure 5.12**).

To deselect all objects:

◆ Click once in the background of a view to deselect all objects.

SELECTING OBJECTS

Selection Modes and Masks

Maya has three *selection modes*: select by hierarchy, select by object, and select by component. Each mode has its own *selection mask*, also called a *pick mask*. The selection mask can be used to avoid selecting certain types of objects or components. Together, the selection mode and mask determine what you can select when you click in the view, and they don't affect your ability to select objects in the Outliner or Hypergraph. The buttons that control the selection mode and mask can be found in the Status Line, which is the toolbar at the top of the Maya interface.

Selecting objects using object type mode

Object type mode, commonly called *object mode*, is the default selection mode in Maya. If you're in a different mode, you can switch to object mode by clicking the middle of the three selection mode icons in the Status Line (**Figure 5.13**). Object mode lets you select entire objects and, optionally, use the selection mask to make specific types of objects non-selectable.

This mode is extremely useful when you want to select an object of one type that has an object of another type overlapping it. For example, if you have a NURBS curve that you used to create a NURBS surface, you may find it difficult to select the curve, because it's overlapped by the surface. To more easily select the curve, you can turn off surfaces in the object selection mask (**Figure 5.14**). Alternately, if other objects might get in the way, you can turn off *all* object types and then turn curves back on (**Figure 5.15**).

Figure 5.13 Object mode, the default selection mode, is represented by the middle of the three selection mode icons.

Figure 5.14 You can click one of the selection mask icons to turn off selection for that object type.

Figure 5.15 After turning off all object types, you can click any selection mask icon to turn on selection for that object type.

Table 5.1

ICON	NAME	FUNCTION
Object Mode Selection Masks		
+	Handles	Selects selection handles and IK handles
(icon)	Joints	Selects skeleton joints
(icon)	Curves	Selects NURBS curves, curves on surfaces, and paint effects strokes
(icon)	Surfaces	Selects NURBS, poly, and subdivision surfaces, as well as planes
(icon)	Deformations	Selects lattices, clusters, non-linears, and sculpt objects
(icon)	Dynamics	Selects particles, emitters, fields, springs, rigid bodies, and constraints
(icon)	Rendering	Selects lights, cameras, and textures
?	Miscellaneous	Selects IK end effectors, locators, and dimensions

There are eight object type icons for the object mode selection mask, all of which are described in **Table 5.1**. Most of these icons include multiple object types, which you can also turn off and on individually when you need that level of precision.

✔ **Tip**

■ You can see a tool tip describing each selection mask icon by holding your mouse over it.

To turn off selection for surfaces:

1. Choose Create > NURBS Primitives > Sphere, then Create > NURBS Primitives > Circle.

2. If necessary, switch to object mode by clicking its icon 🔳 in the Status Line.

3. Click the Surfaces icon 🔳 from the row of selection mask icons in the Status Line.

4. Drag a marquee around the two objects (**Figure 5.16**).

   Only the circle is selected. The sphere isn't selected because it's a surface (**Figure 5.17**).

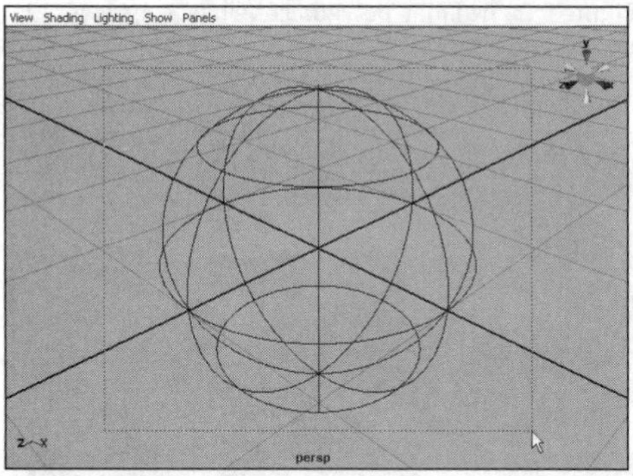

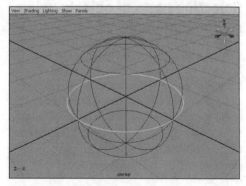

Figure 5.16 The curve in this scene occupies the same space as one of the sphere's curves.

Figure 5.17 Because selection of surfaces is turned off, only the curve is selected.

To turn off selection for all object types:

◆ Click and hold the arrow between the selection mode icons and the selection mask icons, and then select All Objects Off from the pop-up menu (**Figure 5.18**). All object types are turned off in the selection mask. You won't be able to select any objects in the view until you make an object type selectable.

Figure 5.18 You can use this menu to turn all object types on or off in the selection mask.

To turn on selection for curves only:

1. Follow the steps in the previous task for turning off all object types.

2. Click the Curves icon ⊇ from the row of selection mask icons in the Status Line. Only curves will be selectable.

✔ Tips

■ You can use the previous steps to turn selection on or off for any object type. To do so, use the corresponding icon.

■ To turn selection on or off for a subset of the object types represented by an icon, right-click that icon and select or deselect the corresponding types (**Figure 5.19**).

Selecting parts of objects using component mode

Every Maya object is made up of components that define its shape. A simple polygon cube, for example, is made up of 8 vertices, 12 edges, and 6 faces (**Figure 5.20**). Each of these components can be selected and edited individually using Maya's manipulation tools and *component mode*, also referred to as *component type mode* (**Figure 5.21**).

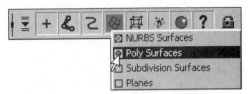

Figure 5.19 You can choose exactly what object types are selectable from each icon's pop-up menu.

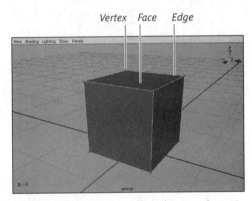

Figure 5.20 A simple polygon cube has 8 vertices, 12 edges, and 6 faces.

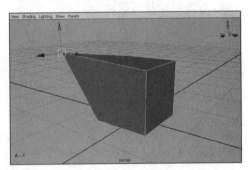

Figure 5.21 You can select and manipulate individual components of objects.

Figure 5.22 The Points icon on the right has turned orange (dark gray) to indicate that only some of its constituent object types are selectable.

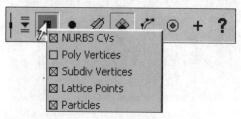

Figure 5.23 You can set exactly which types of components are selectable in the pop-up menu of each selection mask icon.

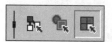

Figure 5.24 Component mode is represented by the right-hand object mode icon.

Like object mode, component mode has its own selection mask that determines what types of components you can and can't select. There are eight component type icons in component mode, all of which are defined in **Table 5.2**.

Unlike in object mode, not all component types can be made selectable at the same time as others. You can't turn on selection for two different component types that would apply to the same object—poly vertices and poly faces, for example. If you click the Faces icon while the Points icon is active, the Points icon turns orange to indicate that it's only partially enabled (**Figure 5.22**). Right-clicking the Points icon indicates that poly vertices have been disabled (**Figure 5.23**).

You can switch to component mode by clicking the selection mode icon to the right of the object mode icon (**Figure 5.24**). You can also toggle between object mode and component mode by pressing F8. Once in component mode, you can select components the same way you select objects: either by clicking them or by clicking and dragging a marquee to select multiple components.

Table 5.2

Component Mode Selection Masks

Icon	Name	Function
■	Points	Selects NURBS CVs, poly vertices, subdiv vertices, lattice points, and particles
•	Parm Points	Selects NURBS edit, curve, and surface points; and poly, NURBS, and subdiv UVs
⬦	Lines	Selects NURBS isoparms and trim edges, poly and subdiv edges, and springs
◈	Faces	Selects NURBS patches, and poly and subdiv faces
⬠	Hulls	Selects NURBS hulls
◉	Pivots	Selects rotate, scale, and joint pivots
+	Handles	Selects selection handles
?	Miscellaneous	Selects local rotation axes and image planes

To select and move a face of a polygonal object:

1. Choose Create > Polygon Primitives > Cube.

2. Switch to component mode by clicking its icon ⬛ in the Status Line or by pressing F8 .

3. Click the cube to display its components.

4. Click the Faces icon ◈ .

5. Click the point displayed in the center of a face to select that face (**Figure 5.25**).

6. Click the Move Tool icon 🔩 in the Tool Box, or press w .
   The Move tool manipulator appears.

7. Click and drag the Move tool manipulator to move the face and change the shape of the cube (**Figure 5.26**).

Component mode shortcuts

The following keyboard shortcuts let you quickly switch to selecting specific polygonal and subdiv components:

F9 —Turns on selection of vertices.

F10 —Turns on selection of edges.

F11 —Turns on selection of faces.

F12 —Turns on selection of UVs.

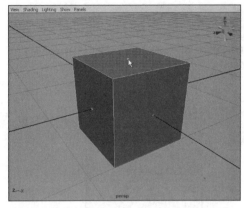

Figure 5.25 Click the point at the center of a face to select it.

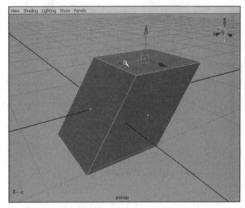

Figure 5.26 Once the component is selected, you can use Maya's Move tool to move it.

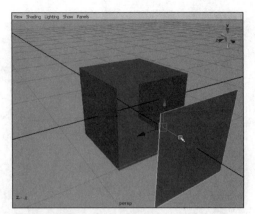

Figure 5.27 If you click a NURBS primitive cube expecting to select and move the entire cube, you may end up taking off one of its faces by accident.

Figure 5.28 Hierarchy mode is represented by the left-hand object mode icon.

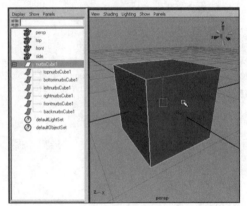

Figure 5.29 Using hierarchy mode, you can click in the view to select a root node (nurbsCube1) rather than the actual object you clicked (frontnurbsCube1).

Selecting objects using hierarchy mode

Hierarchy mode, also referred to as *hierarchy and combinations* mode, can be used to select the top node in the hierarchy the object belongs to rather than the object itself. This can be useful when you want to manipulate several objects as if they were a single object—for example, a NURBS primitive cube, which consists of six surfaces grouped together. Clicking to select a NURBS cube normally selects only one of its surfaces, which isn't usually the result you're looking for (**Figure 5.27**). Using hierarchy mode lets you click any of the surfaces to select its parent.

You can also use the hierarchy mode selection mask to enable the selection of templated objects, which can't be selected in the view in object mode. (See "Hiding and Templating" later in this chapter.)

You can switch to hierarchy mode by clicking the selection mode icon to the left of the object mode icon (**Figure 5.28**).

To select the top object in a hierarchy:

1. Choose Create > NURBS Primitives > Cube.

2. Switch to hierarchy mode by clicking its icon ⊡ in the Status Line.

3. Click the cube.

   The nurbsCube1 group node at the top of the hierarchy is now selected, rather than the specific surface you clicked (**Figure 5.29**).

✔ Tip

■ You can quickly move up the hierarchy by pressing the up ⬆ arrow to select an object's parent. Depending on your task, this may be more convenient than switching to hierarchy mode.

Using Quick Select Sets

You'll often want to select the same group of points or the same objects repeatedly. However, making these selections more than once can be tedious. It's much more time-efficient to save the selection as a *Quick Select Set*. A set allows you to group objects without affecting their position in the hierarchy. Quick Select Sets are also added to the Edit > Quick Select Sets menu, which lets you conveniently select all the objects in that set.

To create a Quick Select Set:

1. Select multiple objects in object mode, or select multiple points in component mode.

2. Choose Create > Sets > Quick Select Set (**Figure 5.30**).

   The Create Quick Select Set dialog box opens.

3. Enter a name in the Enter Quick Select Set Name field (**Figure 5.31**).

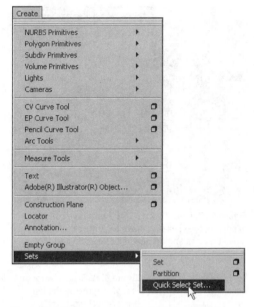

Figure 5.30 You can create a Quick Select Set from the Create > Sets menu.

Figure 5.31 It's a good idea to enter a descriptive name for your set.

Edit		
Undo	Ctrl+z	
Redo	z	
Repeat "Quick Select Set..."	g	
Recent Commands...		
Cut	Ctrl+x	
Copy	Ctrl+c	
Paste	Ctrl+v	
Keys	▶	
Delete		
Delete by Type	▶	
Delete All by Type	▶	
Select All		
Select Hierarchy		
Invert Selection		
Select All by Type	▶	
Quick Select Sets	▶	leftEar
Paint Selection Tool		rightEar
Select Edge Loop Tool		
Select Edge Ring Tool		
Select Border Edge Tool		
Duplicate	Ctrl+d	□
Duplicate with Transform	D	
Group	Ctrl+g	□
Ungroup		□
Level of Detail	▶	
Parent	p	□
Unparent	P	□

Figure 5.32 All of the Quick Select Sets you create are accessible from the Edit > Quick Select Sets menu.

4. Click OK.

The named selection is now selectable by name in the Edit > Quick Select Sets menu (**Figure 5.32**). You can also view the set and its contents in the Outliner (**Figure 5.33**).

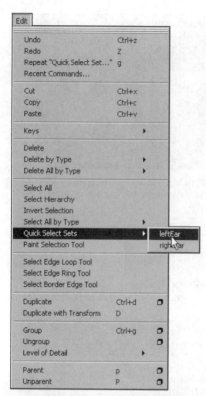

Figure 5.33 You can also use view your Quick Select Sets in the Outliner.

Hiding and Templating

Hiding an object does exactly what it sounds like: It makes the object invisible, allowing you to see any objects behind it. This can be useful when you want to focus on a particular area of a scene.

Templating an object lets you see how it's placed without it getting in the way of viewing or selecting other objects. When you template an object, it's displayed as a gray, non-selectable wireframe. Templated objects can only be selected in the view by switching to hierarchy selection mode and selecting the Template mask.

Both hidden and templated objects can still be selected from the Outliner or Hypergraph.

To hide a selected object:

1. Select an object to hide (**Figure 5.34**).

2. Choose Display > Hide > Hide Selection (**Figure 5.35**), or press Ctrl / Control + h. The selected object is hidden from view (**Figure 5.36**).

✔ Tip

- You can also select multiple objects and hide them using the method described in this task.

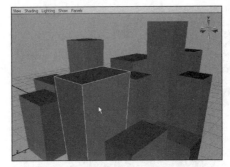

Figure 5.34 Hiding one or more objects can often allow you to view other parts of a scene better.

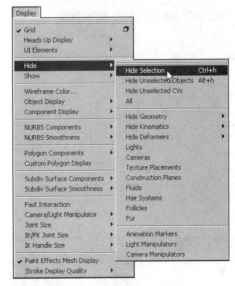

Figure 5.35 You can hide selected objects by choosing Display > Hide > Hide Selection.

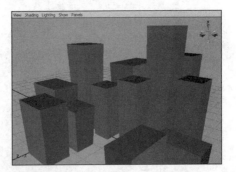

Figure 5.36 The object disappears from the view, allowing you to see the objects behind it.

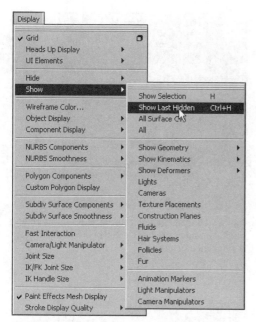

Figure 5.37 Since you can't select hidden objects in the view, the Show Last Hidden option is more likely to be useful than Show Selection.

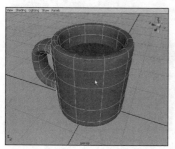

Figure 5.38 You can template an object to make it easier to work with other objects in your scene.

To show the last hidden object:

◆ Choose Display > Show > Show Last Hidden (**Figure 5.37**), or press [Ctrl]/[Control]+[Shift]+[h]

The last object hidden becomes visible.

To show all hidden objects:

◆ Choose Display > Show > All.

All hidden objects become visible.

To template an object:

1. Select the object(s) you want to template (**Figure 5.38**).

2. Choose Display > Object Display > Template (**Figure 5.39**).

continues on next page

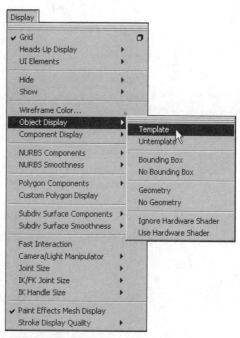

Figure 5.39 To template a selected object, choose Display > Object Display > Template.

3. The object becomes a nonselectable gray wireframe (**Figure 5.40**).

To untemplate an object:

1. Switch to hierarchy mode, and click the template selection mask icon 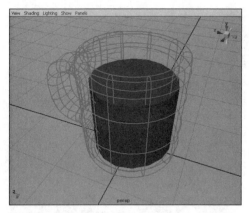 to enable selection of templates.

2. Select the templated object or objects that you want to untemplate.

The selected templated object becomes light pink.

3. Choose Display > Object Display > Untemplate (**Figure 5.41**).

The object becomes untemplated.

Figure 5.40 Templated objects are displayed as gray wireframes and can't be selected in the view in object or component mode.

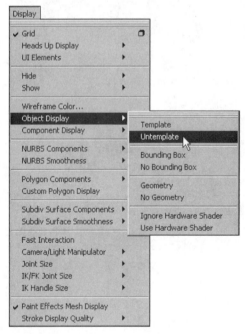

Figure 5.41 You can untemplate selected objects by choosing Display > Object Display > Untemplate.

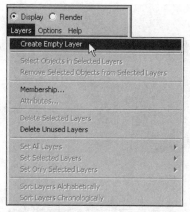

Figure 5.43 By default, a new layer is called *layer* plus a number. You can give your layers more descriptive names from the Edit Layer dialog box.

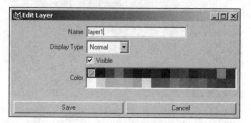

Figure 5.44 The Edit Layer dialog box lets you change an object's name, display type, and color. You can easily change the display type from the Layer Editor as well.

About Layers

Layers are used to associate objects so they can be hidden, templated, or *referenced* as a group. Referencing a layer is similar to templating, but the objects retain their normal appearance in shaded mode, while templated objects display as wireframes. Each layer can also have an associated color, which changes the wireframe color of objects in that layer. This can make objects easier to distinguish from each other in wireframe mode.

To create a layer:

1. Open the Channel Box. If the Layer Editor isn't displayed at the bottom of the Channel Box, click the Show the Channel Box and Layer Editor icon in the top right corner of the Channel Box.

2. From the Layer Editor's Layers menu, select Create Empty Layer (**Figure 5.42**), or click the Create Layer icon.
   A new layer is created (**Figure 5.43**).

To rename and color-code a layer:

1. Double-click the layer to open the Edit Layer dialog box (**Figure 5.44**).

2. Type a descriptive name for the layer in the Name field.

3. Select a color swatch.
   The wireframe of each object on the layer displays in the selected color.

4. Click Save.

To add objects to a layer:

1. Select the objects you want to add.

2. Right-click the layer to which you want to add the objects, and choose Add Selected Objects from the pop-up menu (**Figure 5.45**).

✔ Tips

■ To add all newly created objects to a layer, select that layer and choose Add New Objects to Current Layer from the Layer Editor's Options menu. Objects you create subsequently will be added to that layer.

■ You can choose the order in which the layers are listed by selecting Layers > Sort Layers Alphabetically or Sort Layers Chronologically.

To toggle a layer's visibility:

◆ In the Layer Editor, click the square furthest left of the layer name (**Figure 5.46**).

If the layer is currently visible, it becomes invisible; if the layer is invisible, it becomes visible.

To make a layer templated or referenced:

◆ In the Layer Editor, click the middle square to the left of the layer name (**Figure 5.47**).

Clicking once makes the layer templated, and a T appears in the box. Clicking again makes the layer referenced, and an R appears in the box. Clicking a third time clears the box and restores the layer to normal.

Figure 5.45 You can use a layer's pop-up menu to add objects to that layer.

Figure 5.46 To make a layer invisible, click the left-most box next to the layer's name.

Figure 5.47 To switch a layer between normal, templated, and referenced modes, click the middle box next to the layer's name.

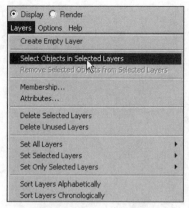

Figure 5.48 You can select all the objects in a layer by selecting the layer and then choosing Layers > Select Objects in Selected Layers.

Figure 5.49 You can delete a layer by right-clicking it and choosing Delete Layer from its pop-up menu.

To select a layer's objects:

1. In the Layer Editor, select the layer(s) whose objects you want to select.

2. Choose Layers > Select Objects in Selected Layers (**Figure 5.48**).

   or

   Right-click the layer, and choose Select Objects from its pop-up menu.

To delete a layer:

1. In the Layer Editor, select the layer(s) you want to delete.

2. Choose Layers > Delete Selected Layers.

   or

   Right-click the layer, and choose Delete Layer from its pop-up menu (**Figure 5.49**).

   The layer is removed from the Layer Editor. Objects in the layer aren't deleted.

✔ Tips

- You can select multiple layers in the Layer Editor by holding down (Shift) and clicking the layers.

- Objects in templated layers cannot be selected by using the Template selection mask. However, you can still select them in the Outliner or the Hypergraph.

GROUPING, PARENTING, AND ALIGNING

Grouping, *parenting*, and *aligning* provide ways of organizing and controlling an object's relationship to other objects. Because construction in Maya almost always consists of multiple objects, it's crucial to have ways to organize, move, and distribute these objects.

Grouping objects is a commonly used organizational and hierarchical tool. Grouping works by gathering individual objects into a set, which you can then move around or duplicate as a whole. In addition, grouped objects provide organization for your scene by creating a common namespace or folder-like structure.

Parenting is similar to grouping, but with a fundamental difference: Parented surfaces (**Figure 6.1**) have a relationship in which one follows the other (**Figure 6.2**), whereas objects in a group can act both independently and as a single, grouped entity. Parenting is used for control structures such as bones.

Aligning objects, surfaces, and curves can be tricky if you're trying to do it by sight alone. To get precise and quick results, Maya offers a few tools to help, including the Align and Snap Together tools.

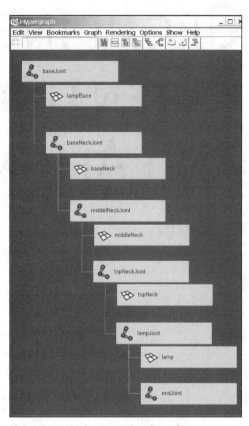

Figure 6.1 Multiple parented surfaces (known as a hierarchy, or chain) are shown in the Hypergraph.

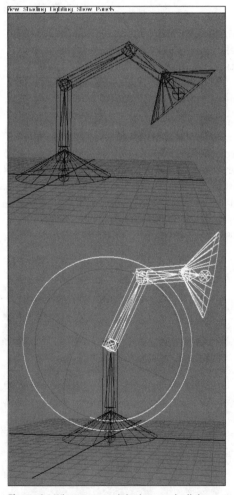

Figure 6.2 When a parent joint is moved, all the children move along with it.

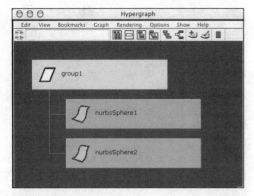

Figure 6.3 The top node is used to change values of the entire group without changing the current values of the individual objects.

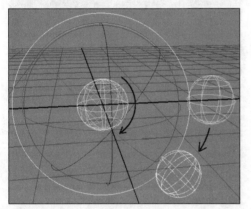

Figure 6.4 Rotating the group node rotates all the surfaces in the group at the same time around the group's pivot point.

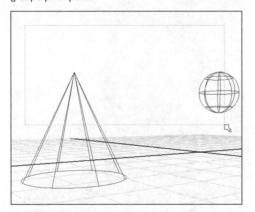

Figure 6.5 You can drag a marquee to select multiple surfaces. The marquee only needs to touch a part of the surface.

Grouping

Grouping two or more objects connects those objects with an additional node, called group(*n*) (**Figure 6.3**); you use this node when you want to perform an action to both objects, such as moving them at the same time. Even though the objects are grouped, you can still select one and move or perform an action on it without affecting the other objects in the group. Alternatively, you can select the group node and have your actions affect the grouped objects as if they were a single object (**Figure 6.4**).

To group two or more objects together:

1. Marquee-select two or more surfaces with the Arrow tool (**Figure 6.5**), or Shift-click to select multiple objects.

2. Choose Edit > Group (**Figure 6.6**), or press Ctrl/Control+g.

   The objects are grouped together with an additional node.

continues on next page

Figure 6.6 Select Edit › Group to group objects together.

119

3. Choose Window > Hypergraph.

The Hypergraph opens in a new window.

4. Press 〔f〕 to zoom the Hypergraph to the selection.

There is now one more node than the number of objects. This additional node is the group node, named group[*n*] (**Figure 6.7**).

✔ Tips

■ You can select the group node and set the Pick mask to hierarchy mode to move the grouped objects together, or you can select a surface's node and set the Pick mask to object mode to move that surface separately from the group.

■ An object can only be part of one group at a time.

To ungroup an object:

1. Select the group node. You can find it in the Hypergraph (**Figure 6.8**).

2. Choose Edit > Ungroup (**Figure 6.9**).

The geometry is no longer grouped, and the group node is deleted.

Groups and the Outliner

The Hypergraph shows the actual node hierarchy, but it can be unwieldy to use for everyday selections. You can also use the Outliner to display, select, and ungroup your objects.

To use the Outliner to manipulate groups:

1. Choose Create > Polygon Primitives > Cube.

Repeat this step three times so you have three cubes.

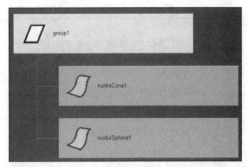

Figure 6.7 The top node is created at the same time the group is created. You use it to control the nodes beneath it.

Figure 6.8 The group node's default name is group[*n*], with *n* representing the number of groups created so far.

Figure 6.9 Select Edit > Ungroup to pull objects out of the group.

GROUPING

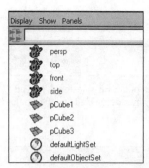

Figure 6.10 Items not in a hierarchy are displayed on the same far-left level in the Outliner, whereas grouped items are shifted right a notch.

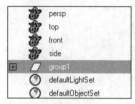

Figure 6.11 Items that are grouped are placed under their group name. You may need to expand the group by clicking the plus sign.

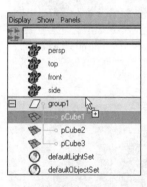

Figure 6.12 A single gray line appears, to indicate the insertion spot for the object.

Figure 6.13 Place an object in any group by dragging and dropping.

2. Choose Window > Outliner.

You can see the three cubes sitting at the scene level, which means they haven't been grouped or parented to anything (**Figure 6.10**).

3. Select all three cubes, and press [Ctrl]/[Control]+[g] to group them.

The cubes are placed under the group node named group1 (**Figure 6.11**).

4. Click the plus next to group1 in the Outliner to expand the group and show its contents.

You're now able to see the cubes. You can select them by clicking them here, rather than clicking in the view or Hypergraph.

5. Click pCube1 with the middle mouse button, and drag up. Don't release the mouse button.

A gray line appears, to indicate where you'll reposition the cube in the hierarchy if you let go of the mouse (**Figure 6.12**).

6. Position the line between the group1 node and the side camera, and release the mouse button.

The cube is removed from the group (**Figure 6.13**). You can also place items *into* a group in a similar manner by dragging them onto the group in the Outliner.

✔ Tip

- When you're dragging objects to be ungrouped, make sure the Outliner displays a single gray line. A double line that brackets an item parents or groups things to that item instead.

GROUPING

You can easily select a group node or move through objects in a group by using the arrow keys. This technique is helpful if the Outliner is closed, or if you have nested groups and wish to quickly select the group directly above without moving to the Outliner.

To move within the hierarchy using the arrow keys:

1. Start with the cubes from the previous task.

2. Select pCube3, and press ⬆.

   The selection moves up in the hierarchy, and the group is selected (**Figure 6.14**).

3. Press ⬇.

   The selection moves back into the group, so pCube2 is selected (**Figure 6.15**).

4. Press ➡.

   pCube3 is selected again (**Figure 6.16**).

Figure 6.14 On the left, pCube3 is selected. After you press ⬆, pCube3 becomes deselected and the whole group is selected.

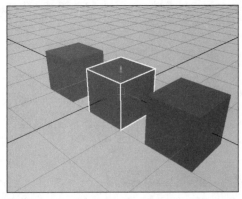

Figure 6.15 ⬇ moves the selection into the next available branch down the hierarchy; in this case, it selects pCube2.

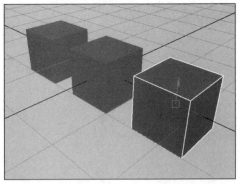

Figure 6.16 Using ➡ and ⬅ cycles through the objects within your group.

GROUPING

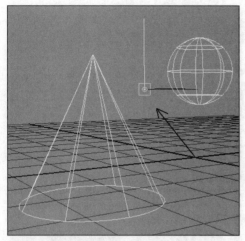

Figure 6.17 The group node's pivot point is used as the center point for the entire group. New groups start with their pivots at the origin.

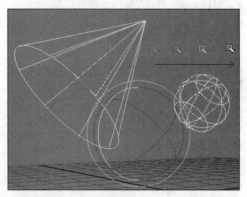

Figure 6.18 You translate, rotate, or scale a group the same way you do an individual object.

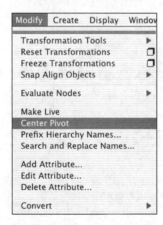

Figure 6.19 The Modify › Center Pivot command is useful for quickly centering the pivot of a group.

Transforming groups

Once objects are grouped together, they can be translated, rotated, or scaled as if they are a single object. Maya creates an extra group node to give you an additional pivot point to use as the center point the objects rotate or scale around. When an object is grouped, the pivot point of the group node is placed at the origin. You can then move the pivot point anywhere in the scene to determine its rotation and scale center point.

To translate, rotate, or scale a group:

1. Select the group node in the Hypergraph or Outliner, or click one of the grouped objects with the Pick mask set to hierarchy mode ![icon] to select the group node.

2. Select the Rotate, Scale, or Move tool in the toolbar, or use its respective hotkey.

3. Press [Insert]/[Home] to go into pivot-point edit mode.

4. Move the pivot point to the position you want the group to rotate around or scale from (**Figure 6.17**).

   You can ignore this step if you're just translating the object.

5. Press [Insert]/[Home] to get out of pivot-point edit mode.

6. Translate, rotate, or scale the group by selecting a manipulator's axis and dragging left or right in the pane with the middle mouse button to change the axes' value (**Figure 6.18**).

✔ Tip

■ You can move the pivot point to the center of a selected group node (or any other object) by selecting Modify > Center Pivot (**Figure 6.19**).

GROUPING

Parenting

Parented objects react differently than objects that are grouped. Parented objects have a child-parent relationship. In real life, when a child is holding a parent's hand, the child must go wherever the parent goes (at least in theory). The same is true in 3D—an object that is parented to another object has to follow the other object around (**Figure 6.20**). This is a direct connection, unlike grouping. When you parent one object to another, no extra node is created. This means the child uses the parent for all its information and treats the parent as its new world space.

Parenting is very important in setting up skeletons for characters because human bone structure follows a natural parenting chain. Your arm starts at your shoulder blade and continues down, connecting your shoulder to your upper arm to your lower arm to your wrist to your palm to your fingers. When the parts are parented together, a relationship is created that forces the fingers to follow the rest of the arm. In this case, the parent is the upper arm, and its child is the lower arm. The lower arm is the parent of the wrist, which itself is the parent of the palm. Whenever the upper arm is moved, all the children beneath it move, creating the whole arm movement (**Figure 6.21**).

The overall relationship of the parts of the skeleton is called a *hierarchy* (**Figure 6.22**). A hierarchy determines which objects control other objects. The order of the hierarchy is important to both selecting and translating.

When you're parenting two objects together, the order in which you select the objects is very important. The second object you select becomes a parent of the first object selected. Once it's parented, the child follows the parent's translations.

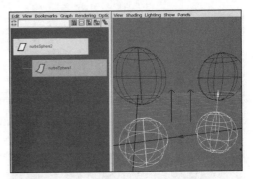

Figure 6.20 The sphere on the left is parented to the sphere on the right. The sphere on the left will inherit any transformations performed on the sphere on the right.

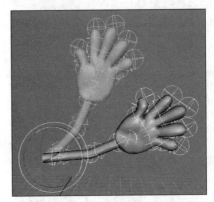

Figure 6.21 The fingers are children of the palm, and the palm is a child of the lower arm. When the upper arm is rotated, all the joints and surfaces below the parent joint follow.

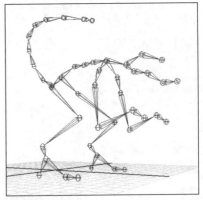

Figure 6.22 An entire hierarchy is formed by parenting one bone to another until they're all connected.

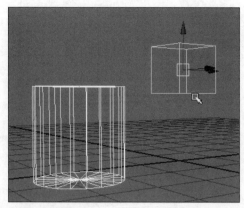

Figure 6.23 (Shift)-click additional objects to add them to the selection.

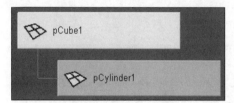

Figure 6.24 The cube is the parent of the cylinder, as shown in the Hypergraph by a connecting line.

Figure 6.25 Select Edit > Unparent to separate two or more parented surfaces.

To parent two objects together:

1. Select the object you want to become the child by clicking it.

2. Select the object you want to become the parent by (Shift)-clicking it (**Figure 6.23**).

3. Choose Edit > Parent, or press (p).

   The second selected object becomes a parent of the first object (**Figure 6.24**).

✔ Tips

- Because no additional node is added when objects are parented, the pivot point of the parent is used as the center point for controlling the entire hierarchy.

- If you select more than two objects, all selected objects become children of the last object selected.

- You can parent one object to another by using the middle mouse button to drag the child onto the parent in the Hypergraph and Outliner.

To unparent objects:

1. Select each of the children you want to unparent.

2. Choose Edit > Unparent to unparent the object, or press (Shift)+(p) (**Figure 6.25**).

   The object is pulled out of the hierarchy, so that it now acts separately from the parented hierarchy.

✔ Tip

- You can also use the middle mouse button to drag the object out of the hierarchy in the Hypergraph and the Outliner, disconnecting the selected object from the rest of the hierarchy.

PARENTING

125

Grouping vs. Parenting

The difference between parenting and grouping is subtle. Both actions create a hierarchy that lets you move grouped objects. In some respects, grouping is like parenting several objects to an object that contains no geometry (know as a *null object*, or *null*). However, you must note a few differences.

When an object becomes a child of another object, it uses its parent as its new world space. That means it no longer looks to the center of your scene to get its position information; instead, it looks to its parent. An object under a group still uses the scene's world space (**Figure 6.26**).

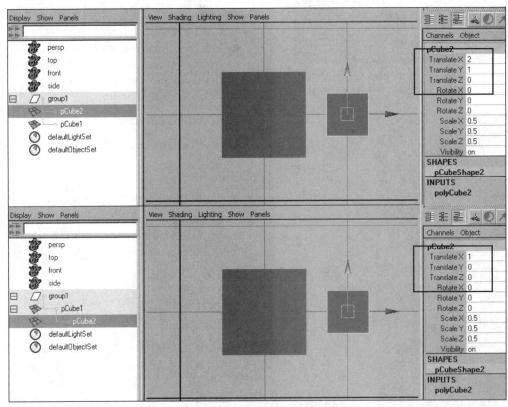

Figure 6.26 On top, the cubes are grouped, and pCube2 is two units over and one unit up. When pCube2 is parented to pCube1 (bottom), the translation values change because pCube2 is only one unit to the right of its parent. The position of the cube hasn't changed, but its transformation values have.

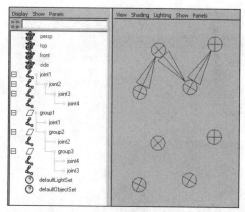

Figure 6.27 The top group of joints is parented together, so the joints appear to be connected. The bottom set of joints has been grouped to behave similarly, but the joints lack the same connections.

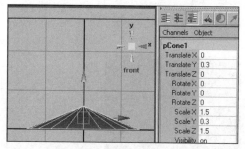

Figure 6.28 This cone will form the base of the lamp.

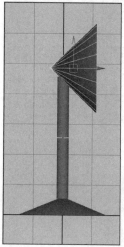

Figure 6.29 A simple lamp arrangement. It needs some structure to allow you to move it.

The parent-child relationship is also used in some elements of Maya to establish how objects are connected. This functionality is especially important in bones (as discussed in Chapter 10). When parented together, bones become connected in a special way that allows them to function like a real skeleton (**Figure 6.27**).

Grouping can do just the opposite: It severs links or the inheriting of information you may not want. For instance, if an object is scaled, all its children are in a scaled world space. This can create odd distortion with rotations. By using groups, you can establish more control over the attributes of your world space, including pivot point, scale, and rotation.

Building a lamp out of objects is a good example to show this contrast.

To build a lamp using parenting:

1. Choose Create > Polygon Primitives > Cone, and enter the settings shown in **Figure 6.28**.

2. Create two poly cylinders, scale them to be long and skinny, and position them on top of each other above the cone.

3. Duplicate the bottom cone, and position it on top of the cylinders like a shade (**Figure 6.29**).

4. Choose Window > Outliner.

   In the resulting view of your objects, you can see that they have no grouping (**Figure 6.30**).

continues on next page

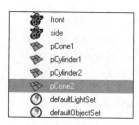

Figure 6.30 The objects aren't grouped.

127

5. In the Outliner, use the middle mouse button to drag pCone2 onto pCylinder2, pCylinder2 onto pCylinder1, and pCylinder1 onto pCone1, creating the structure shown in **Figure 6.31**.

   Now the lamp's parts are parented together so that each piece is moved by those below it, like a real lamp.

6. Select pCone1, and rotate it.

   The whole lamp moves, because the rest of the pieces are children of the base.

7. Select pCylinder1, and rotate it.

   The lamp becomes distorted (**Figure 6.32**) because the rest of the lamp is a child of the cone and inherits the cone's scale values.

You can avoid distortion problems by freezing the transformations and setting new pivot points on the object, or by using grouping instead. Using groups gives you an extra level of control as well. To illustrate the difference between the two, let's opt for grouping.

To build a lamp using grouping:

1. Perform steps 1–4 of the previous task to create the base lamp with no hierarchy.

2. Select the shade and top arm of the lamp, and group them by pressing Ctrl / Control +g or choosing Edit > Group.

3. Press Insert / Home to get into pivot point mode.

   You can now access group1's pivot point, which is at the bend of the lamp.

4. Select the Move tool, and position the pivot point at the joint of the lamp (**Figure 6.33**).

5. With group1 still selected, Shift +select the lower arm of the lamp and group the parts by pressing Ctrl / Control +g or selecting Edit > Group.

   This action creates a nested group consisting of group1 and the lower cylinder (**Figure 6.34**).

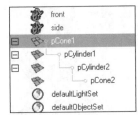

Figure 6.31 Drag and drop each piece onto the next until the structure looks like this.

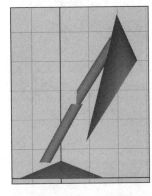

Figure 6.32 This unwanted distortion occurs because the objects inherit scale values from their parents.

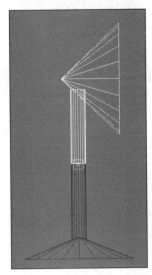

Figure 6.33 Drag the pivot point down to the middle joint. This is the point at which the lamp will bend.

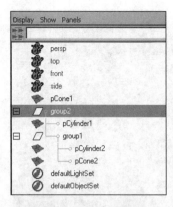

Figure 6.34 A grouped hierarchy is nested differently than a parented hierarchy.

Figure 6.35 Drag the new pivot point down for the base joint.

Figure 6.36 As long as you select the group nodes, you can pose the lamp without distortion.

6. Position the pivot point of group2 at the base of the cylinder (**Figure 6.35**).

7. Select the Rotate tool, and rotate group2.

The entire top of the lamp pivots and moves with the group, and there is no distortion. You can now position your lamp as you desire (**Figure 6.36**).

Freeze Transformations

When you're parenting, it isn't always desirable to have children inherit certain transformations from their parents. For example, an object may become skewed if it's parented to an object with scale transformations. Alternatively, you'll often want to create a way to easily return an object to its original position. Freeze Transformations is a handy tool that helps in both these situations.

Freeze Transformations (available in the Modify menu) resets the transformation values of an object to zero without moving the object. Think of it as establishing a new origin for the object. The most obvious result is that you can easily "zero out" an object (return it to its original position). Using Freeze Transformations also sets scale values to 1, so it avoids distortion in parenting chains.

It's a good idea to perform Freeze Transformations on an object once you've placed it where you need it. Doing so simplifies your scene and makes performing actions on multiple objects easier. Animation controls with logical default positions are simpler to keep track of. As a result, animating with the object is much easier, because you can tell how far the object has moved relative to its starting location instead of looking at random numbers.

GROUPING VS. PARENTING

Aligning and Snapping Objects

Many models require precisely positioned, evenly spaced, or carefully placed objects. The alignment and snap tools ensure that your objects don't overlap or have gaps between them. Maya's Align and Snap Together tools are great for arranging several objects at once in a very precise way (**Figure 6.37**). And when you want to position only one object, you can use Snap shortcuts as a quick way to ensure accurate placement.

Snaps are alignment shortcuts used to quickly align objects or components to gridlines, curves, points, or view planes—for example, moving a selected object to a specific gridline (**Figure 6.38**). You can also use Snaps to make sure curve components and surfaces overlap other curves or surfaces. This is important in Maya because many commands require that curves and/or surfaces touch in order for the command to work properly. The best way to confirm that a selected point is touching the desired curve is to select the point and use Snap to Curves to move the point to the curve. Snapping can also help bring selected, out-of-view surfaces into view by snapping the selected object to a gridline or curve that is within view.

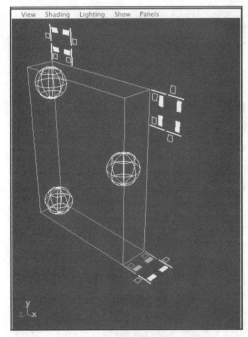

Figure 6.37 The Align tool (shown here) is useful for aligning sets of objects.

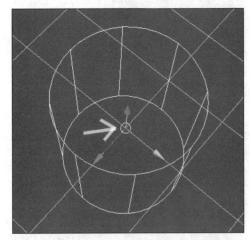

Figure 6.38 Snaps help surfaces jump into alignment with gridlines, curves, and points.

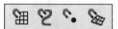

Figure 6.39 The four Snaps, from left to right: Grids, Curves, Points, and View Planes.

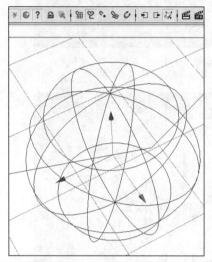

Figure 6.40 Snap to Curves moves the surface into alignment with the curve.

The four Snaps

Let's look at the four Snaps (**Figure 6.39**) available in Maya:

◆ **Snap to Grids** ▦ ([x])—Snaps a CV, pivot point, object, or polygonal vertex to a grid corner. If you turn on this option before you draw a curve, the CVs will snap to the grid corners (Figure 6.38).

◆ **Snap to Curves** ▨ ([c])—Snaps a CV, pivot point, or polygonal vertex to a curve or curve on a surface (**Figure 6.40**).

◆ **Snap to Points** ▨ ([v])—Snaps a CV, pivot point, object, or polygonal vertex to another point or face center (**Figure 6.41**).

◆ **Snap to View Planes** ▨—Snaps a CV, pivot point, object, or polygonal vertex to a view plane (**Figure 6.42**).

To snap an object to the grid:

1. Select an object.

2. Select the Move tool.

continues on next page

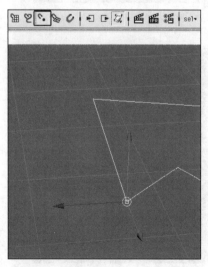

Figure 6.41 The two curve's endpoints are snapped together using Snap to Points.

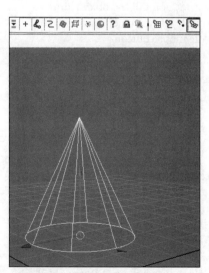

Figure 6.42 Use Snap to View Planes to snap the surface along the plane axis.

3. Hold down ⌧, and drag with the middle mouse button along the grid you would like the object to snap to (**Figure 6.43**).

or

Click 🖳 in the status bar, and drag with the middle mouse button along the grid you would like the object to snap to.

The pivot point of the object snaps to the grid corner where you clicked with the middle mouse button.

4. Release the mouse to finalize the snapping position.

To snap an object to a curve:

1. Select an object.

2. Select the Move tool.

3. Hold down ⌖, and drag with the middle mouse button on the curve you would like the object to snap to (**Figure 6.44**).

or

Click 🖳 in the status bar, and drag with the middle mouse button on the curve you would like the object to snap to.

The pivot point of the object jumps to the curve where you clicked with the middle mouse button.

4. Release the mouse to finalize the snapping position.

To snap an object to a view plane:

1. Select an object.

2. Select the Move tool.

3. Click 🖳 in the status bar, and drag with the middle mouse button on the view plane you would like the object to snap to.

The pivot point of the object snaps to the view plane where you clicked with the middle mouse button (**Figure 6.45**).

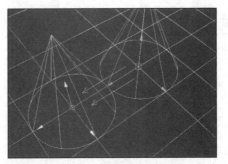

Figure 6.43 The center point of the surface is used to snap from gridline to gridline.

Figure 6.44 The surface's center point slides across the curve until you release the mouse button.

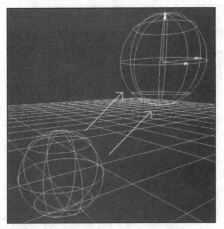

Figure 6.45 Snapping to the view plane keeps the movement of your object perpendicular to the camera.

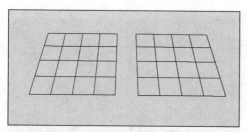

Figure 6.46 Separate two primitive planes so that you can easily view the snapping results.

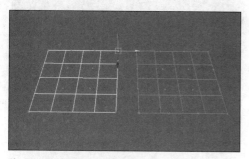

Figure 6.47 Select the point you would like to snap into alignment with another point.

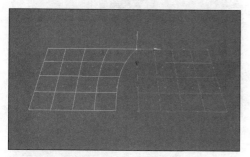

Figure 6.48 Any selected point can be snapped to any edit point, CV, or face center.

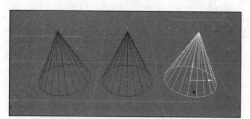

Figure 6.49 These cones have been snapped to the face centers by using Snap to Points.

To snap a point on one surface to a point on another surface:

1. Create two NURBS planes (**Figure 6.46**).

2. Select both planes, and press F8 .
   The selection mode switches into CV components.

3. Select a corner CV on one of the planes (**Figure 6.47**).

4. Select the Move tool.

5. Hold down v , and click and drag with the middle mouse button on a second plane near the CV you would like the object to snap to.

   The pivot point of the selected CV snaps to the CV on the second plane that's closest to where you clicked with your middle mouse button (**Figure 6.48**).

✔ Tips

- Although you can use the left mouse button when snapping, using the middle mouse button prevents unwanted objects from accidentally being selected.

- New in Maya 7.0, Snap to Points can also snap to face centers. Turn on face component display by pressing F8 , and snap away (**Figure 6.49**).

ALIGNING AND SNAPPING OBJECTS

133

The Snap Align Tools

The Snap Align tools are a set of alignment aids for placing multiple objects. Alignment is very important in the world of 3D because an object can appear to be aligned in the Perspective view but be completely off in the orthographic views (**Figure 6.50**). The align tools can help you quickly ensure that your objects really are where you want them.

The Snap Alignment toolbox includes Snap Align Objects, Snap Align, and Snap Together. Many of these function in a similar fashion, so use the tool that suits your particular needs or preferences.

To align two or more objects using the Align Objects tool:

1. Create two primitive cylinders (making one taller along the *y* axis) with some space between them (**Figure 6.51**).

2. Select the cylinders.

3. From the Modify menu, select the box beside Snap Align Objects > Align Objects. The Align Objects Options dialog box opens.

4. Select Min for the Align Mode, and select Align in World Y (deselecting World X and Z) (**Figure 6.52**).

   Setting the World to Y forces the movement to happen along the *y* axis.

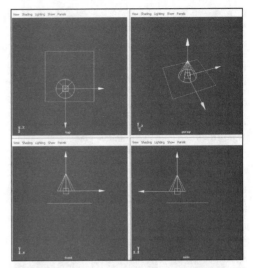

Figure 6.50 The cone seems to be centered on the plane in the Perspective view, but in the orthographic views, you can see that it's actually very much out of alignment.

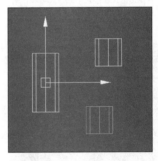

Figure 6.51 The cylinders are different sizes to better illustrate the change after alignment.

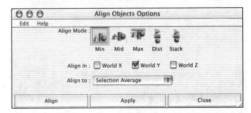

Figure 6.52 Min aligns the surfaces with the minimum *y* value of the two.

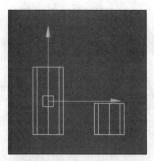

Figure 6.53 The bases of the two surfaces are now placed on the same grid line.

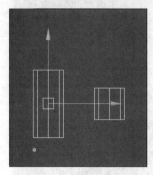

Figure 6.54 The two surfaces are aligned to their centers.

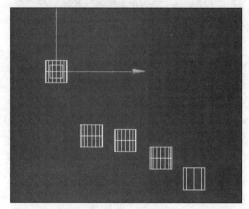

Figure 6.55 Only the placement of the two surfaces furthest away from each other matters, because the rest of the objects will be distributed evenly between them.

5. Click Apply.

One cylinder moves up the *y* axis and the other moves down the *y* axis until the base (the minimum) of each object is aligned with the other (**Figure 6.53**).

6. With the Align Objects Options dialog box still open, select Mid ⬛ for the Align Mode, and select Align in World Y (deselecting World X and Z).

7. Click Align.

One cylinder moves up the *y* axis and the other moves down the *y* axis until their centers are aligned (**Figure 6.54**).

To evenly distribute multiple objects along an axis using the Align Objects tool:

1. Create a primitive cylinder.

2. Duplicate the cylinder four times.

3. Move one of the cylinders up the *y* axis 10 grid units (**Figure 6.55**).

4. Select all of the cylinders.

5. From the Modify menu, select the box beside Snap Align Objects > Align Objects. The Align Objects Options window opens.

continues on next page

6. Select Dist ⬚ as the Align Mode, and select Align in World Y (deselecting World X and Z) (**Figure 6.56**).

Setting the World to Y forces the objects to be distributed along the *Y* axis.

7. Click Apply.

Each of the cylinders moves up the *y* axis until they're evenly spaced between the two cylinders that are furthest from the others (**Figure 6.57**).

✔ Tip

■ Make sure the items you want to distribute are between your outermost objects. You can get arrangements you didn't expect if there is an outlying object.

To align two or more objects using the Align tool:

1. Create five primitive cylinders, and randomly space them away from each other.

2. Select one cylinder by clicking it, and then Shift-select the others one at a time until all are selected.

3. From the Modify menu, select the box beside Snap Align Objects > Align Tool.

A gray box appears around the selected cylinders. On the edges of the box are icon manipulators used to align the objects (**Figure 6.58**).

Figure 6.56 The Dist option can be used to evenly distribute the selected objects along the selected axes.

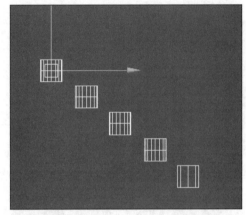

Figure 6.57 The cylinders are perfectly spaced along the *y* axis.

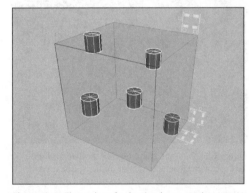

Figure 6.58 The order of selection becomes important because the objects are aligned to the last selected object.

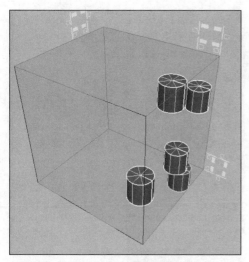

Figure 6.59 The gray bounding box is for visualization purposes only: You need to click the icons for the Align function to work.

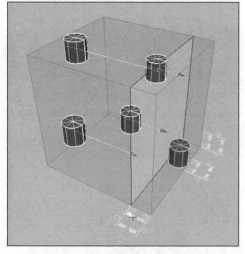

Figure 6.60 The plane shows where the objects are being aligned, and the arrows indicate the path of each object.

4. Click 🖳 or one of the other shapes on the surrounding box (**Figure 6.59**).

The cylinders fall into alignment with the selected icon. The yellow arrows preview the alignment, indicating how each object will move (**Figure 6.60**).

5. Press ⓩ to undo the alignment, and then click another icon to see its alignment type.

6. Repeat the last step until you feel comfortable with each of the alignment icons' functions.

✔ Tip

■ Objects are aligned to the last selected object (blue).

THE SNAP ALIGN TOOLS

To align objects using the Snap Together tool:

1. Create a primitive cylinder and a primitive cone (**Figure 6.61**).

2. Choose Modify > Snap Align Objects > Snap Together Tool.

3. Click the cone.

   A blue arrow appears, denoting the spot you clicked.

4. Click the cylinder.

   A dotted blue line connects the two objects (**Figure 6.62**).

5. Press ⓔ.

   The two objects are drawn together, so that the two selected points touch (**Figure 6.63**).

✔ Tip

■ The Snap Together tool won't function on objects within the same group. Instead, it snaps the whole group to any outside surface.

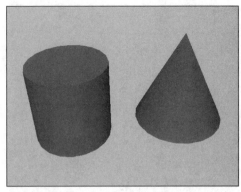

Figure 6.61 Two objects ready for alignment. It helps to have them far enough apart that you can easily click anywhere on their surfaces.

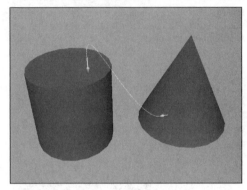

Figure 6.62 The dotted line indicates the path and rotations the object will follow to align the selected points. This is a visual aid only.

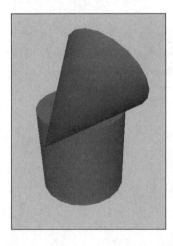

Figure 6.63 The two points on the surfaces are drawn together, like pulling a stitch shut.

NURBS CURVES AND SURFACES

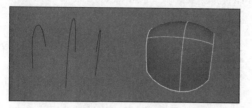

Figure 7.1 A set of NURBS curves and the surface created from them.

NURBS modeling is a powerful technique with a broad variety of uses. NURBS objects can be sharp edged or easily made into complicated multidirectional curved surfaces. These intricate curves and geometric shapes make them well suited to modeling mechanical items such as sports cars, as well as many organic shapes. NURBS modeling can require some forethought and strategy for complicated tasks, but it's often the best choice for objects that are easily defined by profiles, edges, or simple rounded shapes.

NURBS objects are divided into two categories: curves and surfaces. Surfaces are broad areas of geometry that can be planar or form very complicated topography. Most NURBS models are composed of many of these surfaces, which are positioned edge to edge like sheets of paper. Together, they form complete, seemingly unbroken objects. A surface is defined by the curves in or around it, and all NURBS modeling depends on the careful positioning and manipulation of these curves.

Although NURBS curves are different from Bézier curves; you create and edit them similarly. Bézier and NURBS curves represent curved lines whose shape you can define by translating or adding points along the curve. You can use NURBS curves to create a framework for a final surface, much the same way you would make a wire mesh to cover with paper maché (**Figure 7.1**).

About NURBS Objects

NURBS object creation is a Maya strongpoint because of the precise control it affords you over the final surface. There are two types of NURBS objects: *curves* and *surfaces*.

NURBS curves have three main components: *control vertices (CVs)*, *edit points*, and *hulls* (**Figure 7.2**). You use these components to create and edit curves in different ways. As you grow familiar with creating NURBS curves, you'll likely come to prefer one component to the others, making it your primary editing method.

In addition to CVs, edit points, and hulls, NURBS surfaces have the following more advanced components: *isoparms* and *surface patches* (**Figure 7.3**). Both of these components are uneditable pieces of the NURBS surface. You can edit any NURBS surface that was created from a curve (for example, a revolved surface) by editing components of the original curve or by editing the surface's components directly. When a surface is created from one or more curves, it remains linked to that curve through a history connection. Thus, when you modify a curve, you're also editing the surface.

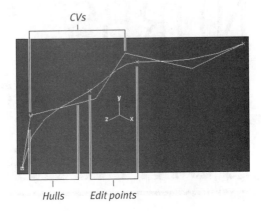

Figure 7.2 NURBS components are used to easily and quickly change the shape of an existing curve or surface.

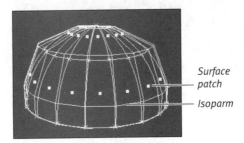

Figure 7.3 NURBS surface components are used to manipulate the shape and composition of the surface.

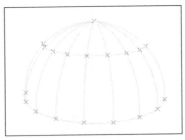

Figure 7.4 Surface edit points can be shown by themselves to make selection and editing easier. You can select each component by clicking its icon, in this case a small *x*.

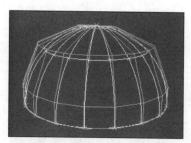

Figure 7.5 Maya lets you show or hide as many components as you want to view at any given time. This helps you narrow down your selection while still getting a good idea of what the object's other components look like.

Each NURBS component (edit point, CV, and so on) can be displayed and edited both individually (**Figure 7.4**; edit points are shown) and with other components (**Figure 7.5**; edit points and hulls are shown). NURBS curves are an integral part of NURBS modeling because they help you create and edit surfaces. This chapter will provide the foundation you need to control the look of NURBS curves and surfaces.

✔ Tip

- You'll find it useful to keep your construction history on when modeling with NURBS. Doing so lets you make adjustments to your surfaces much more easily and often prevents the need to re-create pieces of geometry. Without history, the NURBS object workflow feels rigid and unforgiving.

NURBS Modeling Strategy

NURBS models usually consist of many separate NURBS surfaces, all working together to form the semblance of a continuous surface. This can be a tricky process, because all of these surfaces rely on each other, and your surface construction order can affect your workflow efficiency. Also, the number and direction of your curves and surface components can be important in matching or joining your surfaces.

Luckily, Maya offers many tools to tackle these tasks. When you look over these tools as they're covered in the chapter, keep in mind the following tips: When you first begin working on an object, you may find it easiest to start by laying down all the obvious contour curves and then move on to creating the largest or most important components. Fine-tuning the blends between your components is the last piece of the process.

Try to preserve any curve you make, so that you can use it later if you need to make a new surface. To keep your workflow as simple as possible, use layers to store sets of curves, and be careful when naming your curves and groups. As you get more experienced with the NURBS workflow, you can start deleting curves and finalizing pieces of geometry as you go.

NURBS modeling is akin to building frames to lay your surfaces across. This process, referred to as *edge-based modeling*, can be difficult to master. If you have a hard time with a particular object using NURBS modeling, you may find modeling polygons or subdivision surfaces to be more intuitive. Because you can convert any geometry type—including NURBS—to polygons, a variety of techniques may suit you.

About NURBS Curves

Knowing how to create and edit curves is an important part of understanding Maya. In addition to being used extensively in NURBS modeling, curves are used in animation, as paths and guides, and in rigging as the basis for deformers.

Curves are often used to create a wire representation of a surface. Once you've done this, you can place a skin over the curves to create the final surface (**Figure 7.6**). You can create this final surface using a number of Maya commands, including *lofting*, *extruding*, and *revolving*—all of which we'll examine in depth in this chapter.

Anatomy of a curve

Each NURBS curve has an associated direction, derived from the order in which the CVs were created. A curve's direction is important in determining the look of the final surface. If you don't pay attention to the direction in which a curve is created, you'll often get undesirable results when you go to create the final surface. Curves that are oriented in opposite directions can twist and fold the final surface.

The direction of a curve is determined by the first and second CVs created for the curve. The first CV, or *start point*, is represented by a small square. The second CV is represented by the letter *U*. The start point followed by the *U* shows the user the direction in which the curve is headed; this determines the *U* direction of any surface created from the curve (**Figure 7.7**). Curve direction has nothing to do with the shape of the curve or where it lies on the screen; it only relates to the start and end points.

Because NURBS curves are used mainly as modeling aids, they don't appear when the scene is rendered.

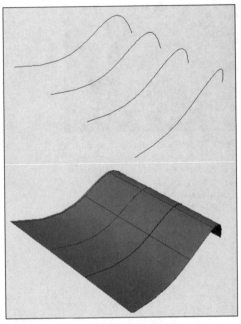

Figure 7.6 Curves used to create a framework for the surface (top), and the same curves with a surface laid over them (bottom).

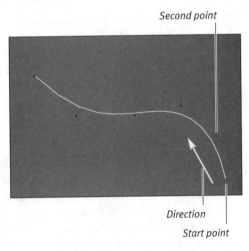

Figure 7.7 The *U* direction of a curve is determined by the first and second CVs created.

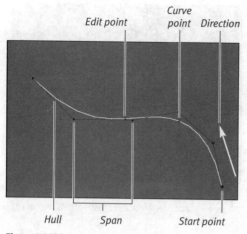

Figure 7.8 This image shows NURBS curve components.

Each curve has the following components (**Figure 7.8**):

◆ **Control vertices**—CVs are points placed slightly away from the curve and are the components most often used to edit a curve's shape.

◆ **Edit points (knots)**—Edit points (EPs), placed directly on the curve and indicated by a small *x*, represent a more direct but limited way of editing a curve's shape. A surface contains an isoparm for each knot on its source curve.

◆ **Hulls**—Hulls are straight lines connecting each CV. Showing the hulls can help clarify how the CVs on your curve or object are connected. By clicking a hull, you select the entire row of CVs along the hull.

◆ **Spans**—A span is the area between two edit points. Each time an edit point is added, a span is added as well. You can't edit spans directly (like edit points); instead, they represent the results of your edits. You use spans to create and rebuild curves and surfaces. The more spans you add when rebuilding a surface, the more edit points you're adding—which means the more spans you have, the more detailed and heavy your surface becomes.

◆ **Curve point**—A curve point is an arbitrary point on a curve, often used as a point to detach a curve from or to align it with. A curve point can be located anywhere along a curve.

◆ **Start point**—The start of a curve is the first CV created for the curve, represented by a small square.

◆ **Curve direction**—The direction of a curve is determined by the first and second CVs created for the curve.

Creating NURBS Curves

Every curve has a certain degree; the higher the degree, the smoother the curve. A curve can have a degree of 1, 2, 3, 5, or 7. The degree represents the complexity of the curve between CVs. A curve with a degree of 1 is a linear curve and requires only two points to define it (**Figure 7.9**). Linear curves and surfaces are characterized by straight lines and sharp corners. A curve degree of 3 produces a smooth curve without using an excessive number of CVs to describe it (**Figure 7.10**). A curve with a degree of 3 is the most common and versatile curve because it requires only four points and is smooth enough to create a high-quality surface. A higher-degree curve holds closer to the CVs, resulting in a smoother, more accurate interpolation. Because of the accuracy needed for manufacturing, car designers often use degrees higher than 5. For animation, however, a degree of 3 is usually enough.

Each curve requires CVs that total one more than its degree. For example, a curve with a degree of 3 requires four CVs (Figure 7.10); a 7-degree curve requires eight CVs, thereby creating a heavier surface (**Figure 7.11**). For this reason, a degree of 3 or 5 is usually ideal.

Typically, you create a curve in one of three ways: with the CV Curve tool, the EP Curve tool, or the Pencil Curve tool.

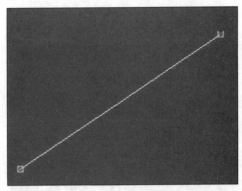

Figure 7.9 A curve degree of 1 creates a linear curve and a linear surface (if a surface is created from the curve).

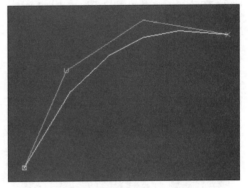

Figure 7.10 A curve degree of 3 produces a smooth curve without using an excessive number of CVs.

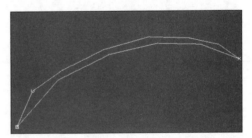

Figure 7.11 This is a 7-degree curve, which means it requires eight CVs.

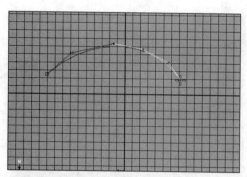

Figure 7.12 This curve was created by placing points using the CV Curve tool.

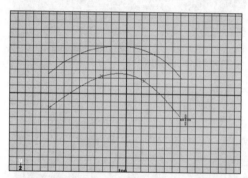

Figure 7.13 This curve was created using the EP Curve tool.

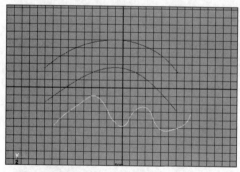

Figure 7.14 The bottom curve was created using the Pencil Curve tool.

To create a curve with the CV Curve tool:

1. Choose Create > CV Curve Tool.

2. In the Top view, click in several places.

   A CV appears with each mouse click, and a curve appears on the fourth click (**Figure 7.12**).

3. Press (Enter) to complete the creation of the curve.

   The curve becomes highlighted to indicate that it's selected.

To create a curve with the EP Curve tool:

1. Choose Create > EP Curve Tool.

2. In the Top view, click in several places.

   A curve is created once the second edit point is placed, and it continues to take shape with each subsequent point (**Figure 7.13**).

3. Press (Enter) to finish creating the curve.

✔ Tip

- The EP tool is better suited when you want precise control over exactly where your curve passes. Use the CV tool for tasks like ensuring tangency, when you care more about the CV placement than the curve location.

To create a curve with the Pencil Curve tool:

1. Choose Create > Pencil Curve Tool.

2. Click and drag in the Top view to draw a line.

   The curve is completed once you release the mouse. The Pencil Curve tool tends to be a less efficient way of creating a curve because you end up with more points than you need to describe the shape (**Figure 7.14**).

Editing NURBS Curves

Once you've laid out your curve, you may wish to insert points into it or add points to the end of the curve for extra detail.

To add edit points to a curve:

1. Right-click a curve, and select Curve Point from the marking menu (**Figure 7.15**).

2. Click the curve where you wish to insert a new EP.

3. Choose Edit Curves > Insert Knot.

   A new EP is created in the spot you've designated. New CVs are automatically created to adjust this new point (**Figure 7.16**).

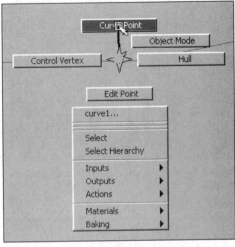

Figure 7.15 The right-click marking menu provides component display options.

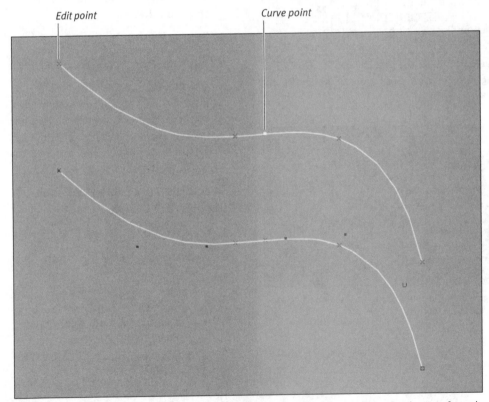

Edit point   *Curve point*

Figure 7.16 The original curve with a curve point selected, and the curve after Insert Knot has been performed.

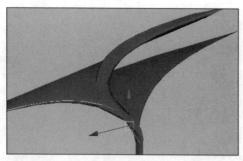

Figure 7.17 Curve direction can cause unwanted surface problems. It's best to keep all curves of the same surface facing in the same direction.

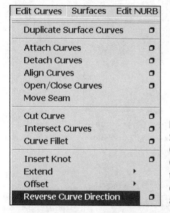

Figure 7.18 Select Edit Curves > Reverse Curve Direction to change the direction of a curve.

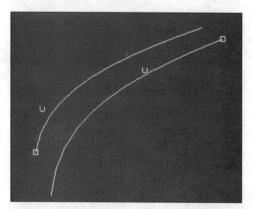

Figure 7.19 The curve on top shows the direction before it was reversed; the curve beneath it shows the direction after the curve has been reversed.

Curve direction

As stated earlier, each curve has a direction, called the *U* direction. Sometimes you'll want to reverse a curve's direction because you're getting undesirable surfaces from the curves (**Figure 7.17**).

To reverse a curve's direction:

1. Select a curve in object mode.

2. Choose Edit Curves > Reverse Curve Direction (**Figure 7.18**).

3. Press F8 to view the new curve direction in component mode (**Figure 7.19**).

EDITING NURBS CURVES

Opening, Closing, and Attaching Curves

A curve that doesn't start and end on the same point is called an *open curve* (**Figure 7.20**). Many Maya commands won't function correctly on open curves, so the curves must be closed. A *closed curve* has the same start and end point, making it continuous (**Figure 7.21**).

You may want to attach two curves to each other, either because it was easier to create them separately or because you want to form a single surface from them. On the other hand, there are occasions when you'll want more control over generating new surfaces by splitting a curve in half in order to perform two separate functions on each half.

To open or close a curve:

◆ Choose Edit Curves > Open/Close Curves (**Figure 7.22**).

An open curve becomes closed, and a closed curve becomes open.

✔ Tip

■ When you perform the close-curve operation, you rely on Maya to interpolate the undefined portion on your curve. You'll get better results if you keep your curves as closed as possible before performing the close curve operation.

To attach two curves:

1. Select the first and then the second curve you want to connect.

   The order in which you select the curves affects certain option settings.

2. Choose Edit Curves > Attach Curves.

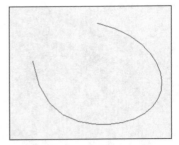

Figure 7.20 An incomplete circle is called an open curve.

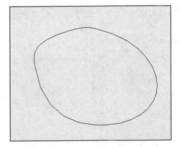

Figure 7.22 The Open/Close Curves command opens a closed curve and closes an open curve.

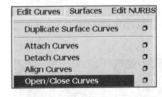

Figure 7.22 The Open/Close Curves command opens a closed curve and closes an open curve.

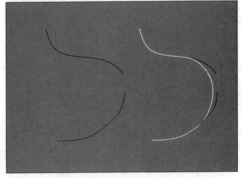

Figure 7.23 The original curves on the left, and the new attached curve on the right. The original curves have been retained in this example.

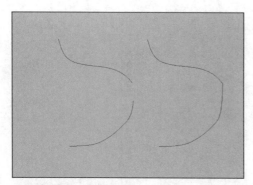

Figure 7.24 The second curve has been connected to the first, instead of blended.

Figure 7.25 An edit point is represented by an *x*; when selected, it can be used as a curve's breaking point.

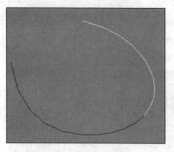

Figure 7.26 Two curves are created out of the detachment at the edit point.

Original Seam   *New Seam*

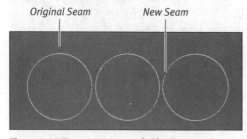

Figure 7.27 The original curve (left), after an edit point is added (middle), and the curve detached and reclosed (right).

The curves blend together in a single curve (**Figure 7.23**). By selecting the box to the right of Attach Curves, you can set the curves to connect instead of blend, which does a better job of preserving the existing curvature (**Figure 7.24**).

To detach a curve:

1. Select a curve with the Pick mask set to Component: Parm Points mode.

   or

   Right-click the curve, and select Curve Point from the marking menu.

2. Select the edit point *x* where you would like to detach the curve (**Figure 7.25**).

   or

   Click the curve to denote a curve point.

3. Choose Edit Curves > Detach Curves.

   The curve is broken into two curves (**Figure 7.26**).

✔ Tips

- If Keep Originals is selected in the Detach Curves Options dialog box, you'll have three curves after detaching—the original curve and two detached curves. Deselect Keep Originals before you detach to automatically delete the original curve (see the "Keep Originals" sidebar later in this chapter).

- If you perform Detach Curves on a closed curve, the curve becomes open with a start and end point where you detached them. Combined with Close Curves, this operation can reposition the seam on a circular curve (**Figure 7.27**).

Altering Whole Curves

Maya has a number of options for automating difficult curve-altering tasks, such as straightening and smoothing. For instance, sometimes curves are too dense and need to be simplified. Or perhaps a curve doesn't have the density it needs for the next operation you wish to perform.

To rebuild a curve to add density:

1. Select a curve to rebuild.

2. From the Edit Curves menu, select the box next to Rebuild Curve (**Figure 7.28**). The Rebuild Curve Options dialog box appears (**Figure 7.29**).

3. Select the Number of Spans box, enter 20, and click Rebuild.

   The curve now has 20 evenly spaced spans (**Figure 7.30**).

✔ Tip

■ You can also use the Rebuild Curves tool to remove density, change linearity, and even out the spans of an existing curve. Explore the options.

Curves are like rubber bands in that you can pull and stretch them apart. That is, you can edit CVs to be any distance from one another. However, for the practical purposes of animation, you're better off making your curve behave like a piece of string that stays the same length while you bend it. You can do that by locking the length of the curve so that the CVs remain the same distance from one another when you animate the curve. Locking a curve also locks the length of the spans. If you think you may want to significantly change the shape of the curve later, add some extra curve density before locking your curve.

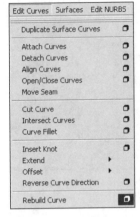

Figure 7.28 Select the option for Edit Curves > Rebuild Curve.

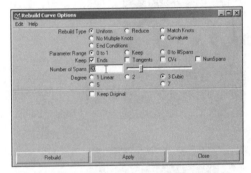

Figure 7.29 Enter 20 in the Number of Spans box.

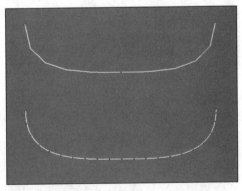

Figure 7.30 The curve on top has been rebuilt from 4 spans to 20 even ones. It can now be adjusted to add greater definition.

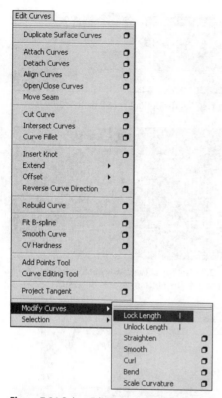

Figure 7.31 Select Edit Curves > Modify Curves > Lock Length.

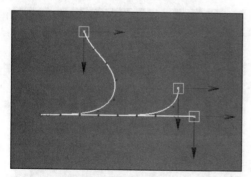

Figure 7.32 With Lock Length enabled, drag a CV to pull the curve like a piece of string.

To lock the length of a curve:

1. Select a curve, and choose Edit Curves > Modify Curves > Lock Length (**Figure 7.31**).

2. Press F8 to switch to component mode, and select the Points component type.

3. Select the first CV in the curve, press W, and move the CV.

   The curve follows the CV you selected like a piece of string (**Figure 7.32**).

✔ Tip

- To unlock a curve, select the curve and choose Edit Curves > Modify Curves > Unlock Length.

To straighten a curve:

1. With a curve selected, choose Edit Curves > Modify Curves, and click the option box next to Straighten (**Figure 7.33**).

   The Straighten Curves Options dialog box opens.

2. Deselect the Preserve Length check box.

continues on next page

Figure 7.33 Select Edit Curves > Modify Curves > Straighten.

3. Adjust the Straightness slider to 1 (or type 1 in the text box) (**Figure 7.34**).

4. Click Apply.

The wavy curve becomes a straight line (**Figure 7.35**). Values less than 1 only partially uncurl the curve, like unrolling a piece of string.

To smooth a curve:

1. With a curve selected, choose Edit Curves > Modify Curves, and click the option box next to Smooth (**Figure 7.36**). The Smooth Curves Options dialog box opens.

2. Set the Smooth Factor to 10 (**Figure 7.37**).

3. Click Apply.

The jagged curve becomes smoother (**Figure 7.38**).

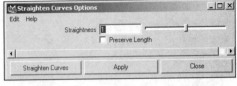

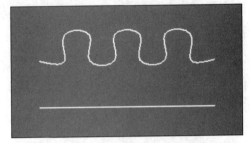

Figure 7.34 Set the options for Straighten Curves.

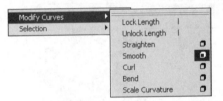

Figure 7.35 The top curve is wavy before being straightened. The bottom curve is the result.

Figure 7.36 Select Smooth from the Edit Curves > Modify Curves menu.

Figure 7.37 Set the Smooth Factor to 10.

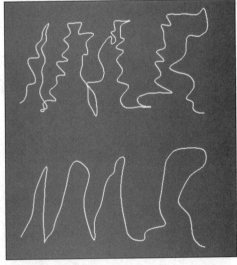

Figure 7.38 The top curve is jagged before applying the Smooth function. The bottom curve is the result.

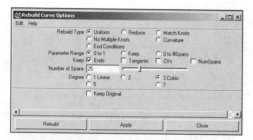

Figure 7.39 Set the Number of Spans to 25.

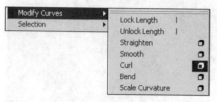

Figure 7.40 Select Edit Curves › Modify Curves › Curl.

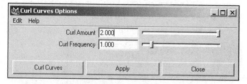

Figure 7.41 Set the options for Curl Curves.

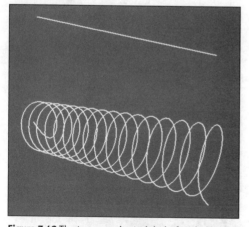

Figure 7.42 The top curve is straight before being curled. The bottom curve is the result.

To curl a curve:

1. With a curve selected, choose Edit Curves, and click the option box next to Rebuild Curve.

   The Rebuild Curve Options dialog box opens.

2. Set the Number of Spans to 25 (**Figure 7.39**).

3. Click Rebuild.

   The effect of the curl is more apparent if your curve has many CVs in it.

4. Choose Edit Curves > Modify Curves, and click the option box next to Curl (**Figure 7.40**).

   The Curl Curves Options dialog box opens.

5. Set the Curl Amount to 2 and the Curl Frequency to 1 (**Figure 7.41**).

6. Click Apply.

   The curve becomes a spiral (**Figure 7.42**).

To bend a curve:

1. With a curve selected, choose Edit Curves > Modify Curves, and click the option box next to Bend (**Figure 7.43**).

   The Bend Curves Options dialog box opens.

continues on next page

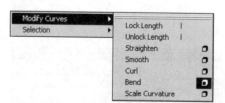

Figure 7.43 Select Edit Curves › Modify Curves › Bend.

ALTERING WHOLE CURVES

2. Set the Bend Amount to .15 (**Figure 7.44**).

3. Click Apply.

The curve becomes more like a circle (**Figure 7.45**).

To scale curvature:

1. With a curve selected, choose Edit Curves > Modify Curves, and click the option box next to Scale Curvature (**Figure 7.46**).

The Scale Curvature Options dialog box opens.

2. Set the Scale Factor to .5 and the Max Curvature to 1 (**Figure 7.47**).

3. Click Apply.

The curve expands (**Figure 7.48**).

✔ Tip

■ You can also apply the Straighten, Smooth, Curl, Bend, and Scale Curvature effects to selected CVs instead of to the entire curve.

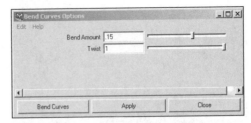

Figure 7.44 Set the options for Bend Curves.

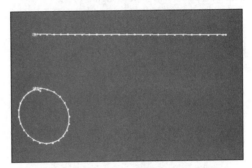

Figure 7.45 The top curve is straight before being bent. The bottom curve is the result.

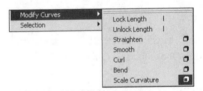

Figure 7.46 Select Edit Curves > Modify Curves > Scale Curvature.

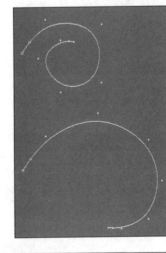

Figure 7.48 The top curve is tighter before applying Scale Curvature. The bottom curve is the result.

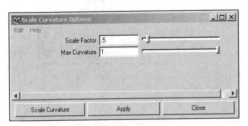

Figure 7.47 Set the options for Scale Curvature.

Figure 7.49
This spiral was created easily by curling a curve and then offsetting it to create the second curve needed to loft a surface.

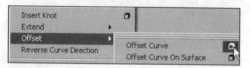

Figure 7.50 Select Edit Curves > Offset, and select the box next to Offset Curve.

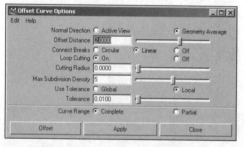

Figure 7.51 Enter 2 in the Offset Distance box.

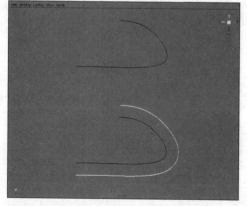

Figure 7.52 The new curve is 2 units away in all perpendicular locations. Note that this is different than duplicating and scaling a curve.

Interactions Between Curves

Maya contains several operations that are based on the relationships between preexisting curves. The Offset and 2d Fillet functions are perhaps the most common of these.

Creating a new curve that parallels an existing one (like a spiral ramp, or a rounded edge) can be difficult if the original curve has complicated or spiral topology. The Offset Curve function creates a copy of your curve a fixed distance from the original at all points (**Figure 7.49**).

To offset a curve:

1. Select a curve, choose Edit Curves > Offset, and click the option box next to Offset Curve (**Figure 7.50**).

   The Offset Curve Options dialog box opens.

2. Set the Offset Distance to 2 (**Figure 7.51**).

3. Click Offset.

   A new curve is created that is exactly 2 units from the original (**Figure 7.52**).

   Like many functions in Maya, you can scale the distance interactively using the Channel Box. To do so, select the input node, and change the value until the new curve is the desired distance away from the source curve (**Figure 7.53**).

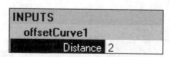

Figure 7.53 Using the Channel Box, you can adjust the distance of the existing offset easily rather than performing the operation again.

Circular 2D fillets

A *fillet* is a concave junction where two curves or surfaces meet. You can create 2D fillets to combine multiple curves with an arc between them. Sometimes it's easier to create two curves and fillet them together in order to create a corner than it is to draw out one curve with the corner in it. An example might be when you need to create a corner out of two perpendicular curves (**Figure 7.54**).

To create a circular 2D fillet:

1. Create two curves to fillet between (**Figure 7.55**).

2. Right-click the first curve, and select Curve Point from the marking menu.

3. Click the first curve, and drag the point to where you want the fillet to arc (**Figure 7.56**).

Fillet

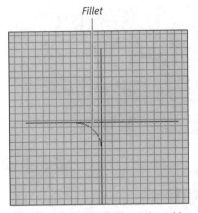

Figure 7.54 Use the 2D Fillet tool to add smooth corners to a set of curves.

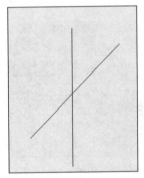

Figure 7.55 Two curves intersecting.

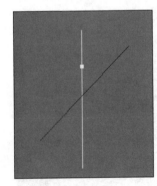

Figure 7.56 Click and drag a curve point into the place where you would like the arc to begin.

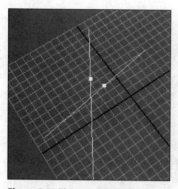

Figure 7.57 The two curve points determine the start and end points of the arc.

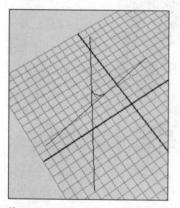

Figure 7.58 An arc is created between the two curve points selected on each curve.

4. Right-click the second curve, and select Curve Point from the marking menu.

5. [Shift]-click the second curve, and drag the point to where you want the fillet to arc (**Figure 7.57**).

6. Choose Edit Curves > Curve Fillet.

An arc is created between the two curve points (**Figure 7.58**).

Keep Originals

Many of the curve and surface manipulation and rebuild commands have a Keep Originals option. When you rebuild a curve using a command such as Detach, the Keep Originals option lets you retain the original curve in addition to creating the new curve(s) as a result of the specific rebuild command.

Be aware that you may not notice that the original curve or surface is still present because the new curves or surfaces will sit directly on top of the original.

Creating Surfaces from Curves

Curves don't render, so in order to get visible geometry from your NURBS curves, you must use them to create a NURBS surface. All NURBS surfaces originate from one or more profile or edge curves.

You can use several commands in Maya to create surfaces from curves. They include Revolve, Planar, Loft, Extrude, Birail, and Boundary.

Each command has strengths and limitations, and each has a set of requirements. If one surface type doesn't seem to be suited for the area you're defining, there is usually another type that works just as well.

Several of the tools (Revolve, Extrude, Birail) use profile curves to define their shapes. A *profile curve* is any curve that defines the outline of an object. The most common and obvious use of this is in the Revolve tool, where the curve is rotated around an axis to form an object. This functions similarly to a woodworker's lathe (**Figure 7.59**). In addition, you can alter the profile curve to tweak the object's shape after the final surface has been created. You can do this because the profile curve and final surface are connected through the object's construction history (**Figure 7.60**).

If you're drawing a profile curve for a vase or any other object that has thickness to it, you should draw the profile of both the inside and the outside (**Figure 7.61**). If you don't draw both profiles, your object will be paper-thin. Because most real objects have some depth or dimension, you need to re-create that thickness in Maya to keep your objects looking realistic. If you plan to make your object transparent, pay special attention to the thickness. Some shaders rely on the actual thickness to calculate appearance, and it will be noticeable if the object is too thick or thin.

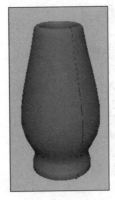

Figure 7.59 This surface was created with one revolved curve.

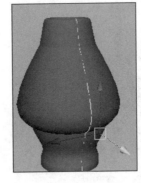

Figure 7.60 By tweaking a point of the curve—part of the construction history—you can interactively sculpt the object.

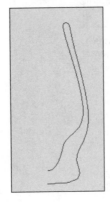

Figure 7.61 A profile of a pot. When drawing a profile curve, make sure you add the inside of the surface to add thickness to the final object.

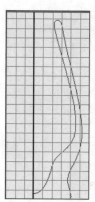

Figure 7.62 A profile curve illustrates the outline of the object used for revolving.

Figure 7.63 From the Surfaces menu, select the box next to Revolve to open the Revolve Options window.

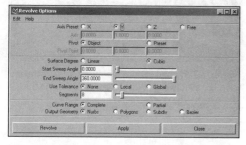

Figure 7.64 The revolve axis is very important to the look of the final surface. Choose the axis that goes through the middle of the final surface.

To revolve a curve to make a vase:

1. In the Front or Side view, draw a curve for the shape of the vase's profile (**Figure 7.62**).

2. Select the curve in object mode.

3. In the Surfaces menu, select the box next to Revolve (**Figure 7.63**).
   The Revolve Options window opens.

4. Select the axis around which you want the object to revolve (**Figure 7.64**).
   This example uses the y axis.

5. Click Revolve to create the surface of the vase.
   If you get unexpected results, you may have the object revolving around the wrong axis.

6. Press ③ to increase the smoothness to see the full surface (**Figure 7.65**).

✔ Tips

■ You can adjust Start Sweep Angle and End Sweep Angle in Revolve Options to create a revolved surface that isn't a complete 360 degrees.

■ To interactively change the shape of a revolved surface by changing the angle of the axis revolution, you can use the Show Manipulator tool.

Figure 7.65 Increasing surface smoothness helps clarify where the actual revolved surface lies.

CREATING SURFACES FROM CURVES

One of the best ways to create a surface from multiple curves is to use the Loft command. This command creates a surface that extends from one selected curve to the next until each curve is covered with a surface. Each of the isoparms on the final surface is derived from the edit point placement on each curve. As a general rule, you should have the same number of edit points on each curve.

To loft across multiple curves:

1. Create two or more curves with which to create a surface (**Figure 7.66**).

2. Shift-select each curve in the order in which you want the surface to loft across them.

   The order in which you select curves is important. The surface starts at the first selected curve and covers each additional curve in the order you select them.

3. With all the curves selected, choose Surfaces > Loft to create a surface over the curves (**Figure 7.67**).

✔ Tips

- A new surface displays in rough mode and looks as if it isn't fully touching the curves used to create it. Select the surface and press ③ to view the surface in smooth display mode.

- The curves you use to loft can be in any position, but lofts work best when the shift in curve orientation doesn't exceed 90 degrees and when all curves have the same *U* direction. If the surface doesn't look the way you expected, insert more curves or double-check the curve directions and selection order.

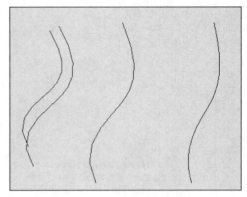

Figure 7.66 When creating curves to loft across, you must consider each curve describing the contour of the final surface.

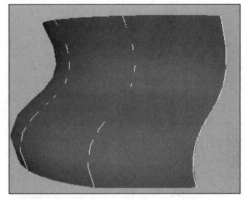

Figure 7.67 A lofted surface maintains a connection to the original curves so that you can edit them in the future using the original curves.

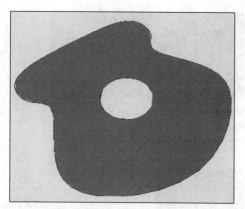

Figure 7.68 The Make Planar command works well for any closed, flat curve out of which you want to make a flat surface.

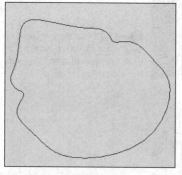

Figure 7.69 This closed curve determines the outline of the surface. Use grid snap to be sure all the points of the curve lie on the same plane.

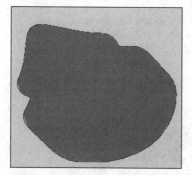

Figure 7.70 A flat surface is created, with the curve used as the border of the surface.

The Make Planar command is used to make a flat surface out of a curve. An example of its use would be to create the flat top of a guitar (that is, the part with the hole in it) (**Figure 7.68**). You could create the outline of the guitar's body with a curve, and then use the Make Planar command to complete the flat surface.

To make a curve planar:

1. Create a closed curve with all the CVs on the same axis (**Figure 7.69**).

2. Choose Surfaces > Planar.

   A planar surface is created from the curve (**Figure 7.70**).

✔ Tips

- The curve must be closed or self-intersecting for the Planar command to work.

- All CVs must lie on the same axis for the command to work. To ensure that this is the case, you can grid-snap each CV to a grid plane.

- To make a plane with holes in it, select multiple closed curves.

CREATING SURFACES FROM CURVES

The Extrude command creates a surface by sweeping one curve (the profile) along another curve (the path). This command is suited to long skinny objects such as cords or wires, as well as branches, limbs, and more.

To extrude a curve:

1. Create a profile curve that is the shape you'd like the final extruded surface to be.

   For example, to extrude a tube, create a circle (**Figure 7.71**).

2. Starting from the already created curve, create a CV curve the length of the final surface you want to create (**Figure 7.72**). This is referred to as the *path curve*.

3. Select the circle, and then Shift-select the path curve.

4. Choose Surfaces > Extrude to sweep the profile curve along the path curve.

   A new extruded surface is created (**Figure 7.73**).

✔ Tip

■ By default, the new surface starts at the angle of the profile curve and mimics its angles. With this default setting, the extruded surface only follows the path curve if the profile curve is perpendicular to the path curve. To ignore the angle of the profile curve and have the curve follow the path curve, select At Path in the Extrude Options window.

The Birail tool is similar to Extrude, except that instead of having one path curve and one profile curve, it has two path curves (rails) and any number of profile curves. The hull of a boat provides a good example: Two path curves can determine the hull's outline, and profile curves can determine its depth and shape (**Figure 7.74**).

Figure 7.71 Any curve shape can be used for an extrude—for example, if you're looking for a tubelike shape, you could use a closed curve.

Figure 7.72 The second curve you create for an extrude is used for the path and length of the extruded surface.

Figure 7.73 The surface created from the extrude follows the angle of the profile curve.

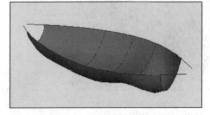

Figure 7.74 The hull of a boat can be created from a few profile curves and two rail curves.

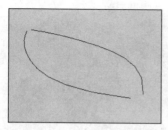

Figure 7.75 You always use two curves for the rails.

Rail curves   Profile curve

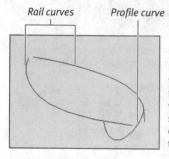

Figure 7.76 For the command to function correctly, your must curve-snap the ends of each profile curve to the rails.

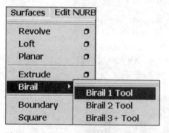

Figure 7.77 Choose Surfaces › Birail › Birail 1 Tool.

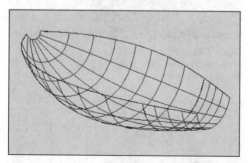

Figure 7.78 A surface is created from the three curves using the Birail tool.

The various Birail tools (Birail, Birail 2, Birail 3+) apply depending on how many profile curves you plan to have. The following task assumes one profile. If you want more, you can just select the appropriate tool.

To create a birail surface:

1. Draw two curves to use for the rails of the surface (**Figure 7.75**).

2. Draw a new curve that extends from the first curve to the second curve using curve snap (hold down ⒸⒸ, and click and drag the rail curve) for the first and last points (**Figure 7.76**).

   The curves must touch each other for the operation to work. Curve snap helps ensure that the profile curve touches both rails.

3. Choose Surfaces > Birail > Birail 1 Tool (**Figure 7.77**).

   Use Birail 2 Tool if you have two profile curves. Use Birail 3+ if you're using three or more profile curves.

4. Click the profile curves, and then click the rail curves (**Figure 7.78**).

   The birail surface is created.

✔ Tip

- Birail creates a surface along the entire length of the rails. To limit this to a section of the rails, use a Birail 2 and put your profile curves at the beginning and end of where you want your surface to be.

CREATING SURFACES FROM CURVES

The Boundary command requires three or four curves that intersect or meet at each other's ends. You might use a boundary surface when you have three surfaces connecting at a corner and you want to use three of the edges to complete a rounded corner between the surfaces (**Figure 7.79**).

To create a boundary surface:

1. Draw three or four curves with intersecting ends (**Figure 7.80**).

   You can make sure the ends intersect by curve-snapping the first and last CVs to the other curves.

2. Select all the curves that complete the boundary (**Figure 7.81**).

3. Choose Surfaces > Boundary.

   The boundary surface is created (**Figure 7.82**).

Figure 7.79 The gap between these surfaces would be a good candidate for filling via the Boundary command.

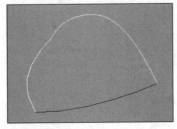

Figure 7.80 With boundary surfaces, as with birail surfaces, it's essential to curve-snap each end point.

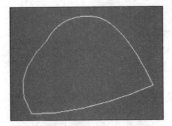

Figure 7.81 You can select curves or isoparms on which to use the Boundary command.

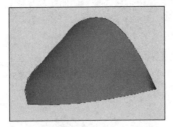

Figure 7.82 A surface is created across the three curves.

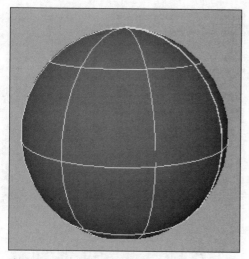

Figure 7.83 The sphere has been selected to make it live so that a curve can be drawn on it. Any surface can be made live.

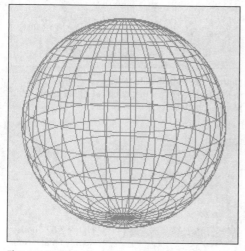

Figure 7.84 When the surface is live, the wireframe turns green.

Surface Curves and Trims

Many NURBS surface operations, like the Planar and Trim commands, require curves to be on or in a surface. You can generate these curves a few different ways: by intersecting two objects, projecting them from the view, or drawing them directly.

To draw a curve directly on a surface, you must make the surface *live*. This means the surface becomes the new world space for all operations. Once a surface is live, a curve can be created and edited directly on the surface.

To make a surface live:

1. Select a surface (**Figure 7.83**).

2. Choose Modify > Make Live, or click ⟳.
   The surface wireframe turns dark green to indicate that it is a live surface (**Figure 7.84**).

✔ Tip

■ To deactivate a surface that's live, select Modify > Make Not Live.

To draw a curve on a live surface:

1. Make the surface live.

2. Choose Create > CV or EP Curve Tool (**Figure 7.85**).

3. Click points on the surface where you want to create the curve (**Figure 7.86**).

4. Press ⌈Enter⌉ to complete the curve. A curve is created on the surface.

5. Choose Modify > Make Not Live to bring the surface back into normal mode (**Figure 7.87**).

✔ Tips

■ You can move the curve along the surface in the *U* or *V* direction using the Move tool.

■ If you cross the seam (the area on cylindrical NURBS objects where the surface loops back to itself) when drawing a curve on a live surface such as a cylinder, the curve takes the long way around your object when going from point to point. Use the Move Seam command to put the seam out of the way.

Sometimes a surface is hard to draw on, or you may already have a curve and want to put it on a surface. The simplest way to do this is to project the curve onto the surface. Projecting a curve creates a new curve on the selected surface. Imagine projecting the image of a curve at an object from a slide projector. The shape of the object may warp the image of the curve. Likewise, when you project a curve in Maya, the resulting curve projected on an object's surface is warped to some degree.

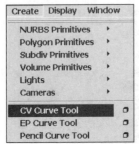

Figure 7.85 Choose Create > CV Curve Tool.

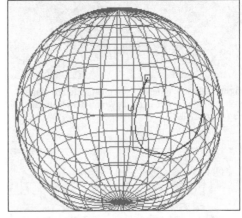

Figure 7.86 It's helpful to tumble your view around the surface to get a straight look at where you want to place each CV.

Figure 7.87 Choose Modify > Make Not Live to return to normal mode.

Figure 7.88 Curves on surfaces work well when you want to later trim out part of a surface, as with this pumpkin.

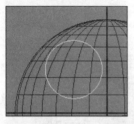

Figure 7.89 This circle will be projected onto the surface of the sphere.

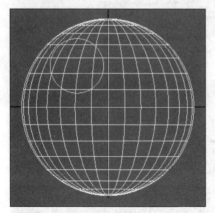

Figure 7.90 Both the curve and the surface must be selected for the projection to work.

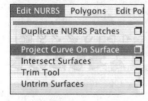

Figure 7.91 The active view becomes the angle from which the curve is projected.

A pumpkin's eyes provide a good example: You can draw the shape of the eyes you want to cut out of a pumpkin in the Front view and project these curves onto the pumpkin shape so that you can later trim them out of the surface (**Figure 7.88**). The trim function is often used after projecting a curve onto a surface to cut out the curve shape.

To project a curve onto a surface:

1. Create a NURBS surface for the curve to be projected onto—a primitive sphere, for example.

2. In the Front view, create a curve to project onto the surface; this example uses a primitive circle (**Figure 7.89**).

3. Select the curve to be projected, and select the surface (**Figure 7.90**).

4. With the Front view active, select Edit NURBS > Project Curve On Surface (**Figure 7.91**).

   The curve becomes projected on both sides of the sphere's surface (**Figure 7.92**).

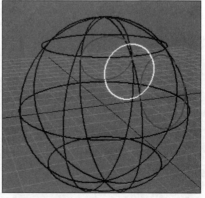

Figure 7.92 The curve is projected on both sides of the object.

167

To trim out a hole in a surface:

1. Follow the steps outlined in the previous task, "To project a curve onto a surface."

2. Choose Edit NURBS > Trim Tool.

3. Click the sphere.

   The object becomes transparent, and the lines turn white to indicate that you're in the Trim tool (**Figure 7.93**).

4. Click in an area you want to keep—*not* the area in which you want a hole.

   A yellow diamond indicates the area you want to retain (**Figure 7.94**).

5. Click (Enter) to trim the surface.

   Because the curve was projected on both sides of the sphere, there are now two holes in the surface (**Figure 7.95**).

✔ Tip

- You can click each area you want to retain. In our sphere example, you can click the main surface of the sphere and inside the area of one of the circles to create only one hole in the surface.

Figure 7.93 The object becomes transparent, and each area that has an option to trim is filled with a grid.

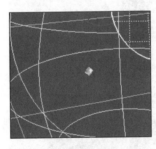

Figure 7.94
The small, yellow diamond indicates that the region will be kept intact.

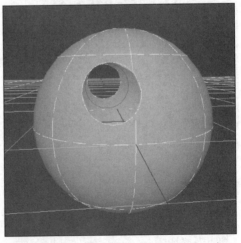

Figure 7.95 The surface now includes two holes where the original curve originally appeared on the surface.

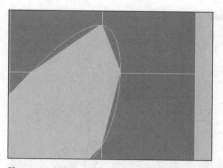

Figure 7.96 The surface here is not falling within the bounds of the smooth trim curve.

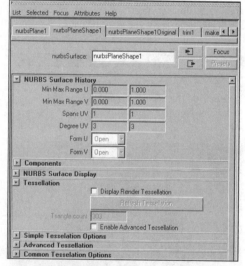

Figure 7.97 The Shape tab controls many attributes that affect the appearance of your object.

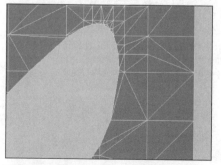

Figure 7.98 Displaying the render tessellation lets you see a more accurate representation of your model. However, displaying tessellation can slow down performance.

Sometimes a Trim or Planar operation displays slight inaccuracies in the way your surface is shown in real time, particularly on surfaces where the isoparms are placed far apart (**Figure 7.96**). You can sometimes remedy this problem by switching to Smooth Shaded mode (press ③), whereas other times you need to display the way the object will be tessellated at render time to get an accurate display of your trim.

To display render tessellation:

1. With a NURBS object selected, press Ctrl+a.

   This brings up the Attribute Editor for your object.

2. Select the second tab (nurbsPlaneShape1) in the Attribute Editor. In the first input box, you'll see the name of your object, followed by its shape (in this case, nurbsPlaneShape1) (**Figure 7.97**).

3. Click the arrow next to Tessellation to display the options, and select the Display Render Tessellation box.

   The object is triangulated and displays all the polys it will use at render time (**Figure 7.98**). You can adjust the settings to change how it will tessellate.

Modifying and Matching NURBS Surfaces

Generating surfaces from curves is only one way to create the shape you want. There are many options for blending, joining, and matching two or more surfaces, including attaching, aligning, Booleans, and filleting. These tools let you make complicated shapes that would not be achievable from a single NURBS surface.

Boolean operations take two objects and create a new object based on the inter-section of those objects. There are three type of Booleans: Intersection, Union, and Subtraction.

To create a Boolean surface:

1. Create two overlapping NURBS objects.

   In this example, we've created a primitive sphere and cylinder (**Figure 7.99**).

2. Choose Edit NURBS > Booleans > Subtract tool.

3. Click the sphere, and press Enter.

   The sphere is now your base object, and Maya prompts you (**Figure 7.100**) to select a second object.

Sculpt Geometry Tool

Maya has a Sculpt Geometry tool for all three geometry types (polygons, NURBS, and subdivision surfaces). This tool lets you "paint" on your surface, pushing and pulling like a sculptor. Sculpting geometry can be much more intuitive than building something piece by piece, and you can quickly use it to rough out an organic shape, or add details to an existing model. Keep in mind that your surface geometry must be very dense for this tool to work correctly.

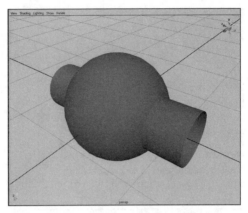

Figure 7.99 Boolean objects must intersect, because the operation is based on the overlapping areas.

Figure 7.100 The helpline prompts you with instructions for multi-part tools.

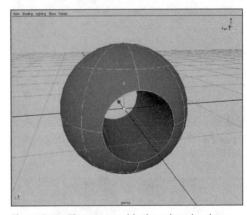

Figure 7.101 The area outside the sphere has been trimmed from the cylinder, and the area inside the cylinder has been trimmed from the sphere.

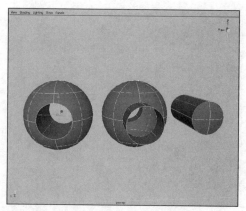

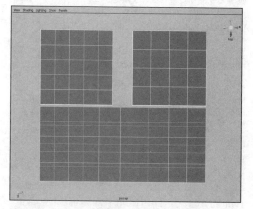

Figure 7.102 From left to right: Subtraction, Union, Intersection.

Figure 7.103 The mismatched isoparms in these planes create a mesh that is too dense when attached.

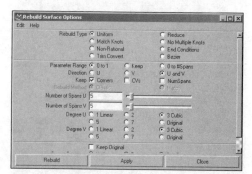

Figure 7.104 The Rebuild Surface tool is a powerful option for matching and adjusting surfaces.

4. Click the cylinder, and press Enter.

   The area where the cylinder overlapped the sphere is subtracted from the sphere (**Figure 7.101**).

   Selecting one of the other operations, such as Union or Intersection, results in different geometry outputs (**Figure 7.102**).

✔ Tip

■ Selecting the objects in the reverse order will subtract the sphere from the cylinder. Be sure you click the objects in the correct order.

Joining together or aligning two surfaces is important in maintaining an object that doesn't appear to have seams or creases. The surface direction and number of isoparms can affect how surfaces attach or align. Objects can be difficult to stitch together if they have different numbers of isoparms or surface directions that aren't the same (**Figure 7.103**). Rebuilding a surface can help match surfaces in surface direction, in the number of isoparms they contain, or both.

To rebuild a surface for stitching:

1. Select an open NURBS surface you wish to rebuild.

   For this example, the surface is a plane, and the target surface to match is an additional plane with five spans per side.

2. From the Edit NURBS menu, select the box next to Rebuild Surfaces.

   The Rebuild Surface Options dialog box appears (**Figure 7.104**).

   continues on next page

3. Enter **5** in both the Number of Spans U and Number of Spans V input fields, and click Rebuild.

The surface (see Figure 7.102) now matches the other plane (**Figure 7.105**).

To attach two surfaces:

1. Select two NURBS surfaces you want to attach (**Figure 7.106**).

Your selection order determines which surfaces will be moved or altered during the attachment process.

2. From the Edit NURBS menu, select the box next to Attach Surfaces.

The Attach Surface Options dialog box appears.

3. Deselect Keep Originals, and click Attach.

The two surfaces are blended into one surface (**Figure 7.107**).

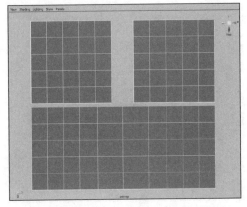

Figure 7.105 The right-hand plane now matches the left-hand plane, and will attach efficiently.

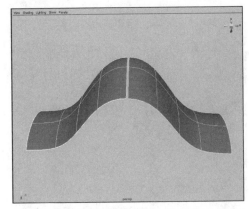

Figure 7.106 Select two NURBS surfaces you want to connect.

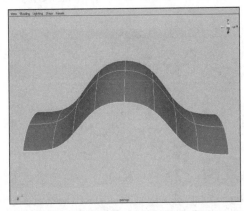

Figure 7.107 Two NURBS surfaces attached into one. The center isoparm is by default an even average of the two edges that were joined.

MODIFYING AND MATCHING NURBS SURFACES

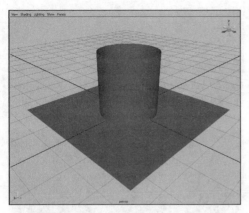

Figure 7.108 Position the objects so that they're touching.

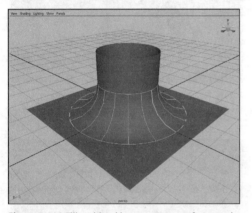

Figure 7.109 Fillets blend between two surfaces and maintain tangency.

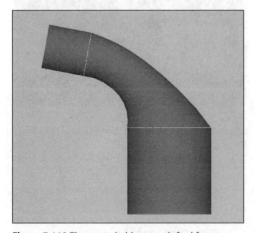

Figure 7.110 The central object was lofted from curves generated from the basic cylinders.

To fillet two surfaces:

1. Create a primitive NURBS plane and cylinder.

2. In the Channel Box, enter 5 for the Scale X and Scale Z attributes of the plane and 1 for the Translate Y attribute of the cylinder.

   The cylinder now rests on the plane (**Figure 7.108**).

3. Choose Edit NURBS > Surface Fillet > Circular Fillet.

   A new surface smoothly blends between the cylinder and the plane (**Figure 7.109**).

✔ Tip

- You can have the fillet appear on the inside or outside of either object by adjusting the Reverse Primary and Secondary Surface Normal options. Using the Create Curves on Surface option, you can also draw curves on the objects for trimming or other operations.

Duplicating surface curves

Generating curves from an existing surface is a good way to place curves precisely where you need them. For example, you can loft a new surface so that it matches up with another surface you have created. Doing so effectively adds to the original object and makes the two surfaces easy to attach later if you want (**Figure 7.110**).

To duplicate surface curves:

1. Create and select a primitive cylinder.

2. From the Edit Curves menu, select the box next to Duplicate Surface Curves. The Duplicate Surface Curves Options dialog box appears (**Figure 7.111**).

3. Select the U direction, and click Duplicate.

The circular curves are duplicated (**Figure 7.112**) and can now be used to form surfaces (**Figure 7.113**).

Figure 7.111 Select the *U* direction. This only duplicates curves that run in the *U* direction of the surface.

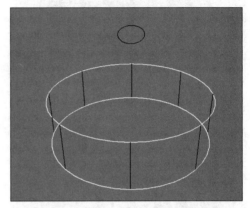

Figure 7.112 A curve has been created for each isoparm that spanned the *U* direction of the surface.

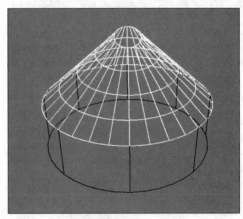

Figure 7.113 Selecting the curve at the top and lofting from it creates a surface that is exactly lined up with the original.

POLYGONS

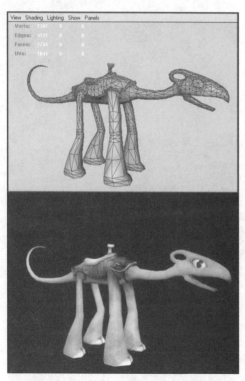

Figure 8.1 This polygon model was designed to have the fewest faces possible. The textures make up for the lack of detail. (Modeled and textured by Toby Marvin.)

Poly (short for polygon, or polygonal) modeling can be fun and quick, giving you a lot of freedom and control over any section of your model at any time. Polygonal modeling is older than NURBS modeling, but Alias is constantly improving the poly tools to make this approach one of the more powerful modeling choices in Maya 7.0.

Polygonal objects are made up of many small planar surfaces, referred to as *faces* or *polys*. These faces are commonly three or four sided, but they sometimes have more sides. A complete poly object consists of a handful to hundreds of thousands of these surfaces. In general, the more faces a model contains, the smoother the surface appears.

Games make extensive use of polygons because the complexity of a game must be limited if it is to offer fast interaction with real-time rendering. If your character has a low poly count—that is, a low number of faces—it will render and interact quickly. A character in a game is usually limited to a certain number of polygons so that the game can run in real time (**Figure 8.1**).

You can, however, use polygons to make smooth, highly detailed, even organic surfaces (**Figure 8.2**). Some surfaces are easier to build in polygons than in NURBS surfaces. For example, you can create a character's body from a single seamless polygon surface—something you can't achieve without using many NURBS surfaces.

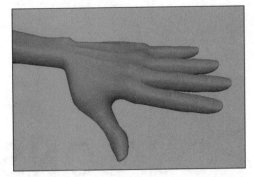

Figure 8.2 You can use polygons to make complicated, organic, or smooth shapes, such as this hand.

Figure 8.3 The faces are displayed on this sphere. The highlighted face was selected by clicking the dot in the center of the face.

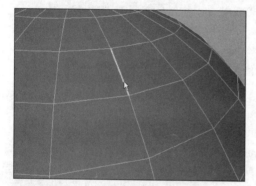

Figure 8.4 The selected edge is shared by the faces on either side of it. Any change to the position or size of this edge will affect all the faces it touches.

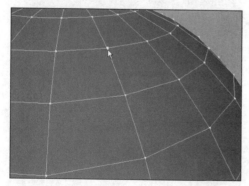

Figure 8.5 The selected vertex is at the corner of four faces.

Modeling Polygons

The most common way to create a complex polygon model is to start with a primitive poly object—a cube or cylinder, for instance. By transforming this simple object and manipulating its existing components, you can get the basic shape for your model. From there, you can build on the object by adding more complexity to the surface.

Polygons include the following four types of components, which are important for both modeling and texturing:

◆ A **face** is one of the many smaller surfaces that make up the polygon object as a whole. You can choose a face by selecting the point in its center (**Figure 8.3**).

◆ An **edge** is one border of a polygonal face (**Figure 8.4**). Edges always connect exactly two vertices.

◆ A **vertex** is at the corner of a face. Vertices become yellow when selected (**Figure 8.5**). Moving a vertex changes the shape of the faces that include it.

◆ **UVs** are used for creating texture, not for modeling; they become green when selected (see Chapter 14, "Shaders, Materials, and Mapping").

These components aren't actually separate objects; rather, they're different ways of accessing the same pieces. Moving an edge would have the same effect as moving both vertices that that edge runs between. Moving a face has the same effect as moving all the edges that define the face. Some operations, like Extrude Face, can only be performed on certain components.

✔ Tip

■ Once a face, vertex, or edge is selected, you can move, rotate, or scale the component. For the fastest workflow, use the marking menu.

Polygon Strategy

Working with polygons has a very different feel than modeling NURBS surfaces. It's common to start with a single piece of geometry and then push, pull, cut, and merge the components of that object, so modeling with polys can be similar to working with clay. Because you can adjust any component of a polygonal object without worrying about breaking seams or matching surfaces, adjustments are easy to make. This means polygonal modeling is a great option for doing a quick 3D sketch of a model or making a temporary low-resolution version of a model you intend to complete later.

When you're poly modeling, it's often a good idea to start by roughing out a shape and add detail later. Consider your end goal when choosing your starting shape and when deciding how much detail to begin with. A table might start with a cube, whereas a tree trunk, which is fairly irregular, might start with a 10-sided cylinder. The more faces your object has, the harder it is to make adjustments. By starting with a basic object, you'll only add the faces that you need. Cylinders make good beginnings for arms and legs, cubes for buildings, spheres for faces, and so forth.

When you're cutting up or creating new faces, keep track of what sort of polygons you're creating. Although Maya supports *n-gons* (faces with five or more sides) it's best to stick with tris and quads (three- and four-sided faces, short for triangles and quadrangles). Some operations only work on surfaces made of tris and quads, and n-gons can cause these tools to operate unexpectedly. At render time, everything is converted into tris anyway; and for games, the triangle count determines the real-time playback.

Because poly modeling makes it easy to create everything from one surface, it makes a good choice for complicated contiguous organic shapes, such as characters. On the other hand, polys are also well suited to simple blocky shapes such as buildings and square tables. In these cases, constructing your model out of many different polygonal options may be just as easy (such as making a table out of five separate cubes—one for the top, and four for the legs).

Polygons don't work as well on shapes with many complicated geometric curves, or very round objects. A poly model must always be very dense to mimic a round surface, while NURBS objects only tessellate and become dense at render time. Round or curving objects are often best approached with NURBS, where the toolset and working surface density are more suited to the task.

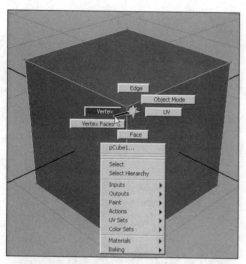

Figure 8.6 Generally, only one kind of component is displayed at a time. This marking menu, accessible with the right mouse button, provides a convenient way to switch among the different component displays.

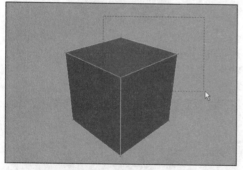

Figure 8.7 Three vertices are selected simultaneously using marquee-select.

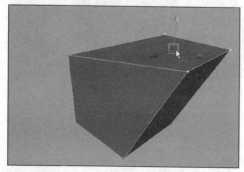

Figure 8.8 Move the selected vertices using the Move tool. The shape of every face that shares these vertices is changed.

To select and transform polygon components:

1. Create any polygon primitive (see Chapter 3, "Creating Primitives and Text").

2. Right-click a polygon surface to open the marking menu.

3. From the marking menu, select Vertex (**Figure 8.6**).

4. Select some vertices.

   You can marquee-select by clicking and dragging (**Figure 8.7**).

5. Press w, or click the Move tool icon in the toolbar.

6. Move the vertices (**Figure 8.8**).

✔ Tips

- If you're in wireframe mode, you must click a component of the surface, such as an edge, for the marking menu to show up. If you're in shaded mode, you can click anywhere on the surface.

- You can use the method described here to select and transform any of the polygon components except UVs. You can select UVs in a 3D view, but you can only move them in the UV Texture Editor. For more information about UV textures, see Chapter 14, "Shaders, Materials, and Mapping."

When using polygons, you often work with a large number of components. Maya has several tools to help you select components and to prevent you from selecting components by mistake. These include the Select Edge Loop and Select Edge Ring tools, backface culling, and other quick methods to expand, contract, and convert your existing selections.

MODELING POLYGONS

The Select Edge Ring and Select Edge Loop tools are new in this version of Maya; they let you select a cross-section of polygonal components. In previous versions of the application, this had to be done by hand.

To use the Select Edge Ring and Select Edge Loop tools:

1. Choose Create > Polygon Primitives > Cylinder.

2. Set Subdivisions Height to 3, which creates extra cross sections (**Figure 8.9**).

3. Choose Edit > Select Edge Loop Tool or Select Edge Ring Tool (**Figure 8.10**).

4. Double click an edge.

   If you choose the Edge Loop, all connected edges in that direction are selected. If you choose the Edge Ring, all parallel edges around the object are selected (**Figure 8.11**).

   or

   Click an edge, and then click a separate edge in the same loop or ring (depending on the tool you chose.)

   All the edges between the two are now selected (**Figure 8.12**).

✔ Tips

- To deselect a component, click somewhere away from your object to clear your selection.

- You can make as many ring or loop selections as you want. Click any new edges, in any direction, to add them to your selection.

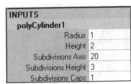

Figure 8.9 Using the Channel Box, set the cube to be divided into thirds.

Figure 8.10 Select the tool you want from the Edit menu.

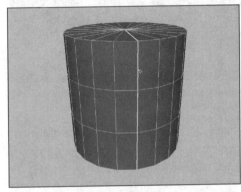

Figure 8.11 All the edges in a loop or right around the object are selected.

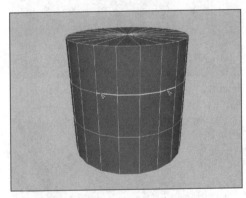

Figure 8.12 All the edges between the two you choose are selected.

INPUTS	
polyCylinder1	
Radius	1
Height	2
Subdivisions Axis	20
Subdivisions Height	3
Subdivisions Caps	0

Figure 8.13 Set Subdivisions Cap to 0, making the cap just one face across the top.

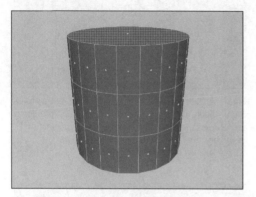

Figure 8.14 Delete the cap to form a hole.

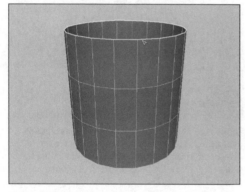

Figure 8.15 All the border edges have been selected. This works around any sort of hole or border.

The Select Border Edge tool functions like the Edge Ring and Edge Loop versions, but it works only on border edges. A *border* edge is an edge that isn't surrounded by faces. For example, the tool is ideal for selecting the edges of a hole in your object, such as a mouth or eye socket; you can then use Extrude Edge to fill in geometry behind the hole.

To use the Select Border Edge tool:

1. Using the cylinder from the previous task, set Subdivisions Caps to 0 (**Figure 8.13**).

2. Select the face on the top of the cylinder, and press (Delete) (**Figure 8.14**).

   Removing this face creates a border edge along the top of the cylinder.

3. Choose Edit > Select Border Edge.

4. Double click an edge of the new hole.

   All connected edges around that border are selected (**Figure 8.15**).

Once a model becomes complex, it can be difficult to make accurate selections or view particular components. Backface culling hides components of your model that aren't facing the camera. This makes the view cleaner and prevents you from selecting those faces. It's also useful for spotting surfaces with normals facing the wrong way (we'll explain normals at the end of this chapter).

MODELING POLYGONS

To use backface culling:

1. Choose Create > Polygon Primitives > Torus.

2. Right-click a polygon surface to open the marking menu, and select Face.

3. In the Side view, marquee-select the top half of the torus, and then delete the faces (**Figure 8.16**).

4. Choose Display > Custom Polygon Display. The Custom Polygon Display Options dialog box opens (**Figure 8.17**).

5. From the Backface Culling menu, select On, and click Apply.

   The portions of the torus on the far side of the camera view disappear. They can't be selected (**Figure 8.18**).

6. From the Backface Culling menu, select Keep Wire. Click Apply.

   You can see the wireframe of the back side, but you can't select components from that part of the surface (**Figure 8.19**).

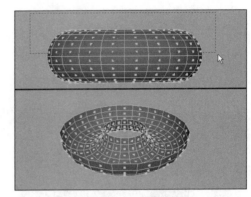

Figure 8.16 In the top image, the faces of a torus have been selected in the Side view. (It's often helpful to switch views to get a better angle on your selection.) In the bottom image, you see the torus after the selected faces have been deleted.

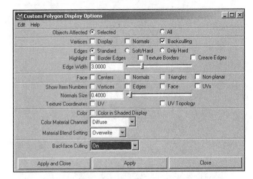

Figure 8.17 In the Custom Polygon Display Options dialog box, you can choose whether to have the display options affect all polygon objects or just the selected one(s)—for Objects Affected, choose Selected or All.

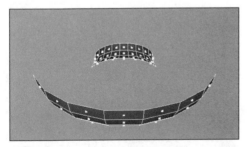

Figure 8.18 When Backface Culling is turned on, the components on the far side of the object disappear so you can't select them. This feature works for all kinds of polygon components.

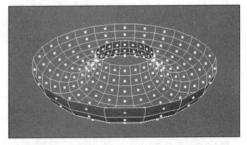

Figure 8.19 Backface Culling is set to Keep Wire. This setting lets you see the shape of the object while preventing you from selecting unwanted components on the object's back side.

MODELING POLYGONS

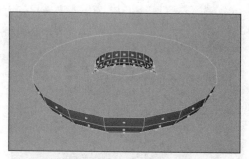

Figure 8.20 Keep Hard Edges lets you see the object's basic shape, but only the edges that border a hole in the object.

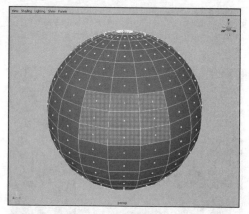

Figure 8.21 Select several faces on a sphere, but leave some room for expanding and shrinking.

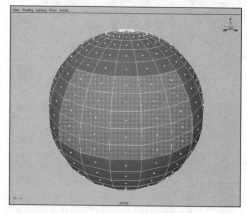

Figure 8.22 Hand-selecting poly vertices one by one can be tedious and difficult. Using ⟨>⟩, you can select the points surrounding the ones that are currently selected, making the selected area larger.

7. From the Backface Culling menu, select Keep Hard Edges. Click Apply.

   You can see the hard edges of the back side only—that is, the edges along the sides of holes in the surface (**Figure 8.20**).

8. From the Backface Culling menu, select Off. Click Apply.

   The Custom Polygon Display Options are reset to their default values. You can once again select the back sides of polygon surfaces.

To grow, shrink, and convert a selection:

1. Choose Create > Polygon Primitives > Sphere.

2. Right-click a polygon surface, and select Face from the marking menu.

3. Select one or more faces, but not all of them (**Figure 8.21**).

4. Press ⟨>⟩.

   The faces surrounding the existing selection are selected. Repeat this step to increase the size of the selected area (**Figure 8.22**).

   continues on next page

MODELING POLYGONS

5. Press $\boxed{<}$.

The region of selected faces becomes smaller. Repeat this step to further shrink the region (**Figure 8.23**).

6. Hold $\boxed{\text{Ctrl}}$/$\boxed{\text{Control}}$ and right-click to bring up the marking menu. Select To Vertices (**Figure 8.24**).

The faces are deselected, and the vertices they surrounded are selected.

✔ Tips

■ A selection of any kind of polygon component can similarly be converted to edges, vertices, or UVs.

■ Some polygon-modeling tools, such as Extrude Face, work only on faces. If you've already selected the region as vertices, Convert Selection saves you the time of meticulously selecting the faces one by one in order to run this tool on the faces.

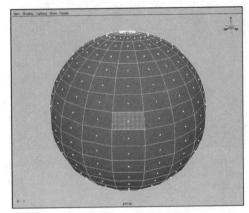

Figure 8.23 The original selection has been shrunk down to just one face. You can shrink a selection to nothing or expand it to the whole object.

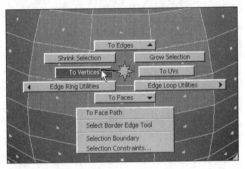

Figure 8.24 Using the marking menu to switch selections can save you a lot of time when a selection is easier to make with one component type than another.

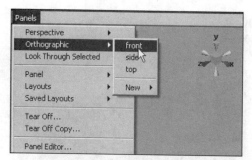

Figure 8.25 Switch to the Front orthographic view.

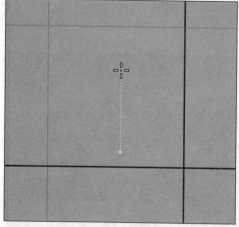

Figure 8.26 Place the second vertex in a face using the Create Face tool.

Creating and Deleting Polygon Components

You can start a model by creating a single face using the Create Polygon tool. You might use single faces to define complicated profiles or to trace background images that you wish to apply to the new faces later. For example, you can use a poly face to make a background building.

To create a polygonal house using the Create Polygon tool:

1. Select Panels > Orthographic > front to switch to the Front orthographic view (**Figure 8.25**).

   or

   Click the *z*-axis on the View Compass (the blue cone).

   The orthographic view makes it easier to draw a planar face (where all the vertices of the surface fall onto one plane).

2. From the Polygons menu, choose the Create Polygon tool.

   The cursor changes to a crosshairs icon, indicating you're ready to create a polygon.

3. In the Front view, click where you want to create the first vertex in the face.

   A light green square represents the current vertex.

4. Click and hold to create the next vertex, and then drag to see the connection to the previous vertex (**Figure 8.26**).

   You can hold ⊠ before you click to snap your vertices to the grid.

5. Release the mouse button to finish the creation of the second vertex.

   Once you've created the second vertex, click and drag to see the connection between two vertices.

continues on next page

6. Repeat steps 4 and 5 to create the third vertex (**Figure 8.27**).

7. Create the fourth vertex (**Figure 8.28**), and press Enter.

This simple polygonal face is the first step in creating any number of models.

Now let's add some "windows" to your polygonal house.

To make windows for the house:

1. Follow the previous set of steps to create a four-sided polygonal face, with one exception: Don't press Enter to finish the face.

2. Hold Ctrl / Control, and click inside the face to create a single vertex, and then release Ctrl / Control (**Figure 8.29**).

3. Create at least three more vertices to make a square hole inside the face (**Figure 8.30**).

4. Repeat steps 2 and 3 to create another hole, and press Enter.

✔ Tip

■ Holding Shift while placing new vertices keeps the cursor aligned to 90-degree angles, making it easier to create straight edges and right corners.

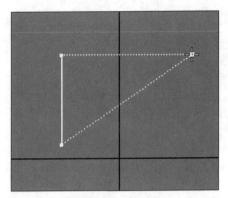

Figure 8.27 Place the third vertex to form a right angle.

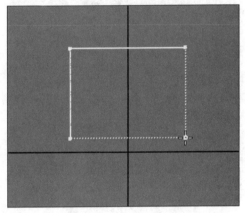

Figure 8.28 Place the fourth vertex to form a square.

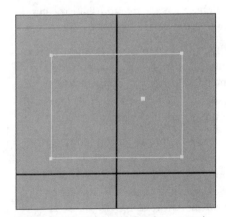

Figure 8.29 Click inside the first face created to begin creating a window.

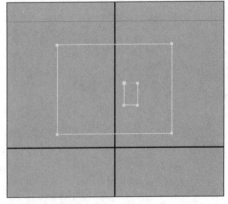

Figure 8.30 Place the fourth vertex in a window using the Create Face tool.

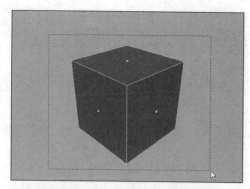

Figure 8.31 When you marquee-select around the entire object, even the faces on the far side of the object are selected.

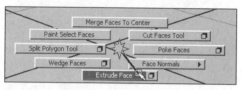

Figure 8.32 The marking menu lets you access common tasks much more quickly.

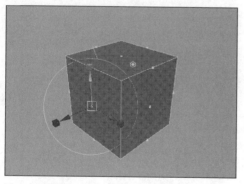

Figure 8.33 This manipulator appears when you select Edit Polygons > Extrude Face.

Extruding

Extrude Face is a commonly used tool for constructing new surfaces. It allows you to pull additional geometry from the surface. You select a face or faces, extrude them, and then manipulate the new faces.

To extrude faces of a cube:

1. Choose Create > Polygon Primitives > Cube.

2. Right-click the cube, and select Face from the marking menu.

3. Marquee-select all the faces (**Figure 8.31**).

4. Choose Edit Polygons > Extrude Face.

   or

   Shift -right-click to bring up the marking menu, and select Extrude Face (**Figure 8.32**).

   A manipulator appears that you can use to move, rotate, and scale the new faces (**Figure 8.33**). Even though the manipulator shows up on only one face, it affects all the faces that were just extruded. It transforms them locally, which means they move relative to their *surface normal* (a line perpendicular to the center of each individual face).

   continues on next page

5. Move one face out from the center of the cube with the Translate axis of the new manipulator.

All newly extruded faces move out from the center as well (**Figure 8.34**). This procedure is helpful for creating symmetrical objects.

✔ Tips

- When you first extrude a face, points appear on the center of each edge of the face you chose (see Figure 8.33). These points are new faces that remain one-dimensional until you move or scale the selected face. Beware any time you see these points along an edge: They can cause problems later in the final rendering because you have two surfaces sitting directly on top of each other. To avoid this, make sure you scale or move a face after every extrusion.

- After extruding a face, you'll often want to scale it proportionally. Click any of the scale manipulators, and a proportional scale manipulator appears in the center. To rotate along a single axis, click the outside rotate manipulator, and three rotate manipulators (one for each axis) appear.

- When you extrude more than one face at a time, Maya extrudes those faces separately. To extrude them as one piece, choose Polygons > Tool Options > Keep Faces Together.

Extruding edges works similarly to faces. This technique is useful for extruding new geometry from a border or a hole. For example, you might extrude the edges of a pipe to create more segments, or extrude flaps from a box.

To extrude edges:

1. Choose Create > Polygon Primitives > Cube.

2. Right-click the cube, and select Face from the marking menu.

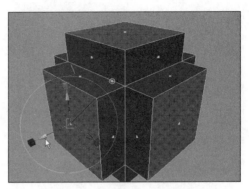

Figure 8.34 When one face is moved outward, all the faces move outward. When you scale with the Extrude Face tool, all the selected faces are scaled simultaneously, relative to their centers.

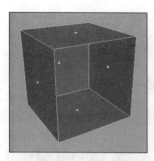

Figure 8.35 One face of the cube is deleted, creating an opening.

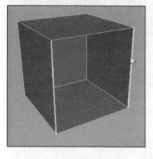

Figure 8.36 The edges on the left and right sides of the opening are selected.

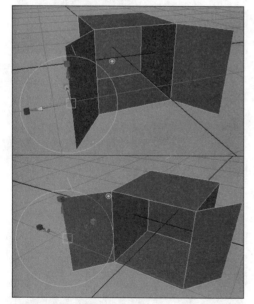

Figure 8.37 The edges have been extruded, which creates new faces. When one edge is moved, the other edge moves in the same direction for one axis but in the opposite direction for the other axis (depending on which side of the cube is removed). This figure shows two possible results.

3. Select a face on the side of the cube, and press Delete.

The face disappears, and you see the inside of the cube (**Figure 8.35**).

4. Right-click the cube, and select Edge from the marking menu.

5. Select the left edge, and press Shift to select the right edge of the hole you created (**Figure 8.36**).

6. Choose Edit Polygons > Extrude Edge.

or

Shift-right-click to bring up the marking menu, and select Extrude Vertex.

7. Move the edge out and away from the cube.

Two new faces are created, and the cube looks like an open box (**Figure 8.37**).

✔ Tips

■ An edge should not be shared by more than two faces. This means you should extrude only edges that are adjacent to an opening in the polygon. Although you can do otherwise, many operations don't work if your object contains such arrangements (**Figure 8.38**).

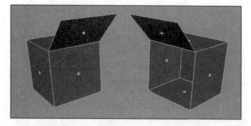

Figure 8.38 The object on the left has an edge that is shared by three faces; the object on the right doesn't, because it has an opening in the front. It's not good construction to have an edge shared by more than two faces. One problem is that the polygon object can't be converted to subdivision surfaces.

The Extrude Vertex tool creates additional polygons around the selected vertex in a pyramid-like shape, moving the vertex away from the surface at a user-defined length. It's useful in low-poly modeling, because it creates fewer polygons than Extrude Face does.

To extrude faces from a vertex:

1. Choose Create > Polygon Primitives > Cube.

2. Right-click the cube, and select Vertex from the marking menu.

3. Select the vertex you want to extrude (**Figure 8.39**).

4. Choose Edit Polygons > Extrude Vertex. The Polygon Extrude Vertex Options dialog opens.

5. Set Extrude Length to 2 (**Figure 8.40**). The Extrude Length setting determines how far the selected vertex is moved away from the surface.

6. Click Extrude Vertex. The vertex is extruded, and additional faces are created to produce a pyramid-like shape (**Figure 8.41**).

✔ Tips

- Changing the Extrude Width setting adjusts the percentage of supporting edges used to create the extrusion, making the pyramid-like shape wider.

- Changing the Divisions setting to a higher number divides the extruded surface into additional polygons (**Figure 8.42**).

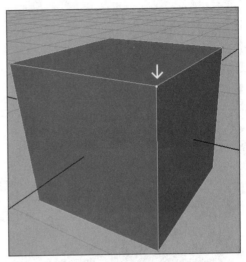

Figure 8.39 The corner vertex is selected in preparation for the extrusion.

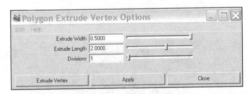

Figure 8.40 The Extrude Length setting determines how far the selected vertex is moved away from the surface.

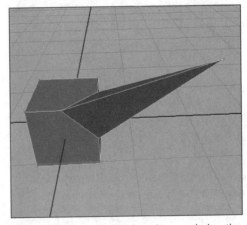

Figure 8.41 A pyramid-like shape is created when the vertex is extruded.

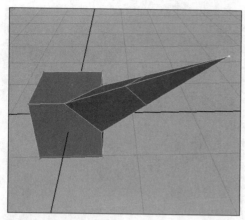

Figure 8.42 Divisions is set to 2, creating additional surface geometry on the extrusion.

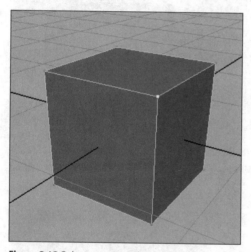

Figure 8.43 Select a vertex to be chamfered.

Edit Polygons	Subdiv Surfaces
Texture	▶
Subdivide	▢
Split Polygon Tool	▢
Extrude Face	▢
Extrude Edge	▢
Extrude Vertex	▢
Chamfer Vertex	▢
Bevel	▢

Figure 8.44
Select Chamfer Vertex to chamfer the selected vertex.

Removing corners and holes

The Chamfer Vertex tool removes a selected vertex and creates a chamfered corner; a three-sided polygon is created, and the original vertex is removed.

To chamfer the corner of a polygon:

1. Choose Create > Polygon Primitives > Cube.

2. Right-click the cube, and select Vertex from the marking menu.

3. Select the vertex on the corner you want to chamfer (**Figure 8.43**).

4. Choose Edit Polygons > Chamfer Vertex (**Figure 8.44**).

   The corner of the polygon becomes chamfered, creating a three-sided triangle to replace the corner vertex (**Figure 8.45**).

✔ Tips

- When the Delete Faces option in the Chamfer Vertex options is selected, Chamfer Vertex leaves a triangular hole for the chamfered corner instead of creating a new face.

- Adjusting the Width option in the Chamfer Vertex options changes the distance the chamfer runs down the edges, making the newly created triangle wider.

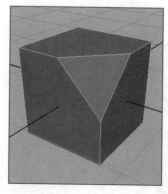

Figure 8.45
The completed chamfer.

When you're deleting or cutting faces, you'll often end up with holes or gaps in your model. The Fill Hole tool closes these holes. You can use this tool to patch up your model or create faces that you can then extrude. Doing so saves you the trouble of selecting all the edges around the hole if you want to extrude a face.

To fill in a hole in a polygonal object:

1. Choose Create > Polygon Primitives > Sphere.

2. Right-click the sphere, and select Faces from the marking menu.

3. Select the top third of the faces, and press Delete (**Figure 8.46**).

    By slicing open the sphere, you have created a hole (**Figure 8.47**).

4. Right-click the sphere, and select Edges from the marking menu.

5. Select a border edge along the hole.

6. Choose Edit Polygons > Fill Hole.

    The hole is capped off with an n-gon (**Figure 8.48**).

✔ Tip

- If there is only one hole in your model, you don't need to select the border edge. Maya fills in all holes it finds when you perform Fill Hole on your object.

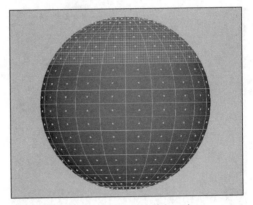

Figure 8.46 Delete the top third of the sphere.

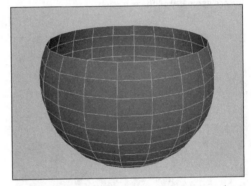

Figure 8.47 You have created a hole with many edges, something that is tedious to cover by hand.

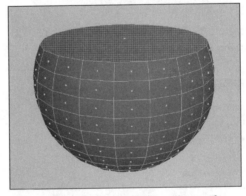

Figure 8.48 The hole is now filled in with a new face, which you can subdivide or extrude as needed.

Figure 8.49 Select half of an object.

Figure 8.50 Select +X as the Mirror Direction.

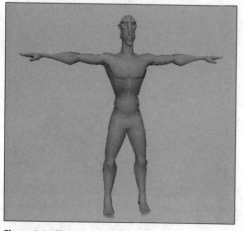

Figure 8.51 The symmetrical object.

Mirroring

When modeling, you often create symmetrical objects. Humans, for example, are bisymmetrical: One half looks like the other half, but flipped. The Mirror Geometry command flips one half of an object so you have two symmetrical parts. That means you only have to model one half of a body and then use Mirror Geometry to make a whole person.

To mirror geometry:

1. Select the object to be mirrored (**Figure 8.49**).

2. Choose Polygons > Mirror Geometry.
   The Polygon Mirror Options dialog box opens (**Figure 8.50**).

3. Select a Mirror Direction of +X, and click Apply.
   The model becomes two halves joined in the middle (**Figure 8.51**).

✔ Tip

■ Once you've mirrored a piece of geometry, you can perform adjustments on both sides of the model. Set your Move tool settings to Reflection, and any translation changes made to one side will be reflected on the other side. This technique can be useful even on objects you haven't mirrored.

Deleting polygon components

Deleting faces is as simple as pressing $\boxed{\text{Delete}}$; but special operations are required to delete vertices or edges from inside a model.

To delete a vertex:

1. Select the object from which you want to delete a vertex.

2. Right-click the object, and select Vertex from the marking menu.

3. Select the vertex or vertices you want to delete (**Figure 8.52**).

4. Choose Edit Polygons > Delete Vertex (**Figure 8.53**).

    The selected vertices and any edges they defined are deleted (**Figure 8.54**).

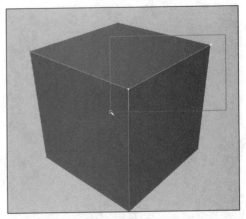

Figure 8.52 Select the vertices you wish to remove. Be careful not to accidentally select any on the rear of your object.

Figure 8.53 Select Delete Vertex. You can't delete vertices with more than two edges without using this tool.

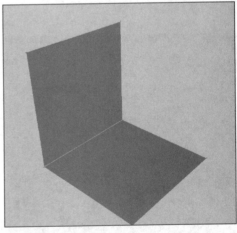

Figure 8.54 The vertices and all the edges touching them have been deleted. In this case, only two faces are left.

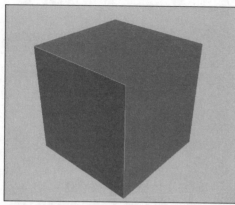

Figure 8.55 Deleting an edge from this cube doesn't change its shape, which results in a poorly constructed cube containing an n-gon.

Although you can delete edges by pressing (Delete), doing so leaves vertices behind, often resulting in n-gons (**Figure 8.55**). To remove an edge and any vertices attached to that edge, perform the following task.

To delete an edge:

1. Select the object from which you want to delete an edge.

2. Right-click the object, and select Edge from the marking menu.

3. Select the edge or edges you want to delete (**Figure 8.56**).

4. Choose Edit Polygons > Delete Edge.

    The selected edges and any vertices they share are deleted (**Figure 8.57**).

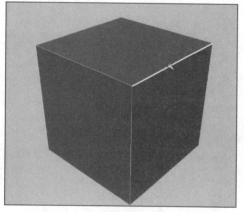

Figure 8.56 Select the edges you wish to delete.

Figure 8.57 Removing the edge removes associated vertices to maintain proper construction and therefore changes the shape of the cube.

Splitting and Merging Polygon Components

Splitting and merging the existing components in your model lets you add detail where you need it. There are many ways of refining your polygonal mesh, including the Split Polygon tool, the Split Edge Ring tool, subdividing faces, and others. By adding more components, you increase the density of your model in a specific area or cross section and can add detail in those areas.

The merge operations—Combine, Merge Vertex, Merge Edge, and Merge to Center—allow for the removal of detail where the model is too dense. They're also used to stitch together separate poly models and parts.

Splitting polygon components

The Split Polygon tool is used extensively in polygon modeling—so much so that two new tools, Split Edge Ring and Duplicate Edge Loop, duplicate functions of this flexible tool. The Split Polygon tool lets you split one face into two or more faces along an edge that you create. You can split multiple faces simultaneously to save time or use the tool to prepare for Split Edge Ring or other poly functions.

Because of the way perspective distorts the view of an object, it can be difficult to select the center of an edge. To help you split a face in the right place, the Split Polygon tool snaps to the center of an edge or to a user-defined point along an edge.

In general, it's best to limit yourself to three- and four-sided faces, known as *tris* and *quads*, respectively. Quads and tris respond more predictably to other polygon modeling tools (especially Split Edge Ring). If a face has five or more sides, you should split it into multiple faces with fewer sides each.

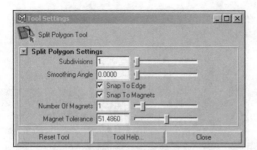

Figure 8.58 The options for the Split Polygon tool make it easy to split a polygon in halves, thirds, quarters, and so on.

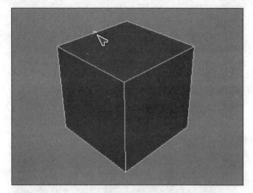

Figure 8.59 Using the Split Polygon tool, you can place a point at the center of an edge.

Figure 8.60 The new edge is defined by the two points placed by the Split Polygon tool. Pressing [Enter] completes the command. To continue splitting and go all the way around the cube, click a point one edge at a time.

To split a face:

1. Choose Create > Polygon Primitives > Cube.

2. Choose Edit Polygons > Split Polygon Tool.

   The Tool Settings dialog box opens with Split Polygon tool options.

3. Select Snap To Magnets and Snap To Edge, and adjust the Magnet Tolerance slider to the middle of the range (**Figure 8.58**).

4. Click and drag along a top edge to the center.

   The point should snap to the center of the edge (**Figure 8.59**).

5. Release the mouse button.

6. Click and drag along the edge on the opposite side of the top of the cube to the center of that edge (**Figure 8.60**).

   With Snap To Edge selected, only points along an edge can be selected.

7. Press [Enter].

   The face is now split in half.

8. Right-click the cube, and select Edge from the marking menu.

continues on next page

9. Select the new edge you created, and move it up so that the object looks like a simple house (**Figure 8.61**).

10. Choose Edit Polygons > Split Polygon Tool.

11. Click and drag up the left side of the cube until the point snaps to the corner. Repeat for the right side (**Figure 8.62**).

12. Press (Enter).

    The five-sided face, which formed the front of the house, is split into a three-sided face and a four-sided face.

✔ Tips

- Make sure your split always creates an edge. If you click an edge and press (Enter) without successfully clicking another edge of the same face, you'll put a vertex on that edge—another example of bad construction. To avoid this problem, make sure to undo the action if the Split Polygon tool doesn't create a new edge.

- Snapping can make it difficult to create a split where you want, especially near edges. To turn off snapping, under the Split Polygon tool options in the Tool Settings dialog box, deselected Snap To Edge.

- You aren't limited to snapping to the middle of an edge—you can snap to more than one point of an edge. To split a polygon into thirds, snap to a point one-third of the way along an edge. You can enter 2 for Number Of Magnets in the Split Polygon tool options in the Tool Settings dialog box. Doing so creates two points, evenly spaced along the edge, to which the tool will snap (Snap To Magnets must also be selected).

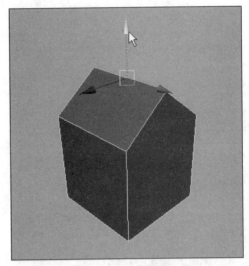

Figure 8.61 The new edge is moved up, creating a simple house shape. Note that the front of the house has five edges. More than four edges is generally considered bad construction.

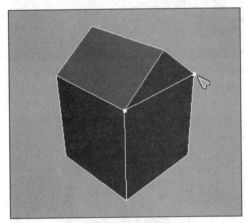

Figure 8.62 A new edge is created, splitting the front face into two separate faces.

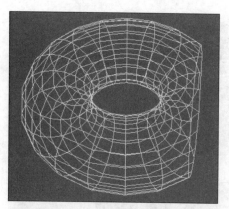

Figure 8.63 The Cut Face tool is an interactive surface-cutting tool that either deletes one side of the cut surface (shown here) or slices the surface, leaving you with both sides.

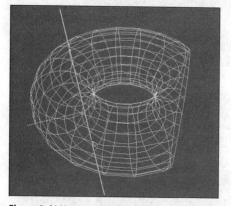

Figure 8.64 You can use the Cut Face tool to slice a piece of a surface by directing the cutting line into the exact position on the surface where you want the cut made. The short line defines which side of the cutting line will be deleted.

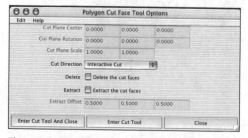

Figure 8.65 The Polygon Cut Face Tool Options dialog box provides many commands for cutting the surface in an exact, numeric position, or for interactively placing a cutting line. You can adjust the direction (or the plane) in which the cut is made.

The Cut Face tool can cut through a surface in any direction, regardless of component orientation. It performs a straight cut through your model like a saw (**Figure 8.63**). To be more specific, the Cut Face tool adds edges to a poly (or an entire polygonal object) through a projected line that you position to your liking (**Figure 8.64**). The line is projected from the view angle of the camera, slicing through all the selected intersecting polygons.

With the Cut Face Delete option selected, one side of the cut object is deleted. This option is useful if you later want to create an instance of the object or mirror the object to complete it (as you would the head of a character).

To slice a surface using the Cut Face tool:

1. Create a primitive polygon cube, and select it.

2. Choose Edit Polygons > Cut Faces.

   The Polygon Cut Face Tool Options dialog box opens (**Figure 8.65**).

   continues on next page

3. Click Enter Cut Tool, and then click and hold in the view.

A line appears that is used as the cutting plane (**Figure 8.66**).

The first point you click will be the center of rotation for the line; the line will always pass through the cursor and this point.

4. Drag the line to position the cutting plane on the surface.

5. Release the mouse to cut the surface (**Figure 8.67**).

The line is projected across the object, and cuts are made where it crosses a surface. Notice that no surfaces are deleted—just split.

6. In the Cut Face options, select Delete the Cut Faces (**Figure 8.68**).

7. Click Enter Cut Tool and Close.

8. Click and drag the line across a surface to choose another cutting plane.

9. Release the mouse to cut the surface.

The surface on one side of the cutting line is deleted (**Figure 8.69**).

✔ Tips

- A short line, perpendicular to the cutting line, appears to show you which side of the line will be deleted (see Figure 8.64).

- Hold (Shift) to snap the cutting line horizontally, vertically, or at a 45-degree angle, to make a more precise cut.

- Both polygonal objects and their components can be cut. When you use the cut tools on selected faces in component mode, only those faces are cut.

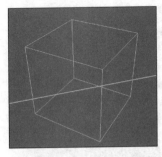

Figure 8.66
You can move and rotate the cut line until it's perfectly aligned with your cut.

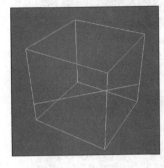

Figure 8.67
The cut line is projected from the selected camera angle to make a cut straight through the surface.

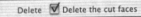

Figure 8.68 Deleting cut faces removes part of the original surface.

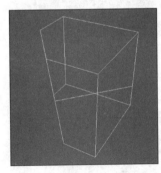

Figure 8.69
The surface on one side of the cutting line is deleted, leaving only a portion of the original surface.

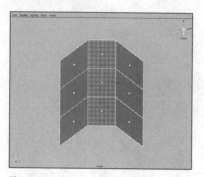

```
INPUTS
  polyCube1
              Width   1
             Height   1
              Depth   1
   Subdivisions Width  3
  Subdivisions Height  3
   Subdivisions Depth  1
```

Figure 8.70 Create a cube split into a three-by-three grid.

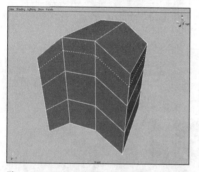

Figure 8.71 Move some faces up to make an uneven cross section, or edge ring.

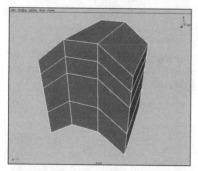

Figure 8.72 The dotted indicator indicates which faces will be affected and where they will be split.

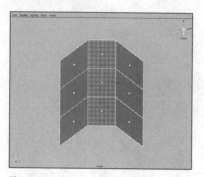

Figure 8.73 Each face is split proportionally instead of absolutely (in this case, each face was split approximately in half).

The Cut Face tool doesn't take into account curves or bends in your model. The Split Edge Ring tool is ideal if you want to add a cross-section to your model that evenly splits a set of faces and the Cut Face tool can't be positioned evenly.

New in Maya 7.0, the Split Edge Ring tool evenly divides all faces in a loop around your model. It contains options for spacing and can be used to perform many common Split Poly options easily and precisely.

To add a cross section using the Split Edge Ring tool:

1. Create a poly cube primitive with Subdivisions Width and Subdivisions Height set to 3 (**Figure 8.70**).

2. Right-click the cube, and select Faces from the marking menu.

3. From the Front view, select the middle faces and drag them up (**Figure 8.71**).

4. Choose Edit Polygons > Split Edge Ring Tool.

5. Click and hold a vertical edge of the cube. Don't let go yet.

   Maya highlights an edge ring to show you which faces will be cut, and a green indicator line appears, showing where the cut will occur (**Figure 8.72**).

6. Drag the mouse up and down to position the line to your liking. Release the mouse button to cut the faces.

   Notice that the Split Edge Ring tool divides all the faces proportionally instead of straight across (**Figure 8.73**).

To split any face using the Split Edge Ring tool:

1. Select the cube from the previous task.

2. Choose Edit Polygons > Split Edge Ring Tool (**Figure 8.74**).

   The Split Edge Ring Tool options appear.

3. Deselect the Auto-complete option.

   The tool waits for your manual input, versus searching for a ring automatically as in the previous task.

4. Click an edge on the left side of the cube and then a corresponding edge on the right side of the cube.

   All the faces between those two edges are selected and ready to cut (**Figure 8.75**).

5. Press (Enter) to complete the split; or click along the edge ring to add to the selection, and then press (Enter).

   The faces are split.

✔ Tips

- By default, the tool splits all faces at the same proportionate distance. If you wish it to instead maintain a set distance from an edge, change the tool settings from Relative to Absolute.

- You can bend the Split Edge Ring tool at right angles. Click an adjacent edge, and the tool turns (**Figure 8.76**).

Figure 8.74 Use the tool options to adjust the tools to suit your specific task.

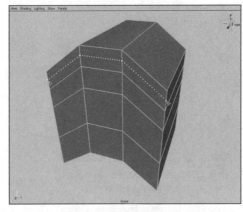

Figure 8.75 With auto-complete off, you click either end of the selection you wish to split.

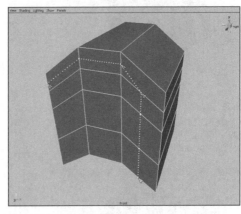

Figure 8.76 The ability to turn corners extends the usefulness of the tool and lets you specify complicated paths around irregular borders.

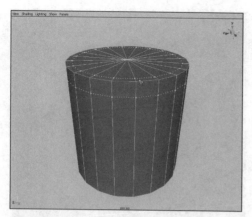

Figure 8.77 Position the indicators where the new edge loops should be created. Notice the positioning of each edge loop is proportional to the length of the faces it's splitting.

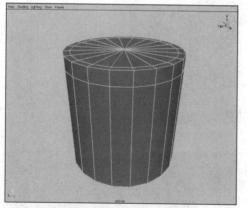

Figure 8.78 Once the mouse button is released, the positioning guides become new edge loops.

Similar to Split Edge Ring, Duplicate Edge Loop creates two new edge loops around your object, offset from the first. This tool is immensely useful when you're adding creases and sharp corners to smooth poly or subdivision surfaces.

To duplicate an edge loop:

1. Create a poly cylinder primitive.

2. Choose Edit Polygons > Duplicate Edge Loop Tool.

3. Click and hold a horizontal edge that runs along the outside of the cylinder cap. Don't release the mouse.

   An edge loop is selected, and two indicators appear to show where the new edge loops will be placed (**Figure 8. 77**).

4. Drag the mouse up and down to position the line to your liking. Release the mouse button to cut the faces (**Figure 8.78**).

✔ Tip

■ You can also use the Duplicate Edge Loop tool to duplicate part of an edge loop. Turn off Auto-complete in the tool options, just as you did for the Split Edge Ring tool.

The Bevel tool removes an edge and replaces it with an angled face. This is similar to the Duplicate Edge Loop tool's function, but it removes the original by default and places the new edges equidistant (and not proportionally) from the source edge. Because most real-life objects don't have perfectly sharp edges, you'll probably use the Bevel tool a lot.

To bevel an edge:

1. Choose Create > Polygon Primitives > Cube.

2. Right-click the cube, and select Edge from the marking menu.

3. On the cube, select the edges you want to bevel (**Figure 8.79**).

4. Choose Edit Polygons > Bevel (**Figure 8.80**).

   The edges become beveled, creating angled faces (**Figure 8.81**).

You can also use the Bevel Plus tool to create objects with bevels. Bevel Plus uses curves to extrude objects and give them caps and beveled edges.

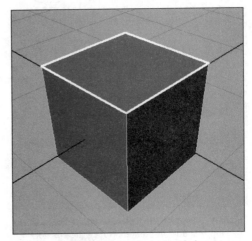

Figure 8.79 Select the edges to be beveled.

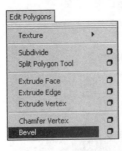

Figure 8.80 Select the Bevel command.

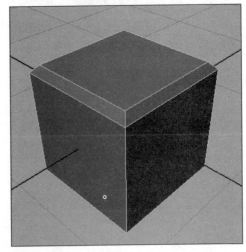

Figure 8.81 The beveled box.

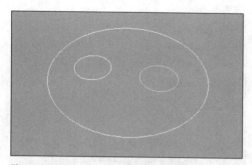

Figure 8.82 Select the curves you want to bevel.

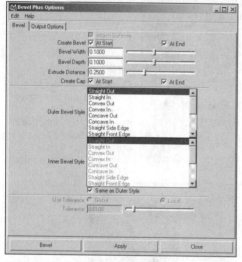

Figure 8.83 Select the Surfaces > Bevel Plus command options.

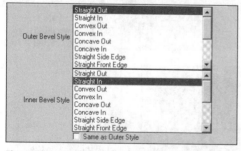

Figure 8.84 Select Straight In for the Inner Bevel Style.

To create a beveled object with a hole:

1. Create two closed curves.

   For more information about creating NURBS primitives, see Chapter 3.

2. Select the outer curve first and the inner curve(s) next (**Figure 8.82**).

3. Choose Surfaces > Bevel Plus.

   The Bevel Plus Options dialog box opens (**Figure 8.83**).

4. In the Bevel tab, set the Bevel Width and Bevel Depth to 0.1 and the Extrude Distance to 0.25.

5. From the Outer Bevel Style list, select Straight Out.

6. Deselect the Same as Outer Style check box.

   The Inner Bevel Style list becomes active.

7. From the Inner Bevel Style list, select Straight In (**Figure 8.84**).

8. In the Output Options tab, select Polygons.

9. Click Apply to create the beveled object (**Figure 8.85**).

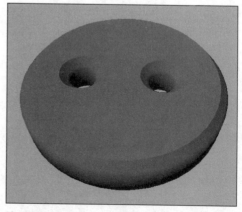

Figure 8.85 The beveled button.

Subdividing and Merging

The Subdivide tool splits a face into quads (four-sided faces) or tris (three-sided faces). This tool provides a quick way to add detail to your surface in the form of additional faces. These faces should not, however, be confused with subdivision surfaces (covered in Chapter 9). In the next task, you'll combine the Subdivide and Extrude Face tools to create a door.

To subdivide a polygon face:

1. Choose Create > Polygon Primitives > Cube.

2. Scale the cube to the shape of a door (**Figure 8.86**).

3. Right-click the cube, and select Face from the marking menu.

4. Select the face on the front of the cube.

5. Choose Edit Polygons > Subdivide.
   The face splits into four faces (**Figure 8.87**).

6. Choose Edit Polygons > Extrude Face.
   The manipulator and new faces appear.

7. Scale the faces down a little using the Manipulator tool (**Figure 8.88**).

8. Choose Edit Polygons > Extrude Face again.
   The manipulator and new faces appear.

9. Scale the new faces down a little, and move them in toward the middle of the object, which should now look like a door with four panels (**Figure 8.89**).

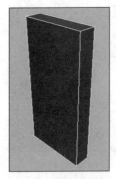

Figure 8.86 The cube is scaled to the shape of a door.

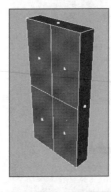

Figure 8.87 The face is subdivided into four smaller faces. To subdivide a face into more faces, select Edit Polygons > Subdivide > Options, and adjust the Subdivision Levels setting.

Figure 8.88 The extruded faces are scaled down relative to their centers.

Figure 8.89 A completed four-panel door. If you selected the face on the opposite side of the door before performing the Subdivide function, the same steps would model the back side of the door simultaneously.

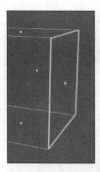

Figure 8.90 The selected face is the face that will be split with the Poke Faces command.

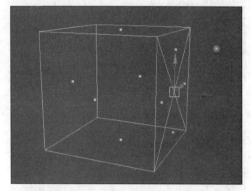

Figure 8.91 Each selected face is split into four faces, each one a perfect triangle.

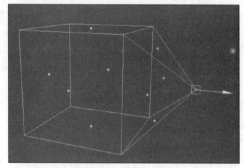

Figure 8.92 The Poke Faces tool creates a manipulator at the center point of the poked face, which is used to push the new geometry into, or pull it away from, the surface.

The Poke Faces tool is similar to Subdivide in that it cuts the selected face into new faces. However, unlike the Subdivide tool, which cuts quad faces into quads, the Poke Faces tool subdivides quad faces into tris. This is useful in low poly modeling when you wish to round off a face a bit or create tris instead of quads.

To poke the face of a polygon using the Poke Faces tool:

1. Create a primitive polygon cube.

2. Right-click the cube's surface, and select Face from the marking menu.

3. Select one or more faces to poke (**Figure 8.90**).

4. Choose Edit Polygons > Poke Faces.
   Each selected face is split into four faces (**Figure 8.91**).

5. Select the manipulator, and move it away from the surface.
   A pyramid-like shape appears as the manipulator is pulled away from the surface (**Figure 8.92**).

When you build a polygonal model one face at a time, you need to connect those faces by merging two vertices or edges into one. However, the polygon tools only work on components in the same mesh, so you must first combine the separate faces into one mesh.

To combine two poly objects:

◆ With both objects selected, select Polygons > Combine. The surfaces are highlighted in one color, indicating that they're one mesh.

To merge vertices:

1. Select the surfaces (**Figure 8.93**), and choose Polygons > Combine.

2. Right-click the surface, and select Vertex from the marking menu.

3. Select the vertices you wish to merge (**Figure 8.94**).

4. Choose Edit Polygons > Merge Vertices. The Merge Vertex Options dialog box opens (**Figure 8.95**).

5. In the Merge Vertex Options dialog box, adjust the Distance slider so that it spans the space between the selected vertices (in this case, a value of 1).

6. Click Apply.
   The two vertices merge (**Figure 8.96**).

✔ Tip

■ When you're merging multiple vertices, don't set the distance too high. Your points will merge if the distance between them is smaller than the distance set by the slider. To ensure this doesn't happen in unwanted areas, make sure the vertices you're joining are positioned close together and that the Distance slider is set as low as possible.

To merge edges:

1. Select the surfaces, and choose Polygons > Combine.
   The surfaces are highlighted in one color, indicating that they're one mesh.

2. Choose Edit Polygons > Merge Edges Tool.
   The cursor changes to an arrowhead (**Figure 8.97**).

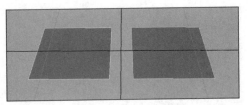

Figure 8.93 Select two separate polygon meshes.

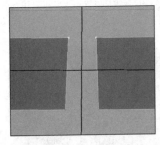

Figure 8.94 Select two vertices to merge using the Merge Vertices tool.

Figure 8.95 Set the Distance to 1 in the Merge Vertex Options dialog box.

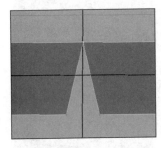

Figure 8.96 The result of merging two vertices.

Figure 8.97 The cursor changes to an arrowhead when you select the Merge Edges tool.

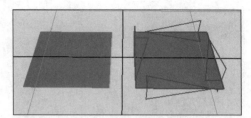

Figure 8.98 The potential target edges have arrows assigned to them.

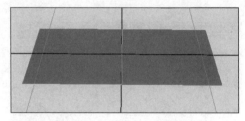

Figure 8.99 The result of merging edges.

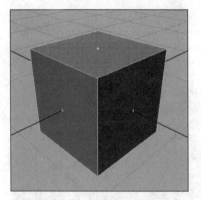

Figure 8.100 Select a face to merge.

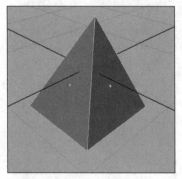

Figure 8.101 The result of merging the face.

3. Click a border edge of one of the faces.

The selected edge turns tan, and violet arrow shapes appear on all the edges that are available for merging (**Figure 8.98**).

4. Click one of the available edges, and press Enter.

The two edges merge, if they're close enough (**Figure 8.99**).

✔ Tip

◆ When you're merging vertices, you can accidentally create faces on the inside of your model (merging the vertices surrounding the faces of two cubes, for instance). Doing so creates geometry that can't be converted, among other things. To avoid this situation, use Merge Edges as much as possible, and keep alert when using Merge Vertices. Look at things in wireframe to ensure no internal geometry.

When you're editing a mesh, you may wish to remove a face without deleting it. You can select and delete most component types of a polygonal mesh, but deleting a face usually leaves a hole. However, the Merge to Center tool combines Delete Face and Merge Vertices into one command. This tool removes the selected faces or edges and then draws the surrounding vertices into a point without leaving a hole. The Merge to Center tool is very useful in low poly modeling.

To merge the faces of a cube:

1. Choose Create > Polygon Primitives > Cube.

2. Right-click the cube, and select Face from the marking menu.

3. Select a single face on the cube (**Figure 8.100**).

4. Select Edit Polygons > Merge to Center.

The selected face is removed, and the remaining vertices are drawn into a single point (**Figure 8.101**).

Refining Polygons

When you're modeling low-poly objects, the basic polygon tools are sufficient. However, adding faces and controlling the number of faces required to get a smooth piece of geometry can be prohibitively difficult. Maya provides options to smooth your surfaces so you don't have to do it by hand.

Polygons start with sharp edges and corners. You can round them by using the Polygons > Smooth function, which subdivides surfaces into many smaller polygons to round their corners and edges.

To smooth a polygon:

1. Create a cylinder primitive, and set the options as shown (**Figure 8.102**).

2. Choose Polygons > Smooth.

   The Polygon Smooth Options dialog box opens (**Figure 8.103**). A higher Subdivision Levels value in the Polygon Smooth Options dialog box creates a smoother object with more faces. The Continuity setting determines how closely the new shape resembles the original (versus how rounded it is). A low Continuity setting makes the object appear more similar to the original shape; a high Continuity setting produces a very rounded shape.

3. Adjust the Subdivision Levels slider to set it to 3.

4. Click Smooth.

   The object becomes smooth (**Figure 8.104**).

✔ Tips

- The basic structure of a polygon object should be complete before you apply the Smooth function. Smoothing produces a dense object with many faces, making it more difficult to work with.

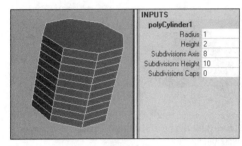

Figure 8.102 Create a poly cylinder like this one.

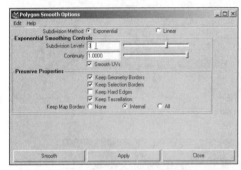

Figure 8.103 The Polygon Smooth Options dialog box.

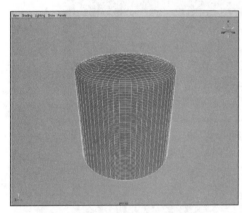

Figure 8.104 The new cylinder is much smoother and also much denser.

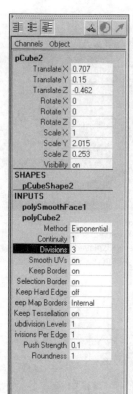

Figure 8.105
The inputs in the Channel Box let you change the Smooth options after the function has been run. However, once you make additional tweaks to the surface, going back and changing the options in the polySmoothFace input field will produce undesirable results.

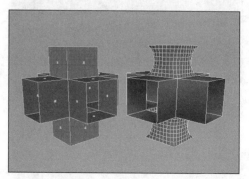

Figure 8.106 (Left) The faces on the top and bottom of the object have been selected. (Right) The result of the Smooth function, which works by selecting whole polygon objects or faces of the object.

- You can set Subdivision Levels in the Polygon Smooth Options dialog box as high as 4; however, 3 is generally high enough (and a higher value can give you a cumbersome surface due to an abundance of point information).

- You can change the level of smoothing after the function is complete by clicking polySmoothFace1, which should be at the top of the list of inputs in your Channel Box. You'll see a field labeled Divisions, which you can change from 0 (no smoothing) to 4 (very smooth) (**Figure 8.105**).

- You can smooth a portion of a polygon surface by selecting the faces of the part of the surface you want smoothed and then applying the Smooth operation (**Figure 8.106**).

Smooth proxies

The Smooth Proxy tool is ideal for situations when you want to work on a low-res model but still want to see how the model will look when it's smoothed or converted to a subdivison surface. With the addition of the Poly Crease, Split Edge Ring, and Duplicate Edge Loop tools, the Smooth Proxy function has become an even more powerful option for poly modeling. Poly Crease lets you add detail without adding more faces, whereas Split Edge Ring and Duplicate Edge Loop let you quickly stitch in geometry where you most often need to define your smooth mesh.

Using the Smooth Proxy tool, you can preview a smoothed version of your low-res model (just as if you had applied the Smooth command to it). The original low-res surface remains visible, allowing you to manipulate fewer points while still viewing the final smoothed shape.

REFINING POLYGONS

The low-res and high-res surfaces are linked; edits to the low-res mesh are reflected in the hi-res mesh, but not vice versa. For this reason, you should avoid adjusting the hi-res mesh until you're certain you don't need the low-res mesh, or you may have unwanted results.

To facilitate poly modeling using the Smooth Proxy tool:

1. Select a polygonal object in object mode—in this case, the base cylinder from the previous task.

2. Choose Polygons > Smooth Proxy, and set the Subdivisions Level value to 3.

3. Click Smooth.

   Maya creates a new, smooth version of the model while also retaining the original (**Figure 8.107**).

   Because you set Subdivisions Level to 3, the smooth version looks the same as if you'd performed Poly Smooth on it.

4. Right-click the original object, and select Vertex from the marking menu.

5. Select and move one or more of the vertices.

   The hi-res version of the model mirrors the manipulations of the low-res model (**Figure 8.108**).

✔ Tips

■ You can quickly define a smooth proxy for an object by pressing [Ctrl][`]. The same command can be used to turn the proxy off again.

■ You can also toggle the display back and forth by pressing the [`] key. To show both displays simultaneously, press [~].

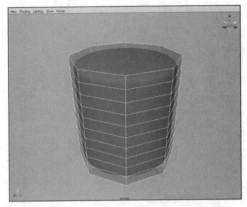

Figure 8.107 Smooth Proxy lets you view a smooth version of your model while you work on a lower-res version. The original cylinder is displayed as transparent cage, and the smoothed cylinder rests in the center.

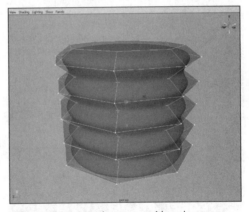

Figure 8.108 A smooth proxy provides a low-res control cage to control many hi-res points. This allows for easy and smooth adjustments to dense surfaces.

REFINING POLYGONS

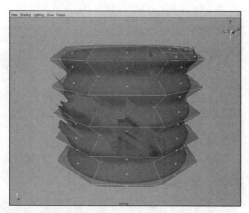

Figure 8.109 The high-res points on this model were adjusted, and then a low-res face was subdivided. As you can see, the results are messy.

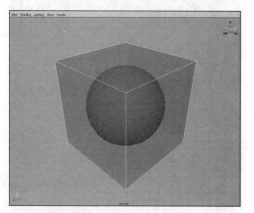

Figure 8.110 A smooth version of a cube looks like a sphere. You'll crease its edges to change that.

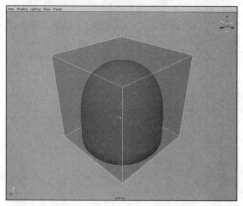

Figure 8.111 Creasing the bottom edge draws the object toward the corner, which makes it sharper and sharper.

- Only adjust the low-res, or unsmoothed surface. Adjusting points on the smooth (high-res) mesh will cause problems if you later add or remove faces on the low-res mesh (**Figure 8.109**).

- Select the Proxy or Smooth Mesh In Layer check box in the tool options to place the new objects on separate layers. Doing so lets you hide all your low-res objects, to easily ensure they don't render. It also ensures you don't accidentally modify your hi-res mesh.

In some cases, you'll want to smooth your poly model but keep certain edges sharp. Smoothing a circular glass tabletop, for instance, results in a lozenge shape. In previous versions of Maya, you could only retain your sharp edges by duplicating them, which could be tedious and costly in terms of face density. To avoid adding extra geometry, Maya now lets you crease poly edges, which makes them sharper and pulls the object towards them.

To crease a polygonal edge:

1. Choose Create > Polygon Primitives > Cube.

2. Choose Polygon > Smooth Proxy (**Figure 8.110**).

3. Choose Polygon > Poly Crease Tool.
   The object is automatically brought into edge mode.

4. Select the bottom edges of the cube. With the middle mouse button, drag to the right.
   The edges become sharper, drawing the smooth version of the model down toward the corners. Because the side edges aren't creased, the object remains round on the sides (**Figure 8.111**).

continues on next page

5. Repeat step 4 for the top edges (**Figure 8.112**).

6. Select the top and bottom edges, and scale them down until the cylinder looks like a tabletop (**Figure 8.113**).

✔ Tips

■ Dragging to the left lessens the amount of creasing. Even an edge that has no influence remains highlighted if you have creased it previously.

■ The Poly Crease tool can create easy bevels on an object. Crease the edges until they're as sharp or round as you want.

■ By adjusting different edges different amounts, you can use the Poly Crease tool to blend between a sharp corner and a rounded object—something that is difficult with polygons (**Figure 8.114**)

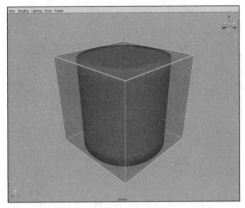

Figure 8.112 With both top and bottom creased, the sphere has turned into a cylinder.

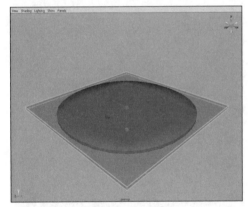

Figure 8.113 This circular disk is defined by only six control surfaces, making it easy to adjust.

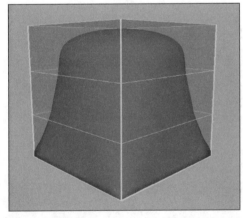

Figure 8.114 Creasing makes this otherwise awkward object easy to form with poly modeling.

Figure 8.115 A poly object with too many polygons.

Reducing the poly count

The Polygons > Reduce command reduces the number of faces in a selected mesh or subset of a mesh by a user-defined percentage. Keeping the polygon count as low as possible is important in games and interactive media to keep rendering time to a minimum. The Reduce tool can help you achieve this.

To reduce the number of faces in a polygonal mesh:

1. Select the polygon object or the set of faces you want to take polygons away from (**Figure 8.115**).

2. Choose Polygons > Reduce.

   The Polygon Reduce Options dialog box opens.

continues on next page

Modeling for Proxies

Smooth Proxy is a powerful tool because it lets you make a smooth surface, retain high-end control over that surface, and still enjoy the freedom and responsiveness of poly modeling.

If you want to use Poly Smooth or a smooth proxy to make your model, it's a good idea to do some advance planning. Keep these points in mind while you're working:

◆ Smoothing your model almost always makes it smaller in volume, so the low-res mesh may sometimes need to overlap. The closer the edges are, the closer the smoothed geometry will be. Plan big.

◆ Edges that are close together will form harder edges in your smoothed model. Use the Duplicate Edge Loop tool to add edges near each other.

◆ Check your smooth version often if you don't have it displayed.

◆ Fairly low-res geometry can form very smooth surfaces (a cube turns into a sphere, for instance), so don't add more detail than you need to your low-res mesh. Start low, and go up if you need to.

◆ If something is smoothing strangely, ensure there are no n-gons in your control mesh, or add more geometry to your control mesh so you can better manage that area.

◆ Remember that the Poly Crease tool can sharpen edges. Keep in mind which edges you plan to adjust and which you plan to keep smooth as you work on your low-res mesh.

◆ Don't put too much stock in how the low-res object looks. In many cases, the low-res object won't closely resemble your goal object. It's the smooth version people will see.

3. Set the Reduce by (%) field to the percentage of polygons by which you want to reduce the mesh—80%, for example (**Figure 8.116**).

4. Click Reduce.

The polygonal mesh is reduced to 20% of the original number of polygons (**Figure 8.117**).

✔ Tips

■ To keep a copy of the original, higher-res surface, select Keep Original in the Polygon Reduce Options dialog box.

■ Reducing your mesh too much can result in ugly geometry. If you need to cut a lot of faces out of a model, concentrate on reducing in the less important areas, so you can preserve detail where it counts.

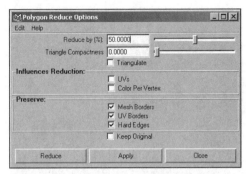

Figure 8.116 Set Reduce by (%) to the desired percentage of reduction; here, 80% is used.

Figure 8.117 The poly object now has 80% fewer polygons than before the reduction.

Surface Normals and Display

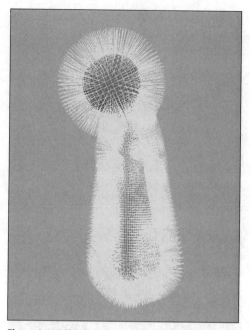

Figure 8.118 This simple shape has both vertex and face normal display turned on, making it appear fuzzy.

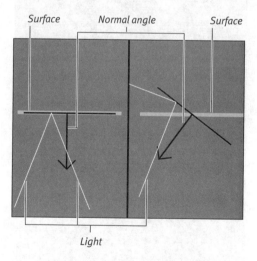

Figure 8.119 On the left, the normal is aligned with the surface, and light bounces back in a realistic way. On the right, the normal is rotated, so light bounces off the surface as if it were perpendicular to the normal. Because less light comes back, the surface appears darker (as if it were turned away from the camera).

Every surface in Maya has normals (**Figure 8.118**). A *normal* is the line perpendicular to the plane tangent to the surface. In other words, the normal always points away from the surface. By default, a normal is also perpendicular to the face or vertex it's associated with.

Normals are important because they tell the renderer how to shade the surface. How bright a surface is depends on the angle at which light hits the surface. Flatter angles reflect more light and are brighter than obtuse angles. If you rotate a vertex normal, the renderer shades the area near it as if the surface was rotated (making it lighter or darker) (**Figure 8.119**). However, the actual surface remains unchanged. Only the apparent angle of the surface is adjusted by the normal.

With polygon objects, you have a good deal of control over the normals. You can do things like average the normals across a surface to give the appearance of smoothing, or adjust the angle of the normals to put the appearance of detail where there is none.

Adjusting and smoothing normals is a crucial part of low-poly modeling, which is used frequently in game production.

To display vertex normals:

1. Select a polygon object.

2. Choose Display > Custom Polygon Display.
   The Custom Polygon Display Options dialog box opens (**Figure 8.120**).

3. In the Vertices section, select Normals, and then click Apply.
   The selected object displays the vertex normals with lines pointing from the vertices (**Figure 8.121**).

By controlling the angle of the vertex normals, you can make a low-res surface look smoother than it actually is.

To soften or harden vertex normals:

1. Create a polygon sphere by selecting Create > Polygon Primitives > Sphere.

2. Press ⑤ to switch to shaded mode.

3. Choose Polygon > Edit > Normals > Soften/Harden.
   The Polygon Soften/Harden Edge Options dialog box opens (**Figure 8.122**).

4. Click All Hard (0), and then click Apply.
   The sphere now has the appearance of a faceted surface (**Figure 8.123**)

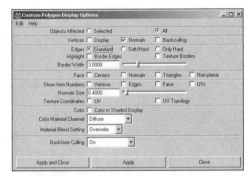

Figure 8.120 Use the Custom Polygon Display Options dialog box to display vertex normals.

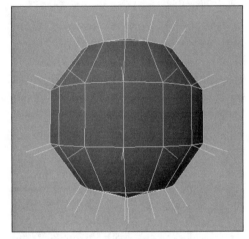

Figure 8.121 The selected object displays the vertex normals with lines pointing from the vertices.

Figure 8.123 Click All Hard (0) to make the sphere look a little like the Death Star.

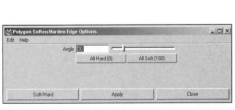

Figure 8.122 Change the appearance of your object in the Polygon Soften/Harden Edge Options dialog box.

SURFACE NORMALS AND DISPLAY

Figure 8.124 Click All Soft (180) to make the sphere look smooth again.

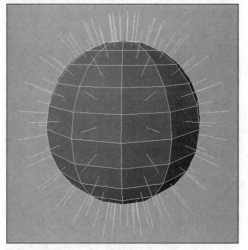

Figure 8.125 Face normals project from the center of each face in a polygon object.

5. Click All Soft (180), and then click Apply.

The sphere again has the appearance of a smooth surface (**Figure 8.124**).

Notice that the edges of the sphere don't smooth. Averaging the vertex normals to make things appear smooth is just a mathematical trick; it doesn't affect the actual geometry, so border edges are still sharp.

✔ Tip

■ The slider hardens any edge more acute than the angle the slider is set to and leaves the rest soft. To soften gentle surfaces in your model but leave the right angles hard, set the slider angle to 90.

Face normals

The face normal determines which side of the surface to render. This is important when you're working on models for real-time display, because most real-time engines won't show a face from the back.

To display face normals:

1. Select a polygon object.

2. Choose Display > Polygon Components > Normals.

The face normals are displayed as perpendicular lines pointing up from the center of each face (**Figure 8.125**).

By default, Maya creates double-sided polygons. If you create a single-sided polygon, the side of the face that has the normal is displayed. If you look at the polygon from the other side, you see right through it. This is also referred to as *backface culling*, as discussed in the "Modeling Polygons" section of this chapter.

To make a mesh single-sided:

1. Press ⑤ to switch to shaded mode.

2. Select a polygon object (**Figure 8.126**).

3. Press Ctrl/Control+a to open the Attribute Editor for the selected object.

4. In the Render Stats section, deselect Doubled Sided (**Figure 8.127**).

   The object updates, and only one side of the object's surface is visible (**Figure 8.128**).

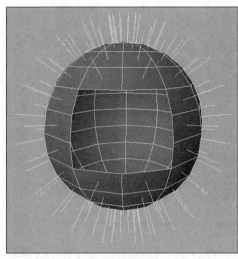

Figure 8.126 Select a double-sided object.

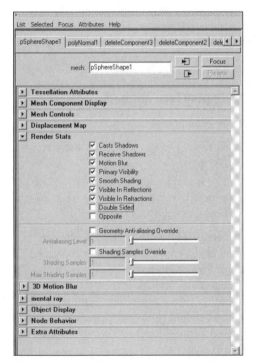

Figure 8.127 Deselect Double Sided in the polygon's Attribute Editor.

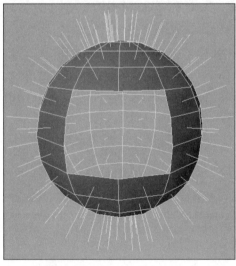

Figure 8.128 You can see through the back face of a single-sided surface.

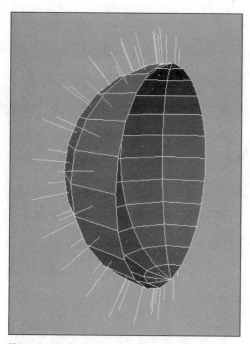

Figure 8.129 The face normals point outward ...

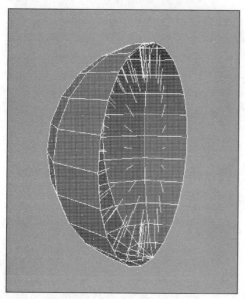

Figure 8.130 ... until they're reversed.

Whether you're working with single- or double-sided polygons, it's important that normals on the same mesh all point in the same direction. However, normals on one surface may not face the same direction as those on another surface to which you're attaching. When this happens, many Maya functions (especially vertex normal softening) won't behave as expected. To correct this situation, select the offending faces and reverse their face normal.

To reverse a face normal:

1. Select the polygon object.

2. Display the face normals for the object as described earlier.

   The face normals project from the centers of all the faces (**Figure 8.129**).

3. Choose Edit Polygons > Normals > Reverse.

   The face normals now project in the opposite direction (**Figure 8.130**).

✔ Tips

- You can set Maya to create single-sided polygonal surfaces by selecting Polygons > Tool Options > Create Meshes Single Sided.

- You can apply all the normal tools to an entire object or just to selected faces. Many of these tools also work on selected vertices, faces, and edges.

SURFACE NORMALS AND DISPLAY

SUBDIV SURFACES

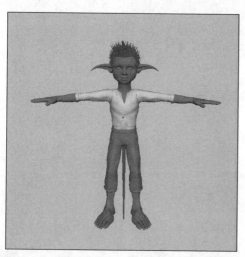

Figure 9.1 This character was modeled in subdivision surfaces. Organic modeling is well suited to subdivs. Modeled by Raf Anzovin.

Subdivision surface modeling—also known as *subdiv modeling* or *sub-Ds*—combines the freedom and utility of poly modeling with the smooth surfaces of NURBS objects (**Figure 9.1**). Subdivision surfaces share many attributes with smooth poly proxies: At the base level, both types of models have a low-res poly control cage, which surrounds a subdivided (smooth) higher-res mesh. The key difference between these model types is that subdivision surfaces are nested like a set of Russian dolls, with finer and finer detailed surfaces controlled by the rougher surfaces around them.

Subdivision surfaces have two edit modes: standard and polygon. Polygon mode behaves similarly to polygon modeling and is nearly identical to a smooth proxy. In standard mode, you work primarily with vertices, which act similarly to NURBS control vertices (CVs). Standard mode allows you to switch back and forth between display levels, so you can toggle between low and high levels of detail on an object. This means you can add detail precisely where it's needed. Maya's subdivision surfaces are called *hierarchical subdivs* because each layer affects the ones beneath it

In polygon mode, you see the edges of a polygon shape surrounding a smooth surface, which is the subdiv surface. In this mode, all the components are the same as in any other polygon, which means that they respond to polygon modeling tools and behave like poly objects.

Standard mode includes a different set of components that can be manipulated at different display levels. Note that subdiv surfaces, like NURBS surfaces, have smoothness levels of Rough, Medium, and Fine, which you can activate using the 1, 2, and 3 keys, respectively (**Figure 9.2**). Don't confuse these smoothness levels with display levels, which make the surface more complex.

Figure 9.2 These are three copies of a subdivision cylinder. From left to right, they increase from display level 1 to 3.

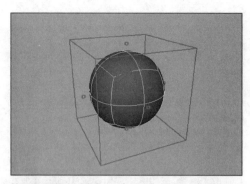

Figure 9.3 This subdiv surface sphere is at display level-0 and has its faces displayed.

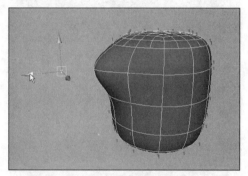

Figure 9.4 A subdiv vertex, at display level-1, has been moved. The surface responds much as a NURBS surface responds to movement of a control vertex.

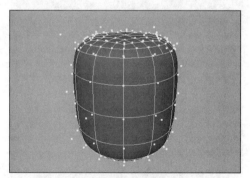

Figure 9.5 UVs don't have associated display levels. Thus they show up as points, not numbers.

Subdiv Surface Components

Subdiv surfaces have four types of components in standard mode: face, vertex, UV, and edge. These are similar to the poly equivalents, but they don't behave exactly the same (poly tools won't work on them):

◆ A **face** generally appears offset from the subdiv surface. It can have three or more sides; however, the most efficient subdiv surfaces have faces with four sides. Optionally, Maya can display a number in the center of the face to indicate the display level (**Figure 9.3**).

◆ A **vertex** generally appears offset from the surface. Depending on the display settings, a vertex is represented by the number of the display level it occupies or a standard vertex. When moved, the vertex controls the area of surface nearest to it (**Figure 9.4**).

◆ **UVs** are used for texturing rather than modeling. These points turn green when selected (**Figure 9.5**). See Chapter 15, "Shaders, Materials, and Mapping."

◆ An **edge** is one border of a face (**Figure 9.6**).

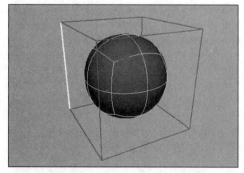

Figure 9.6 An edge of the sphere is selected in standard mode.

225

By default, Maya displays the subdiv components like their poly equivalents. Previous versions of Maya showed numbers denoting the subdivision display level. You can turn on this feature in your preferences to make it clear which level you're working on.

To change subdiv display properties:

1. Choose Window > Settings/Preferences > Preferences.

2. Select the Subdivs category, choose Numbers, and then click Save (**Figure 9.7**).

To select a subdiv surface component:

1. Choose Create > Subdiv Primitives > Sphere.

2. Press ③ to select the Fine level of subdiv surface display smoothness (**Figure 9.8**).

   The surface appears smoother in the view. Changing these settings doesn't affect the construction of the model, just its display.

3. Right-click the sphere, and select Face from the marking menu that appears (**Figure 9.9**).

   The faces appear surrounding the sphere.

4. Select and move the face (**Figure 9.10**).

Figure 9.7 Setting the display options to show numbers instead of dots can make it clearer which level you're working on.

Figure 9.8 From left to right: Rough, Medium, and Fine subdiv smoothness settings.

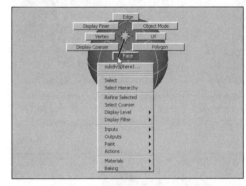

Figure 9.9 To access the marking menu for subdiv surfaces, right-click the sphere's surface. Much of what you need to work with subdiv surfaces is right here.

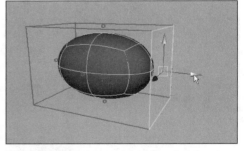

Figure 9.10 A face is moved, and the sphere is elongated.

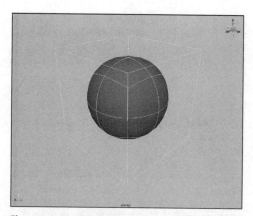

Figure 9.11 A poly cage appears around the object. Notice the faces have dots instead of zeros at their center.

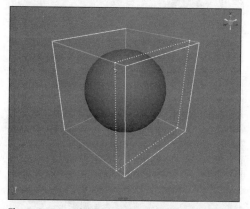

Figure 9.12 In polygon proxy mode, the polygon editing tools, such as Split Edge Ring, work on the components.

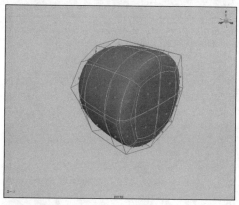

Figure 9.13 The subdiv object reflects the changes made in poly mode and has new faces.

Working with subdivs requires flipping back and forth between standard and polygon proxy mode. Standard mode is ideal for adding detail to your mode, and poly proxy mode lets you use poly tools to add geometry or perform large-scale changes to your model.

To change edit modes:

1. Choose Create > Subdiv Primitives > Sphere.

2. Choose Subdiv Surfaces > Polygon Proxy Mode.

    A poly cube surrounds the sphere; you can edit it with poly tools (**Figure 9.11**).

3. Choose Edit Polygons > Split Edge Ring, and make an edit to the poly mesh (**Figure 9.12**).

4. Choose Subdiv Surfaces > Standard Mode.

    Your object is back in subdiv mode, and you can edit the new geometry you created in poly proxy mode (**Figure 9.13**).

✔ Tip

- It's generally better to add new sections of geometry in poly proxy mode instead of grabbing and pulling out subdiv faces. This approach prevents you from refining too deeply, which in turn slows down performance.

SUBDIV SURFACE COMPONENTS

Refining Subdiv Surfaces

Subdiv surfaces let you move back and forth between different levels of detail, crease edges, and maintain a high level of control over your object. Maya provides a few options dealing just with this aspect of subdivs:

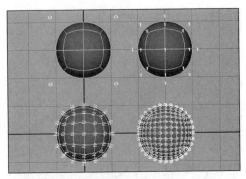

Figure 9.14 A subdiv surface sphere is shown at display levels 0 (from top left), 1, 2, and 3. By default, the sphere has only levels 0 and 1. It needs to be refined to access higher levels.

◆ **Display level**. Subdiv surface objects have different display levels—that is, different levels of refinement. This means you can work with many points close together on a surface that affect only a small area, or with fewer points farther apart on a surface that affect a large area. You can move back and forth between levels (**Figure 9.14**). Level-0 is the base mesh; it's the first level on which you work, because it's where all the polygonal components exist. These components can only be adjusted using the Polygon tool set in polygon mode. When you start adding detail to your model, the subdivision edits (which have their own tools and workflows and are available in standard mode) go on subsequent levels—level-1, level-2, level-3, and so on.

◆ **Refine**. This function gives the selected area of the surface a higher level of detail. If the surface is at level-1, Refine shows the selected area with level-2 points.

◆ **Finer and Coarser**. These functions allow you to move quickly to a higher (Finer) or lower (Coarser) level of detail.

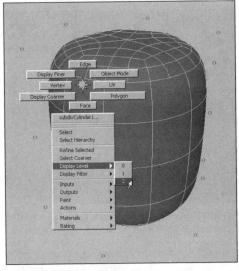

Figure 9.15 Display Level allows you to choose from any of the existing levels.

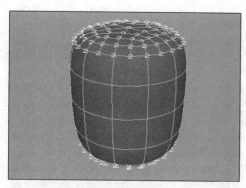

Figure 9.16 The level-2 vertices show up on the default cylinder where detail is needed. If you need the 2s to be evenly distributed, go to display level-1 and refine.

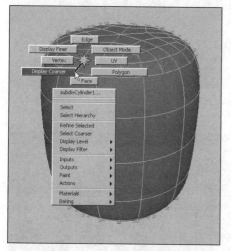

Figure 9.17 You can also select Display Coarser and Display Finer to change the display level.

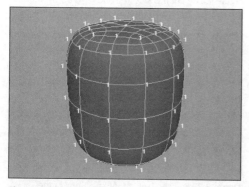

Figure 9.18 The subdiv surface cylinder at display level-1.

To change display levels on a subdiv surface:

1. Choose Create > Subdiv Primitives > Cylinder.

2. Press ③ to select the Fine level of subdiv surface smoothness.

3. Right-click the cylinder, and select Vertex from the marking menu.

4. Right-click the cylinder, and select Display Level > 2 from the marking menu (**Figure 9.15**).

   Many more points appear, labeled 2 (**Figure 9.16**).

5. Right-click the cylinder, and select Display Coarser from the marking menu (**Figure 9.17**).

   The display level is reduced to 1 (**Figure 9.18**).

6. Right-click the cylinder, and select Display Finer from the marking menu.

   The display level goes back up to 2.

To add detail to a subdiv surface:

1. Choose Create > Subdiv Primitives > Cube.

2. Press ③ to select the Fine level of subdiv surface smoothness.

3. Right-click the cube, and select Vertex from the marking menu.

4. Select a vertex (**Figure 9.19**).

5. Right-click the cube, and select Refine from the marking menu.

   The zeros are replaced by ones in the area around the original point, and there are more numbers (**Figure 9.20**).

6. Right-click the cube, and again select Refine from the marking menu.

7. Select and move a point (**Figure 9.21**).

8. Right-click the cube, and select Display Level > 0 from the marking menu.

9. Select and move a point (**Figure 9.22**).

   The changes to the level-2 points remain while you work with level-0 points. You can move back and forth between the display levels.

✔ Tips

- The Refine function also works with edges and faces.

- You can refine up to a display level of 13. However, we don't recommend that you go above 3 because the speed of interactivity decreases dramatically as the level increases.

- You can't delete a subdiv surface component. However, if you transform any component at a display level of 1 or higher and then try to delete it, the component returns to its original position.

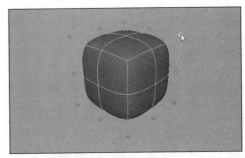

Figure 9.19 A vertex is selected to determine the area to be refined.

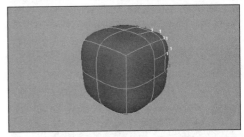

Figure 9.20 With the Refine function, detail is added only around the selected component.

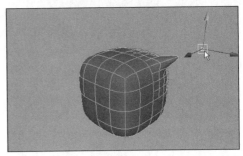

Figure 9.21 A point is selected and moved. This refined area allows tweaks to small portions of the surface.

Figure 9.22 You can tweak large portions of the surface by returning the display level to 0.

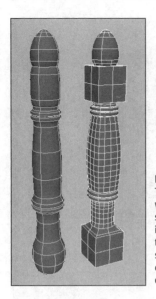

Figure 9.23
These balusters were made with subdivs. On the left is the raw shape; on the right is the same shape after using creasing to flesh out the detail.

Creasing Subdiv Surfaces

Subdiv surfaces support two types of creasing: Partial Crease and Full Crease. Creasing gives an edge more weight, making it appear sharper. Partial creases use finer display levels to adjust the surface, whereas full creases make edges hard. You can use creasing to add extra detail to an object quickly (**Figure 9.23**).

To add a partial crease:

1. Choose Create > Subdiv Primitives > Sphere.

2. Right-click the sphere, and select Edge from the marking menu.

3. Select the top four edges of the cubic cage (**Figure 9.24**).

4. Choose Subdiv Surfaces > Partial Crease Edge/Vertex.

   The surface is refined, and the new components draw up toward the corner (**Figure 9.25**).

5. Without deselecting anything, partial-crease the edges a few more times.

   Notice that the surface becomes sharper and more creased but also gets increasingly dense (**Figure 9.26**).

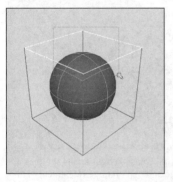

Figure 9.24
Select the top four edges of the cube only.

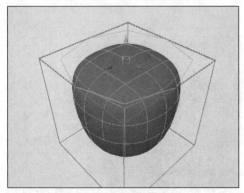

Figure 9.25 Partial creases draw the geometry toward the edge of vertex and also refine the area to allow for the sharper corner.

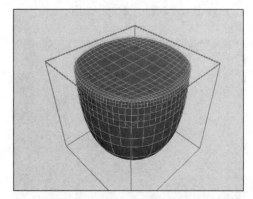

Figure 9.26 This corner has been creased many times. The result is a nice beveled corner, but it's very dense and may perform slowly.

CREASING SUBDIV SURFACES

231

To add a full crease:

1. Continue with the sphere from the previous task.

2. Select the uncreased edges of the cubic cage (**Figure 9.27**).

3. Choose Subdiv Surfaces > Full Crease Edge/Vertex.

   The edges are sharpened, and the sphere now resembles a tile. Note that the edges don't refine the surface (**Figure 9.28**).

4. Select the middle edges of the tile.

5. Choose Subdiv Surfaces > Uncrease Edge/Vertex.

   The tile now looks like a cylinder (**Figure 9.29**).

✔ Tips

- You can also crease vertices. This technique is useful for filling corners between creased edges or pulling spiky geometry smoothly from a surface (**Figure 9.30**).

- If you use Partial Crease Edge/Vertex more than a few times, the dense geometry added from the multiple creases can cause significant slowdown. To make a corner sharper than what one or two creases provide, you can instead add detail to the poly cage as you would for a smooth proxy.

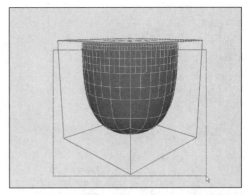

Figure 9.27 Use the Marquee Select tool to select the rest of the cube's edges.

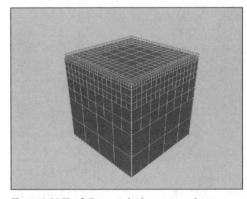

Figure 9.28 The full creased edges are as sharp as a normal poly edge and don't require refinement of the model.

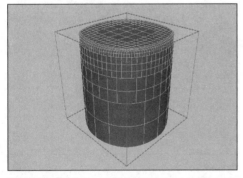

Figure 9.29 With the sides uncreased, the surface smoothes back into a cylinder in the vertical direction.

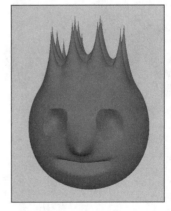

Figure 9.30 This silly face was made with full and partial creases. Vertices were pulled out of the head and creased to make the hair spiky.

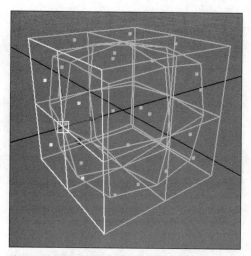

Figure 9.31 Select four faces on one side of the cube.

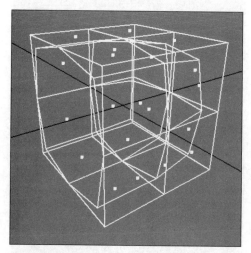

Figure 9.32 The deleted faces create an open-ended subdiv surface.

Figure 9.33 For Mirror, choose X in the Subdiv Mirror Options dialog box.

Mirroring and Subdivs

When you're making symmetrical models, you can use the Mirror command to copy and flip the subdiv surface. This takes a few more steps than with polygons because you can't mirror a subdiv surface directly.

To mirror a subdiv surface:

1. Choose Create > Subdiv Primitives > Cube.

2. Right-click the cube, and select Polygon from the marking menu.

3. Right-click the cube, and select Face from the marking menu.

4. Select and delete the faces from the right side (**Figure 9.31**).

   The subdiv surface is now open on one end (**Figure 9.32**).

5. Select the subdiv surface, and then select the box next to Mirror in the Subdiv Surfaces menu.

   The Subdiv Mirror Options dialog box opens (**Figure 9.33**).

6. Select X to mirror the object across that axis, and click Apply.

   A flipped copy of the surface is created (**Figure 9.34**).

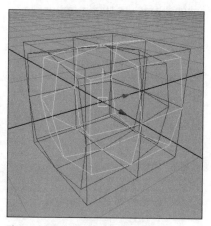

Figure 9.34 The mirrored subdiv surface.

When your model is made up of many separate pieces, you can use the Attach command to join them as one piece. However, any edges you attach must have the same number of vertices.

To attach two subdiv surfaces:

1. Arrange the surfaces from the previous task, "To mirror a subdiv surface," so that their openings are near one another (**Figure 9.35**).

2. Select both surfaces, and make sure you're in standard mode.

3. From the Subdiv Surfaces menu, select the box next to Attach.

   The Subdiv Attach Options dialog box opens (**Figure 9.36**).

4. Set the Threshold amount to 5 to close the gap between the surfaces.

5. Click Apply.

   The two surfaces become one surface (**Figure 9. 37**).

✔ Tip

- Subdiv operations like Attach only work in standard mode. When you're in poly proxy mode, Maya doesn't consider your object to be a subdiv surface (although it provides subdiv options in the marking menu).

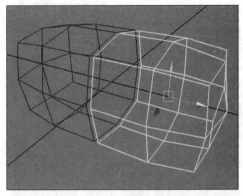

Figure 9.35 Place the openings of the surfaces you want to attach near one another.

Figure 9.36 Set the Threshold to 5 in the Subdiv Attach Options dialog box.

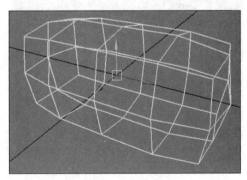

Figure 9.37 The attached subdiv surface.

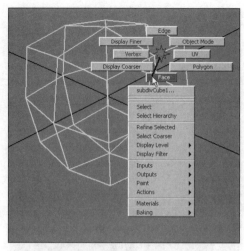

Figure 9.38 Select Face from the marking menu.

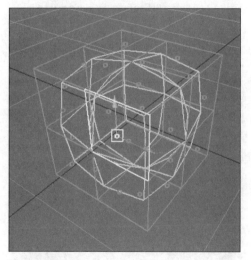

Figure 9.39 Select a face.

Subdiv Hierarchies

As you refine your subdiv models, they can quickly become complex and begin to slow down. Once you're sure you won't be making more large changes, you can simplify things by collapsing your model. Collapsing lets you convert your subdivision changes to polygonal components that can be edited in polygon mode with the polygon tool set. When you collapse the mesh, your base model becomes more complex, but your levels of refinement decrease.

The Collapse Hierarchy command reduces the number of levels in a subdiv surface. Collapse Hierarchy lets you specify the number of levels you wish to collapse and moves the edits from those levels to the level above. Collapsing by one level removes the 0 level of control, makes the 1 level your new 0 level, and so on until there are no more levels.

To collapse the subdiv hierarchy:

1. Choose Create > Subdiv Primitives > Cube.

2. Right-click the cube, and select Face from the marking menu (**Figure 9.38**).

3. Select a face on one side of the cube (**Figure 9.39**).

continues on next page

4. Right-click the cube, and select Refine Selected from the marking menu (**Figure 9.40**).

A level-1 is added to the mesh (**Figure 9.41**).

5. Right-click the cube, and select Polygon from the marking menu.

Notice that the polygon cage doesn't show the detail that was created by adding level-1 (**Figure 9.42**).

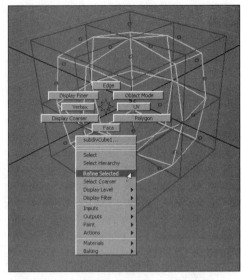

Figure 9.40 Select Refine from the marking menu.

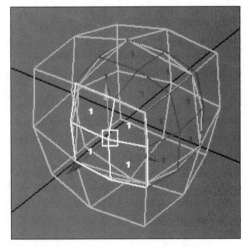

Figure 9.41 By refining the face, you've added a level to the model.

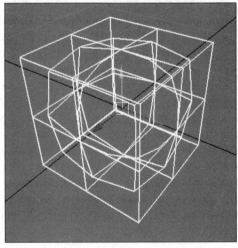

Figure 9.42 Polygon mode doesn't show the added detail of level-1.

Figure 9.43 Set Number of Levels to 1 in the Subdiv Collapse Options dialog box.

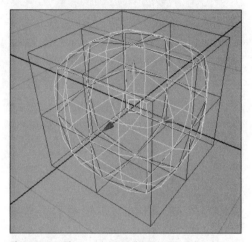

Figure 9.44 After applying Collapse Hierarchy, the surface has level-1 detail in level-0.

New control cage   *Old control cage*

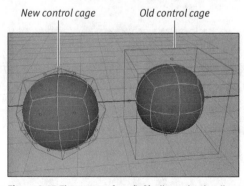

Figure 9.45 The new surface (left) allows the detail that was in level-1 to become the new level-0, and therefore be editable in polygon mode.

6. From the Subdiv Surfaces menu, select the box next to Collapse Hierarchy.

The Subdiv Collapse Options dialog box opens (**Figure 9.43**).

7. Set Number of Levels to 1, and click Apply.

A collapsed copy of the selected surface is made (**Figure 9.44**).

8. Move the copy away from the original subdiv, right-click new the cube, and select Polygon from the marking menu.

The polygon cage is now equivalent to the level-1 display and shows the detail added through refining (**Figure 9.45**).

✔ Tips

■ Collapsing is a one-way operation. Use it only if you no longer need level-0 control over your mesh.

■ Maya's Mental Ray renderer only renders subdiv surfaces that are quadrilateral. This means the faces involved in the mesh can have only four sides. Maya's renderer, however, renders non-quadrilateral subdiv surfaces. Collapse Hierarchy will fix non-quad subdivs so that Mental Ray can render them.

SUBDIV HIERARCHIES

237

Working in Polygon Mode

Subdiv surfaces can speed the modeling process because you can choose between viewing the surface in high-res with many points or low-res with just a few points. If you know how to model polygons, you can model subdiv surfaces as well, because they use many of the same tools.

Standard mode is good for adding fine details, but polygon mode is essential for creating the basic structure of the surface. One common tactic is to model a polygon to get the rough form and then convert it to subdiv surfaces. This approach is helpful because it lets you work quickly, and the polygon primitive cube has a simpler construction than the subdiv primitive cube.

It's good practice to finish all the manipulation you plan to do in polygon mode before you begin refining the surface in standard mode. You can lose changes made to the surface if you frequently switch between modes.

To model a turtle out of subdiv surfaces using polygon mode:

1. Choose Create > Subdiv Primitives > Sphere.

2. Press ③ to select the Fine level of subdivision surface smoothness.

3. Scale the sphere down the *y* axis to make it flatter (**Figure 9.46**).

4. Right-click the sphere, and select Polygon from the marking menu.

   A rectangular polygon shell appears around the sphere.

5. Right-click the sphere, select Face from the marking menu, and select the face on the front side of the polygon (**Figure 9.47**).

6. Choose Edit Polygons > Extrude Face, and scale down the face (**Figure 9.48**).

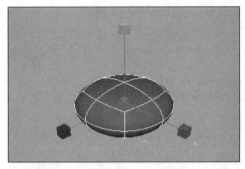

Figure 9.46 The sphere is scaled flatter to resemble a turtle shell.

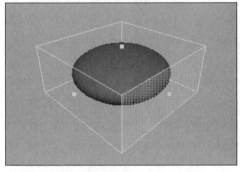

Figure 9.47 The front face is selected.

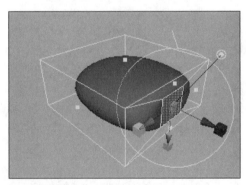

Figure 9.48 The face is scaled down. To get the proportional scale manipulator in the center, click any of the other scale manipulators.

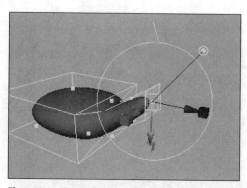

Figure 9.49 The neck is formed by moving the face out and up.

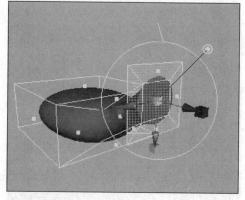

Figure 9.50 The scale of this face determines the size of the back of the turtle's head.

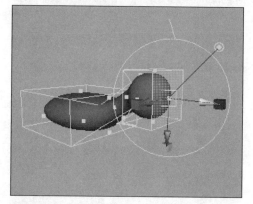

Figure 9.51 Move this face forward to give the head some length.

7. Choose Edit Polygons > Extrude Face again, and move the face forward and up (**Figure 9.49**).

   This is the turtle's neck.

8. Choose Edit Polygons > Extrude Face, and proportionally scale the face up (**Figure 9.50**).

9. Choose Edit Polygons > Extrude Face, and move the face forward (**Figure 9.51**).

   This is the turtle's head.

10. Select the face on the bottom of the sphere.

11. Choose Edit Polygons > Subdivide (**Figure 9.52**).

   continues on next page

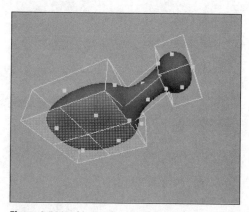

Figure 9.52 Looking at the object from below, you can see that the bottom has been subdivided.

WORKING IN POLYGON MODE

12. Choose Edit Polygons > Extrude Face, and proportionally scale the faces smaller (**Figure 9.53**).

13. Choose Edit Polygons > Extrude Face again, and move the faces down (**Figure 9.54**).

You've created a turtle!

✔ Tips

■ You can add extra detail to your poly cage by using any of the polygon tools discussed earlier, such as Split Polygon, Split Edge Ring, Bevel, and more.

■ You can flip back and forth between polygon and standard mode while working. However, if you make edits deeper than display level-1 in standard mode, splitting or extruding faces in polygon mode can cause the smooth surface to become jagged or otherwise distorted.

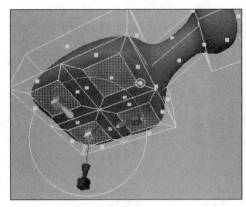

Figure 9.53 The bases of the legs are scaled down simultaneously.

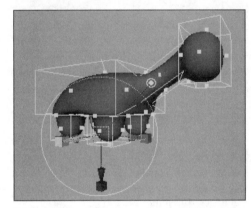

Figure 9.54 Move these faces down to determine the length of the legs. A simple turtle shape is completed.

Figure 9.55 Scale up the sphere. This is the start of your head.

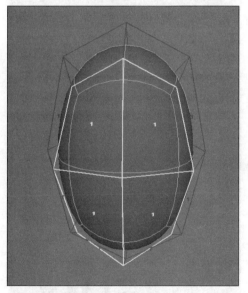

Figure 9.56 Refine the front of the sphere where the face will be...

Sculpting Subdivs

Beginning in Maya 7.0, you can use the Sculpt Geometry tool on a subdiv surface. Previously, you could only use this tool effectively on very dense poly or NURBS surfaces. Because you can add density anywhere it's needed with Maya subdivs, using the Sculpt Geometry tool doesn't mean your object must be dense all over. Instead, you can add detail wherever you wish to sculpt.

You can sculpt a head from a simple subdiv sphere if you plan ahead and add detail only where needed.

To prepare a surface for sculpting:

1. Choose Create > Subdiv Primitives > Sphere.

2. Scale the sphere up to 1.5 in the *y* direction (**Figure 9.55**).

3. Press ⒊ to select the Fine level of subdivision surface smoothness.

4. Right-click the sphere, and select Face from the marking menu.

5. Select the front face, and refine it (**Figure 9.56**).

   Now the front of the head, where the face will be, has more detail.

continues on next page

SCULPTING SUBDIVS

6. Select the top two faces on the front, and refine twice more (**Figure 9.57**).

The eye area of the head has more detail.

7. Select two groups of faces where you want the eyes to be (**Figure 9.58**), and refine them twice (**Figure 9.59**).

To sculpt subdiv surfaces using the Sculpt Geometry tool:

1. Start with the head from the previous task.

2. Right-click the head, and select Vertex from the marking menu.

3. Right-click the head, and select Display Level > 4 from the marking menu.

4. Select all the vertices you wish to sculpt (**Figure 9.60**).

5. From the Subdiv Surfaces menu, select the box next to Sculpt Geometry.

The Sculpt Geometry Tool options appear.

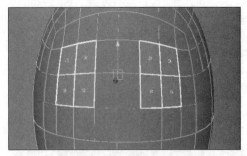

Figure 9.57 ...and refine twice more for the eyes.

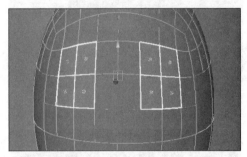

Figure 9.58 Refine again more precisely for the eyes...

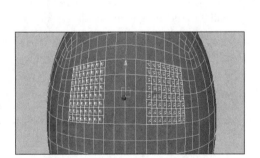

Figure 9.59 ...and again to make the resolution even finer.

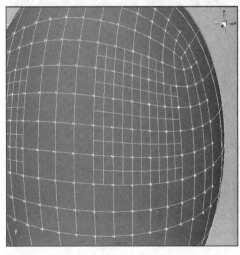

Figure 9.60 You must have an object or components selected when choosing the Sculpt Geometry tool. The tool only works within that selection.

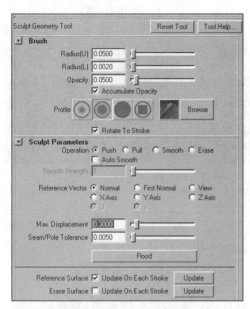

Figure 9.61 Set the options as shown. The brush is much too large and heavy at first if you leave it at the defaults.

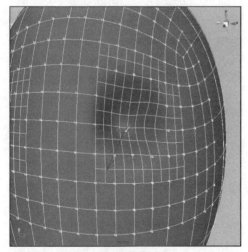

Figure 9.62 Paint on an eye socket. It may take several brush strokes to get the shape and depth you want.

Figure 9.63 With the Pull setting, you can drag geometry away from the surface—an advantage over real sculpting.

6. Set Radius(U) and Opacity to .05, set Max. Displacement to .3, and ensure that Operation is set to Push (**Figure 9.61**).

7. Click and drag in the middle of one of your model's dense patches, and begin sculpting an eye socket.

   The Sculpt Geometry tool pushes in your level-4 points as you move the mouse (**Figure 9.62**).

8. Set the Sculpt Geometry tool to Pull (**Figure 9.63**).

   The tool now pulls up geometry instead of pushing it in.

9. Paint eyebrows over the eyes (**Figure 9.64**).

10. Set the display level of the head to 5, and select the finer vertices.

    Now you can paint on a finer resolution surface to adjust the eyebrows more precisely.

continues on next page

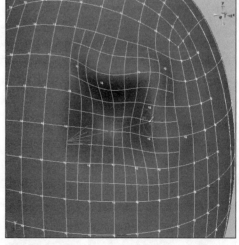

Figure 9.64 The Pull setting allows you to pull up ridges for eyebrows.

SCULPTING SUBDIVS

243

11. Sculpt the eyebrows until you're satisfied.
Note that if you sculpt close to the
edge of the refined surface, Maya automatically refines the surface for you
(**Figure 9.65**).

12. Repeat steps 4–11 for the other eye
(**Figure 9.66**).

You now have the start of the face. You
can use similar steps to add a nose, a
mouth, ears, warts, and wrinkles.

✔ Tips

■ It's best to use the Sculpt Geometry tool
to add details to a model, as opposed to
trying to create complicated shapes.
Start with a basic form, and then sculpt
to give it an organic look.

■ You can sculpt in object mode, and Maya
will auto-refine and select new faces for
you. However, when sculpting in this
mode, you won't be able to tell which display level you're painting in.

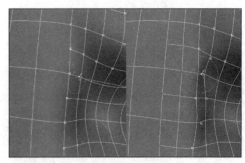

Figure 9.65 Painting near the edge of your surface
(left) creates new refinement automatically (right).

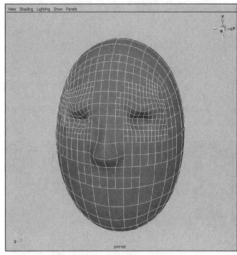

Figure 9.66 The start of a face. You can use the Sculpt
Geometry and Refine tools hand in hand to add many
features to your models.

SKELETONS AND RIGGING

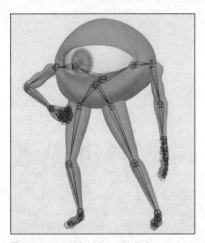

Figure 10.1 Inside this eyeball character, you can see the skeleton, which is used to pose and animate the character.

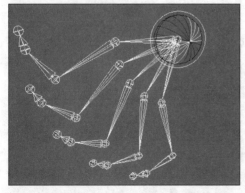

Figure 10.2 Illustrating the principle of forward kinematics. When the hip joint is rotated, all the joints below rotate with it.

Once you model a character, you need to place a skeleton inside it in order to animate it (**Figure 10.1**). The skeleton is built as a hierarchy of individual joints connected by bones.

These bones typically aren't used directly to animate. Instead, you place a set of constraints on the bones. These constraints limit or alter the movement of the bones and allow you both greater control of the whole skeleton and the ability to pose the character with just a few bones or curves.

In general, nature serves as the best template for placing joints: Use pictures of skeletons, human or animal. A shoulder joint should go at the shoulder; an elbow joint should go at the elbow; and so on. However, you don't need to be too literal. For example, although the human foot has 26 bones, you can animate a shoe with three bones. Wherever you want something to bend, that's where you need a joint.

Joints are hierarchical—that is, the joints at the top of the hierarchy move those beneath them. The first joint you place is at the top of the hierarchy and is often referred to as the *root joint*. This joint moves the whole skeleton. Because the knee, ankle, and foot joints are below the hip joint, the rest of the leg moves when the hip joint is rotated. This type of character posing uses *forward kinematics* (FK) (**Figure 10.2**).

Inverse kinematics (IK) refers to posing from the bottom of the hierarchy up. In this type of rig, if you move the foot around, the knee and hip rotate accordingly (**Figure 10.3**). Sections of your skeleton must specifically be set up for IK use, whereas FK control is inherent in the bone hierarchy.

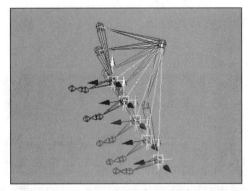

Figure 10.3 The foot is moved using an IK handle. Some animators avoid IK because it tends to move limbs in straight lines rather than natural arcs.

FK or IK?

New animators always wonder which is better—FK or IK? The answer is that they both have advantages and weaknesses.

Forward kinematics allows for very precise motion, smooth arcs, and easy layering of rotations. FK can be more troublesome for posing because each joint must be rotated into position. As such, FK is best suited for posing freely moving objects, because it's difficult to maintain the end of an FK chain in one location.

Inverse kinematics is best used when you need precise control over the end of a chain, because you animate the handle rather than adjusting each joint in the skeleton. It's easy to put the joints exactly where you want, so you might use IK when placing the hand or foot of a character on an immobile object. However, there are drawbacks: IK handles have a tendency to flip, create floaty or disconnected animation, and leave flat arcs. Plus, positioning the intermediate joints can be difficult.

Spline IK (discussed later in this chapter) is good for tentacles and spinal columns or any skeleton that has many joints that need to move in a fluid, organic manner.

Full Body IK, new in Maya 7.0, is a quick and powerful rigging option. Full Body IK connects the whole skeleton together, allowing you to pose the character from the end of any chain. It suffers from the same drawbacks of any IK rig, but it has a lot more flexibility than the standard IK options.

A complex character employs all of these methods to give you the greatest amount of freedom and control.

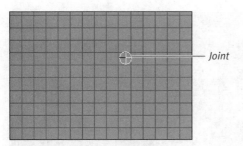

Figure 10.4 A joint is created in an orthographic view by selecting Skeleton › Joint Tool.

About Joints

When you create joints, the bones appear automatically between them. The order in which you create joints is important: The first joint that's created resides at the top of the hierarchy; the second joint is parented to the first (making it a child of that joint and forcing it to follow the parent's movement); the third is parented to the second; and so on down the line.

A joint is like a pivot point in a hierarchy. You can't take a joint's pivot point away: The joint always remains with its pivot point. A joint's position in the hierarchy determines which joints transform with it: The joints below it transform with that joint; the joints above it aren't affected by that joint's movements. Don't confuse this hierarchy with joints that are above or below each other *physically:* One joint can be above another in the *y* direction but below it within the hierarchy.

You can think of bones as a visual representation of your skeleton's joint hierarchy. When you parent one joint to another, a bone appears. If you unparent a joint, the bone disappears. Sometimes it's easier to create separate hierarchies and then piece them together, or to branch out from an existing hierarchy. For instance, a character's neck and arms branch out from its spine. It may be easier to make an arm and then parent it to the spine, while the simpler structure of the neck could just be added to the spine directly.

To create joints:

1. Choose Skeleton > Joint Tool.

2. In the Side view, click to place the joint.

You should generally use an orthographic view when you create joints to avoid the imprecise placement of perspective views (**Figure 10.4**).

continues on next page

3. Click where you want the next joint to be placed.

A bone appears between the two joints (**Figure 10.5**).

4. Click and drag to place the third joint. When you release the mouse button, the joint is placed.

5. Press [Enter].

The skeleton is complete, and you're no longer in the Joint tool. The top joint of the hierarchy is selected, which causes the whole skeleton to be highlighted.

✔ Tips

- It's often a good idea to build a skeleton with grid snap turned on so that all your joints are securely aligned. A convenient way to do this is by holding down [x] when you place joints.

- You can make the joints appear bigger or smaller by selecting Display > Joint Size and choosing a size from the list.

- To delete a joint, select the joint and then press [Delete]. That joint is deleted along with any joints below it in the hierarchy.

To parent joints:

1. Create the skeleton of a leg and foot out of five joints in the Side view (**Figure 10.6**).

Press [Enter] to complete the creation.

2. As a separate hierarchy, create spine joints in the Side view, starting from the bottom and working your way up (**Figure 10.7**).

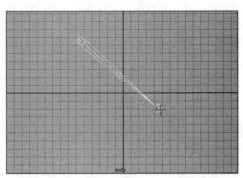

Figure 10.5 The second joint is created. A bone appears between the two joints, demonstrating that they are parented together. The bone is thicker at the parent joint than at the child joint.

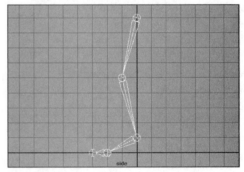

Figure 10.6 This is a typical leg skeleton. Starting from the top, the joints are named hip, knee, ankle, ball, and toe. If the character is wearing shoes, you don't need bones for each toe; one bone is sufficient to rotate the front of the shoe.

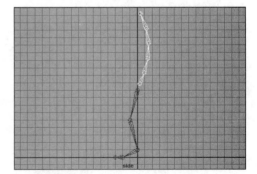

Figure 10.7 A spine is created from the bottom up. This makes the bottom joint the parent of the rest of the spine. The rest of the joints are beneath it in the hierarchy even though they're above it in space.

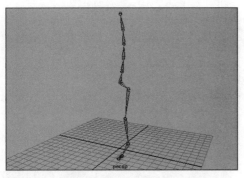

Figure 10.8 The leg has been parented to the spine. Now the bottom joint of the skeleton is the root joint for the whole character. When this joint is moved, the whole character moves.

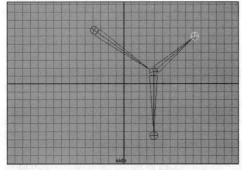

Figure 10.9 A new joint branches off from the existing joints.

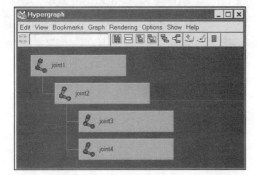

Figure 10.10 Joint3 and joint4 are both children of joint2. That means that if joint2 is rotated, joint3 and joint4 rotate with it.

3. In the Front view, move the leg to the side.

4. Select the top joint of the leg, Shift-select the bottom joint of the spine, and press p.

A bone appears between the leg and the spine. It's now one hierarchy (**Figure 10.8**).

Save this skeleton; you'll use it shortly for another task.

✔ Tips

■ You can similarly unparent joints. Select the joint you want to unparent, and press Shift + p. The joint becomes unparented, and the bone disappears.

■ You can also parent and unparent joints in the Outliner: Drag the joints around by clicking them with the middle mouse button. If you drag one joint on top of another, you parent them together. To unparent, drag the joint to the base level of the scene.

To branch off from an existing skeleton:

1. Using the skeleton from the task "To create joints," click the Joint tool icon.

2. Click the joint from which you want to branch.

Doing so *selects* the joint rather than creating a new one.

3. Click where you want the new joint to be placed.

A new joint appears, with the bone branched off from the original skeleton (**Figure 10.9**).

4. Choose Window > Hypergraph to view the resulting hierarchy.

Note that two joints are at the same level in the hierarchy and both are parented under the same joint (**Figure 10.10**).

ABOUT JOINTS

Adjusting Hierarchies

When skeletons become complex, you need to work with the joint hierarchies as they are, instead of taking them apart and putting them back together again and again. Maya provide a number of useful tools to help you work within a complicated skeleton. These tools let you mirror, move, insert, and delete joints inside the existing hierarchy.

To save time, once you create a leg or an arm, you can *mirror* the joint, which makes a duplicate leg or arm appear on the other side of the body.

To mirror joints:

1. Using the leg from the "To parent joints" task, select the hip joint (**Figure 10.11**).

2. From the Skeleton menu, select the box next to Mirror Joint.

   The Mirror Joint Options dialog box opens.

3. For Mirror Across, select YZ (**Figure 10.12**).

4. Click Mirror.

   A new leg appears on the other side (**Figure 10.13**).

✔ Tips

- If the leg was built in the Side view, you should mirror it across the *yz* plane. To figure out which plane you should use, look at the View axis in the corner of the panel and imagine two of the axes forming a plane that you want to mirror across. If the new leg doesn't appear in the correct location, undo the mirror joint and try choosing a different plane to mirror across in the Mirror Joint Options dialog box.

- Don't mirror a joint that falls on the center line of the body: If you do, you'll end up with two joints on top of each other.

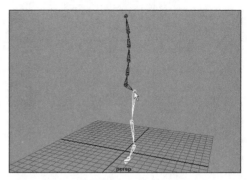

Figure 10.11 The hip joint is selected so that the leg can be mirrored over to the other side.

Figure 10.12 The YZ option is chosen so that the leg will mirror across the *YZ* plane.

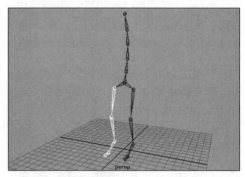

Figure 10.13 The opposite leg is created using the Mirror Joint Options dialog box from the Skeleton menu.

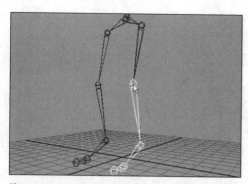

Figure 10.14 The knee joint of the leg has been selected so that it can be moved.

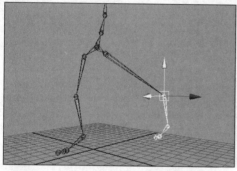

Figure 10.15 As the knee is moved back, the foot bones move with it. Note that the bone between the hip and the knee becomes longer.

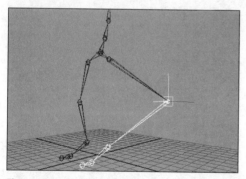

Figure 10.16 When the knee joint is moved in pivot move mode, the foot, which is below it in the hierarchy, stays put.

When you move a joint to position it, all the joints beneath it in the hierarchy move along with it. You can move a joint *independently* of its position in the hierarchy by using pivot move mode.

To move a joint:

1. Start with your skeleton from the previous task.

2. Select the knee joint (**Figure 10.14**).

3. Press [w].

4. Move the knee backward.

    The rest of the leg moves with it (**Figure 10.15**).

5. Press [z] to undo the last move.

6. Press [Insert]/[Home] on the keyboard. You're now in pivot move mode.

7. Move the knee backward.

    The rest of the leg doesn't move with it (**Figure 10.16**).

8. Press [z] to undo the last move. Press [Insert]/[Home] again to get out of pivot move mode.

Inserting and deleting joints

Sometimes you need to insert a new joint into your skeleton after you've laid it out. Rather than unparenting, adding a new joint, and then re-parenting, use the Insert Joint tool. This handy tool keeps your existing skeleton intact by splitting your bone and inserting a new joint in your hierarchy.

Conversely, you may find that you've created more joints than you need. If so, you can select the joint and remove it from the hierarchy without deleting any additional nodes, like deleting the joint would do.

To insert a joint:

1. Create a skeleton of several joints (**Figure 10.17**).

2. Choose Skeleton > Insert Joint Tool.

3. Click a joint, and drag out the new joint.

   The new joint is inserted between the joint you clicked and the joint beneath it in the hierarchy. It's easiest to do this in an orthographic view (**Figure 10.18**).

4. Press ⏎Enter to finish, and exit the tool.

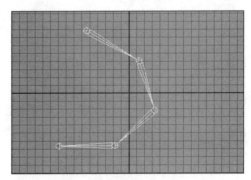

Figure 10.17 A skeleton of several joints is created in an orthographic view.

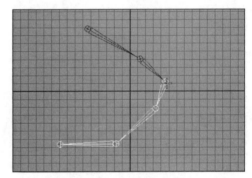

Figure 10.18 A new joint is created between two existing joints. It's positioned between the joints both physically and in the hierarchy.

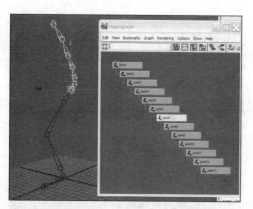

Figure 10.19 You can select a joint by clicking it in the modeling window or by clicking the corresponding joint node in the Hypergraph.

Figure 10.20
Select Skeleton ›
Remove Joint.

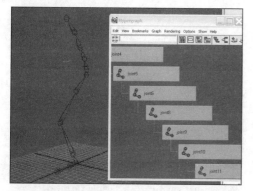

Figure 10.21 The selected joint (joint7) is completely deleted from the scene and can no longer be viewed in the Hypergraph.

To remove a joint from the hierarchy:

1. Click the joint you would like to remove (**Figure 10.19**).

2. Choose Skeleton > Remove Joint (**Figure 10.20**).

   The joint is removed from the hierarchy and deleted from the scene. Now that the selected joint has been removed, the bone from its parent ends at the selected joint's child (**Figure 10.21**).

Sometimes you'll want to disconnect a portion of a previously created skeleton to use it in a new character. For instance, you may want to create a *half-human* character that uses a human joint system—with human-like arms but nonhuman-like legs. By disconnecting the center joint, you can use the upper half of the human skeleton on the human half of the new character.

To disconnect a joint from the hierarchy:

1. Click the joint you would like to disconnect from the hierarchy (**Figure 10.22**).

2. Choose Skeleton > Disconnect Joint (**Figure 10.23**).

   The selected joint and its children are disconnected from the original hierarchy.

3. Choose Window > Hypergraph.

   The Hypergraph opens in a new window.

4. Press a to focus all the joints in the Hypergraph window.

   The skeleton is split into two hierarchies that can be selected and moved independently of each other (**Figure 10.24**).

✔ Tip

■ Disconnecting a joint is different from unparenting it. Disconnecting leaves a new joint where the base of the disconnected hierarchy was removed, whereas unparenting removes the joint (**Figure 10.25**).

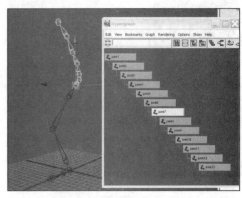

Figure 10.22 You can select a joint by clicking it in the modeling window or by clicking the corresponding joint node in the Hypergraph.

Figure 10.23 Select Skeleton > Disconnect Joint.

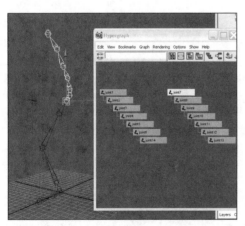

Figure 10.24 Although in the Modeling view the skeleton still appears to be one, you can see in the Hypergraph that there are now two separate hierarchies.

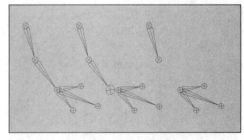

Figure 10.25 On the left is the original skeleton. In the middle, the Disconnect tool has been used and the piece has been moved away slightly. On the right, the joints have become unparented, and a bone is missing.

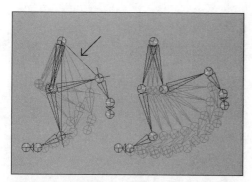

Figure 10.26 On the left, an IK handle moves the foot. On the right, both the hip and ankle are rotated to move the foot.

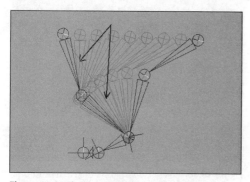

Figure 10.27 The top of the leg is moving, but the ankle stays put because it has an IK handle, which is keyframed. Note that this foot also has an IK handle going from the ankle to the ball and from the ball to the toe. These IK handles keep the rest of the foot in place.

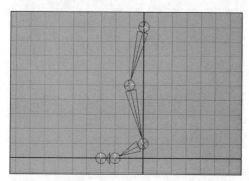

Figure 10.28 This is a typical leg skeleton. Sometimes a heel joint is added, but it's used as a placeholder; the ankle and toe joints bend, but the heel joint is just used as a rotation pivot.

About IK Handles and Solvers

Inverse kinematics makes animation easier in many situations. For example, to put a foot in a certain position using forward kinematics, you need to rotate the hip, knee, and ankle. However, by using an IK handle on the ankle, you can move the ankle into position, and the hip and knee rotate accordingly (**Figure 10.26**).

You can also use an IK handle to make a foot or hand stick in one spot. When your character is walking and you want one foot to remain planted on the ground, IK handles make it much easier to keep that foot in place (because multiple rotations in the joints connected to the IK handle help to keep it that way) (**Figure 10.27**). Once it's keyframed, the foot does its best to stay where it is even though the joints in the IK chain are rotating. The same goes for arms and hands. If your character is climbing a ladder or leaning against a wall, an IK handle will help keep it in place.

To add an IK handle:

1. Create a leg out of five joints (**Figure 10.28**).

2. Choose Skeleton > IK Handle Tool.

3. Click the hip joint.

4. Click the ankle joint.
   An IK handle is created.

continues on next page

5. Move the IK handle around
(**Figure 10.29**).

6. Select Twist in the Channel Box.

7. With the middle mouse button, drag
from left to right in the Perspective view.

The leg rotates around the IK chain
(**Figure 10.30**).

The Twist attribute only works on a Rotate
Plane (RP) type of IK handle. By default, a
Rotate Plane solver is created when you
make an IK handle. If you move the IK handle too high, however, the leg flips around,
and the knee points in the opposite direction (**Figure 10.31**). You can solve this
problem by adjusting the Pole Vector attributes, which are in the Channel Box for the
IK handle.

Another alternative is to create a Single
Chain solver. Although it doesn't permit the
Twist attribute like the Rotate Plane solver
does, the Single Chain solver doesn't have
the same flipping problem that Rotate Plane
has. When using a Single Chain solver, you
can rotate the limb by rotating the IK handle. However, the Rotate Plane solver is considered more predictable because it's not
affected by the rotation of the IK handle.

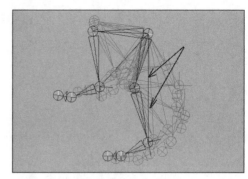

Figure 10.29 The IK handle is moved around, allowing
for easy placement of the foot.

Figure 10.30 The leg is rotated via the Twist attribute.

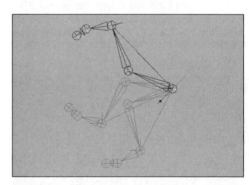

Figure 10.31 When a leg is lifted too high, it can flip
over if you're using an RP IK handle.

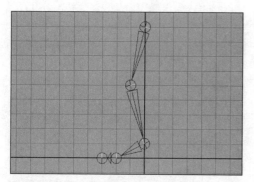

Figure 10.32 This is the basic skeleton for a leg.

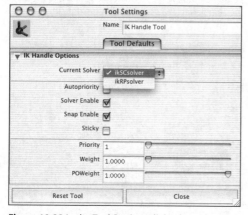

Figure 10.33 In the Tool Settings dialog box, choose ikSCsolver. This type of IK handle doesn't cause the flipping problem that an RP handle can cause.

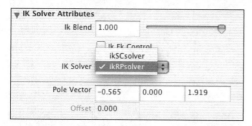

Figure 10.34 In the Attribute Editor for the IK handle, you can change the type of solver after it's created.

To create a Single Chain IK handle:

1. Create a leg out of five joints (**Figure 10.32**).

2. From the Skeleton menu, select the box next to IK Handle Tool.

   This opens the Tool Settings dialog box.

3. Select ikSCsolver from the Current Solver pop-up menu (**Figure 10.33**).

4. Click the hip joint.

5. Click the ankle joint.

   An IK handle is created with a Single Chain solver.

6. Rotate the IK handle.

   The limb rotates.

✔ Tips

- You can also change the type of solver after you've created the IK handle: Select the IK handle, and open the Attribute Editor. Click IK Solver Attributes, and then choose the solver type from the IK Solver pop-up menu (**Figure 10.34**).

- IK handles can also flip when a character turns 180 or 360 degrees. To avoid this problem, you can constrain the orientation of the Pole Vector of an IK handle to the joint above it. Constraints are covered later in this chapter.

ABOUT IK HANDLES AND SOLVERS

About Spline IK

Spline IK gives you a way of controlling many joints using a curve rather than by rotating them directly. This approach is especially useful when you have many joints in a continuous chain (such as in a spine or a tail), because you can move the skeleton quickly into the shape you desire without rotating each individual joint (**Figure 10.35**).

To create a Spline IK:

1. Create a spine skeleton, starting from the bottom and working your way up (**Figure 10.36**).

2. Choose Skeleton > IK_Spline Handle Tool.

3. Click the top joint of the skeleton.

4. Click the second joint from the bottom of the skeleton.

   Two things are created: the Spline IK handle and a curve. By default, the curve is automatically parented to the joints.

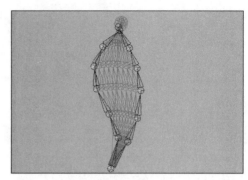

Figure 10.35 By creating an IK spline on these joints, you can animate a spine skeleton by moving just one point. Keyframing the rotation of each joint to achieve the same effect would be much more difficult.

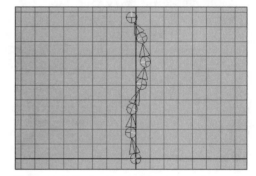

Figure 10.36 The human spine has a natural curve. When you're creating a spine for a character, it's helpful to match the shape of the character's back.

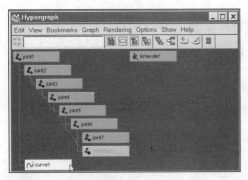

Figure 10.37 It's easier to select the curve in the Hypergraph because the icon can be isolated.

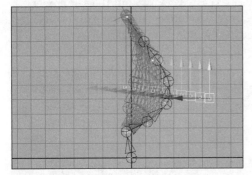

Figure 10.38 When the CV is moved, the spine bends to form the shape of the control curve.

5. From the Hypergraph or Outliner, select the curve you just created (**Figure 10.37**).

6. In the Pick mask, select component mode. You can now see the CVs of the curve.

7. Select and move a CV (**Figure 10.38**). The joints rotate in response and stick to the shape of the control curve.

✔ Tips

■ In general, you shouldn't use the root joint of the skeleton as part of your Spline IK chain. If you do, when you move the CVs, the whole skeleton will rotate. To avoid this, choose the joint that's one above the root joint of the skeleton as the base of your Spline IK.

■ Because CVs don't have their own node, they don't leave keyframes in the timeline. To see the keys controlling your spline, create a cluster for each CV, and animate the cluster. See Chapter 12 ("Animation") and Chapter 13 ("Deformers") for more information on keyframes and clusters.

Understanding the Hypergraph and Skeletons

When you're creating characters, the Hypergraph plays an important role in hierarchy order and selection. It's the best tool Maya offers to help you understand the way hierarchies are formed as well as how Maya's various elements relate to one another.

The Hypergraph provides two layout options: Freeform and Automatic (the default). If you choose the Automatic option, Maya lays out the Hypergraph for you, with the root node at the top of the hierarchy and each child indented below its parent with a line connecting child and parent. In addition, nodes are locked in place so that the hierarchies remain visually consistent and organized.

In contrast, if you select Freeform from the Options > Layout menu, you can move the nodes around and organize them to your liking. In addition, you can import an image of your character into the background of the Hypergraph so that you can align its joints to their proper positions on top of the image, making it much easier to select individual joints. In a simple hierarchy, this may not be necessary; but when you have hundreds of joints and surfaces, selection can become cumbersome without this aid.

The Hypergraph displays each of your joints with a blue joint icon [image]. When a single joint is selected in the view pane, all of its children are highlighted to indicate their relationship to the selected joint. As children of the joint, they are affected if the selected joint is rotated. Be aware that although the children are highlighted in the view pane, they haven't been *individually* selected.

Select a joint, and open the Hypergraph. The joint you clicked is selected (yellow), but the joints underneath it (its children) aren't. Because the parent is selected, the children will follow. If, in the Hypergraph, you [Shift]-select the children and then rotate the joints, each joint will rotate. Although you'll rarely select joints in this fashion, it's important to understand what is and isn't selected in a hierarchy.

You can move joints from one hierarchy to another or disconnect them from a hierarchy—all from within the Hypergraph. You use the middle mouse button to move joints in and out of hierarchies. To move a joint (and its children) into another hierarchy, drag the joint (using the middle mouse button) onto the node you want to serve as its parent. Once you do this, the selected node (and its children) is connected to the new hierarchy.

To remove a joint (and its children) from a hierarchy, select its node with the middle mouse button, and drag it away from the hierarchy (releasing the mouse when the node has been moved away from the hierarchy). This technique also works well for removing objects from a group within the Hypergraph.

About Constraints

Constraints in Maya direct or limit the motion of objects by connecting their attributes. You can constrain objects together so that they behave in similar ways. For instance, you can constrain the hour hand of a clock to rotate slightly whenever the minute hand moves, or you can constrain many pistons to move up and down when the first one is moved.

Constraints can also be used to ensure a certain behavior from an object—having eyes always point at a target or a ship always point up from the ocean, for example.

Constraints are very useful when you need to connect only certain attributes. For instance, objects can be connected in translation but rotate differently. Additionally, you can turn the constraints on and off (or partially off) as you need to, even in the middle of animation. Neither of these capabilities is available through parenting.

Constraint types

Maya offers the following constraint types:

◆ **Point**—A point constraint connects the translate values of one object to another.

◆ **Orient**—An orient constraint connects the rotate values of one object to another.

◆ **Scale**—A scale constraint connects the scale values of one object to another.

◆ **Aim**—An aim constraint aims one object at another object. This type of constraint can be useful for controlling where a character is looking, for example.

◆ **Parent**—The parent constraint works similar to the parent function in Maya but lets you offset the child object from the parent. You can also turn the constraint on and off and choose which attributes are being affected, which you can't do with the parent function.

◆ **Geometry**—A geometry constraint constrains the position of one object to the surface of another object. The pivot point of the constrained object determines where the constrained object sits on the surface.

◆ **Normal**—A normal constraint constrains an object's orientation values so that they align with the normals of another surface. When used in conjunction with a geometry constraint, the normal constraint is very useful for moving characters or vehicles over bumpy surfaces.

◆ **Tangent**—A tangent constraint constrains an object's orientation in the direction of a curve. If the constrained object is attached to a path, a tangent constraint ensures that the object always points in the direction of the path curve.

◆ **Pole Vector**—A pole vector constraint allows you to use an object to control the pole vector value of an IK Rotate Plane handle.

Creating constraints

Most constraints are created in the same manner: You select the object that will control the constraint and then the object you wish to be constrained. Options such as offsets and weight give you flexibility.

To create a point constraint:

1. Create a poly sphere and cube.

2. Translate the cube a few units away from the sphere (**Figure 10.39**).

3. Select the sphere, and Shift-select the cube.

4. Choose Constraint > Point.

   The cube jumps so that its center point is now at the same location as the sphere's center point (**Figure 10.40**). This is a good way to ensure that your objects are positioned at the exact same location.

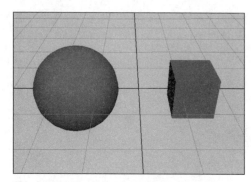

Figure 10.39 Constraints let you control one object with another, even if they're in different hierarchies.

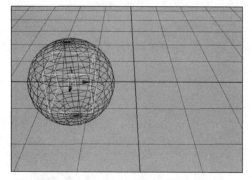

Figure 10.40 When Maintain Offset is deselected, a point constraint causes one object to jump to the exact location of another.

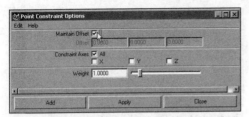

Figure 10.41 Maintain Offset applies the constraint relative to the object's current position, not its absolute position.

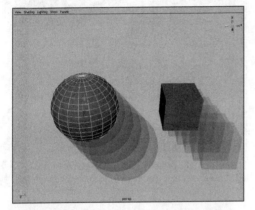

Figure 10.42 When the sphere is moved, the cube moves as well. Because the cube's location is now defined by the sphere, it can't be moved alone.

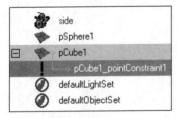

Figure 10.43 You can find a constraint node under the object that is being constrained or by graphing connections in the Hypergraph.

5. Undo once, so that the objects are separated again.

6. Select the sphere, and (Shift)-select the cube.

7. From the Constraint menu, select the box next to Point.

   The Point Constraint Options dialog box opens.

8. Select Maintain Offset (**Figure 10.41**).

   This option ensures that the initial position of the cube remains the same.

9. Click Apply.

   The cube's wireframe becomes pink when the sphere is selected. This means the sphere is influencing the cube in some way.

10. Select the sphere, and translate it in any direction using the Move tool.

    The cube translates exactly the same way automatically (**Figure 10.42**).

✔ Tips

- Try adding an orient constraint using the same method as described in the preceding task. Then, when you rotate the sphere, the cube will rotate in the same manner.

- The object that gets constrained is determined by which object is selected first. If you want the cube to control the sphere, you select the cube first and (Shift)-select the sphere before creating the constraint.

- Constraints show up in the Outliner and Hypergraph underneath the object they're applied to (**Figure 10.43**). You can select this node and adjust the constraint parameters or delete it to remove the constraint.

The Connection Editor

Similar to constraints, the Connection Editor is another way to link attributes together. It sets up direct relationships between any two attributes, and you can use the translation values of one object to drive the translation values of another. Although connections can form a broader variety of relationships than constraints, they can't be turned on and off as constraints can.

Figure 10.44 The Connection Editor links left-side attributes that control right-side attributes.

The Connection Editor also supports linking of non-similar attributes. Translation values can be linked to rotations, scale, IK Twist, or any other attribute. This lets you set up powerful control systems for your models (see also "Basic Rigging," later in this chapter).

To link two attributes with the Connection Editor:

1. Create a poly sphere and cube.

2. Choose Window > General Editors > Connection Editor.

   The empty Connection Editor window appears (**Figure 10.44**).

3. Select the sphere, and then click Reload Left.

   This loads the sphere's attributes into the Connection Editor. The output, or left side of the editor, controls the connection.

4. Select the cube, and then click Reload Right.

   The cube's attributes are loaded into the Connection Editor (**Figure 10.45**). The input, or right side, is controlled (much like a child object).

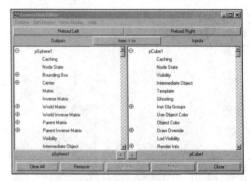

Figure 10.45 Both sides are loaded. Many more attributes are displayed here than in the Channel Box.

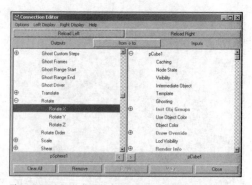

Figure 10.46 Click an attribute on the left side. Connections are always made left to right.

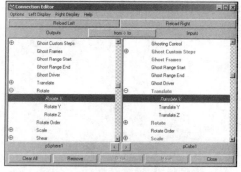

Figure 10.47 Attributes in italics are currently connected to something. In this case, they are both connected and selected.

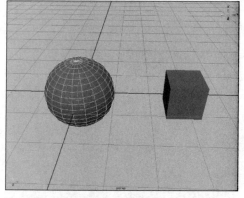

Figure 10.48 With the Connection Editor, you can control any attribute with almost any other attribute.

5. Scroll down the left side until you find Rotation. Expand it by clicking the plus sign, and then click Rotate X.

The text becomes highlighted in purple, which indicates that you may now connect this attribute to an attribute on the right side (**Figure 10.46**).

6. Scroll down the right side until you find Translation. Expand this attribute, and then click Translate X.

The attributes become italicized, indicating that they are connected (**Figure 10.47**).

7. Select the sphere in your Perspective view, and rotate it three degrees along the *x* axis.

The cube moves three units along its *x* axis (**Figure 10.48**).

✔ Tips

■ To remove a connection, select the attribute on the left. Any attributes it's connected to are automatically selected on the right. Then, click the attributes on the right to remove any unwanted connections.

■ You can also connect groups of attributes. To do so, connect any expandable attributes as you would single attributes. Both sides must have the same number of attributes, and unavailable connections are grayed out.

■ You can amplify or reduce the effect of a connection by inserting a multiply node in the Hypergraph. This technique is useful when you're linking attributes that operate on different orders of magnitude, such as rotation to translation. (See Chapter 14, "Shaders, Materials, and Mapping," for more on how to use the Hypergraph.)

Basic Rigging

Models alone can be difficult to pose. They often have too many parts to position properly (such as a tank), or too few (such as a character made from one poly mesh). To help with this issue, animators often build a control structure with which to pose their model. This control structure is referred to as a *rig,*

A rig is usually constructed from joints, curves, and the model itself. Constraints, connections, and parenting are all used to control the behavior of the rig. In a typical rig, geometry is attached to joints, and the motion of those joints is limited through constraints and connections.

Additional elements are often brought into the rig, such as NURBS curves. These curves are then linked to the rest of the rig and used by the animator to pose the model. These curves are often referred to as *controls.* Using controls, you simplify the number of objects you must move to pose the character. Also, since you are not manipulating the joints directly, you can hide the skeleton of the character to avoid accidentally selecting it.

One common use of a rig is to automate behavior that you don't wish to animate, such as the movement of machine parts. You can use constraints and connections to ensure accurate driven motion, such as on the wheels of a locomotive.

To rig a drive shaft:

1. From the Front view, create two NURBS or poly wheels, and rotate them so they stand on edge (**Figure 10.49**).

2. Select the Joint tool, and place joints at the top of the right wheel, at the top of the left wheel, and to the left of both wheels.

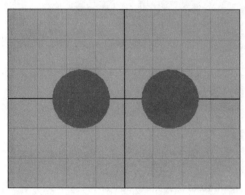

Figure 10.49 Create two locomotive wheels. Old locomotives are driven by a driveshaft, which is connected to a piston that goes in, out, and around as the wheels rotate.

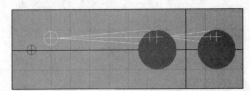

Figure 10.50 Place the joints near the top of each wheel, at the same height. The last joint should rest on the axis a distance away.

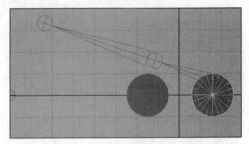

Figure 10.51 The parent constraint ensures that the first bone in the chain moves with the first wheel. The wheel is shown here rotated away temporarily to illustrate the behavior.

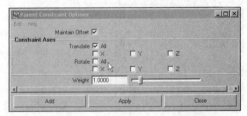

Figure 10.52 An aim constraint drives rotation channels and would conflict with a parent constraint by default. Removing the rotation channels from the parent constraint allows them to be controlled by the aim constraint without conflicting.

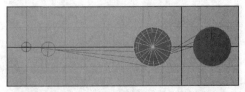

Figure 10.53 The left-hand wheel is rotated slightly here. The aim constraint only adjusts rotation; so, the driveshaft bone maintains its length while it always aims toward joint4, where the piston would lie.

3. Select the Joint tool again, and place a single joint on the axis underneath joint3 (**Figure 10.50**).

4. Select the right-hand wheel, Shift-select joint1, and choose the box next to Constrain > Parent.

   The Parent Constraint Options dialog box opens.

5. Make sure that Maintain Offset, Translate All, and Rotate All are selected, and click Apply.

   The joint and hierarchy now rotate with the wheel (**Figure 10.51**).

6. Select the left-hand wheel, and Shift-select joint2. In the Parent Constraint Options dialog box, deselect Rotate All, and then click Add (**Figure 10.52**).

7. Select joint4, Shift-select joint2, and choose Constrain > Aim.

   Now, when the left wheel rotates, the drive shaft points at a single goal, whereas joint2 maintains its translation relative to the wheel (**Figure 10.53**).

8. Create a NURBS circle for use as a control curve, and position it over the right wheel.

   It's usually a good idea to place your control curves in logical places, such as foot controls on the bottom of feet, hip controls around the hips, and so on.

continues on next page

BASIC RIGGING

9. Select the circle, Shift-select the right wheel, and choose Constrain > Orient.

10. Repeat step 9 for the left wheel.

This binds the orientation of the wheels to that of the circle. Now, when you rotate the circle, the whole drive apparatus moves appropriately (**Figure 10.54**).

✔ Tip

■ Because they have the same rotation values, you could connect the wheels' rotation axis to the control curve instead of constraining them. Choose whatever method works best for you in any given situation.

Character skeletons can become very complex, consisting of hundreds of bones. For instance, the spine of a character may include several bones to ensure a smooth bend—but rotating each bone individually would be time-consuming. Making a spine rig that rotates all the bones at once can save you a lot of time.

To rig an FK spine:

1. Press and hold x to snap the grid, and create six evenly spaced joints pointing up along the *y* axis (**Figure 10.55**).

2. Create a NURBS circle, and scale uniformly to 4 units.

Rename this circle *Body Control*.

3. Create another NURBS circle, rotate it 180 degrees on the *y* axis, and scale it uniformly to 2 units.

Rename this circle *Spine Control*.

4. Select Spine Control, Shift-select Body Control, and press p to parent them together (**Figure 10.56**).

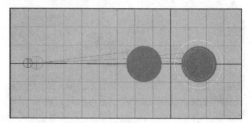

Figure 10.54 Rotating the control rotates the wheels and moves the two shafts all at once.

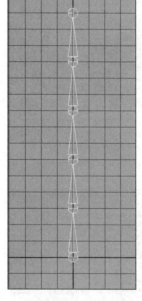

Figure 10.55 Spines should be constructed from the hips up, because the motion of the spine is driven more often from the hips than from the shoulders.

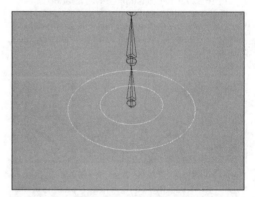

Figure 10.56 The controls should be parented together to ensure the Spine Control circle stays at the same location and isn't left behind when the body moves.

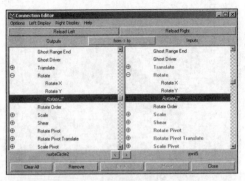

Figure 10.57 Link the Z rotations together.

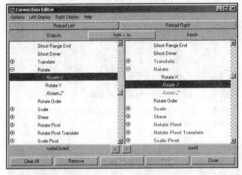

Figure 10.58 The local axes of rotation are different for the circle and the bones, so to keep things intuitive, the channels are cross-linked.

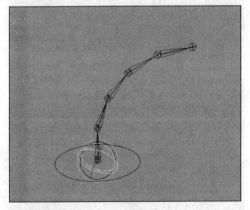

Figure 10.59 With a spine control, only one curve has to be moved to get a smooth rotation from all five joints.

5. Choose Window > General Editors > Connection Editor.

   The Connection Editor opens.

6. Select the Spine Control circle, and click Reload Left. Then, select joint5 and click Reload Right.

7. Select Rotate Z on the left side and Rotate Z on the right side to link the two (**Figure 10.57**).

8. On the left side, select Rotate X, and link it to Rotate Y on the right side (**Figure 10.58**).

9. Repeat step 8 for joint2, joint3, and joint4.

   You only need to reload the right side each time, because the Output side is always the Spine Control circle.

10. Select Spine Control, and rotate it on the *x* or *z* axis.

    The whole spine bends smoothly (**Figure 10.59**).

11. Select Body Control, (Shift)-select joint1, and choose Constrain > Parent.

    Be sure the default options are selected.

    Now you have a control to move the whole spine and hips of a character, and a control to bend the spine. Notice that Spine Control doesn't bend the hips (joint1) because the rotation of Body Control adjusts them instead.

✔ Tip

■ It's a good idea to perform a Freeze Transformations operation on any control before you start making constraints on or connections to it. This way, you can easily return the control to its starting location.

BASIC RIGGING

269

Legs can be very complicated to rig. The motion of the leg can pivot on the ball of the foot or the heel, and it's important to have control over the placement of the knee. Because the leg is often pinned to the ground, most legs are rigged using IK by default. Doing so allows the foot to be placed easily when animating and lets the rest of the body move without disturbing the feet.

To rig an IK leg:

1. Start with the spine rig from the previous task.

2. Select the Joint tool, click the first joint of the spine (joint1), and construct a five-joint leg (**Figure 10.60**).

3. Select the IK Handle tool, and add a rotate plane IK handle from the hip to the ankle (**Figure 10.61**).

4. Create a NURBS circle, and position it directly under the foot.

   Rename this circle *Foot Control*.

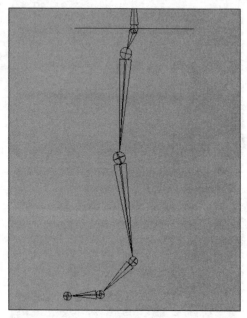

Figure 10.60 Ensure the leg is placed properly in the Front view as well.

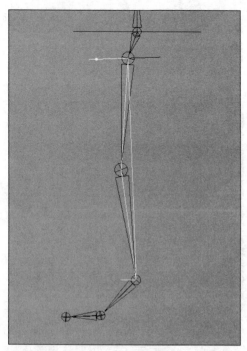

Figure 10.61 Because feet often rest on the ground, it's usually best to have legs rigged as IK.

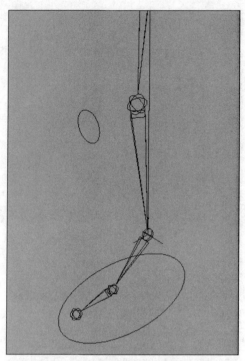

Figure 10.62 Foot Control should be at the bottom of the foot, and Knee Pointer goes directly in front of the knee.

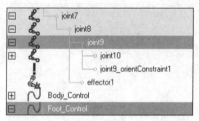

Figure 10.63 The orient constraint ensures the foot stays still unless the control curve is also rotated.

5. Create a second circle, and position it in front of the knee (**Figure 10.62**). Rename this circle *Knee Pointer*.

6. Select Knee Pointer, [Shift]-select Foot Control, and press [p] to parent the pointer to the control.

7. Select the pointer and control, and choose Modify > "Freeze transformations".

   This option ensures the controls can easily be returned to their starting locations after animation by setting all transformation values back to zero.

8. Select Foot Control, [Shift]-select the IK handle, and choose Constrain > Parent.

   or

   Select them in the reverse order, and press [p] to parent them.

   This ensures the ankle translates with the foot control.

9. Select Foot Control, [Shift]-select the ankle bone, and choose Constrain > Orient (**Figure 10.63**).

continues on next page

10. Move the foot control around.

The leg follows the control, but there is no control over the placement of the knee.

11. Select Knee Pointer, [Shift]-select the IK handle, and choose Constrain > Pole Vector (**Figure 10.64**).

This option lets you aim the knee by moving the pointer. Because Knee Pointer is parented to the foot control, by default the knee rotates with the foot as well (**Figure 10.65**).

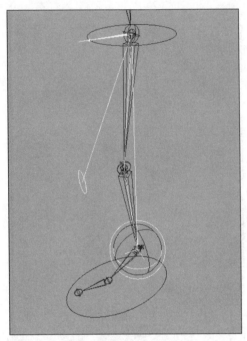

Figure 10.64 Use Knee Pointer to avoid the common IK problem of directing where the solver places the middle joints.

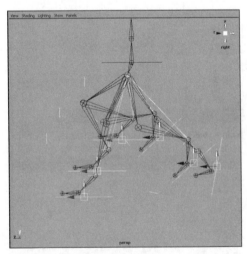

Figure 10.65 In conjunction with the spine, the foot rig now allows independent placement of the hips, knee, ankle, and toe, as well as quick placement of the foot and leg wherever needed.

Effectors

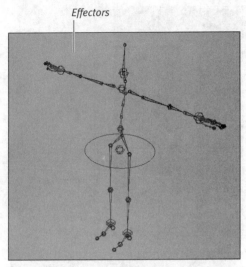

Figure 10.66 The FBIK skeleton and its accompanying effectors. The circles and boxes around the joints can be used to pin parts of the model in place while posing.

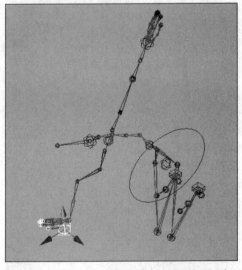

Figure 10.67 FBIK can be a powerful animation tool, giving you quick and precise control over your character.

About Full Body IK

Full Body IK, a new feature in Maya 7.0, is a character rig designed for bipeds and quadrupeds. Full Body IK (FBIK) utilizes pinnable IK handles and a fully interconnected skeleton (**Figure 10.66**) that makes posing your character quick and easy. Additionally, FBIK automatically adds the complicated set of constraints and connections to your skeleton, saving you from doing it yourself.

Whereas a normal IK solver only affects a portion of the body, the IK rig of FBIK is entirely interconnected. If you over-extend an IK control, the body adjusts itself to ensure an accurate pose. If you want your character to pick something up, you can drag the hand down to the ground, and the skeleton will bend at the waist and knees to ensure the hand reaches (**Figure 10.67**).

Maya provides a built-in FBIK skeleton that you can use to explore the way FBIK works.

To import an example FBIK rig:

1. Choose Skeleton > Full Body IK > Get FBIK example.

   The Visor opens with two models displayed (**Figure 10.68**).

2. With the middle mouse button, drag the example you want into your view.

   Now you have an example of FBIK you can bind geometry to or use to explore FBIK options.

Setting up for FBIK

To use FBIK, you must create a properly named skeleton. FBIK uses the names of your joints to determine what features to add to the rig and where to add them.

To create a skeleton for your character, you need to ensure it has a proper hierarchy as well as joints in all the places you need it to bend.

To create a skeleton for your character:

1. Start with the character model you wish to rig (**Figure 10.69**).

   Characters should have their arms out flat, with palms facing straight down.

2. From the Side view, and starting at the hips of the character, insert a four-bone spine (**Figure 10.70**).

3. From the Front view, build a three-bone arm with joints at the shoulder, elbow, wrist and hand (**Figure 10.71**).

   Make sure the bones line up from the Top view as well.

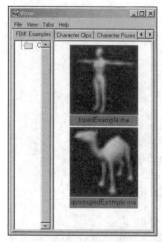

Figure 10.68 The Visor contains a prerigged biped and quadruped skeleton.

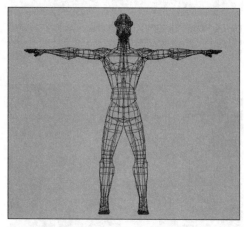

Figure 10.69 If you intend to use FBIK, you should model your character in the appropriate T pose.

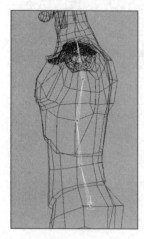

Figure 10.70 It generally helps to have the spine follow the curve of the back. Any number of bones may be used.

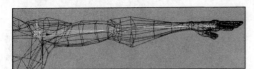

Figure 10.71 The arms should line up from both views, and the bones should face straight away from the body.

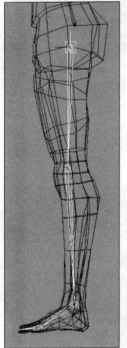

Figure 10.72 Keep the legs straight, and try not to have the knee bend backward; otherwise, the default interpolation may be reversed (and painful looking).

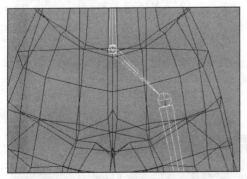

Figure 10.73 When parented correctly, a new bone should appear to connect the two joints.

4. From the Side view, build a four-bone leg with joints at the hip, knee, ankle and toe (**Figure 10.72**).

   Make sure the bones line up from the Front view as well.

5. Select the hip joint, Shift-select joint1, and then press p to parent the leg to the spine (**Figure 10.73**).

6. Select joint4, Shift-select the shoulder joint, and then press p to parent the arm to the spine.

7. Select the shoulder joint, and choose Skeleton > Mirror Joint.

   The arm is duplicated on the other side of the body.

8. Select the hip joint, and choose Skeleton > Mirror Joint.

9. Choose Skeleton > Joint Tool. From the Side view, click joint5, and then build a head and neck for your character (**Figure 10.74**).

   Now you have a skeleton with a suitable hierarchy for FBIK or another type of rig.

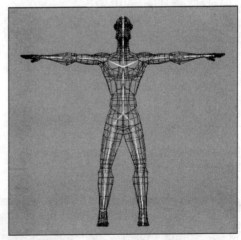

Figure 10.74 Everything is mirrored and ready to go. This skeleton contains the bare minimum for an FBIK setup.

ABOUT FULL BODY IK

275

To label your skeleton:

1. Start with the skeleton you prepared in the previous task.

2. Select joint1, and choose Skeleton > Joint Labelling > FBIK Labels > Label Root.

   The joint is now labeled, but you see no change.

3. Choose Skeleton > Joint Labelling > Show All Labels.

   The word *Root* becomes visible next to the joint you labeled in the previous step (**Figure 10.75**).

4. One at a time, select the rest of the joints of the spine, and choose Skeleton > Joint Labelling > FBIK Labels > Label Spine (**Figure 10.76**).

5. Select the shoulder joint, and choose Skeleton > Joint Labelling > FBIK Labels > Label Arm.

   The joints are automatically labeled down the arm.

6. With the shoulder still selected, choose Skeleton > Joint Labelling > FBIK Labels > Label Left (**Figure 10.77**).

   Now the arm is completely labeled, including designations for left and right. Characters are always labeled relative to the character, not how the character is oriented in relation to the user.

7. Select the hip joint, label it *Leg*, and then label it *Left*.

8. Repeat steps 5–7 on the right side of the body, labeling the arm and leg *Right*.

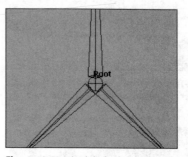

Figure 10.75 Joint labels clearly show the role of each joint as part of the heads up display.

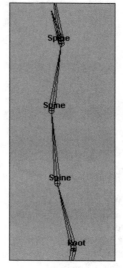

Figure 10.76 Label each spine bone individually, stopping at the neck.

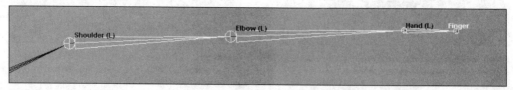

Figure 10.77 Labeling the arm saves you the trouble of naming each bone within the arm.

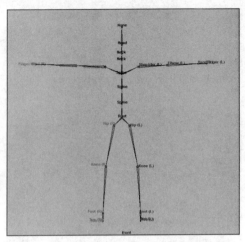

Figure 10.78 Once everything is labeled, the rig can be applied. FBIK uses the joint names or labels to build its rig, so double-check for accuracy.

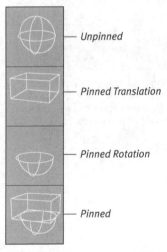

— Unpinned

— Pinned Translation

— Pinned Rotation

— Pinned

Figure 10.79 The four different displays for effectors.

9. Select the neck joint or joints, and label them *Neck*.

10. Select the head joint, and label it *Head*. Now your model is fully labeled and ready to rig (**Figure 10.78**).

✔ Tip

- To tidy up your joint names, you can choose Skeleton > Joint Labelling > "Rename joints from labels". Doing so gives all your joints names equal to their labels, making it easier to keep track of them.

Using FBIK

Once your character is properly prepared, the placement of the rig is entirely automated. Maya creates controls called *effectors*, which you can position like IK handles to move the character around or pin in space to pose the rest of the character.

Effectors can have four states (**Figure 10.79**):

- **Unpinned**—Displayed as a sphere, an unpinned effector can be influenced by any other adjustment to the body.

- **Translation**—(Alt + w). Displayed as a cube, an effector pinned on translation attempts to maintain its position in space, although the joint may still rotate freely. Pinning the translation is useful for a character who is tied at the wrists or who is losing his grip on an object.

- **Rotation**—(Alt + e). Displayed as a half-circle, pinned rotation prevents the joint from rotating relative to its parent. This is useful for a character that who is running while holding something up.

- **Fully Pinned**—Displayed as a box with a half-circle under it, a fully pinned control doesn't move at all. This function is effective if you have a character whose hands are gripping or resting on an immovable object.

To add FBIK to a skeleton:

1. Start with the skeleton from the previous task. Select the root joint.

2. Select the option box next to Skeleton > Full Body IK > Add Full Body IK.

3. Ensure that By Label and Biped are selected, and click Apply (**Figure 10.80**).

   Maya adds the constraints and effectors to your skeleton automatically. Your character is now rigged (**Figure 10.81**)!

Figure 10.80 Set the options you wish to use.

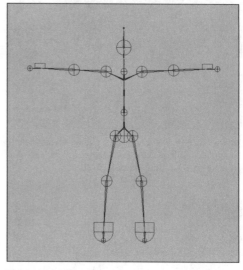

Figure 10.81 The effectors appear on your model in the appropriate spots. Take a moment to double-check that all the effectors you wanted were added, and that they are in the correct places.

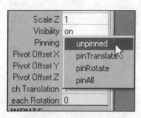

Figure 10.82 Setting the hand to unpinned frees it to move with the rest of the body.

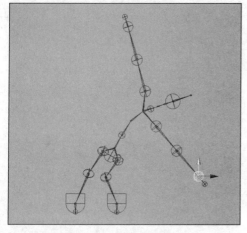

Figure 10.83 The body adjusts itself to reach the hand properly.

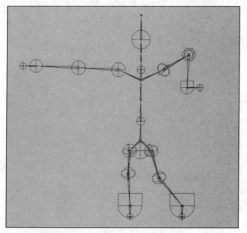

Figure 10.84 Pinning both translation and rotation is ideal for posing characters who are gripping, climbing, or walking.

4. Select a hand effector, and set Pinning to unpinned in the Channel Box (**Figure 10.82**).

5. Select the other hand, and translate it around in the view.

The rest of the body follows the lead of the hand (**Figure 10.83**).

6. Select a hand, and press [Alt]+[e] and [Alt]+[w] to pin it in translation and rotation.

7. Drag the body around using the hips effector.

The pinned hand remains in place, as if it's holding on to something (**Figure 10.84**).

PARENTING AND BINDING TO A SKELETON

11

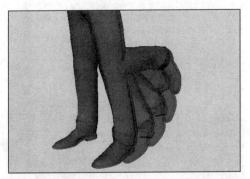

Figure 11.1 For the leg to bend at the knee, it needs to be bound to a skeleton.

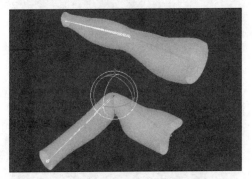

Figure 11.2 When the elbow joint is rotated, only the forearm rotates with it.

Once you've created a skeleton, you need to either *parent* or *bind* your surfaces to the joints in order for them to move with the skeleton. Anything that doesn't need to bend, like a hat or glasses, can be parented to the joints. Anything that does need to bend, like an arm, leg, or torso, must be bound to the skeleton (**Figure 11.1**). Surfaces that are bound are referred to as *skins*.

Parenting to joints works the same way as parenting to anything else: When you move or rotate the joint, its child object(s) move or rotate as well. Binding, however, is a bit different. When a surface is bound to a skeleton, you can determine which portion of that surface moves with which joint. For example, in an arm, only the forearm should move when the elbow joint is rotated; the shoulder and biceps should remain in place (**Figure 11.2**).

There are two kinds of binding: *rigid bind* and *smooth bind*. Rigid bind assigns each of the object's points to one joint, although you can use *flexors* to create smooth deformations. Smooth bind allows each point to be influenced by any number of joints. A rigid bind can be easier to set up, but a smooth bind works better for areas that are affected by more than two joints, like a spine or a tail.

Parenting to a Skeleton

The geometry of a character made out of rigid, nonflexible parts, such as a robot, can be parented to a skeleton rather than bound. You can also use parenting for specific parts of a character, like eyes or teeth, even if the character's primary surface needs to be bound to the skeleton.

To parent surfaces to joints:

1. Use the Create > NURBS Primitives menu to create three spheres and two cylinders, and then scale and position them to represent an arm (**Figure 11.3**).

2. Select the Joint tool from the Skeleton menu, and create three joints to fit the arm (**Figure 11.4**).

3. Select a surface.

4. Shift-select the joint to which the surface should be parented.

5. Press p.

   Now, when you select and rotate that joint, the surface rotates with it.

6. Repeat steps 3–5 for the other surfaces. When any joint is rotated, the parented surface moves with it (**Figure 11.5**).

✔ Tip

■ Because parented geometry takes less time for Maya to calculate than bound geometry, complex characters often have segmented *stand-in* or *proxy* geometry that's parented to the skeleton. You can use the proxy for faster interaction while you're animating and hide the character's actual geometry until you're ready to render.

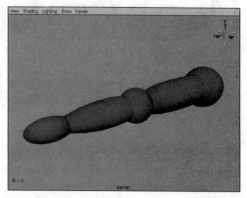

Figure 11.3 These five NURBS primitives form a simple arm. Because the arm is segmented, the individual objects don't need to bend, so they can be parented to a skeleton instead of being bound.

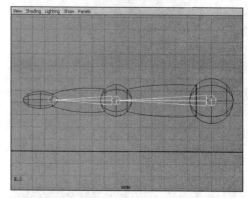

Figure 11.4 Adding three joints to the arm forms two bones.

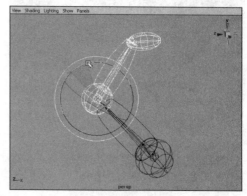

Figure 11.5 Rotating any joint rotates its child object(s), allowing you to animate the arm.

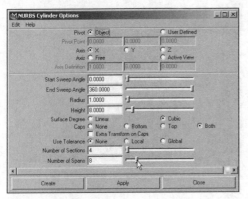

Figure 11.6 A cylinder of eight spans has enough CVs to represent a simple arm.

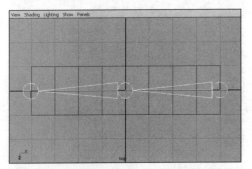

Figure 11.7 The placement of the joints determines where the cylinder will bend.

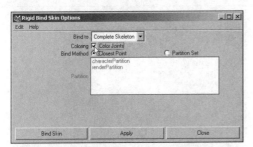

Figure 11.8 The Color Joints option can be useful for determining the joint to which specific points are assigned by the rigid bind.

Using Rigid Bind

Using rigid bind is like parenting the component points of a surface to different joints rather than parenting the entire surface to a single joint. Unlike when you parent objects to joints, Maya automatically calculates which points should be assigned to which bones. Once bound, the surface is referred to as a *rigid skin*, and each set of points that has been assigned to a specific bone is called a *skin group*.

To bind skin using rigid bind:

1. Select the box next to Cylinder in the Create > NURBS Primitives menu.

   The NURBS Cylinder Options window is displayed.

2. In the NURBS Cylinder Options window, change the Axis value to X and the Height and Number of Spans values to 8 (**Figure 11.6**).

   Click the Create button to finalize the cylinder, which will represent a simple arm in this task.

3. Choose Skeleton > Joint Tool, and create three joints to fit the arm (**Figure 11.7**).

4. Select one of the joints, and then Shift-select the surface.

5. From the Skin > Bind Skin menu, select the box next to Rigid Bind.

   The Rigid Bind Skin Options dialog box opens.

6. Select the Color Joints check box (**Figure 11.8**).

   With this option selected, points are color-coded to match the joints they're assigned to, once the skin is bound.

7. Click the Bind Skin button.

continues on next page

8. Select the middle joint, and rotate it. Half of the cylinder moves with the bone (**Figure 11.9**).

✔ Tips

■ Any kind of surface can be bound to a skeleton. You can follow the steps in this task to bind polygons or subdivs as well as NURBS.

■ You can bind a whole character with multiple surfaces at once. To do this, select the root joint of the skeleton and all of the surfaces involved, and then bind the skin.

■ By default, rigid bind uses the entire skeleton. If you'd like to use a specific portion of the skeleton, select the root joint of that portion and choose Selected Joints from the Bind To drop-down in the Rigid Bind Options dialog box.

Editing rigid skins

When you first use rigid bind, the resulting rigid skin often doesn't deform exactly the way you'd like (**Figure 11.10**). If you need to make changes to the positioning of the skeleton, you can detach the skin entirely, modify the joints, and then re-apply the rigid bind. If you don't detach the skin, any changes you make to the joints after binding will affect it, which isn't usually the desired effect (**Figure 11.11**).

Alternately, you can detach the skeleton while still preserving the skin groups that determine which points are assigned to which bones. This allows you to reposition the skeleton and then reattach it, without affecting the way its points are bound to it.

Once you have a skin that's closer to what you want, you can fine-tune it by adjusting which joints affect which points, and to what extent. The degree to which a joint

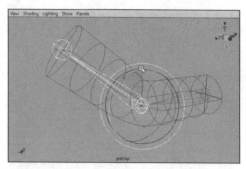

Figure 11.9 Half of the cylinder moves with the second bone when you rotate the middle joint.

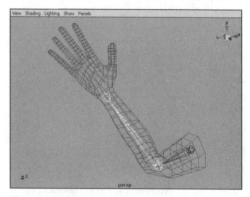

Figure 11.10 This elbow joint is incorrectly positioned, and it's also deforming the skin too sharply.

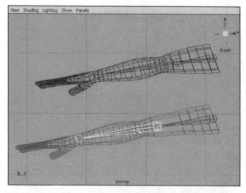

Figure 11.11 The elbow joint in the top arm is too far to the right. However, attempting to move this joint to the left will have undesirable results on the skin. You can avoid this by detaching the skin first.

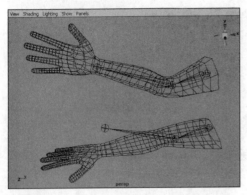

Figure 11.12 Detaching a skin from a repositioned skeleton will result in the skin returning to its original position, while the skeleton remains in place.

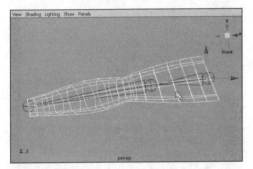

Figure 11.13 By detaching this geometry, we can reposition the misplaced elbow joint.

Figure 11.14. Choose Detach Skin to remove the influence of the bones from the selected surface.

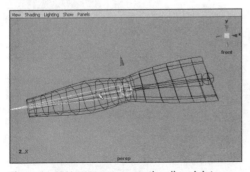

Figure 11.15 You can now move the elbow joint without affecting the surface.

affects a point is referred to as its *weight*, and can be any value up to 1.0. You can also create flexors to gain more precise control of the way the surface bends when specific joints are rotated.

One important technique when modifying rigid skins is setting the skeleton to the *bind pose*. This means that if you've moved or rotated any of the joints, they'll be put back where they were when you bound the skin to the skeleton. It's a good idea to do this before adding a flexor or detaching a skin, or you may get undesirable results (**Figure 11.12**).

To set a skeleton to its bind pose:

1. Using a skeleton with a rigid bound skin, move one or more of the joints. (You can create a skin by following the steps described in "To bind skin using rigid bind," earlier in this chapter.)

2. Select one of the joints.

3. From the Skin menu, select Go to Bind Pose.

   All of the skeleton's joints are reset to the position and rotation they were in when its skin was bound.

To detach a skin:

1. Select the skin geometry that you want to detach from its skeleton (**Figure 11.13**). (You can create a skin by following the steps described in "To bind skin using rigid bind," earlier in this chapter.)

2. From the Skin menu, choose Detach Skin (**Figure 11.14**).

   The geometry becomes detached from the skeleton. You can re-attach the geometry in the same that way you originally bound it.

3. Select a joint, and move it.

   The joint moves, but the surface remains in place (**Figure 11.15**).

To detach a skeleton and preserve skin groups:

1. Select the skeleton that you want to detach from its skin. (You can create a skin by following the steps described in "To bind skin using rigid bind," earlier in this chapter.)

2. From the Skin > Edit Rigid Skin > Preserve Skin Groups submenu, select Detach Skeleton (**Figure 11.16**).

   The skeleton becomes detached from the skin, but the skin groups are preserved.

To reattach a skeleton to its skin:

1. Follow the steps in "To detach a skeleton and preserve skin groups," above, and make any desired modifications to the skeleton or skin.

2. Select the detached skeleton.

3. From the Skin > Edit Rigid Skin > Preserve Skin Groups submenu, select Reattach Skeleton (**Figure 11.17**).

   The skeleton is reattached to the skin, using the same skin groups that it had before.

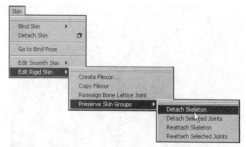

Figure 11.16 You can use this menu to temporarily detach a skeleton. Its point assignment and weighting will be maintained when you reattach it.

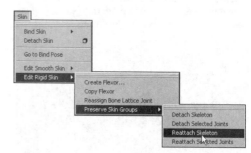

Figure 11.17 You can only reattach a skeleton if you previously used this menu to detach the skeleton. Skeletons detached using Detach Skin must be re-bound.

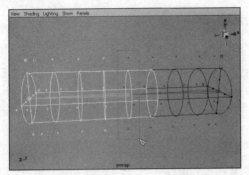

Figure 11.18 Be sure to hold down (Shift) as you click or click and drag to select points.

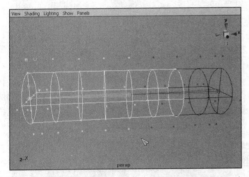

Figure 11.19 The points you've added are highlighted like the other points in the selected joint's skin group.

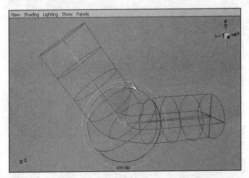

Figure 11.20 Because the middle row of points has been added to the middle joint, it rotates with that joint.

To assign rigid-bound points to a different joint:

1. Create a rigid skin by following the steps described in "To bind skin using rigid bind," earlier in this chapter.

2. Choose Deform > Edit Membership Tool.

   The cursor changes.

3. Click one of the joints.

   The points that are members of that joint are selected.

4. (Shift)-select the points you'd like to assign to the joint. You can click and drag a marquee to select multiple points at once (**Figure 11.18**).

   The points are added to the skin group of the selected joint (**Figure 11.19**).

5. Select and rotate the joint.

   The points that you added now rotate with the joint (**Figure 11.20**).

✔ Tips

- While using the Edit Membership tool, you can switch to adding points to a different bone by clicking on that bone.

- If you (Ctrl)/(Control)-select points while using the Edit Membership tool, they're removed from the joint's skin group. However, if they aren't assigned to another joint, the points are left behind when the character moves.

- The Edit Membership tool can be used for any deformer, such as a lattice or a blend shape.

USING RIGID BIND

To edit rigid skin weights:

1. Create a rigid skin by following the steps described in "To bind skin using rigid bind," earlier in this chapter.

2. In component mode, select the points whose weights you'd like to edit (**Figure 11.21**). You can switch to component mode by pressing F8 .

3. Choose Window > General Editors > Component Editor.

4. In the Component Editor, click the Rigid Skins tab.

5. Click the top numeric field, and drag down to highlight all the weights (**Figure 11.22**).

6. Enter the new value for the weights.

   All the weights for the selected points take on the new value. Rotate the joint to see what effect this has. For example, if you enter 0.5, the points now rotate half the distance of the joint (**Figure 11.23**).

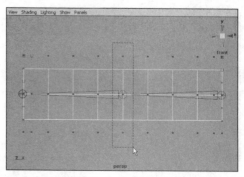

Figure 11.21 It's difficult to determine which points are which in the Component Editor, so you should select a group of points that you want to change to be the same value.

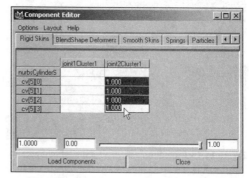

Figure 11.22 The Component Editor displays the bone weights of the selected points.

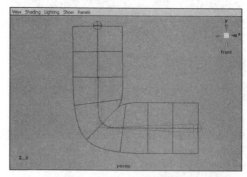

Figure 11.23 By setting the points around the joint to a weight of 0.5, you can create a smoother bend.

Using Rigid Bind

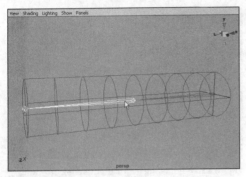

Figure 11.24 The joint to which you plan on adding a flexor should be in its bind pose. If not, choose Go to Bind Pose from the Skin menu after selecting it.

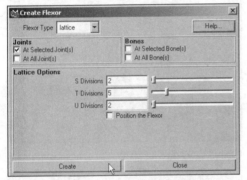

Figure 11.25 The default settings in the Create Flexor dialog box work well for most joints.

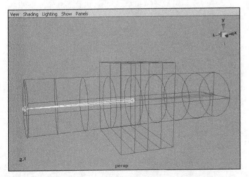

Figure 11.26 A *lattice* is a grid that deforms when its joint moves and influences the joint's skin group.

To create a flexor:

1. Create a rigid skin by following the steps described in "To bind skin using rigid bind," earlier in this chapter.

2. Select the middle joint (**Figure 11.24**).

3. Choose Skin > Edit Rigid Skin > Create Flexor.

   The Create Flexor dialog box appears (**Figure 11.25**).

4. Use this dialog box to change the flexor's type and adjust its settings; the defaults are fine for most circumstances.

   Click Create to finalize the flexor. A lattice is created around the joint (**Figure 11.26**). (For more information on lattices, see Chapter 13, "Deformers.")

5. Rotate the joint about 90 degrees.

   When the joint is rotated, the flexor reshapes the surface to create a smooth bend (**Figure 11.27**).

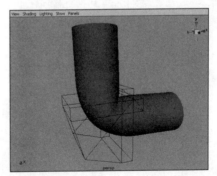

Figure 11.27 A lattice creates a smooth, controllable deformation at a joint.

To change a flexor's attributes:

1. Follow the steps in the previous task to create a flexor.

2. Select the lattice that appears when the flexor is created.

3. In the Channel Box under the Shapes heading, click Creasing.

4. With the middle mouse button, click and drag back and forth in the view to change the value in the Creasing field, which in turn affects the inner part of the bend (**Figure 11.28**).

5. In the Channel Box under the Shapes heading, click Rounding.

6. With the middle mouse button, click and drag back and forth in the view to change the value for Rounding, which affects the outer part of the bend (**Figure 11.29**).

✔ Tip

- You can select a flexor's LatticeGroup node in the Outliner to position and scale the lattice without affecting the geometry.

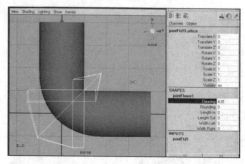

Figure 11.28 Adjusting a lattice's Creasing attribute makes the surface on the inside of the bend more or less creased.

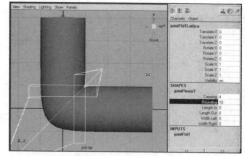

Figure 11.29 Adjusting a lattice's Rounding attribute makes the surface on the outside of the bend more or less rounded.

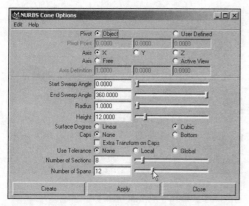

Figure 11.30 By changing some values in the NURBS Cone Options dialog box, you can quickly create a surface that represents a tail.

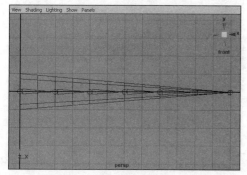

Figure 11.31 Adding seven joints results in six bones.

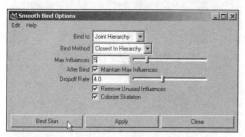

Figure 11.32 In this case, the default smooth bind options are fine.

Using Smooth Bind

Using smooth bind creates a skin in which each point is influenced by a number of joints. This allows the skin to deform smoothly with the skeleton. As with rigid bind, Maya automatically calculates which points should be influenced by which joints, based on their hierarchy and proximity.

To bind skin using smooth bind:

1. To create a cone to represent a tail, choose Create > NURBS Primitives and select the box next to Cone.

2. In the NURBS Cone Options dialog box, change the Axis value to X, and change the Height and Number of Spans values to 12 (**Figure 11.30**).

   Click the Create button to finalize the cone.

3. Create a skeleton of seven joints to fit the tail (**Figure 11.31**).

4. Select the surface, and then (Shift)-select the root joint.

5. Choose Skin > Bind Skin, and select the box next to Smooth Bind.

   The Smooth Bind Options dialog box appears (**Figure 11.32**).

6. If necessary, use the Smooth Bind Options dialog box to adjust the settings for the smooth bind.

   The Max Influences setting lets you choose how many joints can affect any given point, and the Dropoff Rate value controls how far a given joint's influence extends.

   continues on next page

7. Click Bind Skin to apply the smooth bind.

8. Rotate the joints to test the skin.

The surface moves with the joints and bends smoothly (**Figure 11.33**).

Editing smooth skins

When you use smooth bind to create a skin, Maya automatically calculates which points should be influenced by which bones and to what extent. The generated result is likely to work well in some areas but not so well in others (**Figure 11.34**). Fortunately, Maya provides several tools for you to edit a smooth skin.

The degree to which a particular point is influenced by a particular joint is referred to as the joint's *weight*. A weight of 1.0 means the point is influenced exclusively by that joint, whereas a weight of 0.0 means the joint has no influence. A point with a weight of 0.5 for two different bones is influenced equally by both (**Figure 11.35**). All the weights on a point must add up to 1.0, so if you change the weight of one bone, Maya automatically adjusts the other weight(s) for that point.

You can adjust weights numerically in the Component Editor, similar to the way you adjust the weights of a rigid skin. You can also *paint* weights on a skin with the Paint Weights tool. Painting gives you an intuitive way to modify weights. It also provides visual feedback on the strength of a particular bone's weight across the surface; the paint shade darkens progressively from white to black as the weight varies from 1.0 to 0.0.

If your model is symmetrical, as most characters are, you can *mirror* any skin weights that you modify from one side to the other. Doing so saves you the extra time of making identical changes to both sides.

As with a rigid skin, you can select a smooth skin and apply Go to Bind Pose or Detach

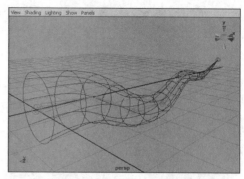

Figure 11.33 As its name suggests, smooth bind provides smooth deformations.

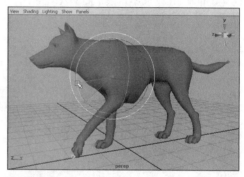

Figure 11.34 When the shoulder joint of this smooth-bound wolf is rotated, it moves part of the torso as well as the shoulder.

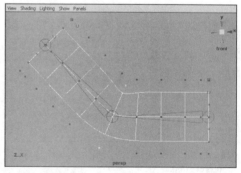

Figure 11.35 The highlighted points at the center of this cylinder have a weight of 0.5 for both the first and second joints, so the points are equally influenced by both joints.

USING SMOOTH BIND

Skin

Bind Skin
Detach Skin

Go to Bind Pose

Edit Smooth Skin
Edit Rigid Skin

Figure 11.36 The Detach Skin and Go to Bind Pose functions apply to both rigid and smooth skins.

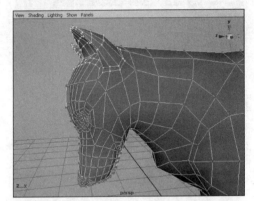

Figure 11.37 Because they're weighted to both the head and neck, the wolf's ears are left behind when the head joint is rotated. They should be weighted entirely to the head.

	head	left_back_hip	left_back_kne	left_back_kne	left_back_paw	
vtx[2543]	0.407	0.000	0.000	0.000	0.000	
vtx[2544]	0.443	0.000	0.000	0.000	0.000	
vtx[2545]	0.455	0.000	0.000	0.000	0.000	
vtx[2546]	0.454	0.000	0.000	0.000	0.000	
vtx[2547]	0.461	0.000	0.000	0.000	0.000	
vtx[2548]	0.450	0.000	0.000	0.000	0.000	
vtx[2549]	0.458	0.000	0.000	0.000	0.000	
vtx[2550]	0.452	0.000	0.000	0.000	0.000	
vtx[2551]	0.410	0.000	0.000	0.000	0.000	
vtx[2552]	0.448	0.000	0.000	0.000	0.000	

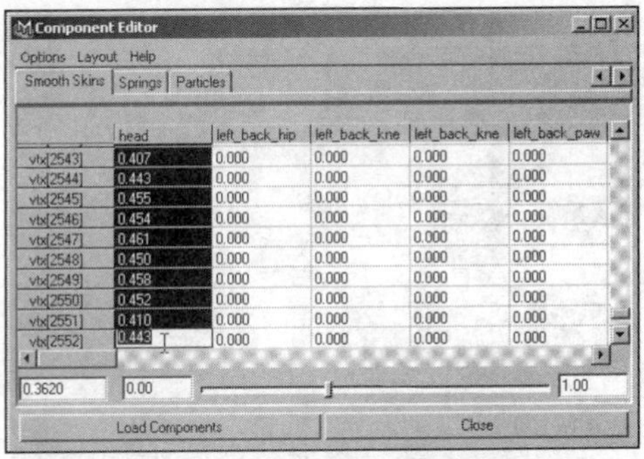

Figure 11.38 Here the weights for the head joint are highlighted. Entering 1.0 in the last field will change all of the weights to one. Maya will automatically reduce the other weights for these points to zero.

Skin from the Skin menu (**Figure 11.36**). Go to Bind Pose puts the skeleton back where it was when you first bound the skin, and Detach Skin removes the connections between the skeleton and the skin.

To edit smooth skin weights in the Component Editor:

1. Select the skin you want to modify. You can create a smooth skin by following the steps described in "To bind skin using smooth bind," earlier in this chapter.

2. In component mode, select the points whose weights you want to modify (**Figure 11.37**). You can switch to component mode by pressing F8 .

3. Choose Window > General Editors > Component Editor.

4. In the Component Editor, click the Smooth Skins tab.

5. Click the top field under the name of the joint whose weights you want to modify, and then drag down to highlight all the weights (**Figure 11.38**).

6. Enter the new value for the weights. All the weights for the selected points become the new value (**Figure 11.39**).

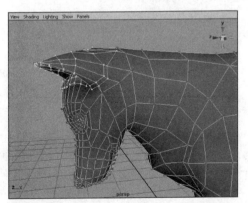

Figure 11.39 Now the ears are weighted entirely to the head joint, so they move with the rest of the head.

To paint skin weights on a smooth skin:

1. Select the skin you want to modify. You can create a smooth skin by following the steps described in "To bind skin using smooth bind," earlier in this chapter.

2. Choose Skin > Edit Smooth Skin, and select the box next to Paint Skin Weights.

   The Paint Skin Weights tool is activated, and its settings are displayed in the Tool Settings window (**Figure 11.40**).

3. If it isn't already selected, choose Smooth Shade All from your view's Shading menu.

   This setting lets you see the weights on your model (**Figure 11.41**).

4. In the tool settings dialog box, select the joint for which you want to paint weights, and, if necessary, choose a different Paint Operation and/or Value to paint with.

5. Adjust the brush size by holding down ⓑ and dragging from right to left with the middle mouse button.

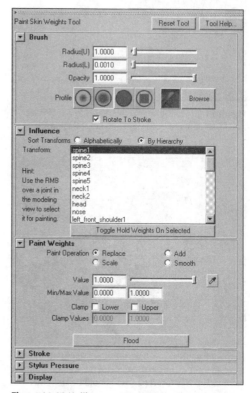

Figure 11.40 Unlike some Maya tools, the Paint Skin Weights tool's settings are vital to its use.

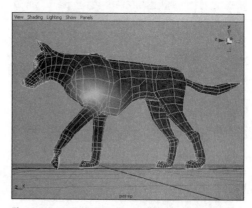

Figure 11.41 The lighter patch on the model's shoulder and part of the torso represents the weights of the left shoulder.

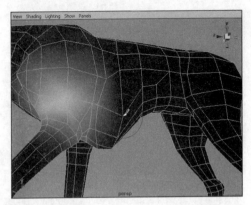

Figure 11.42 Here we have set the value to 0.0 and painted to remove the shoulder's effect on the torso. Because the torso is black, we know the weight is 0.0; but rather than move back into place, the torso geometry has moved slightly forward. This indicates that it's still partially weighted to an incorrect joint, most likely the leg.

6. Using your chosen settings, paint the area you wish to change.

   If you're painting weights for a joint that has been moved, the surface adjusts dynamically to reflect the changes (**Figure 11.42**).

7. To continue painting weights on other joints without accidentally affecting the weights of the selected joint, click Toggle Hold Weights On Selected (**Figure 11.43**).

8. Repeat steps 4–7 until the surface deforms the way you want it to (**Figure 11.44**).

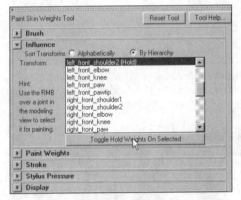

Figure 11.43 By holding the weight of the shoulder, you can paint out the weight of the leg without Maya automatically assigning some of the recalculated weights to the shoulder.

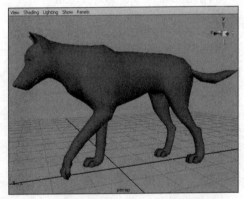

Figure 11.44 Painting the torso with a value of 0.0 for both the shoulder and leg removes its unwanted deformation. Painting the torso with a value of 1.0 for the closest spine joint would have a similar effect.

To mirror skin weights on a smooth skin:

1. Select a joint from the skeleton of the skin you want to modify. You can create a smooth skin by following the steps described in "To bind skin using smooth bind," earlier in this chapter, but you will need to use a symmetrical mesh and skeleton for this task (**Figure 11.45**).

2. Select Skin > Go to Bind Pose.

   The skeleton returns to the position it was in when you bound the skin to it. This is necessary for the weights to mirror correctly.

3. Select the skin.

4. From the Skin > Edit Smooth Skin menu, click the box next to Mirror Skin Weights.

   The Mirror Skin Weights Options dialog box is displayed (**Figure 11.46**).

5. Select the plane you want to mirror across (the plane that divides your character into two symmetrical halves).

6. If you made your changes on the positive side of the axis you're mirroring on, select the Positive to Negative check box. If they're on the negative side, deselect it.

7. Click Mirror to mirror the skin's weights.

   The skin deforms the same way on both sides (**Figure 11.47**).

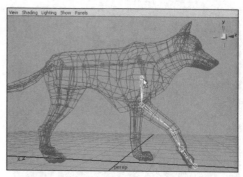

Figure 11.45 Because the unwanted weighting on the right side of the wolf is identical to the problem you fixed on the left side, the mirror command can save time. However, the skeleton must be returned to its bind pose first.

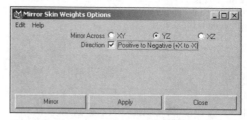

Figure 11.46 The Mirror Skin Weights Options dialog box lets you pick the plane and direction on which to mirror the weights.

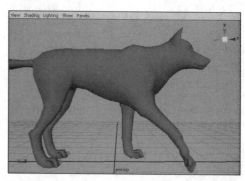

Figure 11.47 After mirroring the weights, the unwanted weighting is removed from the right side of the wolf's torso.

ANIMATION

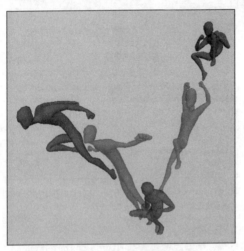

Figure 12.1 Raf Anzovin animated this leaping character with Maya's animation tools.

Maya was built for animation. Almost anything you encounter can be animated, such as a color, a texture, an object's shape, or the intensity of a light. When combined with the techniques explored in Chapters 10 and 11, Maya allows you to undertake complex character animation (**Figure 12.1**).

Most animation is accomplished by setting keyframes. The term *keyframe* has its origin in traditional hand-drawn animation, in which a lead animator creates key poses of a character—drawings at the beginning and end and other vital points of an action—and an assistant then draws the in-between frames, making the final result a smooth motion. When using Maya, you're the lead animator and the program is your assistant. To animate, you set keyframes—that is, you tell an object or attribute where to be at certain points in time—and the program does the in-betweening for you.

Animations are easy to tweak: You can change the timing or distance covered by existing keyframes, you can add or remove keyframes, and you can adjust the acceleration between keyframes by tweaking the animation curve between them.

Animation Controls

The Time and Range Sliders are Maya's primary controls for creating and fine-tuning your animation (**Figure 12.2**):

◆ **Time Slider**—The Time Slider determines your position in time. It's the area at the bottom of the screen that includes the playback buttons and timeline (**Figure 12.3**). You can click any frame to go to that point in time, or you can click and drag to preview a region of animation. You also use the Time Slider to select, move, and scale keyframes.

◆ **Current Time indicator**—This indicator shows the present position in time (**Figure 12.4**).

◆ **Current Time field**—This field also shows the current position in time. You can type a number in this field to change the current time (**Figure 12.5**).

◆ **Start Time/End Time fields**—These values show the time span for the entire animation. The numbers establish the length of time within which the Range Slider can move (**Figure 12.6**).

◆ **Range Slider**—This slider controls the portion of time you're viewing (**Figure 12.7**). It lets you quickly adjust which portion of the animation shows up in the timeline. You can use the buttons on the ends to change the playback start and end times, or you can drag the range forward or backward as a whole. This is helpful when you want to work on only small portions of an animation. The smaller the range, the easier it is to pick individual frames.

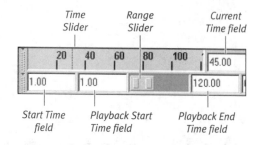

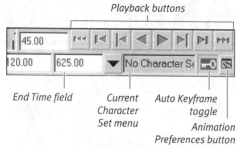

Figure 12.2 The Time and Range Sliders allow you to play back animation, control your position in time, and choose the portion of the animation you're looking at.

Figure 12.3 Click any point in the timeline to go to that time.

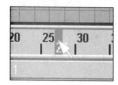

Figure 12.4 The Current Time indicator shows what frame you're on. If you want to cut, copy, or delete a frame in the timeline, the Current Time indicator must be over that frame.

Figure 12.5 The Current Time field also tells you where you are in time. You can type any time here (even one that's not included in the playback range) and go to that time.

Figure 12.6 The number fields on the far left and far right show the start and end times. You should generally set these to the start and end of your entire animation. They can be changed at any time.

Figure 12.7 The Range Slider provides a convenient means of changing which portion of the animation is currently in the timeline.

Figure 12.8 The playback start and end times appear in the fields on the left and right. You can type the times to change the beginning and end of your timeline.

Figure 12.9 From left to right, the playback buttons do the following: go to the start of the playback range, step back one frame, step back one key, play backward, play forward, step forward one key, step forward one frame, go to the end of the playback range.

Figure 12.10 The Auto Keyframe function is on when the button looks like this.

Figure 12.11 This is the Animation Preferences button.

Figure 12.12 You can create and choose character sets here.

◆ **Playback Start Time/Playback End Time fields**—These values control the range of animation that plays back, much like the Range Slider (**Figure 12.8**).

◆ **Playback buttons**—These controls are like the buttons on a CD player (**Figure 12.9**). The Rewind and Fast Forward buttons change the current time to the start or end of the playback range. You can step forward one frame at a time or move to the next or previous keyframe. There is a Play button to go forward or backward; it toggles to a Stop button during playback.

◆ **Auto Keyframe toggle**—This button turns Auto Keyframing on and off (**Figure 12.10**). If it's on, any attribute that is already keyframed is automatically keyframed again when you change its value.

◆ **Animation Preferences button**—This button opens a window to set animation preferences (**Figure 12.11**). It also provides a convenient way to access all general preferences in Maya.

◆ **Current Character Set menu**—This menu lets you choose which character set you're currently working on (**Figure 12.12**). When you're working with more than one character, it's helpful to be able to access individual characters' attributes.

About Setting Keyframes

Keyframes are at the heart of animation in Maya. Setting a keyframe means that you want a certain attribute to have a specific value at a point in time. For example, a ball could begin at –2 along the x axis at frame 1 and end at a Translate X of 2 at frame 10. Between those frames, it would gradually move across the screen (**Figure 12.13**).

There are many ways to set keyframes and adjust them once they've been set. When you set a keyframe, a couple of things happen: The channels that were keyframed are highlighted orange in the Channel Box. In addition, key ticks appear in the timeline—thin, red lines indicating where each keyframe is (**Figure 12.14**). Keyframes also show up in the Graph Editor and the Dope Sheet, discussed later in this chapter.

The following task covers most of the ways to set a keyframe.

To set a keyframe:

1. Choose Create > NURBS Primitives > Sphere.

2. Press (Shift)+(w).

   This keyframes the translates only. Press (Shift)+(e) to keyframe the rotates and (Shift)+(r) to keyframe the scales. These correspond to the hotkeys for the Move, Rotate, and Scale tools.

3. In the Channel Box, select Rotate X, and (Shift)-select Rotate Y and Rotate Z (**Figure 12.15**).

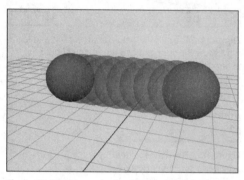

Figure 12.13 As you play back the animation, the sphere moves across the panel.

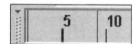

Figure 12.14 The thin line near the 10 is a key tick. It lets you know there is a keyframe for the selected object at that time.

Channels	Object	
nurbsSphere1		
Translate X		0
Translate Y		0
Translate Z		0
Rotate X		0
Rotate Y		0
Rotate Z		0
Scale X		1
Scale Y		1
Scale Z		1
Visibility		on

Figure 12.15 Rotate X, Y, and Z are selected in the Channel Box so that they can be keyframed. You can easily select multiple attributes in the Channel Box by dragging the names.

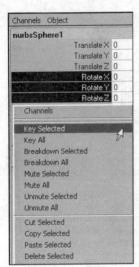

Figure 12.16
When you click in the Channel Box with the right mouse button, you can keyframe the selected attributes.

Figure 12.17 You can change the current time to 20 by typing this value in the field. When you have a particularly long playback range, entering a frame number can be easier than clicking it in the timeline.

4. Right-click the Channel Box, and choose Key Selected from the marking menu that appears (**Figure 12.16**).

   Any channels that are selected (in this case, the rotate channels) are keyframed.

5. Go to frame 10 by clicking that number in the timeline.

6. Move and rotate the sphere.

7. Press ⓢ.

   All attributes in the Channel Box are keyframed.

8. Turn on Auto Keyframe ⬛.

   The button looks pressed down and becomes highlighted.

9. Type 20 in the Current Time field to change the time in the timeline; then, press Enter (**Figure 12.17**).

10. Move the sphere.

    A new keyframe appears. When Auto Keyframe is turned on, it sets a keyframe any time an attribute is changed.

✔ Tip

■ You can set keyframes on an object only when that object is selected. Likewise, you can see the key ticks in the timeline only when the keyframed object is selected. You can also select more than one object and view frame ticks of all selected objects at once.

ABOUT SETTING KEYFRAMES

Although much of the advanced editing of keyframes can be done in the Graph Editor and Dope Sheet windows (discussed later in this chapter), you can access the most frequently used editing tools directly from the timeline.

To edit keyframes in the timeline:

1. Choose Create > NURBS Primitives > Sphere.

2. Change the playback start time to 1 and the playback end time to 30.

3. Set keyframes on the sphere every five frames, starting with the first frame.

4. Move the sphere, and change the current time each time you set a keyframe.

   If Auto Keyframe is still on, you can press [Shift]+[w] in the first frame, and all of the other frames will automatically be keyed (**Figure 12.18**).

5. Click a frame in the timeline where there is a key tick. With the right mouse button, click the timeline; select Delete from the pop-up menu (**Figure 12.19**).

   The keyframe is removed.

6. Hold down [Shift], and drag over the range of two key ticks in the timeline.

   A red area appears, with two small arrows near the middle and two small arrows at the edges (**Figure 12.20**).

7. Drag from left to right on the two small arrows in the center of the selected area.

   The keyframes move together without being scaled. You can do this with an individual keyframe as well.

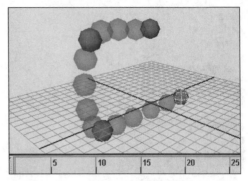

Figure 12.18 This is an example of some simple motion you can add to an object. Select the sphere, and press [Shift]+[w] to keyframe it. With Auto Keyframe turned on, Maya automatically keyframes the sphere every time you move it.

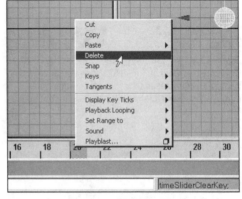

Figure 12.19 Clicking the timeline with the right mouse button gives you access to a variety of convenient commands.

Figure 12.20 The highlighted section of the timeline is selected. The outside arrows allow you to scale the time, and the inside arrows allow you to move several keyframes at once.

Figure 12.21 Double-clicking the timeline is a convenient way to select all the keyframes in the playback range.

8. Double-click the timeline.

   All the keyframes in the playback range are selected. However, the arrows used for scaling end up just outside the playback range, so you must change the playback end time to access them.

9. Change the playback end time to 31.

   An arrow appears at the end of the selected range (**Figure 12.21**).

10. Drag the arrow to the left.

    The animation is scaled down, which makes the sphere move faster. Note that the key ticks no longer fall on whole-number frames.

11. With the right mouse button, click the timeline; select Snap from the marking menu that appears.

    The keyframes are moved to the nearest whole-number frame.

✔ Tips

■ If you want to ensure that the timeline is sitting on a keyframe, use the back and forward arrows with the red marks on them in the animation controls. These jump the timeline to the preceding and next keyframe, respectively.

■ When you're working on the timing of your animation, it's often fastest, and easiest, to select, move, and scale keyframes in the timeline.

ABOUT SETTING KEYFRAMES

Setting Animation Preferences

A few animation preferences are essential for you to set. They affect the way your animation is played back and how you see and work with the timeline.

When a scene gets extremely complicated, with many animated surfaces, Maya may not be able to play back every frame of the animation at full speed. This leaves you with two choices: You can either play back at full speed or play every frame. In some cases, you'll want to see the detail in the motion; other times, you'll want to see the overall pace.

Maya is used to make animations for films, television, games, and the Internet. Films run at 24 frames per second (fps), television runs at 30 (US) or 25 fps, and animation on the Internet often runs at 15 fps. Maya's animation timeline is frame-independent, so you can change the framerate after animation is complete without changing the pacing of the motion. However, it's usually best to choose the framerate beforehand to prevent keyframes from falling on fractional frames.

To set the animation playback speed:

1. Click the Animation Preferences button 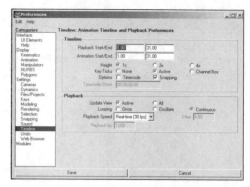, which is near the lower-right corner of the interface.

   The Preferences window opens (**Figure 12.22**).

2. Select Timeline from the Categories list, and then select Real-time in the pop-up menu next to Playback Speed.

3. Select Settings from the Categories list.

4. Select your frame rate from the pop-up menu next to Time (**Figure 12.23**).

5. Click Save so that these settings will be recalled the next time you open Maya.

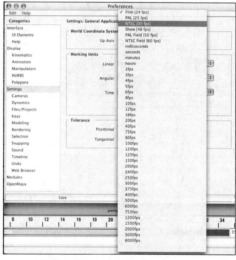

Figure 12.22 It's important to set Playback Speed before you start animating. Choosing the wrong playback speed can cause the audio to go out of sync with the animation when it's rendered.

Figure 12.23 NTSC (30 fps) is a fairly standard setting for video.

Key ticks are the red lines that appear on the timeline when you set a keyframe. Set them to appear only for the selected channels if you want to make changes to some attributes and not others in the timeline.

To change key ticks options:

1. Keyframe an object.

2. Click the Animation Preferences button 🔲 in the lower-right corner of the interface.

3. In the Preferences window, select the Channel Box option next to Key Ticks. Any key ticks in the timeline disappear.

4. Select any keyframed channels in the Channel Box.
   The key ticks for those channels appear.

5. Open the Preferences window again, change the Key Ticks setting back to Active, and click Save.

✔ Tips

- Click the Animation Preferences button to access many of Maya's preferences. Once the window is open, try selecting different categories.

- If the Key Ticks option is set to Channel Box, only the attributes selected are affected when you edit them. If you keyframe both an object's scale and rotate attributes, you can move the keyframes of the scale alone by selecting those attributes in the Channel Box and moving the key ticks. The rotate keyframes will be left behind.

Importing Sound Files

Maya lets you import a sound file so you can animate to spoken dialogue or to the beat of a song. The file must be in AIFF or WAV format.

To import a sound file:

1. Choose File > Import (**Figure 12.24**).

2. Navigate to the sound file you want to use, and click Import.

   The sound file doesn't automatically appear in the timeline.

3. To hear the sound file and see the wave-form, right-click the timeline, select Sound, and select your imported file (**Figure 12.25**).

   The waveform becomes visible in the timeline.

4. Click Play to hear the sound file.

   If the sound file doesn't play back, the animation preferences may need to be adjusted.

5. Click the Animation Preferences button [symbol] near the lower-right corner of the interface.

6. Check to make sure Playback Speed is set to Real-time. If it isn't, select Real-time from the pull-down menu, and then click Save (**Figure 12.26**).

   You should now be able to play back the sound. By default, Maya imports the sound file at frame 0 of the timeline.

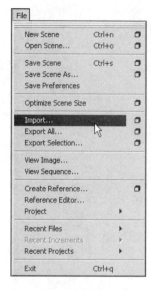

Figure 12.24 Importing sound using the File menu.

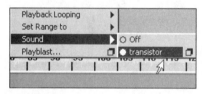

Figure 12.25 Change the current sound file, or adjust the setting by right-clicking in the timeline.

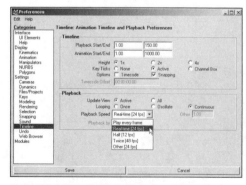

Figure 12.26 For playback, the animation settings must be set to Real-time playback speed.

IMPORTING SOUND FILES

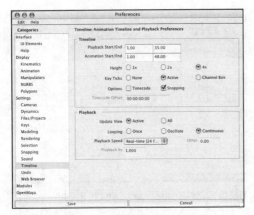

Figure 12.27 You can change the height of the timeline in the animation Preferences window.

Figure 12.28 This is a timeline at the height of 4x. Increase the height only if you need to see the audio more clearly, because the extra height takes up valuable real estate.

7. To change where the sound file begins to play, right-click the timeline, select Sound, and open the options box next to your sound file.

8. Adjust the Offset value to move the beginning of the sound file that number of frames; the value can be positive or negative.

✔ Tip

- You can also import a file by dragging it directly onto the timeline, where it appears immediately.

You can see the sound waves better if you increase the timeline's height.

To set the timeline height:

1. Click the Animation Preferences button 🔲 near the lower-right corner of the interface.

2. Click a Height setting of 2x or 4x (**Figure 12.27**).
   The timeline gets taller (**Figure 12.28**).

3. Click 1x to return the timeline to the normal height.

4. Click Save to keep these preferences.

About the Graph Editor

The Graph Editor is a window that shows a graphic representation of your animation. It has points that represent the time and position in which a keyframe was set, and curves between the keyframes that show the acceleration (**Figure 12.29**).

By changing the distance between keyframes, you can change an object's speed. However, you must adjust the curve that represents the object's motion between keyframes to change its acceleration.

You can use the tangent types in the Graph Editor to quickly change the shapes of the curves (**Figure 12.30**). By default, the keyframes you set are clamped tangents. You can also manually adjust the shapes of the tangents. The Graph Editor is helpful for editing, copying, and looping animation.

Tangent types

There are seven tangent types, all of which you can set by selecting a keyframe or an animation curve and choosing from the Tangent menu in the Graph Editor. You can also change which tangent type is automatically assigned to keyframes before they are set, in the Keys section of the Preferences window. The tangent types are as follows:

◆ **Spline**—Keyframes with spline tangents have smooth curves between and through them (**Figure 12.31**). When animating a fish through water, you might use a spline tangent.

◆ **Linear**—This tangent type draws a straight line from one keyframe to the next. It creates jerky movement with sudden changes, which might be good for something mechanical (**Figure 12.32**).

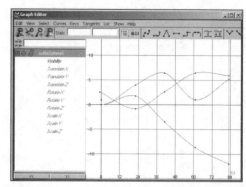

Figure 12.29 Use the Graph Editor to fine-tune your animation once you get the basic timing down.

Figure 12.30 From left to right, these tangent types are spline, linear, and flat.

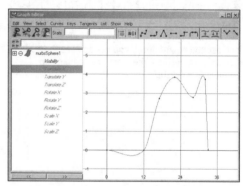

Figure 12.31 These keyframes are set to the spline tangent type. Note that although the values at frames 1 and 12 are the same, there is still a curve between those points because the keyframes aren't set flat. This causes drifting, which can be problematic if you want an object to stay still.

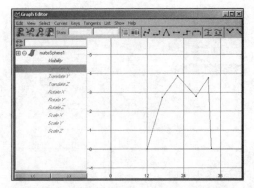

Figure 12.32 These keyframes are set to the linear tangent type.

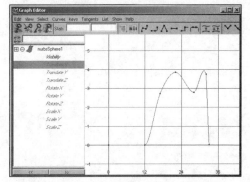

Figure 12.33 These keyframes are set to the clamped tangent type. This tangent type is similar to the spline tangent except that the drifting problem between frames 1 and 12 is fixed.

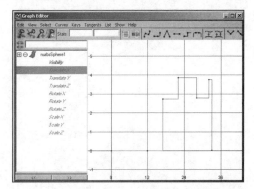

Figure 12.34 These keyframes are set to the Stepped tangent type.

◆ **Clamped**—This is the default tangent type. Keyframes with clamped tangents act just like spline tangents, with one very useful exception: If two adjacent keyframes are set at the same value at different points in time, the tangents of both will act like flat tangents (**Figure 12.33**). Using clamped tangents prevents a problem that sometimes occurs with spline tangents, when an object you want to be still drifts slightly between keyframes.

◆ **Stepped**—This tangent type ensures that a value remains the same until it gets to the next keyframe, when it jumps to that position. It This type makes the curve look like a step—hence, the name (**Figure 12.34**). One use for this tangent is for producing camera cuts. If you want a camera to hold in one position and then cut to another position, keyframe using a stepped tangent.

◆ **Flat**—The tangent itself becomes horizontal when using this tangent type. Flat tangents typically create "slow-in, slow-out"—which means the animation gradually accelerates between keyframes, goes quickly in the middle of the curve, and then gradually decelerates as it moves to the next keyframe (**Figure 12.35**).

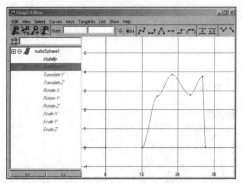

Figure 12.35 These keyframes are set to the Flat tangent type.

ABOUT THE GRAPH EDITOR

◆ **Fixed**—The tangent doesn't change when you edit the keyframe.

◆ **Plateau**—This tangent type is similar to Clamped, but it doesn't merely flatten tangents when two adjacent keyframes have the same value—it also flattens them whenever the curve reaches a hill or valley, preventing any possibility that an object will drift farther then the key you've set for it. For instance, if an object is animated to bump into a wall and then drift back, spline or clamped tangent types will likely exhibit spline interpolation between keyframes that causes the object to drift slightly past the key you set and intersect the wall. Plateau prevents that possibility (**Figure 12.36**).

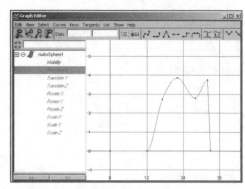

Figure 12.36 These keyframes are set to the Plateau tangent type. Notice that the peaks at the top of the curve are flattened by this type.

Creating a bouncing-ball animation is a good way to learn some of the functions of the Graph Editor.

To use the Graph Editor to change tangent types:

1. Choose Create > NURBS Primitives > Sphere.

2. Move the sphere up 10 grid units.

   An easy way to do this is to type **10** in the field next to Translate Y in the Channel Box.

3. Make sure that you're at frame 1 in the timeline and that Auto Keyframe is turned on.

   The key icon ⟦🔑⟧ appears red and pressed down.

4. Press ⟦Shift⟧+⟦w⟧ to keyframe only the translate attributes.

5. Go to frame 15, and translate the sphere down to 1 along the *y* axis.

   The ball is keyframed once it's moved, because Auto Keyframe is on.

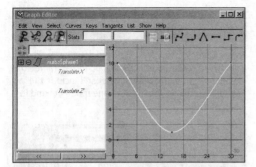

Figure 12.37 The keyframes at the top of the curve are being selected. The ball is at its highest between these points, and it needs to slow down on the way in and out of them—a perfect use for the Flat tangent type.

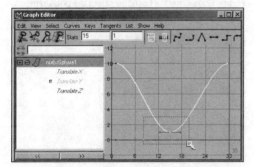

Figure 12.38 This keyframe is at the point when the ball hits the ground. As it is now, the ball doesn't seem to bounce; it just kisses the ground.

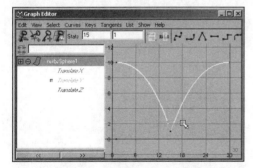

Figure 12.39 Now that the tangents have been adjusted, the ball appears to really bounce.

6. Go to frame 30, and translate the sphere back up to 10 along the *y* axis.

Rewind and play back the animation. The ball's bounce isn't convincing.

7. Choose Window > Animation Editors > Graph Editor.

The Graph Editor window opens. The curve for the sphere's animation appears as long as the sphere is still selected.

8. Marquee-select the two keyframes at the top of the graph (**Figure 12.37**).

9. Click the Flat Tangents button ⊟ in the Graph Editor window.

10. Select the keyframe at the bottom of the curve (**Figure 12.38**).

Because you're trying to click such a small point, it helps to marquee-select, even when you're only selecting one keyframe.

11. Click the Break Tangents button ⋁.

This lets you move the tangents on either side individually.

12. Select the tangent on the left of the keyframe; then [Shift]-select the tangent on the right.

13. Click the Move Nearest Picked Key tool button, which is at the top-left corner of the Graph Editor ⋩.

14. With the middle mouse button, drag the tangents and move them up one at a time to form a V shape (**Figure 12.39**).

Play back the animation. It now looks more like a real bouncing ball.

Adjusting keyframes with the Graph Editor

Perhaps you want your ball to bounce again. One easy way to accomplish this is to copy and paste keyframes in the timeline.

To copy and paste in the timeline:

1. Animate the bouncing ball as described in the previous task.

2. Make sure that the playback end time is set to at least 60.

   You can do this by typing 60 in the Playback End Time field.

3. Hold down [Shift], and drag in the time-line from 1 to at least 31 (**Figure 12.40**).

4. Right-click the timeline; select Copy from the pop-up menu (**Figure 12.41**).

5. Click frame 30.

   The frame you're on when you paste sets the time at which the range of keyframes you paste will begin.

6. Choose Edit > Keys, and select the check box next to Paste.

   The Paste Keys Options dialog box opens.

7. In the Paste Method section, click Merge (**Figure 12.42**) to paste the keyframe at the current frame without moving any adjacent keyframes.

8. Click Apply.

   A new keyframe marker appears on the timeline.

9. Rewind and play the animation.

   The ball now bounces twice.

Figure 12.40 You can [Shift]-click and drag the keyframes from which you want to copy. If you stop at frame 30 in your selection, the selection doesn't include the keyframe at 30, so you must go one frame beyond it.

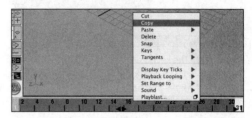

Figure 12.41 Copy the keyframes from the pop-up menu.

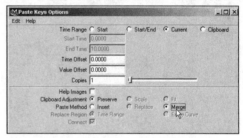

Figure 12.42 In the Paste Keys Options dialog box, click Merge to place the keyframe at the current frame without offsetting any adjacent frames.

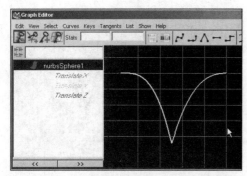

Figure 12.43 Be sure the current time is at the point where you want to begin the paste operation. Otherwise, when you paste, the keyframes will end up wherever the Current Time indicator happens to be and will overwrite the existing frames.

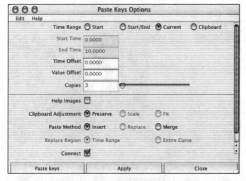

Figure 12.44 Using the Paste Keys Options, you can make several copies at once.

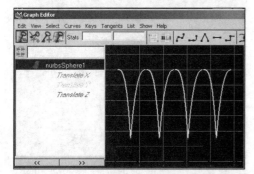

Figure 12.45 This is the result of the paste operation. The ball bounces four times instead of once.

Sometimes you want an animation to repeat several times. You can use the Graph Editor to perform multiple paste operations at once.

To copy and paste in the Graph Editor:

1. Animate a bouncing ball.

2. Make sure that the timeline goes to at least 120.

   You can do this by typing 120 in the Playback End Time field.

3. Choose Window > Animation Editors > Graph Editor.

   The curve for the sphere's animation should appear. If it doesn't, select the sphere and marquee-select all keys.

4. From the Edit menu in the Graph Editor, select Copy.

5. Hold down k, and drag in the Graph Editor window until the red line (the time indicator) is at the end of the curve (**Figure 12.43**).

6. From the Edit menu in the Graph Editor, select the check box next to Paste.

   The Paste Keys Options window opens.

7. In the Copies field, type 3 (**Figure 12.44**). Click Paste Keys.

8. While the mouse is in the Graph Editor, press f.

   The entire animation curve fits within the window. There are now three additional bounces (**Figure 12.45**).

9. Rewind and play the animation.

   The ball bounces four times.

If you want to speed up or slow down your animation, you can scale the time in the Graph Editor. A longer time for the same distance means slower movement, and vice versa.

You can also scale values. Perhaps all your bounces are too high, or none of your arm swings extend far enough. Scaling a value is just as easy as scaling an object's size.

To scale in the Graph Editor:

1. Create a bouncing ball with four bounces, as in the previous task.

2. Choose Window > Animation Editors > Graph Editor.

3. From the column on the left, select Translate Y.

   This isolates the Y translate curve.

4. Marquee-select the whole curve.

5. Press $\boxed{r}$ to switch to scale mode.

6. Move the mouse over the first keyframe on the left side of the curve (**Figure 12.46**).

   The mouse's location when you begin to scale serves as the scale's pivot point.

7. With the middle mouse button, drag to the left.

8. Move the mouse over one of the low points of the bounces (**Figure 12.47**).

9. With the middle mouse button, drag down.

   The bounces get shorter (**Figure 12.48**).

✔ Tip

■ You can also scale just a portion of a curve by selecting only those keyframes you want to scale. You can likewise scale multiple animated objects at the same time, which is often desirable so that their actions remain synchronized.

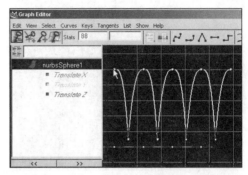

Figure 12.46 It's important to have the mouse at the correct position when you start to scale keyframes in the Graph Editor. Wherever you begin to scale is where the pivot point of the scale will be.

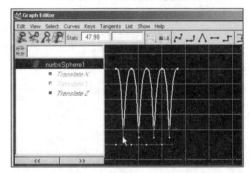

Figure 12.47 Here the time has been scaled down so that the ball bounces faster. The mouse has been carefully placed at the bottom of the bounce, so that position will be the pivot point of the scale.

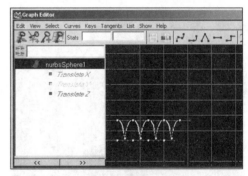

Figure 12.48 The value has been scaled down—that is, the bounces don't go as high as they did. Because the pivot point was at the bottom of the curve, the position at which it bounces hasn't changed—which means the ball appears to be bouncing on the ground, not above or below it.

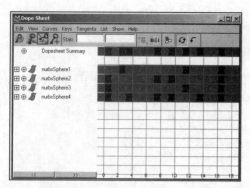

Figure 12.49 The Dope Sheet is especially helpful when working on the timing of a large number of objects.

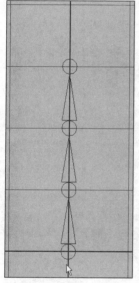

Figure 12.50
Four joints used to represent a tail.

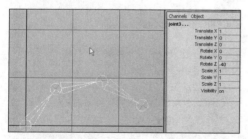

Figure 12.51 The first three joints rotated –40 degrees on the *z* axis.

About the Dope Sheet

The Dope Sheet is another window used for editing keyframes. You can move, scale, cut, copy, paste, and delete in it, much as you can in the timeline and the Graph Editor. It has the advantage of offering a simple, clear way to move the keyframes of multiple objects in time. For this reason, it's most helpful for adjusting the timing of many objects simultaneously (**Figure 12.49**).

The Dope Sheet can also be useful in creating offset animation. If you set keyframes on a number of objects on the same frame, you can open the Dope Sheet and select those keys easily per object and move them together. In this task, you'll create joints and animation for a wagging tail, offset the keys, and cycle the animation.

To create a cycled animation in the Dope Sheet:

1. Create four joints in the Front view. Start at the center of the grid, and place them one grid unit apart in the positive *y* direction (**Figure 12.50**).

2. At frame 0, select the first three joints, and set a key by pressing ⑤.

3. Move to frame 10, and rotate the three joints –40 degrees along the *z* axis (**Figure 12.51**). Press ⑤.

4. Move to frame 20, and rotate the three joints back to 0 along the *z* axis. Press ⑤.

5. Move to frame 30, and rotate the three joints 40 degrees along the *z* axis. Press ⑤.

6. Move to frame 40, and rotate the three joints back to 0 along the *z* axis. Press ⑤.

   Now you are ready to offset the keyframes for each joint so that the second and third joints start to rotate slightly later than the first.

continues on next page

7. Select Window > Animation Editors > Dope Sheet (**Figure 12.52**).

   You see the three joints and the block representation of the keyframes you created.

8. Click joint2 on the left side of the Dope Sheet.

   The keyframes for joint2 are highlighted in the right panel of the Dope Sheet.

9. In the Dope Sheet toolbar, choose the Select Keyframe tool from the upper-left corner. This tool lets you drag a box around the keyframes you want to move. You can slide or resize the box so that it contains the keyframes you want to select (**Figure 12.53**).

10. Switch to the Move tool, and, with the middle mouse button, move the keyframes to the right three frames (**Figure 12.54**).

11. Click joint3 on the left side of the Dope Sheet.

12. With the middle mouse button, move the keyframes to the right six frames.

13. Select all three joints on the left side of the Dope Sheet.

14. Select Curves > Pre Infinity > Cycle (**Figure 12.55**).

15. Select Curves > Post Infinity > Cycle.

    You now have a cycled and offset tail wag animation.

16. Click Play to see the resulting animation.

Figure 12.52 Select the Dope Sheet.

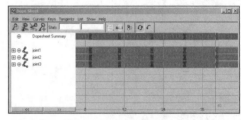

Figure 12.53 Choose the Select Keyframe tool from the upper-left corner of the Dope Sheet, and drag a selection box around the keyframe you want to move.

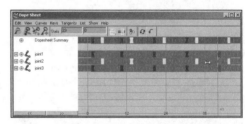

Figure 12.54 The keyframes for joint2 can be moved using the middle mouse button.

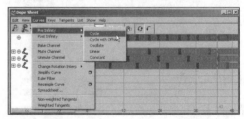

Figure 12.55 Select Pre Infinity or Post Infinity and then Cycle to cycle the animation before or after the keyframed animation.

Muting Animation Channels

The Mute Animation Channel function lets you temporarily turn off specified animation curves for an object, making it easier to focus on a particular aspect of the animation. For example, if a ball is bouncing from the left side of the screen to the right, it may be difficult to focus your attention on the up-and-down motion due to the left-to-right motion. If you mute the left-to-right motion, you can see the up-and-down motion more clearly. When you have adjusted the up-and-down motion as you want, you can unmute the left-to-right motion.

To mute an animation channel:

1. Create a NURBS sphere.

2. Change the playback start time to 1 and the playback end time to 50.

3. At frame 1, select the sphere, and set a keyframe.

4. Move to frame 40, and translate the sphere in the front view 20 units to the right.
   Set another keyframe.

5. Move to frame 20, and set another keyframe.

6. Move to frame 10, and translate the sphere up 10 units.
   Set a keyframe.

continues on next page

7. Move to frame 30, and translate the sphere up 10 units.

   Set a keyframe. You should now have a ball that moves across the screen and bounces up and down.

   To see only the up-and-down motion, you need to mute the Translate X channel in the Channel Box.

8. With the sphere selected, select Translate X in the Channel Box. Right-click the highlighted word, and choose Mute Selected (**Figure 12.56**).

   The channel turns brown, and as you drag through the timeline, the ball moves only up and down.

9. To unmute the channel, select Translate X in the Channel Box. Right-click the highlighted word, and choose Unmute Selected.

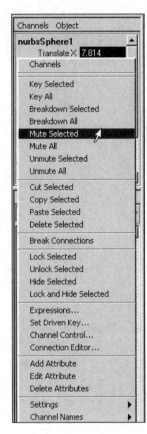

Figure 12.56
Select a channel to mute, right-click, and choose Mute Selected to temporarily disable the animation.

Figure 12.57
Choose Ghost Selected to see the position of your object before and after the current frame.

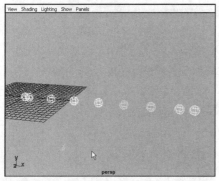

Figure 12.58 The original sphere in the middle is ghosted, showing its position before and after its current frame.

Figure 12.59
Open the Ghost Options dialog box to adjust the display.

Ghosting

Another way to see problem areas in your animation is to apply ghosting to an object. Ghosting leaves a trail showing where your object is going and where it came from. Some animators find ghosting useful because it can provide a snapshot of an entire animation.

To ghost an object:

1. Create a sphere.

2. Go to frame 0 in the timeline, and key the sphere by pressing ⓢ.

3. Go to frame 40, translate the sphere 40 units in the *x* direction, and set another keyframe.

4. Choose Animate > Ghost Selected (**Figure 12.57**).

   You now see multiple spheres. The blue spheres represent where the object was, and the orange spheres represent where it's going (**Figure 12.58**).

5. To change the display of the ghosting, return to the Animate menu and select the options box next to Ghost Selected (**Figure 12.59**).

   The Ghost Options dialog box opens.

continues on next page

6. Change Type of Ghosting to Custom Frame Steps (**Figure 12.60**).

7. Change Steps before Current Frame to 4.

8. Change Steps after Current Frame to 4.

9. Change Step Size to 4.

The step size refers to the number of frames that are skipped between displays of a ghost object. If the step size is 1, a ghost of the object is displayed on every frame.

10. Click Ghost.

Motion Trail is another preview function similar to ghosting. When you apply a motion trail to an animated object, a line traces where the object has been and is going.

To create a motion trail:

1. Create a sphere.

2. Go to frame 0 in the timeline, and press ⑤ to create a keyframe.

3. Go to frame 40, translate the sphere 10 units in the *x* direction, and set another keyframe.

4. Go to frame 20, translate the sphere 5 units in the *y* direction, and set another keyframe.

5. From the Animate menu, select the check box next to Motion Trail.

The Motion Trail Options dialog box opens.

6. Set the Increment to 5, and set the Draw Style to Line (**Figure 12.61**).

7. Click Apply.

A line traces the path that the sphere travels (**Figure 12.62**).

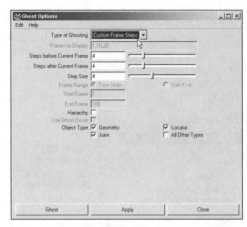

Figure 12.60 Custom settings for the ghosting display.

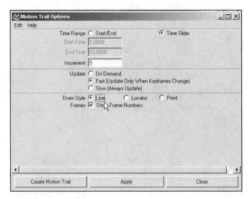

Figure 12.61 Set the Increment to 5 and the Draw Style to Line.

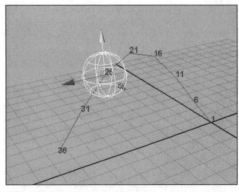

Figure 12.62 A line shows where the object travels and the keyframes at different points on the path.

GHOSTING

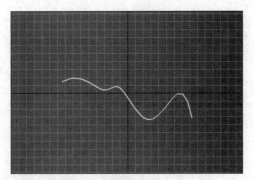

Figure 12.63 This curve is drawn in the Top view.

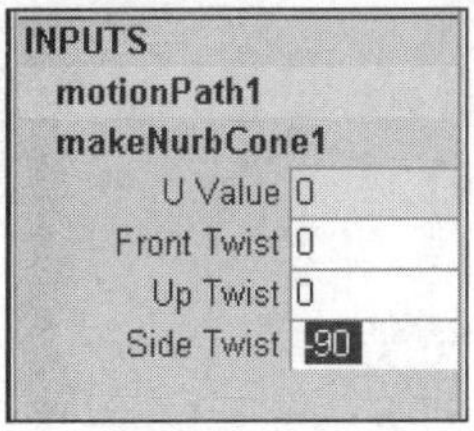

INPUTS
motionPath1
makeNurbCone1
U Value 0
Front Twist 0
Up Twist 0
Side Twist -90

Figure 12.64
The different twists are needed to orient the cone. You can't simply rotate the cone, because its rotate attributes are controlled by the path animation.

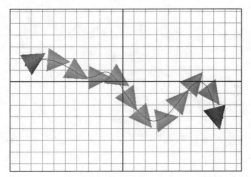

Figure 12.65 This is the resulting path animation.

Path Animation

It can be difficult to animate the flight of an airplane just by setting keyframes because of the number of keyframes required to simulate the detail of the rotation and the direction of the plane. Sometimes you want to establish the path first and then send the object along that path. Maya can even make an object automatically bank around turns and point in the direction of the path.

To animate along a path:

1. Create a curve in the Top view (**Figure 12.63**). (See Chapter 7 for more on creating curves.)

2. Choose Create > NURBS Primitives > Cone.

3. Select the cone; then Shift-select the curve.

4. Choose Animate > Motion Paths > Attach to Motion Path.

   The cone jumps to the beginning of the curve, and when the animation is played back, it moves along the curve.

5. With the cone still selected, click motionPath1 in the Channel Box.

6. Enter −90 in the Side Twist field so that the cone points down the path (**Figure 12.64**).

   When the animation is played back now, you can see how the rotation of the cone follows the path (**Figure 12.65**).

About the Trax Editor

The Trax Editor is another useful animation editor in Maya, incorporating a nonlinear approach to animation. Nonlinear animation lets you create clips of animation and arrange them in any manner you wish. For example, if you have a ball in your scene, you can have a bouncing clip, a rolling clip, and a deflating clip. You can then blend, rearrange, add, duplicate, or delete these clips, making new animations without touching a keyframe, as well as other commonly used functions:

◆ **Cut, Copy, Paste, Duplicate**—Select the clip you want to edit; then, from the Edit menu, select Cut, Copy, Paste, or Duplicate.

◆ **Attribute Editor**—A clip's Attribute Editor lets you adjust the scale, offset, and cycling of the clip you've selected. To see the Attribute Editor, select a clip and select Modify > Attribute Editor.

◆ **Animation Curves**—To see and adjust the original animation curves in the Graph Editor, select a clip and then click the Graph Anim Curves icon .

At the heart of the Trax Editor is the *character set*. The character set defines a set of keyframable attributes. What those attributes are is up to you. A character set isn't necessarily a complex, rigged character; it could just be a sphere. Because the character set lets you treat a complex rig with lots of controls as one object, it's most useful on a character. For instance, when you create a keyframe while using a character set, all the attributes in that character set are keyed, no matter how many objects the attributes belong to. For this reason, many animators like to use character sets even if they're not using the Trax Editor.

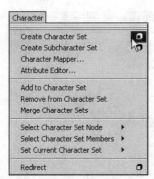

Figure 12.66
Open the Create
Character Set
options.

Figure 12.67 Set the options for the character, including what will be keyable.

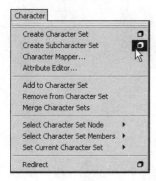

Figure 12.68
Display the options
for creating a
subcharacter set.

To create a character set:

1. Create a NURBS sphere and a polygon cube.

2. Translate the cube 1.5 units above the sphere.
   This will be your character.

3. To create the character set, select the sphere and the cube.

4. From the Character menu, select the check box next to Create Character Set (**Figure 12.66**).
   The Create Character Set Options dialog box opens.

5. Change the name of the character set to All (**Figure 12.67**).

6. Click Create Character Set.
   A character set is created that includes your two objects. Next you'll create subcharacter sets for the sphere and cube individually.

7. Select the sphere.

8. From the Character menu, select the check box next to Create Subcharacter Set (**Figure 12.68**).
   The Create Subcharacter Set Options dialog box opens.

continues on next page

ABOUT THE TRAX EDITOR

9. Change the Name value to Ball, and click Create Subcharacter Set (**Figure 12.69**).

10. Select the cube.

11. From the Character menu, select the check box next to Create Subcharacter Set.

12. Change the Name value to Box, and click Create Subcharacter Set.

13. Navigate to the current character set menu below the playback controls.

14. Click the arrow, and select All (**Figure 12.70**).

This menu is where you choose the character or subcharacter you'll be working with.

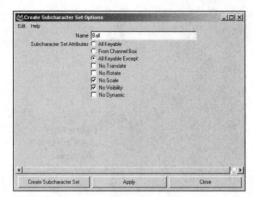

Figure 12.69 Set the options for the subcharacter set.

Figure 12.70 Use the menu in the bottom-right corner of the interface to select the character set you're working with.

To create a clip:

1. With All selected in the Current Character Set menu, go to frame 0 in the timeline.

2. Select the sphere and the cube, and press [s].

3. Move to frame 10 in the timeline.

4. Translate the sphere 1 unit up in the y direction.

5. Translate the cube 0.5 unit up in the y direction; press [s].

This keyframes the sphere and the cube because they're both in the selected character set. When you keyframe any object in a character set, all objects are keyframed automatically.

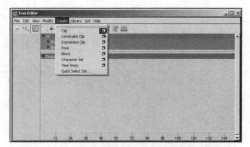

Figure 12.71 Clips contain all the keyframes for all the objects in your character set's animation. The clips can then be manipulated in the Trax Editor.

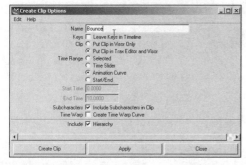

Figure 12.72 In the Create Clip Options dialog box, you can give the clip a unique name and set specific options for the clip's length and content.

6. Move to frame 20 in the timeline.

7. Translate the sphere back down 1 unit so it's back in its original position.

8. Translate the cube back to its original position, and press ⓢ.

Both the sphere and cube move up and back down as you drag through the timeline.

9. Choose Window > Animation Editors > Trax Editor.

The Trax Editor opens.

10. Click the Load Selected Characters icon ⬚.

Two tracks appear, representing your characters.

11. From the Create menu in the Trax Editor, select the check box next to Clip (**Figure 12.71**).

12. Change the Name to Bounce, and click Create Clip (**Figure 12.72**).

Two clips appear in the Trax timeline: Bounce and Bounce1. One clip is assigned to the box and one to the ball.

ABOUT THE TRAX EDITOR

To manipulate a clip:

1. Hold (Shift), and select both clips from the previous task (**Figure 12.73**).

   Arrows appear on both sides of the selected clips, indicating that they can be manipulated together.

2. Scale the clip by clicking the arrow near the right end of the clip and then dragging the clip (**Figure 12.74**).

3. Click the middle of the clip, and drag to move it in the timeline.

4. Click the All character set to deselect the two clips (**Figure 12.75**).

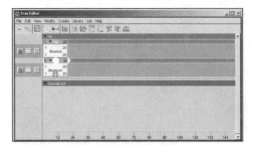

Figure 12.73 Collapsing the All character set lets you work with clips under the main character set. You see one clip as opposed to two subcharacter clips.

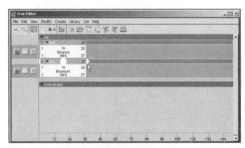

Figure 12.74 Scaling the clip.

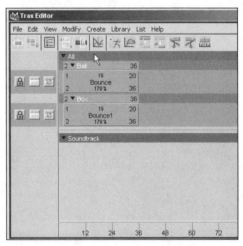

Figure 12.75 Click the arrow next to your main character set to reveal the subcharacter clips.

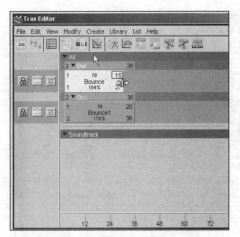

Figure 12.76 Cutting off the clip at a certain point doesn't destroy the original animation. You can adjust this at any time in the Trax Editor.

Figure 12.77 You can duplicate clips and distribute them wherever you need in your timeline.

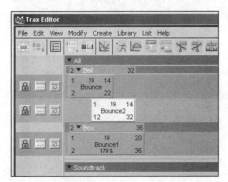

Figure 12.78 Drag Bounce2 to the left so that it overlaps Bounce. The Trax Editor creates a new track for Bounce2.

5. Position the cursor over the upper-right corner of the ball's Bounce clip until you see a double-headed arrow with a line in the middle (**Figure 12.76**). Drag the clip to the left until it becomes smaller.

The animation in that clip is cut off at that point.

or

Position the Current Time indicator at the point in the clip where you would like to trim it, and click the Trim Clip After Current Time icon.

6. Right-click the Bounce clip, and select Duplicate Clip (**Figure 12.77**).

This inserts the same clip at the position of the cursor in the timeline.

7. Drag the new Bounce2 clip to the left so that it overlaps the Bounce clip.

The Trax Editor creates a new track for Bounce2 (**Figure 12.78**).

8. Select Bounce2 and Bounce, and click the Create Blend icon.

The two animation clips are blended together to create a smooth transition between them (**Figure 12.79**).

continues on next page

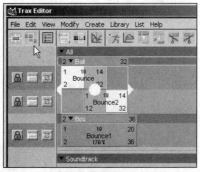

Figure 12.79 The Blend function creates a spline curve between the last frame of one clip and the first frame of another clip.

ABOUT THE TRAX EDITOR

9. Select Bounce2, and drag it to the right so that it no longer overlaps with Bounce (**Figure 12.80**).

There is currently no translation between the two clips, even though a blend has been assigned, because Bounce2 is set to a Relative Offset.

10. Select Bounce2; in the Channel Box, click in the field next to Offset, and select Absolute.

The blend interpolates between the end position of the last clip and the next clip.

11. Right-click Bounce1 in the Box track, and select Duplicate.

12. Select the new clip, position the Current Time indicator so that it's halfway through the clip, and click the Trim Clip After Current Time icon 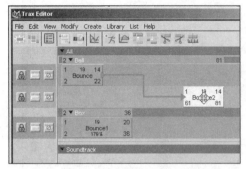 (**Figure 12.81**).

This trims the clip so the Box goes up but doesn't come down.

13. Right-click the new clip, and select Duplicate. Repeat this step several times to add several instances of the shortened clip to the track (**Figure 12.82**).

You now have several clips of the same animation one after each other for the Box subcharacter. The Bounce2 clip has an additive affect because the Offset on each clip is set to Relative; so, the box should bounce higher and higher.

Figure 12.80 Drag Bounce2 to the right so that it doesn't overlap Bounce. Currently there is no interpolation between the two clips because the Offset of Bounce2 is set to Relative.

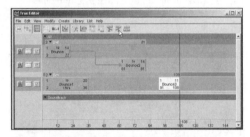

Figure 12.81 The Trax Editor lets you have multiple tracks for each character or subcharacter. By using multiple tracks, you can have more than one clip playing at the same time for the same character.

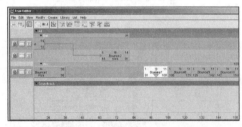

Figure 12.82 The same clip can be imported and moved to a new track. There it can be placed to overlap the original clip, adding to the motion of the original animation.

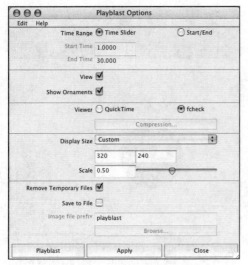

Figure 12.83 You set the Playblast options in this window. If you don't click Save to File and you close your movie player after you watch your animation, you'll have to repeat the Playblast procedure on the animation.

Previewing Your Animation

When you want to preview an animation, you can play it back in the timeline. However, a complex scene won't play smoothly at full speed. In addition, you'll often want to output your animations. For this purpose, Maya provides Playblast, which produces screen snapshots of your animation and turns them into an AVI file on the PC, a Quicktime file on the Mac, or a series of numbered images.

To create a Playblast preview:

1. Create an animation.

2. From the Window menu, select the check box next to Playblast to open the Playblast Options window (**Figure 12.83**).

3. Choose the time range for the movie file you want to create.

   The Time Slider uses your current playback start and end times. The Start Time and End Time fields allow you to enter your own times.

4. Adjust the resolution of the movie.

   If Display Size is set to From Window, the movie uses whichever view panel is currently active as the basis for the size. If you change Display Size to Custom, you can enter whatever resolution you want.

continues on next page

PREVIEWING YOUR ANIMATION

5. Select Save to File if you want Playblast to automatically save your series of numbered frames after you create it.

If Save to File is selected, you can click Browse to choose where you want the files saved. You can also make a movie file instead of a series of numbered frames.

6. Click the Playblast button.

Your animation plays back one frame at a time. A moment later, the FCheck window opens, where you can watch your animation (**Figure 12.84**).

Figure 12.84 You can use Fcheck to watch image sequences, or use your favorite movie player to watch movies you have rendered.

Using Constraints in Animation

Constraints are most often used to set up a character, but sometimes you'll want to use them while animating. For instance, if a character picks up a coffee cup from a table, it would be laborious to try to animate the cup moving wherever the character's hand does—but if you parent the cup to the hand, the cup will follow the hand everywhere even when you don't want it to.

Constraints offer an easy way to re-parent an object in the middle of a scene. Let's return to the coffee cup example. On the frame when the hand first contacts the cup, you can constrain the cup to the hand using a parent constraint. By animating the constraint's Blend Parent value, you can tell the cup when you want it to be attached to the hand and when you don't.

DEFORMERS

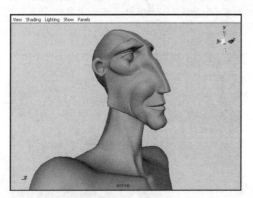

Figure 13.1 This alien's smile was created with a blend shapes deformer.

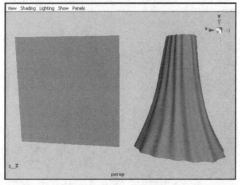

Figure 13.2 Sine, bend, and flare deformers combine to turn a plane (left) into a skirt (right).

Maya's deformers allow you to reshape geometry in a variety of ways. They can speed up many modeling tasks, from adjusting a model's proportions to adding detailed wrinkles to a high-resolution mesh. Deformers are also very useful for animation, whether you want to create ripples across a surface or make a character smile (**Figure 13.1**).

Maya's deformers include the nonlinear deformers bend, flare, sine, squash, twist, and wave; as well as the blend shapes, lattices, clusters, sculpt, jiggle, wire, wrinkle, and wrap deformers. All of these deformers have various settings that allow you to control exactly how they affect the surface to which you apply them. You can combine as many deformers as you need to achieve your desired effect (**Figure 13.2**).

Nonlinear Deformers

You can use nonlinear deformers to quickly distort a surface in a variety of useful ways, greatly speeding tasks that would otherwise require multiple CV selections and transformations. The nonlinear deformers are bend, flare, sine, squash, twist, and wave, each of which alters your surface in a way that matches its name (**Figure 13.3**).

When you create a nonlinear deformer, a special manipulator called a *handle* is added to your object (**Figure 13.4**). It's sized to fit your object initially, but if you scale or move the object, the handle doesn't move with it. However, you can select the deformer handle and translate, rotate, or scale it to change its effect on your object (**Figure 13.5**).

Most of the nonlinear deformer tools have the following options:

- **Envelope**—Scales the deformation, not in area, but in the degree to which it affects the surface. The default value is 1, but you can enter values from −2 to 2. A value of 2 doubles the deformation's effect; a negative value inverts the effect.

- **Low and High Bound**—Change where the effect of the deformation begins and ends along the deformation handle. They default to -1 (for low bound) and 1 (for high bound) and can be set to any negative or positive value, respectively.

In addition, each of the nonlinear deformers has its own set of options, which will be covered in the sections that follow.

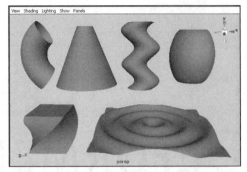

Figure 13.3 Top row, from left to right: Cylinders that have had the bend, flare, sine, and squash deformers applied to them. Bottom row: A cube with a twist deformer applied (left), and a plane with a wave deformer applied (right).

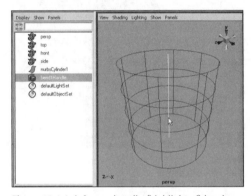

Figure 13.4 A deformer handle (highlighted) has been added to this cylinder.

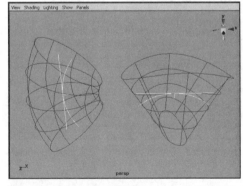

Figure 13.5 Both of these cylinders have had a bend deformer applied to them, but the deformer handle of the cylinder on the right has been rotated 90 degrees.

NONLINEAR DEFORMERS

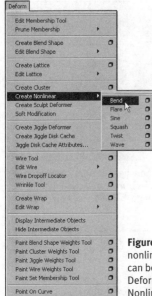

Figure 13.6 All of the nonlinear deformers can be created from the Deform > Create Nonlinear menu.

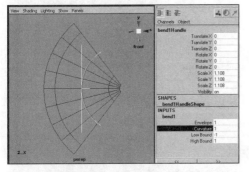

Figure 13.7 The Curvature attribute of the bend deformer controls the degree of the bend.

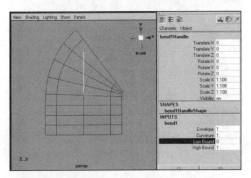

Figure 13.8 The Low Bound attribute, found in most nonlinear deformers, controls where the deformer's effect begins.

Bend deformer

The bend deformer can be a great time saver when you need to bend geometry, but don't want to take the time to move individual CVs or groups of CVs.

An additional option for the bend deformer is Curvature, which determines how much the object bends.

To use the bend deformer:

1. Select the object to be deformed.

2. Choose Deform > Create Nonlinear > Bend (**Figure 13.6**).

   A bend deformer is added to the selected surface.

3. Click the bend1 title under the Inputs section of the Channel Box.

   The bend properties are displayed.

4. Set Curvature to 1.

   The object is now bent around its center (**Figure 13.7**).

5. Set Low Bound to 0.

   The object's bend still starts at its center, but only the top of the object is bent (**Figure 13.8**).

✔ Tip

■ Have your surface geometry ready with the desired number of CVs or vertices before you add a deformer to a surface. Adding geometry after a deformer is applied may cause undesirable results.

Flare deformer

You can add a flare deformer to a surface to quickly taper or flare its geometry. It's useful for surfaces like jugs, bellies, and bell-bottoms.

The additional options for the flare deformer are as follows:

◆ **Start Flare X and Z**—Determine the amount of flare at the start of the low bound along the specified axis.

◆ **End Flare X and Z**—Determine the amount of flare at the start of the high bound along the specified axis.

◆ **Curve**—Determines the amount of curvature between the low and high bound.

To use the flare deformer:

1. Select the object to be deformed.

2. Choose Deform > Create Nonlinear > Flare.

3. Click the flare1 title under the Inputs section of the Channel Box to view the flare properties (**Figure 13.9**).

4. Click Start Flare X.

5. Click and drag with the middle mouse button in the view to dynamically change the attribute's value.

   or

   Type in the desired value.

   The object is flared at the bottom along the x axis (**Figure 13.10**).

6. Adjust the Curve attribute using one of the methods just described.

   The object is curved along the flare (**Figure 13.11**).

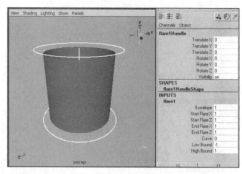

Figure 13.9 When a nonlinear deformer is created, it has no immediate effect on the object. To deform the object, you must change the deformer's properties.

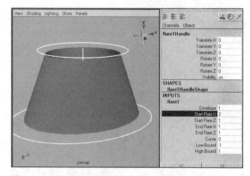

Figure 13.10 Adjusting Start Flare X flares the bottom of the object along the x axis.

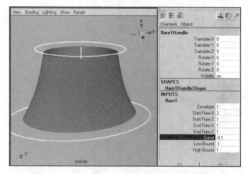

Figure 13.11 Positive values for the Curve attribute create an outward curve along the flare; negative Curve values create an inward curve, as shown here.

NONLINEAR DEFORMERS

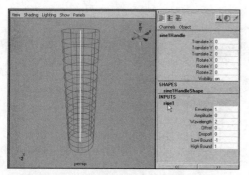

Figures 13.12 Be sure your geometry has enough detail to support the deformation you're trying to create. This cylinder of 16 spans will be used to demonstrate the sine deformer.

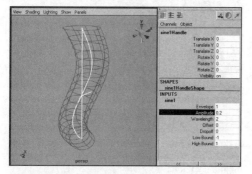

Figure 13.13 Amplitude controls the size of the individual sine waves but not their number.

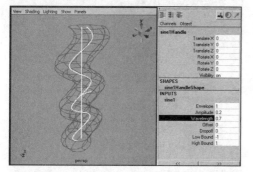

Figure 13.14 Reducing the Wavelength value shortens the waves and increases their frequency, creating more of them in a given area.

Sine deformer

The sine deformer changes the shape of an object along a sine wave, which is a line that follows a regular pattern of hills and valleys. The additional sine options are as follows:

◆ **Amplitude**—Determines the maximum wave amount.

◆ **Wavelength**—Increasing stretches the pattern out over a longer distance. Decreasing this value makes the pattern shorter, creating more repetitions in the same amount of space.

◆ **Offset**—Determines the position of the sine wave relative to the center of the deformer handle.

◆ **Dropoff**—Determines how the amplitude of the sine wave changes along the deformer handle. Positive values cause the amplitude to get increasingly smaller away from the center of the deformer handle, whereas negative values have the opposite effect.

To use the sine deformer:

1. Select the object to be deformed.

2. Choose Deform > Create Nonlinear > Sine.

3. Click the sine1 title under the Inputs section of the Channel Box to view the sine properties (**Figure 13.12**).

4. Click Amplitude.

5. Click and drag with the middle mouse button in the view, or enter a value in the Amplitude field.

   The surface begins to have a wavy shape (**Figure 13.13**).

6. Click Wavelength.

7. Click and drag left with the middle mouse button in the view, or enter a smaller value in the Wavelength field.

   More waves appear on the surface (**Figure 13.14**).

NONLINEAR DEFORMERS

335

Squash deformer

The squash deformer lets you both squash and stretch a surface. This differs from scaling the surface along a single axis in that the squash deformer automatically causes the surface to bulge outward when it's squashed or to get thinner as it's stretched. Thus you can maintain the illusion that the surface is a real object with a fixed volume.

The additional squash options are as follows:

◆ **Factor**—Determines the amount an object is squashed or stretched. Positive values stretch the object, and negative ones squash it.

◆ **Expand**—Determines how much an object expands outward while squashing or inward while stretching.

◆ **Max Expand Position**—Determines where along the deformer handle the expansion is most prominent.

◆ **Start and End Smoothness**—These settings are similar to Dropoff for the sine deformer. These options let you create a smooth transition out of the deformation at their respective ends of the deformation handle.

To use the squash deformer:

1. Select the object to be deformed.

2. Choose Deform > Create Nonlinear > Squash.

3. Click the squash1 title under the Inputs section of the Channel Box to view the squash properties (**Figure 13.15**).

4. Click Factor.

5. Click and drag left and right with the middle mouse button in the view to squash (**Figure 13.16**) and stretch (**Figure 13.17**) the object.

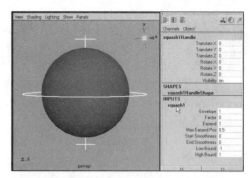

Figure 13.15 A bouncing ball is a common application of squash and stretch in animation.

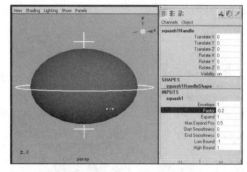

Figure 13.16 Using the squash deformer to squash an object automatically bulges the object outward to maintain volume.

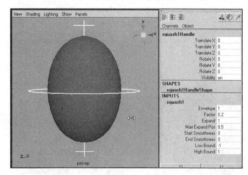

Figure 13.17 Using the squash deformer to stretch an object automatically thins the object to maintain volume.

✔ Tip

■ The squash deformer can be keyframed to squash and stretch an object or character.

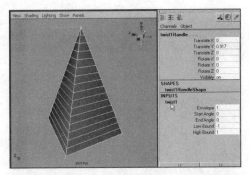

Figure 13.18 Although you can apply a twist deformer to any surface, its effects are less significant on those with round cross-sections. Here a pyramid is selected.

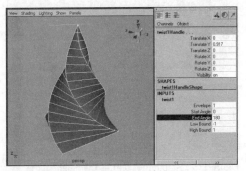

Figure 13.19 Changing the Start or End angle twists the surface.

Twist deformer

The twist deformer is equivalent to selecting and rotating each cross-section of your geometry to create a smooth twist of a specified number of degrees. However, using a twist deformer is much more efficient than doing this by hand.

The twist deformer includes two additional options, Start and End Angle, which determine the degree of twisting at the low or high bound position, respectively.

To use the twist deformer:

1. Select the object to be deformed.

2. Choose Deform > Create Nonlinear > Twist.

3. Click the twist1 title under the Inputs section of the Channel Box to view the twist properties (**Figure 13.18**).

4. Set End Angle to 180.

   The surface twists around the center of the deformer such that the top of the object is rotated 180 degrees (**Figure 13.19**).

Wave deformer

The wave deformer is perfect for creating small waves and expanding rings of ripples. This deformer works best on high-resolution flat surfaces. Additional wave options include the following:

◆ **Amplitude**—Determines the maximum wave amount.

◆ **Wavelength**—Increasing this value makes the waves longer, stretching them out on the surface. Decreasing this value it makes the waves shorter and more frequent.

continues on next page

- **Offset**—Determines the position of the wave pattern relative to the center of the deformer handle. You can animate the offset to make a surface ripple outward.

- **Dropoff**—Determines how the amplitude of the waves changes along the deformer handle. Positive values cause the amplitude to get increasingly smaller away from the center of the deformer handle, and negative values have the opposite effect.

- **Dropoff Position**—Determines where along the deformer handle the Dropoff attribute takes effect.

- **Min and Max Radius**—Determine where the wave begins and ends along the deformer handle.

To use the wave deformer:

1. Select the object to be deformed.

2. Choose Deform > Create Nonlinear > Wave.

3. Click the wave1 title under the Inputs section of the Channel Box to view the wave properties (**Figure 13.20**).

4. Set Amplitude to 0.1.
   The object becomes wavy (**Figure 13.21**).

5. Set Wavelength to 0.2.
   More waves appear on the object.

6. Set Dropoff to 1.0.
   The waves diminish in amplitude away from the center of the object (**Figure 13.22**).

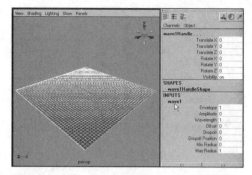

Figure 13.20 The wave deformer works best on flat, detailed surfaces, like this high-resolution plane.

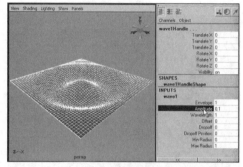

Figure 13.21 Amplitude controls the height of the individual waves, and Wavelength controls their length.

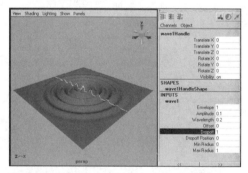

Figure 13.22 Increasing the Dropoff value causes the amplitude of the waves to decrease as they move away from the center of the object.

NONLINEAR DEFORMERS

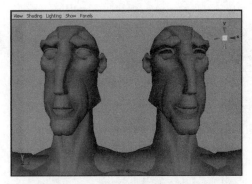

Figure 13.23 The duplicate object (right) has been modified to create a smile.

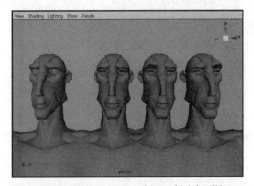

Figure 13.24 The three target objects (right) will be hidden after the blend shape is created, so it doesn't matter that they overlap the original character (left).

Blend Shapes

Maya's blend shapes deformer lets you deform an object to match the shape of one or more objects. These *target objects* are usually copies of the original object, modified in specific areas. For example, you can duplicate a character's geometry, reshape the duplicate's mouth into a smile, and use it as a target object. This technique allows you to animate a smooth transition from a neutral expression to a smile. Because you can have multiple target objects, you can easily add a wink or a raised eyebrow. You can animate the influence of each target independently using the Blend Shape editor.

Blend shapes are most commonly used for facial expressions and *phonemes*, the mouth positions used for lip sync.

To create a blend shape:

1. Select the object to which you want to add a blend shape.

2. Duplicate the object by choosing Edit > Duplicate.

3. Move the duplicate object away from the original so you can easily edit it.

4. Modify the duplicate object's CVs or vertices to create the expression you want (**Figure 13.23**).

5. Rename the object to reflect its expression. This name will be used to label the target object's slider in the Blend Shape window.

6. Repeat steps 1–5 for as many target objects as you want to use in the blend shape (**Figure 13.24**).

continues on next page

7. Select all the duplicate objects.

8. [Shift]-select the original object.

9. Choose Deform > Create Blend Shape (**Figure 13.25**).

A blend shape is created for the original object, using the duplicate objects as targets.

✔ Tips

■ You can modify a blend shape by editing any of its target objects in component mode. The blend shape automatically reflects your changes.

■ Once you've created a blend shape, you can hide or delete the target objects you used to create it. Deleting them reduces the file size and may improve manipulation speed but removes your ability to modify the blend shape.

To animate with a blend shape:

1. Choose Window > Animation Editors > Blend Shape.

2. Under the blend shape you want to animate, move the target slider(s) to create the pose you want (**Figure 13.26**).

3. Key the target weights by clicking the Key button under each target weight you've modified, or click the Key All button on the left side of the Blend Shape editor.

4. Move to another keyframe, and repeat steps 2 and 3 to continue animating.

✔ Tips

■ To view a blend shape's keys in the timeline or Graph Editor, click the Select button below it in the Blend Shape editor.

■ You can multiply a target's effect by entering a value greater than 1 in its field. This creates an exaggerated effect on the object that's being influenced.

Figure 13.25
To create a new blend shape, choose Create Blend Shape from the Deform menu.

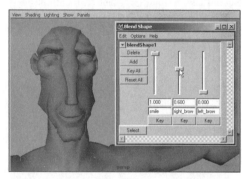

Figure 13.26 Moving a target slider causes the object with the blend shape to deform, taking on the appearance of the associated target object.

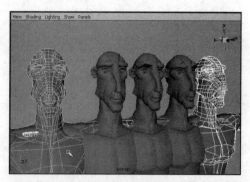

Figure 13.27 You can add additional target objects to a preexisting blend shape at any time.

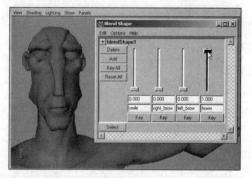

Figure 13.28 A new slider is displayed in the Blend Shape editor.

To add a target to a blend shape:

1. Select the new target object.

   This object should be based on a duplicate of the original, since target objects must have the same number of vertices.

2. [Shift]-select the object with a preexisting blend shape (**Figure 13.27**).

3. Choose Deform > Edit Blend Shape > Add.

   The new target appears in the Blend Shape editor (**Figure 13.28**).

Lattices

The lattice is one of Maya's most useful deformers. It surrounds an object with a box-like wireframe structure; this is the *lattice* the deformer is named for. The points of this structure can be selected and transformed, which also transforms the portion of the surface they enclose. Unlike the handles used to control most deformers, a lattice is itself a deformable object, which means you can modify it using any of Maya's deformers.

Unlike most Maya objects, a lattice deformer's options can be found in its Shape node in the Channel Box. These options are the S, T, and U Divisions, which control the resolution of the lattice. The minimum value for each Divisions setting is 2; increasing this number adds lines across the corresponding faces of the lattice. Where these lines cross, lattice points are created. A higher resolution lattice provides more precise control, whereas a lower resolution lattice is simpler, with fewer points to move.

To use a lattice to deform a surface:

1. Select the surface to be deformed.

2. Choose Deform > Create Lattice.
   A lattice deformer is added to the selected surface (**Figure 13.29**).

3. Switch to component mode by pressing F8 .
   The points of the lattice become visible.

4. Select one or more lattice point(s) (**Figure 13.30**).

5. Move the selected lattice point(s).
   The original surface is deformed by the change in the lattice shape (**Figure 13.31**).

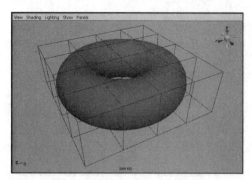

Figure 13.29 A newly created lattice is automatically sized to fit the object it deforms.

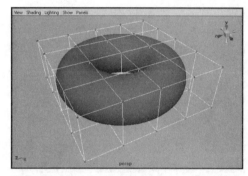

Figure 13.30 To deform an object using a lattice, switch to component mode and transform the lattice's points.

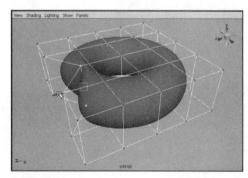

Figure 13.31 Moving the points of a lattice affects the object the lattice deforms.

LATTICES

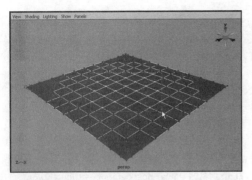

Figure 13.32 The points you select will be added to the cluster when you create it.

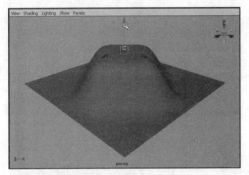

Figure 13.33 Moving a cluster handle moves all the points associated with that cluster.

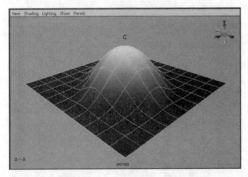

Figure 13.34 By editing a cluster's weights, you can create a smooth transition between the point of maximum influence for the cluster and the surrounding nondeformed surface.

Clusters

Clusters may be the simplest of Maya's deformers, but they can be very useful. A cluster lets you control a set of points from an object. Moving, rotating, or scaling the cluster's handle moves, rotates, or scales the points to a degree that's determined by the cluster's *weight* for each point. At a maximum weight of 1.0, the cluster completely controls a point. At smaller values, it has a proportionately smaller effect: A point with a weight of 0.5 for a cluster moves half as far as a point with a weight of 1.0.

Clusters are most commonly used for animation, whether they're keyframed directly or used indirectly as part of a rig.

To create a cluster:

1. In component mode, select the CVs or vertices from which you want to create a cluster (**Figure 13.32**). You can switch to component mode by pressing F8.

2. Choose Deform > Create Cluster.

   A cluster is created for the object from its selected components.

3. Click the C that appears in the view; this is the cluster's handle.

4. Move the handle to see the effect of the cluster (**Figure 13.33**).

✔ Tip

■ You can adjust a cluster's weights to create a smooth blend between the area affected by the cluster and the rest of the object (**Figure 13.34**). See "About Deformer Weights," later in this chapter.

CLUSTERS

Sculpt Deformers

Sculpt deformers use a spherical influence object called a *sculpt sphere* to deform a surface. Sculpt deformers are useful for creating rounded surface effects when you're modeling. Switching the deformer's mode between flip, project, and stretch produces different surface effects.

To create a sculpt deformer:

1. Select the surface to be deformed.

2. From the Deform menu, click the box next to Create Sculpt Deformer.

   The Sculpt Options window appears (**Figure 13.35**).

3. If necessary, choose a different Mode option.

   In most cases, the default (Stretch) is fine.

4. Click Create to create the deformer.

   A sculpt sphere is added to your object (**Figure 13.36**).

5. Select the sculpt sphere, and move it along the *y* axis.

   The original geometry deforms with it (**Figure 13.37**).

✔ Tips

■ You can select and move the locator (crosshairs) to move the geometry over the sculpt object.

■ You can substitute any NURBS object for the default sculpt when creating a sculpt deformation. To do so, (Shift)-select it after the object to be deformed, and select the Use Secondary NURBS Object as Sculpt Tool check box in the Sculpt Options window.

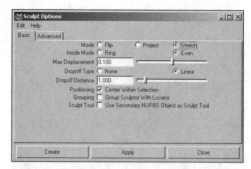

Figure 13.35 Unlike most deformer attributes, you can only change the mode of a sculpt deformer prior to creating the deformer.

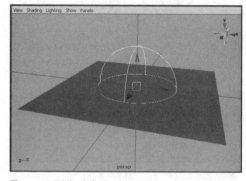

Figure 13.36 By default, the sculpt deformer creates a sphere to control the deformation of the object.

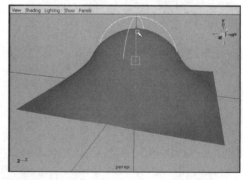

Figure 13.37 Moving the sculpt sphere causes the surface to move with it, conforming to the sculpt sphere's shape.

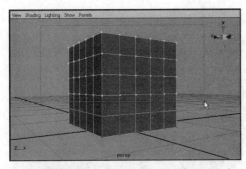

Figure 13.38 When you apply a jiggle deformer to the upper portion of this cube, it appears to be gelatinous when animated.

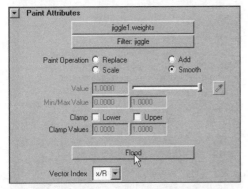

Figure 13.39 You can use the Flood feature of the Paint Attributes tool to quickly smooth out deformer weights, creating a more natural effect.

Figure 13.40 While using the Paint Attributes tool, weights are displayed in shades from white to black on the surface of the selected object.

Jiggle Deformers

Unlike the other deformers we have discussed, jiggle deformers are dynamic, deforming geometry in reaction to motion. When a real object with a fleshy or rubbery surface stops moving, it jiggles back and forth before it eventually settles. Maya's jiggle deformer lets you simulate this effect.

The jiggle deformer has several options. The most commonly used are Stiffness, Damping, and Motion Multiplier. Changing the Stiffness value affects the rigidity of the jiggle, making the object jittery at high values and fluid at low values. Changing the Damping value affects how long the jiggling surface takes to stop moving. The Motion Multiplier attribute scales the overall effect of the jiggle.

Although you can apply a jiggle deformer to an entire object, it's usually more effective to apply it to a specific area, like a character's belly.

To create a jiggle deformer:

1. In component mode, select the CVs or vertices that you want to be affected by the jiggle deformer (**Figure 13.38**). You can switch to component mode by pressing F8.

2. Choose Deform > Create Jiggle Deformer.

3. Switch to object mode by pressing F8.

4. From the Deform menu, choose the box next to Paint Jiggle Weights.

   The Paint Attributes tool settings are displayed.

5. Under the Paint Attributes section, change the Paint Operation to Smooth, and click Flood several times (**Figure 13.39**).

   This smooths out the jiggle weights across the surface of the object (**Figure 13.40**). (See "About Deformer Weights," later in this chapter.)

continues on next page

6. Switch to the Channel Box by clicking its icon at the top right corner of the screen ▦.

7. Click the Enable field, and select Enable Only After Object Stops from the drop-down options (**Figure 13.41**).

This option prevents the jiggle deformer from causing undesirable motion while the object is moving.

8. Select the object, and create a keyframe for it (press ⒮) at frame 1.

9. Go to frame 10 by clicking it in the Time Slider.

10. Press ⒲, and move the object. If Auto Key isn't on, press ⒮ again to keyframe the object in its new position.

11. Make sure the Range Slider is set to display at least 24 frames, to allow enough time to see the full effect of the jiggle deformer.

12. In the timeline, press Play ▶ to view the animation.

The area affected by the jiggle deformer jiggles after the object comes to a stop at frame 10 (**Figure 13.42**). The jiggle gradually diminishes until the object returns to its normal position (**Figure 13.43**).

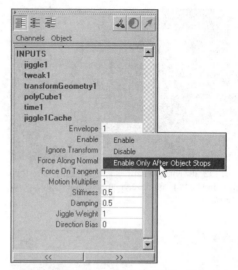

Figure 13.41 Choosing Enable Only After Object Stops means that the jiggle deformer's effects aren't applied when the object is in motion.

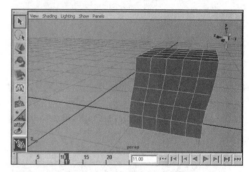

Figure 13.42 When the cube comes to a stop, the upper area of the cube jiggles to an extent determined by the jiggle deformer's weights.

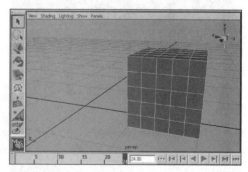

Figure 13.43 The object returns to its normal position once the jiggling subsides.

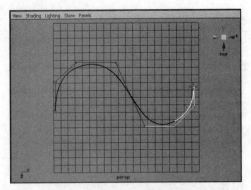

Figure 13.44 Although it isn't necessary for a wire to overlap the surface it will deform, it's helpful for determining what area the wire will effect.

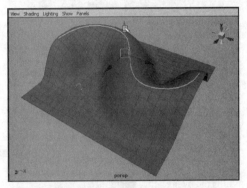

Figure 13.45 Moving the newly created wire deforms the surface. You can control the extent and effect of the deformation with the wire deformer's attributes.

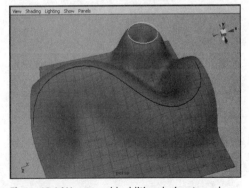

Figure 13.46 You can add additional wires to a wire deformer. Here a NURBS circle (highlighted) has been added.

Wire Deformers

Wire deformers use one or more NURBS curves, called *wires,* to deform the selected surface. This can be useful when you want to deform an area defined by a curve or several curves, such as an eyebrow or a crease.

The wire deformer has several attributes, including Dropoff Distance, which controls how far a wire's influence extends, and Scale, which scales the geometry affected by the wire up or down, creating a sharper or more rounded effect. If you create a wire deformer with multiple wires, each wire has its own Scale and Dropoff Distance attributes.

To create a wire deformer:

1. Create a NURBS curve that overlaps the surface you want to deform (**Figure 13.44**).

2. Choose Deform > Wire Tool.

3. Select the surface, and press Enter.

4. Select the curve, and press Enter.

5. Move the curve.

   The surface deforms as if the curve is pulling or pushing it (**Figure 13.45**).

To add a wire to a wire deformer:

1. Create a wire deformer following the steps in the previous task.

2. Create another NURBS curve.

3. Select the preexisting wire.

4. Shift-select the new NURBS curve.

5. Choose Deform > Edit Wire > Add.

   The second NURBS curve can now be used to deform the surface (**Figure 13.46**).

✔ Tip

■ You can manipulate the individual CVs of wires to further control the deformation of the surface.

Wrinkle Deformers

The wrinkle deformer consists of one or more wire deformers. It automatically creates the wires and combines them under a cluster handle, providing you with a quick and easy way to create wrinkles on a surface.

The wrinkle deformer has options for creating radial wrinkles, which branch out from a center point, and tangential wrinkles, which run parallel to each other along the surface. You can also use the Custom type to create wrinkles based on preexisting NURBS curve(s).

To create a wrinkle deformer:

1. Select the surface you want to deform.

2. From the Deform menu, choose the box next to Wrinkle Tool.

   The Wrinkle tool options appear, and a UV region is displayed on your model.

3. In the Wrinkle tool settings, choose the Type, and adjust any other settings you'd like to change (**Figure 13.47**).

4. In the view, click and drag with the middle mouse button on the control points of the UV region.

   The points on the edges let you resize it, the points on the corners let you rotate it, and the point in the middle lets you position it (**Figure 13.48**).

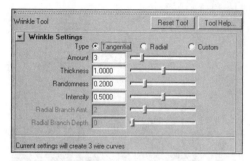

Figure 13.47 The Wrinkle tool settings let you determine what type and number of wrinkles will be created on your surface.

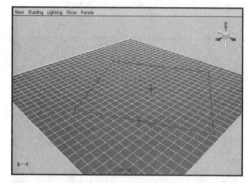

Figure 13.48 By modifying and repositioning this UV region, you can determine what area of your surface is affected by the wrinkle deformer.

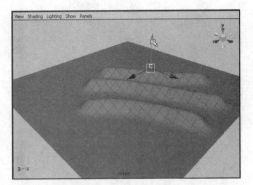

Figure 13.49 Moving the cluster handle causes the wrinkles created by the wrinkle deformer to appear on the surface of your object.

5. Press Enter.

A cluster handle appears over the object.

6. Select and move the cluster handle.

The surface wrinkles in the area you've selected (**Figure 13.49**).

✔ Tip

■ If you're looking for the wires created by the wrinkle deformer, you can view and select them in the Outliner, under their associated clusterHandle. You can display them by choosing Display > Show > Show Selected or by setting their Visibility to On in the Channel Box. As with the wire deformer, you can manipulate a wire's CVs to deform the surface.

Wrap Deformers

Wrap deformers create an effect similar to a lattice, but rather than deforming a surface using a simple grid, any object or objects can be used. The objects used by wrap deformers to deform a surface are referred to as *influence objects*. You may want to display these influence objects as wireframes, even when the view is shaded, so they don't obscure your view of the model.

To create a wrap deformer:

1. Select the object you want to be deformed.

2. Shift-select the object you want to use as an influence object (**Figure 13.50**).

3. Select Deform > Create Wrap.

4. In component mode (press F8), select one or more points of the influence object.

5. Press w, and move the points.

   The points of the object to which the wrap deformer is applied move proportionately (**Figure 13.51**).

To display an influence object as a wireframe:

1. Select the influence object.

2. Open the Attribute Editor by clicking its icon on the right side of the status line or by pressing Ctrl+a.

3. In the Attribute Editor, click the arrow next to Object Display and then the arrow next to Drawing Overrides.

4. Select Enable Overrides, and then deselect Shading.

   The influence object is no longer shaded, and it's visible as a wireframe even in shaded mode (**Figure 13.52**).

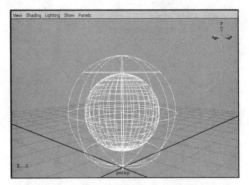

Figure 13.50 Here a low-resolution sphere will be used as an influence object to deform a higher-resolution sphere.

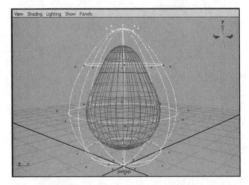

Figure 13.51 Moving the points of a wrap deformer's influence object modifies the object it deforms.

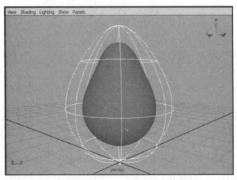

Figure 13.52 The influence object is displayed as a wireframe, even though the view is shaded. This lets you see the object being deformed while using the influence object to deform it.

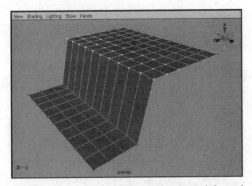

Figure 13.53 A section of this plane has been deformed using a cluster. By changing its weight on the selected points, you can change how much its movement affects those points.

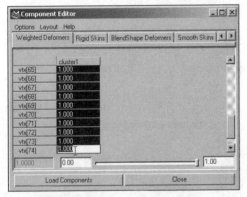

Figure 13.54 By clicking and dragging to select all the fields, you can enter a single value to change all the values at once.

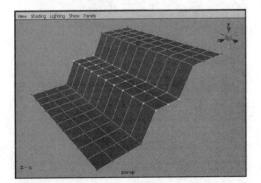

Figure 13.55 With a new cluster weight value of 0.5, the selected points move half as far as they did before.

About Deformer Weights

Several of the deformers we've discussed have *weights*, which determine how much they affect any given point on a surface. In some cases, you may want to change the extent to which a deformer affects specific areas of an object. To do this, you can modify its weights in the Component Editor or paint their values using Maya's Paint Attributes tool.

The Component Editor provides a numeric view of the weights and is most useful when you want to change the weights on a specific group of points to a specific value. The Paint Attributes tool displays the weights on your model, with pure white representing a weight of 1.0 and pure black representing a weight of 0. This tool lets you paint or flood specific values or smooth the transition between values.

To edit deformer weights in the Component Editor:

1. In component mode, select the points whose weights you want to modify (**Figure 13.53**).

2. Choose Window > General Editors > Component Editor.

3. In the Component Editor, click the Weighted Deformers tab.

4. Click the top field under the deformer's name, and then drag down to highlight all of the deformer's weights (**Figure 13.54**).

5. Enter the new value for the weights.

   All the weights for the selected points become the new value (**Figure 13.55**).

To paint skin weights on a smooth skin:

1. Select the surface whose weights you want to modify.

2. From the Deform menu, choose the Paint tool for the type of deformer whose weights you want to change (**Figure 13.56**).

   The Paint Attributes tool is activated.

3. Double-click the Paint Attributes tool button in the Tool Box .

   The Tool Settings window opens for the Paint Attributes tool (**Figure 13.57**).

Figure 13.56 You can paint weights for blend shapes, clusters, and jiggle or wire deformers.

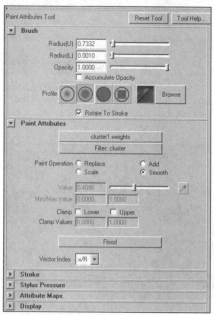

Figure 13.57 The Tool Settings window lets you choose a Paint Operation and Value to paint with, along with other settings.

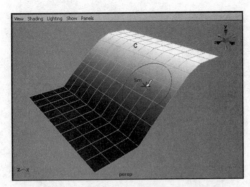

Figure 13.58 Here the Paint Attributes tool has been used to smooth a cluster's weights.

4. If it isn't already selected, choose Smooth Shade All from your view's Shading menu.

This option lets you see the weights on your model.

5. Under Paint Attributes in the Tool Settings, choose a Paint Operation and/or Value to paint with.

6. Adjust the brush size by holding down $\boxed{b}$ and dragging from right to left with the middle mouse button.

7. Using your chosen settings, paint the area you wish to change.

or

Use the Flood button to apply the selected Paint Operation and Value to the entire surface.

If the deformer is currently affecting the object, you can see the object's surface adjust dynamically to reflect the changes (**Figure 13.58**).

About the Deformation Order

The deformation order of a Maya object determines the order in which various operations are applied to that object. For example, if an object has a twist deformer applied and then a bend deformer, the effect is different than if the twist is applied after the bend (**Figure 13.59**).

By default, each new deformation is added to the end of the deformation order; but in some cases, you may realize afterward that you want a particular deformation to take effect earlier (**Figure 13.60**). You can either use the deformer's Options window to choose where to place it in the deformation order when you create it, or use the following method to change the deformation order of any deformers at any time.

To change the deformation order:

1. Right-click over the object whose deformation order you want to change.

2. From the marking menu, select Inputs > All Inputs (**Figure 13.61**).

   The list of input operations appears. The lower in this list an operation appears, the earlier it's applied.

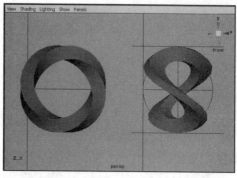

Figure 13.59 Both objects began as elongated cubes, but one was twisted and then bent (left), and the other was bent and then twisted (right).

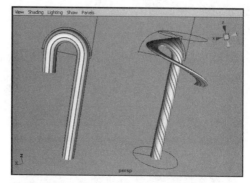

Figure 13.60 This candy cane needs to have a twist applied before the bend, not after (right).

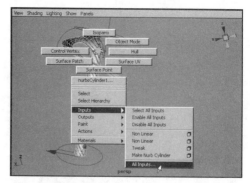

Figure 13.61 Maya's marking menus provide access to context-sensitive functionality.

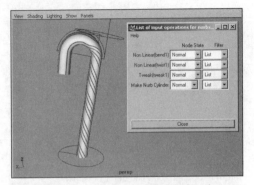

Figure 13.62 The twist is now applied before the bend, but because its deformer handle is positioned to fit the bent model, it isn't quite right.

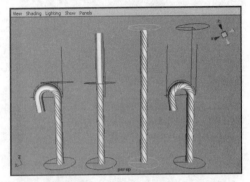

Figure 13.63 By unbending the candy cane, you can see that the twist deformer handle doesn't extend far enough. With a few adjustments, the twist can be extended around the bend (right).

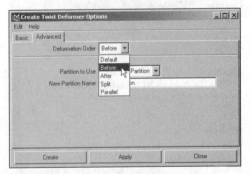

Figure 13.64 In the Advanced tab of a new deformation's Deformer Options window, you can change where in the Deformation Order the deformation is added.

3. Using your middle mouse button, click and drag from the input you want to move to the input you want it to precede.

The object changes to reflect the new deformation order (**Figure 13.62**).

✔ Tip

■ Because deformer handles are placed based on an object's deformed position, you may need to adjust them to create the desired effect (**Figure 13.63**).

To create a deformer that is placed first in the deformation order:

1. When creating the deformer, select the box next to the deformer's name in the Deform menu.

2. In the Deformer Options window, choose the Advanced tab.

3. Select Before from the Deformation Order drop-down options (**Figure 13.64**).

4. The newly created deformer is applied before any existing deformers on the object.

✔ Tip

■ If you delete an object's history, you won't be able to change its deformation order or create deformations that are applied before existing deformations.

Hiding, Showing, and Deleting Deformers

If you're done editing your deformers, or if you just want to view your scene without them, you can hide them for your view. Only the deformer handles will be hidden, so you'll still be able to see the effects of the deformers on your models. You can also delete a deformer, either to remove its deformation from an object, or to make its deformation a part of the mesh itself. This removes your ability to edit the deformation's attributes, but it may speed up manipulation of your scene.

To delete a deformer:

1. Select the deformer handle of the deformer you wish to delete (**Figure 13.65**).

2. Select Edit > Delete, or press (Backspace).
   The deformer is deleted, and any effect it had on the object it was applied to is removed (**Figure 13.66**).

To delete a deformer while keeping its deformations on a surface:

1. Select the object with the deformer you wish to delete.

2. Select Edit > Delete by Type > History.
   The deformer is deleted, but the object remains in its deformed position (**Figure 13.67**).

To hide or show deformers in a view:

◆ From the view's Show menu, select Deformers.

   If this option is selected, it becomes deselected, and deformers are hidden for that view. If it's deselected, it becomes selected, and deformers are displayed for that view.

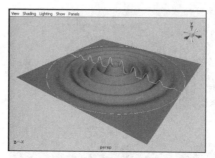

Figure 13.65 This plane has had a wave deformer applied to it. The deformer's handle is selected.

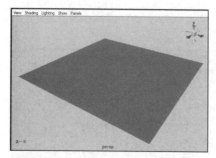

Figure 13.66 By deleting the wave deformer handle, the plane is restored to its undeformed state.

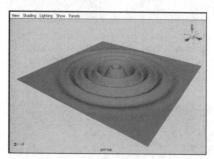

Figure 13.67 By using Delete by Type > History, the wave deformer is removed while its effects on the plane are retained.

✔ Tip

■ You can use the Hide > Hide Deformers and Show > Show Deformers submenus of the Display menu to hide or show deformers in all views. You can also select specific deformer object types to hide or show in these submenus.

SHADERS, MATERIALS, AND MAPPING

Figure 14.1 The objects at left and the objects at right have the same geometry. However, they've been assigned different shaders, which makes them look like they're made from different substances.

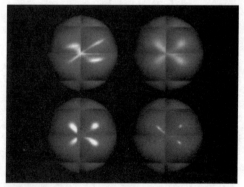

Figure 14.2 Four of the basic materials are shown here (anisotropic, blinn, phong, and phong e). The white specular highlights indicate the difference in how they reflect light.

By default, objects in Maya are a matte gray color. This appearance, like the appearance of all objects in Maya, is controlled by a *shader*. By changing the shader assigned to an object, you can control the object's appearance and surface behaviors.

Shaders control more than just the color of the object: They can make a surface appear shiny and metallic, or rough and rocky (**Figure 14.1**). You can use shaders to make your objects glow, reflect and refract light, appear transparent, and more.

Shaders consist of one or more *materials* or texture nodes linked together. A material controls a number of common attributes of a surface, as well as shininess. *Shininess* is a surface attribute that is determined by how light plays over the object. Maya includes several material types, and they differ primarily in their control over reflection and the *specular highlight*. The specular highlight is the hotspot (bright area) created on a surface by nearby lights. Choosing a material type allows you to change the appearance of the specular highlight: Hard glassy surfaces have tiny, bright highlights; rough surfaces like rubber and plastic have broad, indistinct highlights (**Figure 14.2**).

In addition, Maya materials have other special attributes that provide even greater control with unusual surfaces. Features like incandescence, ambience, and glow all mimic complicated effects. For example, you can make a light bulb seem brighter by adding incandescence or add a soft glow by adding glow attributes (**Figure 14.3**).

Because textures and images have two dimensions, and your object has three, it's important to tell Maya how to wrap your materials around your object. Placing shaders on an object is just as important as creating the correct shader.

There are two primary ways to position a texture: projections and *UV mapping*. UVs, which are stored within an object, tell a texture where it needs to go. NURBs objects come with built in (and un-editable) UVs, but polygonal models don't. Maya provides a special editor for editing UV coordinates.

Projections automate the process somewhat, distributing texture information to the appropriate UV areas. A projection can affect multiple surfaces, making it a good option for objects with many small parts.

Figure 14.3 This light bulb looks lit up when its material is given some incandescence and glow.

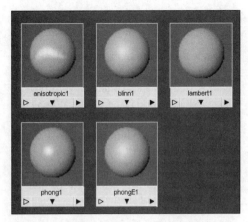

Figure 14.4 These are the basic materials available in the Hypershade.

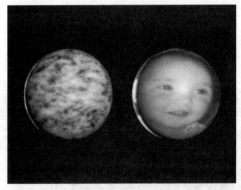

Figure 14.5 The sphere on the left has a fractal texture, which is a procedural texture. The sphere on the right has an image texture.

About the Hypershade

You put together shaders in a workspace called the Hypershade. It displays your *shader network*, which is a collection of nodes such as materials, textures, lights, and utilities. To build a shader, you connect textures and utilities to materials and then assign those materials to your models.

A *material* is a node that contains many of the controls available to the surface. Materials also encapsulate data from other kinds of nodes and are the only kind of node that can be assigned to an object. The kind of material you use also affects the look of the object and which controls are available to it. The Hypershade provides ten kinds of material nodes: five basic materials and five special-case materials (**Figure 14.4**).

A *texture* is an image, either computer generated or bitmapped, like a .jpg or .psd file (**Figure 14.5**). A computer-generated texture is called a *procedural* texture. The use of textures allows for much more detailed control than a simple constant setting offers. The texture image can be mapped to the attributes of a material, and the value or color of the image is then used instead of the original setting. These images can control color, shininess, bump, transparency, and more.

An object in Maya can have only one material assigned to it, but a network can consist of many materials and textures working together. To help keep track of these complicated relationships, Maya provides a third node type, called *utilities*.

Utilities are nodes that take input from a texture or material and alter it in some way. Different Maya utilities adjust shaders in various ways. A couple of common utilities are the bump2d utility, which lets you create a bump map, and the 2D placement utility, which lets you position a texture on a surface.

Using the Hypershade

The Hypershade is split into three areas: the Create and Bins bars, the Hypershade node tabs, and the work-area tabs:

◆ To use the Create bar, click the black triangle below the Create tab, and select Create Maya Nodes from the pull-down menu. This option reveals a long list of nodes you can use to create shaders (you can also use the Create menu to make any of these shaders) (**Figure 14.6**). The nodes you'll need most often are

Surface, 2D Textures, 3D Textures, and Other Textures.

◆ Beside the Create tab is a Bins tab. Click it to reveal the Bins bar. Here you can create virtual folders to organize your project's shaders and other nodes. When you click a bin, the shaders or nodes stored within are displayed in the top part of the Hypershade under the relevant tab. Using bins to store your shaders makes it much easier to work with projects that require a large numbers of shaders.

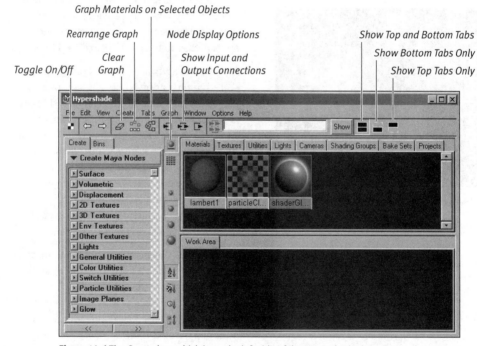

Figure 14.6 The Create bar, which is on the left side of the Hypershade, lets you easily create a variety of different nodes.

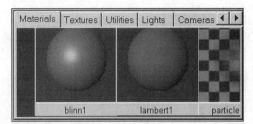

Figure 14.7 The Hypershade tabs let you access all the different nodes, separated by category.

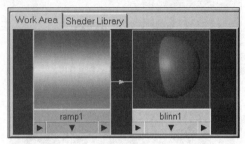

Figure 14.8 In the Hypershade Work Area, you can drag other nodes to make connections. Here a ramp texture is connected to the color of a blinn material.

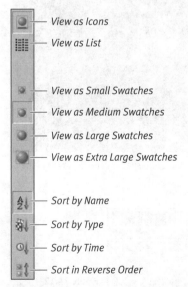

View as Icons

View as List

View as Small Swatches

View as Medium Swatches

View as Large Swatches

View as Extra Large Swatches

Sort by Name

Sort by Type

Sort by Time

Sort in Reverse Order

Figure 14.9 The node display options change the appearance of nodes in the Work Area and hypershade tabs.

◆ The Hypershade tabs let you see all your materials, textures, utilities, lights, or cameras. If you create any of these nodes, they show up under the appropriate tab. For example, if you create a material like blinn by clicking it in the Create bar, it shows up under the Materials tab (**Figure 14.7**). You can make custom tabs to display any node type you specify or even display related files on the hard drive.

◆ The Work Area is a place to work on your materials and texture networks. You can navigate this window like any normal viewport. When you make a new node from the Create bar, it also shows up here. You can middle mouse button-drag nodes from the Hypershade tabs down to the Work Area. Once they're there, you can easily make and view connections (**Figure 14.8**). The networks in this area can be very complicated, so numerous options are available for rearranging the graph (discussed below).

◆ The icons between the Create bar and the Hypershade tabs contains controls for displaying the nodes. This can be useful for improving performance and for quick navigation (**Figure 14.9**).

◆ The Text Filter button and accompanying input box let you limit what is displayed in the Hypershade tabs.

◆ The Toggle On/Off Create Bar button lets you hide or show the Create bar. Hiding it gives you more room to work with other nodes (see Figure 14.6).

◆ The Clear Graph button clears out any nodes in the Work Area. It doesn't delete them; it just clears the area.

◆ The Rearrange Graph button cleans up the Work Area, which tends to get cluttered when you create new nodes.

continues on next page

◆  The Graph Materials on Selected Objects button provides a quick way to find out what material is assigned to a specific object. Select the object, and then click this button, and the material and everything connected to it show up in the Work Area.

◆ The Show Input and Output Connections button shows everything connected to a node. For example, if you select a material and then click this button, the material shows up in the Work Area with all of its connected nodes.

◆ These buttons let you isolate the Hypershade tabs or the Work Area. On the left is Show Top Tabs Only. In the middle is Show Bottom Tabs Only. On the right are Show Top and Bottom Tabs.

To create your own bins:

1. Choose Window > Rendering Editors > Hypershade.

2. Click the Create tab, and expand the Surface category (**Figure 14.10**).

3. Click the Blinn icon four times.

   Four blinn shaders appear in the Work Area and in the Materials tab (**Figure 14.11**).

4. Select Blinn1.

5. Click the Bins tab to reveal the Bins bar (**Figure 14.12**).

Figure 14.10 The Create tab contains a categorized list of nodes to use in creating materials.

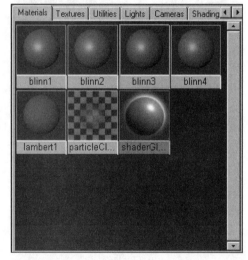

Figure 14.11 Four blinn shaders are displayed in the Work Area.

Figure 14.12 Click the Bins tab to reveal the Bins bar.

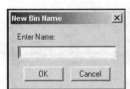

Figure 14.13 Enter a name for the custom bin using the New Bin Name dialog box.

Figure 14.14 A bin called MyBin appears below the Master Bin in the Bin bar.

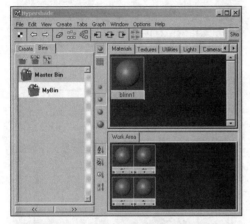

Figure 14.15 Clicking MyBin displays blinn1, which is currently the only node stored in MyBin.

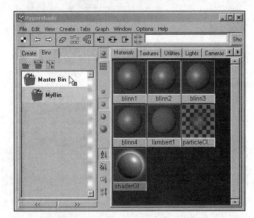

Figure 14.16 Clicking the Master Bin displays all the shaders in the scene.

6. Click the Create Bin from Selection icon at the top of the Bins bar.

The New Bin Name dialog box appears (**Figure 14.13**).

7. Enter a name for the new bin (MyBin), and click OK.

A new bin called MyBin appears below the Master Bin (**Figure 14.14**).

8. Click MyBin.

The Materials tab displays blinn1 alone (**Figure 14.15**).

9. From the Work Area, use the middle mouse button to click and drag blinn2 to MyBin.

Because blinn2 has been added to the bin, the Materials tab displays blinn1 and blinn2.

10. Click Master Bin.

All the shaders are shown in the Materials tab (**Figure 14.16**).

✔ Tips

■ Right-clicking the bin provides a list of useful functions, including removing items and bins (**Figure 14.17**).

■ An object can be placed in as many bins as you want. Bins are just like sets of objects.

Figure 14.17 Right-click MyBin to use functions like Delete and Remove Selected.

ABOUT THE HYPERSHADE

To create your own tabs:

1. Open the Hypershade (Window > Rendering Editors > Hypershade).

2. Choose Tabs > Create New Tab (**Figure 14.18**).

   The Create New Tab dialog opens.

3. For Tab Type, select Disk to display files on the hard drive (**Figure 14.19**).

4. Click the folder icon next to Root Directory.

   The Browse for Folder window opens (**Figure 14.20**).

Figure 14.18 Select Create New Tab from the Tabs menu in the Hypershade to create a new tab.

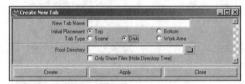

Figure 14.19 Enter a name for the custom tab in the Create New Tab dialog box.

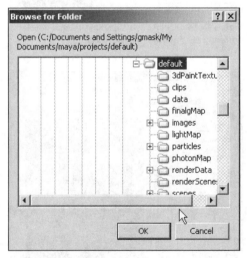

Figure 14.20 The Browse for Folder window opens to the current project directory.

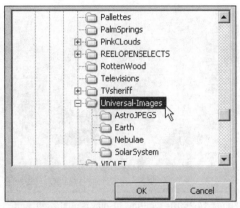

Figure 14.21 Select a folder that contains images or folders of images.

Figure 14.22 Type a name into the New Tab Name field.

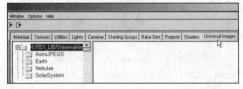

Figure 14.23 The new tab appears in the top half of the Hypershade window.

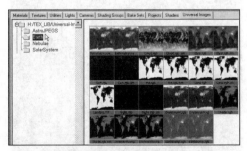

Figure 14.24 Clicking a folder in the new tab displays icons of images stored on the hard drive.

5. Select a folder that contains images or folders of images, and click OK (**Figure 14.21**).

The path to the selected directory is displayed next to Root Directory.

6. Enter the name Universal Images for the tab in New Tab Name field, and click Apply (**Figure 14.22**).

The new tab appears in the top half of the Hypershade (**Figure 14.23**).

7. Click one of the subfolders in your image directory, or click the folder icon next to the Root Directory path.

Icons of the images stored in the directory are created and displayed (**Figure 14.24**).

About IPR Renders

When you're working with shaders in Maya, you can see a rough real-time preview of your object's final appearance. To get a definitive look at what the object looks like, you have to render it (**Figure 14.25**). Rendering is discussed in Chapter 16.

You'll make many changes as you work on your shader. Maya Interactive Photorealistic Renders (IPR) store information so that you can update your render in near real time. Your final rendered image updates as you tweak surface attributes. In some respects, IPR lets you work with a real-time render.

Keep in mind that Maya creates a default light when you perform a render or IPR on your scene. Any scene needs at least one light to render.

To perform an IPR render:

1. Create a scene with a few objects in it—for example, a few primitives (**Figure 14.26**).

2. Position the Perspective view as you want your image framed, and then click the IPR Render button 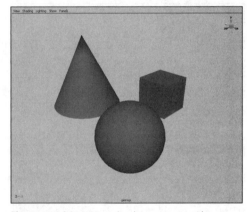.

   The Render View window opens, and, after a moment of calculation, the rendered scene displays (**Figure 14.27**).

Figure 14.25 The real-time display is on the left, and the rendered version on the right. Note the difference in detail.

Figure 14.26 Arrange a simple scene so you have something to render.

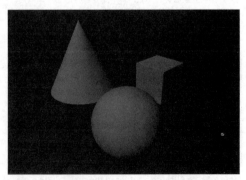

Figure 14.27 Because the textures are simple, the rendered scene looks fairly close to the real-time scene. A default light provides the illumination.

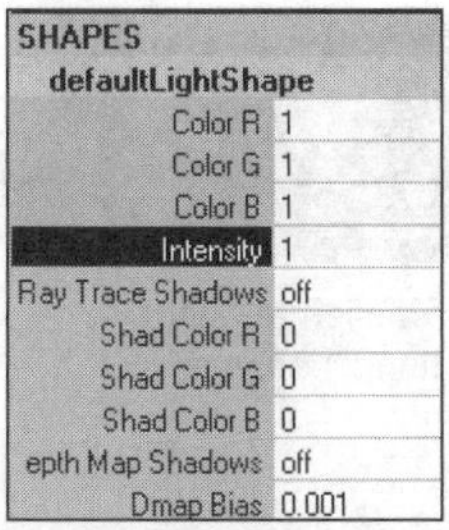

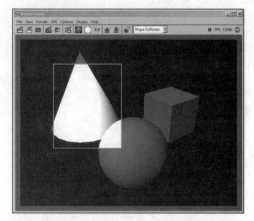

Figure 14.28 Select the light intensity, and adjust it.

Figure 14.29 The IPR render keeps track of light data as well as texture data and can show changes to both without needing to re-render.

3. Left-click, and drag a box around part of your image.

This box indicates the area of the image that will update.

4. Select defaultLight from the Outliner, select the Intensity channel in the Channel Box, and middle mouse button-drag to adjust the brightness of the light (**Figure 14.28**).

The area in the box updates, and you can see the effect of the brighter or darker light on this portion of your image (**Figure 14.29**).

✔ Tip

- IPR renders only update texture and light data. They don't support changes to material assignments or to camera and geometry moves. You must redo your IPR render every time you change one of these characteristics.

About Materials

Maya offers ten types of materials. Five of them are special-case materials, and five are more common, basic, surfaces. The five primary surfaces are anisotropic, blinn, lambert, phong, and phong e (**Figure 14.30**). These material types share basic properties, but they're different in a few ways, primarily in their *specular* and *reflectivity* options (how they reflect light). The more complicated special-purpose materials—including layered and ramp—generally take input from a more basic material.

Figure 14.30 Material types, from left to right: anisotropic, blinn, lambert, phong, phong e.

Common materials

◆ Anisotropic materials are used to simulate microscopic grooves or disturbances on a surface that make the specular highlight perpendicular to the light angle. You use an anisotropic material when creating an object like a CD or something made of brushed metal.

◆ Lambert textures are the simplest shading model mathematically, because they're just matte surfaces. Lambert textures work best on dry rocks, rubber, or basic colors. The default shader in Maya is a lambert called lambert1.

◆ Blinn materials are more complicated than lambert materials but generally represent surfaces more accurately. They're suited to shiny reflective surfaces with small (or complicated) specular highlights, like detailed metals or jewelry.

◆ Phong surfaces are shiny and can be reflective, suited to simple consistent surfaces like glass and plastic.

◆ Phong e materials are similar to phong (as the name indicates), but they give you more control over specular attributes, and generally have a softer highlight.

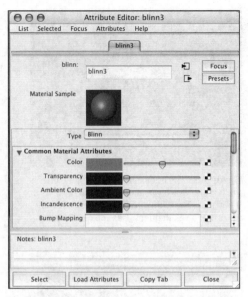

Figure 14.31 This is the Attribute Editor for a blinn material. It holds most of the controls that determine the look of the surface.

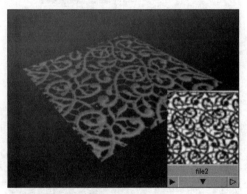

Figure 14.32 The node in the lower-right corner is the texture, which was mapped to the plane as a transparency map. The parts of the image that are white determine the parts of the plane that are transparent.

Several controls are common to the basic materials. They include *color, transparency, ambient color, incandescence,* and *bump mapping.* You can map images to all of these, and most of them can have a color or luminance value assigned to them as well. All are accessible from the Attribute Editor for the corresponding material (**Figure 14.31**).

Common material attributes

◆ Color determines the color of an object. You can pick a color using the Color Chooser, or you can map an image to the color.

◆ Transparency lets you make a surface see-through. You can use the slider to make the surface more or less transparent, or you can map an image to make part of the surface transparent and part of it opaque. This attribute only recognizes luminance—that is, how light or dark an image is. White is transparent; black is opaque (**Figure 14.32**).

◆ Ambient color simulates scattered light as it hits the surface, which brightens the object's diffuse color. You can lighten the whole surface evenly, or you can map an image to lighten only certain parts of a surface. High values tend to make objects look flat or unnatural.

◆ Incandescence gives a material the appearance of emitting its own light (as opposed to ambient, which simulates receiving light from other sources). Objects with incandescence render as illuminated even if there is no light in the scene.

continues on next page

◆ Bump mapping makes a surface appear bumpy. This is an illusion, and the silhouette doesn't change; nor does it display well at acute viewing angles. To affect the surface, this attribute must have an image or texture mapped to it. White on the image creates the illusion of raised bumps; 50 percent gray causes no bumps; and darker colors create divots (**Figure 14.33**).

To change the color of an object:

1. In the Hypershade window, select Create > Materials > Lambert (**Figure 14.34**).

   A new material appears in the Work Area (the lower half of the window).

2. With the middle mouse button, drag the material from the Hypershade onto the surface.

   or

   Select the surface, right-click the material to open the marking menu, and select Assign Material To Selection (**Figure 14.35**).

3. Click the IPR button 📽️.

Figure 14.33 The node in the lower-right corner is the texture, which was mapped to the plane as a bump map. The white areas are higher; the dark areas are lower. Render to see the results of a bump map.

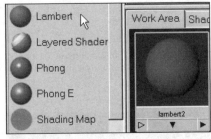

Figure 14.34 This is a portion of the Hypershade. When you click the Lambert button, a new material node called lambert2 appears.

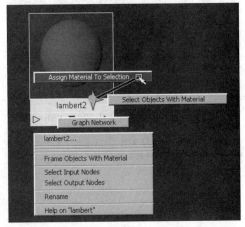

Figure 14.35 When you right-click a material in the Hypershade, a marking menu appears that lets you assign that material to the selected surface. This is particularly convenient if you're assigning shaders to multiple surfaces simultaneously.

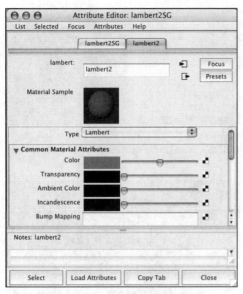

Figure 14.36 This is the Attribute Editor for the material that was just created in the Hypershade.

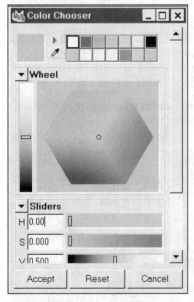

Figure 14.37 The Color Chooser lets you select a color from the swatches at the top or from the color wheel.

4. Double-click the new material.

The Attribute Editor for this material appears (**Figure 14.36**).

5. Click the field next to Color.

The Color Chooser opens (**Figure 14.37**).

6. Choose a color by clicking one of the color swatches at the top of the window or by clicking in the color wheel.

Notice the color update in the IPR window as you click in the color wheel.

7. Click Accept.

The Color Chooser window closes.

✔ Tip

■ If you assign a shader to a surface by using the middle mouse button to drag the shader from the Hypershade, be sure that the view you drag it into is in shaded mode. If it were in wireframe mode, you would need to drag it precisely onto an isoparm or edge of the surface, which is more difficult. However, the drag method of assigning textures only lets you assign a shader to one object at a time. In most cases, it's easier to use the marking menu, because doing so lets you assign a shader to many objects or groups.

About Texture-Mapping NURBS Surfaces

All surfaces in Maya have texture coordinates, called UVs, that show Maya how to place a 2D image on a 3D model (**Figure 14.38**).

A NURBS surface is always four-sided. Even a sphere is four-sided—it's pinched at the top and bottom, and the other two sides meet. In a plane, the U direction extends from left to right, and the V direction extends from bottom to top. This makes the lower-left corner the start point (**Figure 14.39**).

Any image you bring in is also four-sided because image files are square or rectangular. The lower-left corner of the image is placed at the start point of the surface. The bottom of the image is mapped on the surface along the U direction, and the left side of the image is wrapped along the V direction (**Figure 14.40**).

Because all NURBs are four sided, they must be distorted and pinched in order to match the shapes you specify, like the top of a sphere or cone. This means that textures assigned directly to the surface are distorted the same way. To avoid this distortion, NURBS surfaces are often textured using projections. (In addition, most NURBS objects consist of many separate NURBS surfaces.)

Mapping an image or texture to the color attribute lets you put detailed surfaces on your objects. Any attribute with a Map icon ![map icon] next to it can be mapped to a texture, and any attribute with the connection icon ![connection icon] next to it is already mapped to something. Some attributes, like bump mapping, must have a map linked in order to function.

NURBS surfaces' UV coordinates are built in. To shade your NURBS surface, you need to place your textures properly. We'll discuss shading polygonal objects later in this chapter.

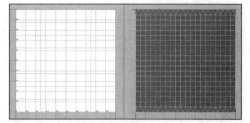

Figure 14.38 On the left are the UV coordinates of a NURBS sphere. On the right are those of a poly sphere.

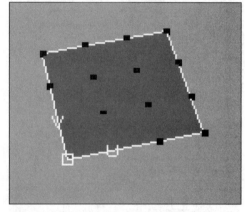

Figure 14.39 On this plane, the CVs are visible, and you can easily see the U and V directions. The square at lower left is the start point; the U is to the right of it, and the V is above it. This means that the U direction goes from left to right, and the V direction runs from bottom to top.

Figure 14.40 The same image is assigned to different NURBS surfaces. It gets wrapped around the surface, and its orientation depends on the U and V directions of the surface.

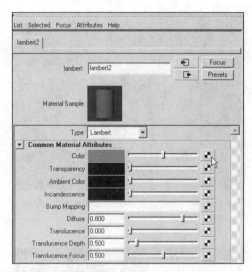

Figure 14.41 By clicking the Map icon (the little checkerboard to the right of the slider), you can map a texture to the color.

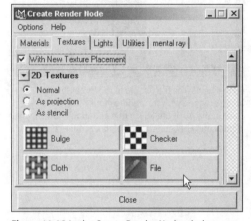

Figure 14.42 In the Create Render Node window, you can choose which new texture you want to map to an attribute of a material.

Figure 14.43 New nodes are created and placed in the workspace. The colored lines indicate connections from one node to another.

To map an image to the color of an object:

1. Choose Create > NURBS Primitives > Plane.

2. Open the Hypershade, and click Lambert to create a new material.

   A new lambert material appears in the Hypershade.

3. Double-click the lambert you just created in the Hypershade.

   The Attribute Editor for the lambert opens.

4. Click the Map icon to the right of the Color slider (**Figure 14.41**).

   The Create Render Node window opens.

5. Make sure the Normal radio button is selected, and then click File (**Figure 14.42**).

   The Attribute Editor for the File node opens.

6. Click the Browse button 📷 next to Image Name.

7. Browse for and open your own image file.

   Maya creates two new nodes (file1 and place2dTexture1) and links them to your lambert material (**Figure 14.43**).

continues on next page

8. With the middle mouse button, drag the lambert you created from the Hypershade onto your surface.

9. Click in the Perspective view, and press ⑥ to switch to textured mode.

The image you chose is now color-mapped to your surface (**Figure 14.44**).

✔ Tips

■ You can also map an image to any of the common material attributes by using the process in the previous task.

■ You can map any existing file node to an attribute by dragging it with the middle mouse button onto a material in the Work Area and selecting color (or any other option).

■ If your color image has an alpha channel, the areas the alpha channel masks out are transparent.

■ You can also map an image by dragging an existing texture onto the name of an attribute in a material's Attribute Editor (**Figure 14.45**).

■ You can find your textures more quickly if you place them in the source images folder of your project directory. Maya defaults to this directory whenever you use an Open dialog box to assign an image file.

Figure 14.44 An image is mapped to the color of the plane.

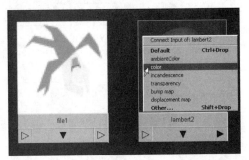

Figure 14.45 The file texture in the Hypershade is being dragged with the middle mouse button to the color in the Attribute Editor of a material. This provides a quick and convenient way to make connections.

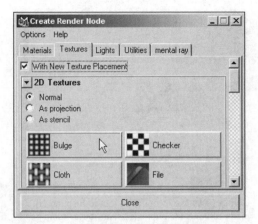

Figure 14.46 Clicking Bulge in the Create Render Node window creates a bulge texture that is mapped to the bump of a material.

Figure 14.47 This is a rendered image of a plane with a bulge texture mapped to its bump. Render to see the bump—it doesn't show up in the Perspective view.

Bump maps need to be mapped in order to function. They work from the value of an image, so they're commonly black and white.

To assign a bump map to a surface:

1. Choose Create > NURBS Primitives > Plane.

2. Open the Hypershade, and create a lambert.

3. Assign the lambert to the plane by using the middle mouse button to drag it from the Hypershade to the plane.

4. Double-click the lambert in the Hypershade.
   The Attribute Editor for the lambert appears.

5. Click the Map button next to Bump Mapping ▣.
   The Create Render Node window appears.

6. Click Bulge (**Figure 14.46**).
   The bulge shows up in the Work Area. You need to render it to see the resulting bump.

7. Frame the plane in your Perspective view, and click the IPR Render button ▣.
   Once you render, the bulges appear on the surface (**Figure 14.47**).

   continues on next page

8. In the Work Area, double-click the bump2d node. It may help to click Rearrange Graph ⊞ to find the node.

The Attribute Editor for the bump2d node appears.

9. Change the bump depth by moving the slider or typing in a number (**Figure 14.48**).

The bulges grow or shrink accordingly (**Figure 14.49**).

✔ Tips

■ Bumps are best used when defining small details, so you should use depth values that range between 1 and -1. Setting the values to extremes can cause the illusion to break down.

■ Bump maps (and other value-based maps) work best if they take full advantage of the 255 shades of gray available in an image. Image-editing software like Adobe Photoshop can help increase the contrast and range of your source images before you apply them, which reduces your reliance on the Bump Depth slider.

When you first map an image on a NURBS surface, it may not be oriented correctly. You can use the place2dTexture node to rotate, move, and scale the texture. You can also use the place2dTexture node for tiling and adjusting coverage.

To use place2dTexture:

1. Create a lambert, and then map a bulge to the color channel.

2. Double-click the place2dTexture node on the left side of the Work Area.

The Attribute Editor for the place2dTexture node appears.

3. Click the Interactive Placement button. A red square with a dot in the middle appears on the surface (**Figure 14.50**).

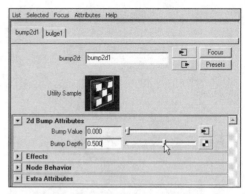

Figure 14.48 The Attribute Editor for the bump2d node contains the bump depth attribute. Bump depth controls the overall height of the bump.

Figure 14.49 The plane on the left has a bump depth of 1; the plane on the right has a bump depth of 0.5.

Figure 14.50 The red square indicates the position, rotation, and relative scale of the texture.

ABOUT TEXTURE-MAPPING NURBS SURFACES

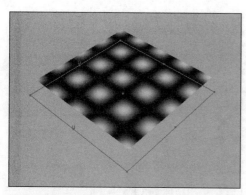

Figure 14.51 The position of the texture is moved via interactive placement. The bulges are now offset so that they don't evenly cover the surface.

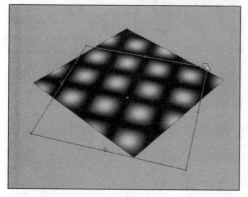

Figure 14.52 The interactive placement was used to rotate the bulge texture.

4. Drag with the middle mouse button, starting from the center point of the interactive placement icon on the object's surface.

   The texture moves on the surface (**Figure 14.51**).

5. With the middle mouse button, drag at the corners of the red square. The texture rotates (**Figure 14.52**).

6. Click in the field next to Repeat UV, type 1, and press Enter.

   The bulges now cover the same distance but with only one bulge, making them longer in the U direction (**Figure 14.53**).

7. In the field two columns to the right of Repeat UV, type 1; press Enter.

   There is now a single bulge on the surface (**Figure 14.54**).

Figure 14.53 The bulges now cover the surface, repeating only once in the U direction. A higher number in the Repeat UV field would result in more numerous, narrower bulges.

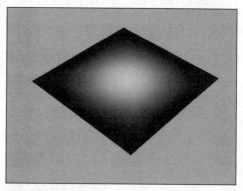

Figure 14.54 With only one repetition, the surface has just one bulge.

Procedural textures

The bulge texture you just used is an example of a *procedural texture*. Procedural textures are images that have their color and value determined mathematically. This means they're easier to place and have infinite resolution.

Procedural textures are used to generate simple surfaces like rubber or concrete, add detail such as dirt or bumps to existing surfaces, make realistic metallic surfaces, and more. One commonly used procedural texture is a ramp, which is like a gradient.

To assign a ramp texture to a surface:

1. Choose Create > NURBS Primitives > Sphere.

2. In the Channel Box, type 90 in the field next to Rotate X, and press Enter.

3. Open the Hypershade, and click Phong E.

   A phong e material shows up in the Work Area.

4. Double-click the phong e material in the Hypershade.

   The Attribute Editor for the phong e material appears.

5. Click the Map button next to the Color slider ▣.

   The Create Render Node window opens.

6. Click the Ramp button (**Figure 14.55**).

   The Attribute Editor for the ramp appears. A ramp texture node also appears in the Hypershade.

Figure 14.55 When you click Ramp in the Create Render Node window, a new ramp texture is created and mapped to a material.

Figure 14.56 A ramp texture is a gradient between one or more inputs. The default is an eye-catching linear RGB gradient, shown here.

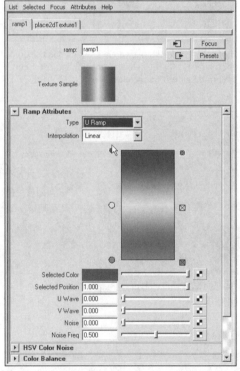

Figure 14.57 The Attribute Editor for the ramp holds the controls for determining the look of the gradient it produces. Position indicators are the circles to the left of the ramp. They determine where a color is positioned within the gradient.

7. With the middle mouse button, drag the phong e from the Hypershade onto the sphere to assign the shader.

   If you have trouble finding the phong e material, click the Work Area and press ⓐ to frame all the nodes.

8. Click the Perspective view, and press ⑥ to see the texture (**Figure 14.56**).

To make the ramp texture look like an eyeball:

1. Create a material with a ramp texture, and assign it to a sphere as in the previous task.

2. Open the Hypershade, and, in the Work Area, double-click the ramp texture.

   The Attribute Editor for the ramp appears.

3. In the Attribute Editor for the ramp, change the type to U Ramp.

4. Click and drag the top position indicator down slightly (**Figure 14.57**).

5. Change the position indicator's color to black by dragging the Selected Color slider all the way to the left.

6. Click and drag the middle position indicator, which is green by default, to just below the top one.

   continues on next page

7. Click the ramp about one-fifth of the way down from the top.

A new position indicator appears (**Figure 14.58**).

8. Click and drag the bottom position indicator up to just below the new one.

9. With the bottom position indicator still selected, click the color swatch next to Selected Color.

The Color Chooser opens.

10. Click the white swatch at the top of the Color Chooser (**Figure 14.59**).

The sphere is now textured like an eyeball (**Figure 14.60**).

Figure 14.58 When you click in the middle of the ramp, a new position indicator is created. By clicking the square with the *X* in it to the right of the ramp, you can delete a position indicator.

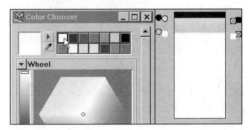

Figure 14.59 The white swatch is selected in the Color Chooser, causing the selected position indicator and the ramp below it to become white.

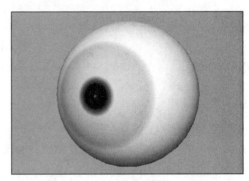

Figure 14.60 The eyeball is complete with a pupil and iris.

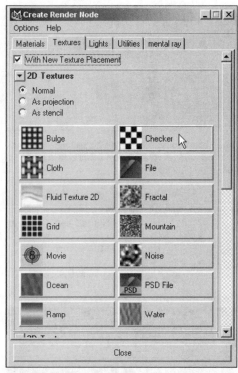

Figure 15.61 You're adding a checker to the Transparency channel so that you can see your red shader through your blue shader.

Figure 14.62 You can click Layered Shader once to create a layered shader, or you can use the middle mouse button to drag the icon into the Hypershade to create it.

Combining Materials

Objects in Maya can have only one material assigned to them. A layered shader is a special case that stacks other materials on top of each other, allowing for more complicated surfaces.

To create a layered shader:

1. Choose Create > NURBS Primitives > Sphere.

2. Create two blinn materials; color one red and one blue.

3. Open the Hypershade, and double-click the blue blinn material.

4. Click the Map icon [■] next to the Transparency slider.

5. Click Checker in the Textures tab of the Create Render Node window (**Figure 14.61**).

6. Under the Create Maya Nodes menu in the Hypershade, click Layered Shader in the Surface section (**Figure 14.62**).

7. Double-click the layered shader material in the Hypershade.

   The Attribute Editor for the layered shader material appears.

   continues on next page

8. With the middle mouse button, drag the red and blue materials from the Hypershade into the red square under Layered Shader Attributes (**Figure 14.63**).

9. Click the x under the original green square to delete it (**Figure 14.64**).

You should now have two blue boxes in the red square under Layered Shader Attributes.

10. Apply the layered shader to the sphere.

11. Click the IPR Render icon [IPR].

The sphere is now red and blue. The red can be seen through the blue because you added checker to its transparency channel (**Figure 14.65**).

✔ Tips

■ You must have transparency in the top shader in the layered shader if any of the bottom shader is to be visible. The first shader on the left is the top shader.

■ You can have as many layers as you need in a layered shader.

■ If you use an image map as a top layer, you can use its alpha channel for automatic transparency (**Figure 14.66**).

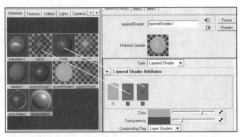

Figure 14.63 You can drag multiple shaders into your layered shader to create layered effects using the transparency of each layer.

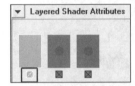

Figure 14.64 The small x at the bottom of each square is used to remove shaders from your layered shader.

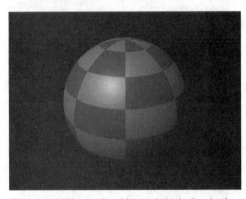

Figure 14.65 The rendered layered shader has both red and blue coloring.

Figure 14.66 The left plane has on it an image with an alpha channel. The middle one has a checker texture. On the right, they're combined in a layered shader. The textures show through the alpha of the first image. This only works in normal application mode.

COMBINING MATERIALS

Figure 14.67 A checkered texture is mapped to spheres using three different projection types: (left to right) cylindrical, planar, and spherical.

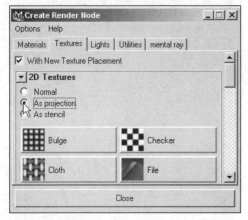

Figure 14.68 A NURBS sphere and a plane.

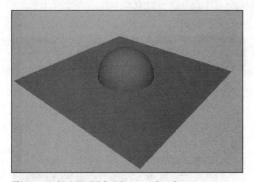

Figure 14.69 The As Projection radio button has been selected in the Create Render Node window.

About Projection Maps

Sometimes you'll want to map one image across two or more surfaces. To do so, you can use a projection map. The default projection type is *planar*, which acts like a slide projector pointed at a surface. Other projection types include *spherical* and *cylindrical*, which project an image from a shape that surrounds the surface (**Figure 14.67**).

To map a texture as a projection:

1. Open the Hypershade, create a lambert material, and assign it to a NURBS plane and a NURBS sphere (**Figure 14.68**).

2. Double-click the lambert in the Hypershade.

   The Attribute Editor for the lambert opens.

3. Click the Map button next to the Color slider ▣.

   The Create Render Node window appears.

4. Click the As Projection radio button (**Figure 14.69**).

5. Click the File button.

   The Attribute Editor for the projection appears. A place3dTexture node appears in the Perspective view.

6. Click the file1 tab at the top of the Attribute Editor.

   The Attribute Editor changes to show the options for the file texture.

7. Click the Folder icon next to Image Name.

   The file browser appears.

   continues on next page

8. Browse for and open an image of your own.

9. Click the Perspective view, and press ⑥ to switch to textured mode.

The place3dTexture node is visible in the Perspective view. The image is visible on the surface, but it's stretched out because it's being projected on from the side (**Figure 14.70**).

✔ Tip

■ If you move a surface with a projection texture mapped to it, the surface will appear to be moving through its texture when it's rendered out. To solve this problem, select the surface and then, from the Texturing menu, select Create Texture Reference Object.

To adjust a projection:

1. Projection-map a texture onto a plane as in the previous task, "To map a texture as a projection."

2. Select the place3dTexture utility in the Perspective view (**Figure 14.71**).

The line coming from the center indicates the projection direction—in this case, on the side of the plane—and you want it to project on the top.

3. Rotate the manipulator so that it points at the surface from above.

The image stretches less as the angle of the projection becomes more perpendicular to the surfaces it's hitting. However, the image still doesn't quite fit the surface.

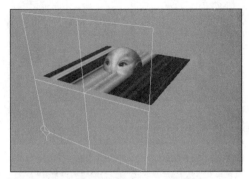

Figure 14.70 The planar projection is projecting the image across the two surfaces from the side. This causes the image to be stretched along the plane.

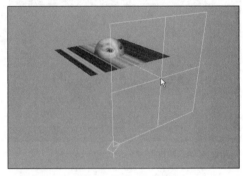

Figure 14.71 The place3dTexture node has been selected in the Perspective view. You can move, rotate, and scale this node the same way you would any object.

Figure 14.72 Now that the place3dTexture node is oriented to the surface, the image is projected across the two surfaces.

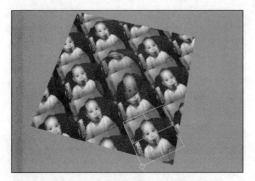

Figure 14.73 The place3dTexture node has been scaled down, rotated, and moved.

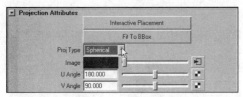

Figure 14.74 You can select a number of different projection methods to minimize the distortion caused by severe angles.

4. With the place3dTexture still selected, press Ctrl+a to open the Attribute Editor.

   The Attribute Editor for the place3dTexture node opens.

5. Click the Fit to Group Box button.

   The place3dTexture is automatically resized to that of the plane, and the image now fits (**Figure 14.72**).

✔ Tips

- If you move or rotate the place3dTexture, the image on the surface moves or rotates. If you scale it up, the image scales up. If you scale it down, the image scales down and is tiled (**Figure 14.73**).

- You can prevent the image from tiling by opening the Attribute Editor and deselecting the Wrap U and Wrap V check boxes in the place2dTexture node associated with your image.

- You may want to change the projection type to suit the shape of your object, To do this, choose an option from the Proj Type drop-down menu on the projection node (**Figure 14.74**).

Textures, especially projected ones, often appear blurry in the view even though they render clearly. However, you often need the image to appear sharper in order to place the texture.

To improve the quality of a texture image in a view:

1. Following the steps in the previous tasks, projection-map a checkered texture onto a sphere (**Figure 14.75**).

   The texture on the surface appears very blurry.

2. Select the sphere.

3. Open the Hypershade, and click the Graph Materials on Selected Objects icon ⬚.

   The material with all of its connections appears in the Work Area.

4. Double-click the material in the Hypershade.

   The Attribute Editor for the material appears.

5. Under Hardware Texturing, click the arrow to expand the options (**Figure 14.76**).

6. Change the Texture Resolution setting to High.

   The blurry checkers on the sphere become sharper (**Figure 14.77**).

✔ Tip

■ Increasing the texture quality slows down Maya's interactivity, especially with a high-resolution image. Once you've finished placing the texture, it's a good idea to reset it to low quality.

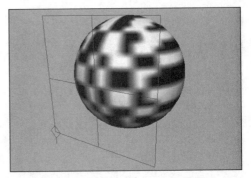

Figure 14.75 A checkered texture is projected onto a sphere. It appears very blurry and doesn't accurately represent how it will look when it's rendered.

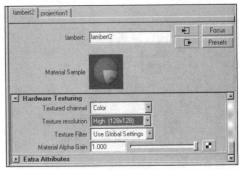

Figure 14.76 Hardware Texturing options are visible in the Attribute Editor for a material. When you increase the Texture Resolution setting to High, the checkers become clear.

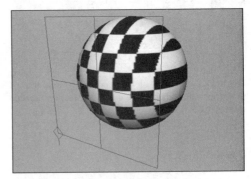

Figure 14.77 The checker texture is much sharper now that the texture quality for Hardware Texturing has been increased.

Figure 14.78 A wrapped-gift texture has been mapped to a cube.

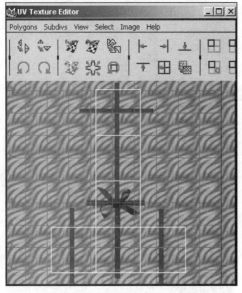

Figure 14.79 The white lines in the UV Texture Editor represent the edges of the cube. You can see how the cube has been "unwrapped." The image beneath these lines is what the actual image file that's mapped to the surface looks like.

About Texturing Polygons

All the techniques covered thus far work on polygon primitives. However, they don't necessarily work on any polygon surfaces you've modeled. Polygon surfaces are made up of many small irregular faces, some of which aren't square. The faces can also be arranged in configurations that aren't grid based, which means applying textures to them isn't as simple as it is on NURBS surfaces.

Think of a wrapped present. Imagine carefully removing the wrapping paper and flattening it out. Once the paper has been flattened, you can easily paint a new image on it (**Figure 14.78**).

This is essentially what you need to do to add a texture to a polygon surface. Before you can successfully texture-map it, you need to "unwrap" the surface. To do this, you create a UV map, which you can see in the UV Texture Editor (**Figure 14.79**).

In most cases, your UV map will consist of several unwrapped pieces. For instance, if you've used the Combine function on a polygon, its surface has more than one discrete part. These UV maps can be difficult and unwieldy to set up because the UVs may all overlap or be tangled. Additionally, special care must be taken to arrange the maps in logical arrangements that are easy to work with.

Maya provides a number of tools to help unfold your objects. If you're texturing with projections, an automatic mapping solution is usually adequate and time-efficient. If you're creating your own maps or working with a low-res character, finessing your own UVs is generally preferable.

One distinct advantage of polygons over NURBS is that you can assign shading groups to individual faces of a polygon surface, whereas a NURBS surface can have only one shading group assigned to it. You do this by selecting polygon faces and assigning the materials to *them*, not to the object as a whole (**Figure 14.80**).

Figure 14.80 Four different textures have been mapped to different parts of the same polygon sphere by assigning the textures to specific faces of the sphere.

To create automatic mapping for a polygon texture:

1. Create a polygon telephone (**Figure 14.81**).

   This one was created by scaling a cube, extruding the top and bottom earpieces, and then smoothing the polygon with a subdivision level of 3 and a continuity of 0.35. Save this model for later use.

2. Create a blinn material, and assign it to the surface.

3. Open the Hypershade, and double-click the blinn material.

   The Attribute Editor for the blinn material opens.

4. Click the Map button 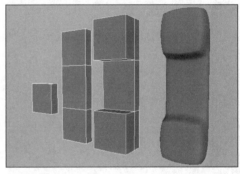 next to the Color slider.

   The Create Render Node window appears.

Figure 14.81 By using Extrude Face and Smooth, you can model a phone from a cube in just a few steps.

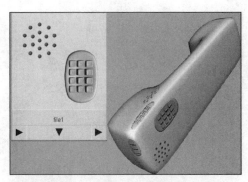

Figure 14.82 On the left is the file texture that is mapped to the phone. On the right, the texture on the phone is stretched out and in the wrong places.

Figure 14.83 Now that a UV map has been created using automatic mapping, the texture is placed on all parts of the surface, but not in the right places.

5. Make sure the Normal radio button is selected, and then click File.

The Attribute Editor for the file node opens.

6. Click the Browse button [📁] next to Image Name.

7. Browse for and open your own image file.

We created one especially for the phone, but any image will do. The image looks messed up and stretched out on the phone in the Perspective view (**Figure 14.82**).

8. Select the surface.

9. Choose Edit Polygons > Texture > Automatic Mapping.

Now the image isn't stretched as much, but the elements aren't in place (**Figure 14.83**).

ABOUT TEXTURING POLYGONS

Editing UVs

Automatic mapping doesn't always produce adequate UVs. Usually you'll need to adjust the UVs by hand before you can shade your model. The UV Texture Editor is a special window for unwrapping, or laying out, your UVs. Using this window, you can translate, scale, rotate, and use a variety of special tools to manipulate the UVs of your model. You navigate the UV Texture Editor just as you would any other panel. Any adjustments made to UVs don't affect the geometry of your model.

The image that is mapped to the surface is tiled in the background of the UV Texture Editor. This lets you move different portions of the surface onto the part of the image you want without a lot of messy overlapping.

To use the UV Texture Editor:

1. Continue using the phone from the previous task.

2. With your object selected, choose Window > UV Texture Editor.

   The UV Texture Editor opens. You can see the image that was assigned to the surface; on top of it is the wireframe of the different parts of the surface (shells) that have been separated.

3. Right-click the surface, and select UV from the marking menu.

4. Choose one UV point from the center of the earpiece of the telephone (**Figure 14.84**).

   The UV shows up as selected both in the UV Texture Editor and in your normal view panels. UVs are always green when selected.

5. Right-click the shell, and choose Select > Select Shell from the marking menu (**Figure 14.85**).

   All the UVs of the shell are selected.

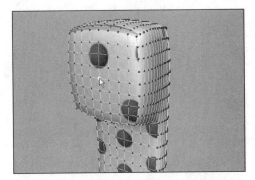

Figure 14.84 One UV point has been selected from the center of the earpiece of the phone.

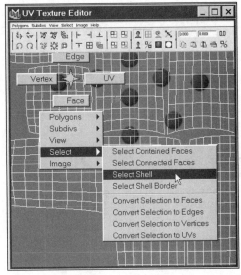

Figure 14.85 Rather than having to carefully select each UV of the shell, you can select the whole shell at once by right-clicking and choosing Select > Select Shell from the marking menu.

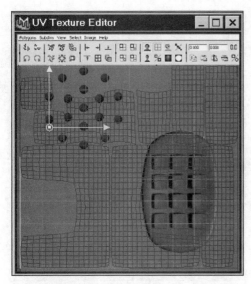

Figure 14.86 In the UV Texture Editor, you can see how the different parts of the surface have been laid out over the image map. The UV point that was selected in the Perspective view is also selected here and displays move manipulators. This makes it easy to recognize which shell is the phone's earpiece.

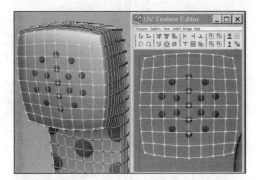

Figure 14.87 While placing the UVs in the Texture view (right), you can see their effect on the surface simultaneously (left).

Figure 14.88 A seam in the texture is apparent along the side of the phone.

6. Move, scale, and rotate the shell over a recognizable part of the image (**Figure 14.86**).

You can watch the image on the selected area of the phone change interactively in the Perspective view.

7. Repeat steps 3–6 for other parts of the phone.

✔ Tip

■ Selecting UVs in the view panel can make it easier to figure out which points on your object correspond to which points in your UV editor. It's helpful to make selections in either window, depending on which view is clearer (**Figure 14.87**).

Because the surface is in many separate pieces (shells) in the UV Texture View, there are seams on the surface (**Figure 14.88**). You can combine two shells and get rid of the seam by using Move and Sew UVs.

To eliminate a seam in a texture using Move and Sew UVs:

1. Continue using the phone from the previous tasks.

2. From the Display menu, choose the box next to Custom Polygon Display.

continues on next page

EDITING UVs

3. Next to Objects Affected, select All, and select Highlight Texture Borders (**Figure 14.89**).

This option displays the seams on your object as thick lines, making them easy to see.

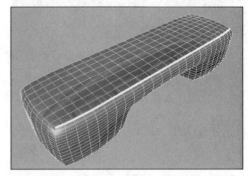

Figure 14.89 Highlight the texture borders to show your UV shells as thick lines.

4. In the Perspective view, use the Select Edge Loop tool to select all the edges along the seam (**Figure 14.90**).

The corresponding edges are automatically selected in the UV Texture Editor when you select them on the object (**Figure 14.91**).

5. Choose Edit Polygons > Texture > Move and Sew UVs.

The seam on the object disappears in the Perspective view (**Figure 14.92**). In the UV Texture Editor, two shells have been combined along that edge (**Figure 14.93**).

Figure 14.90 All of the polygon edges along the edge of the seam have been carefully selected.

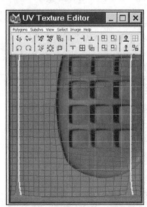

Figure 14.91 The edges of two shells are selected because they are, in fact, one edge shared by both shells.

Figure 13.92 The seam is gone because the edges of the two shells have been sewn together, allowing the texture image to extend across both.

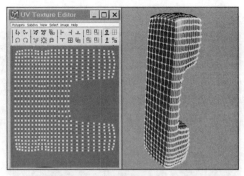

Figure 14.93 Two separate shells have been joined into one bigger shell covering a larger portion of the phone.

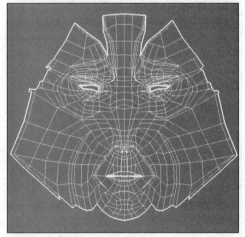

Figure 14.94 This face was laid out using the Unfold tool. To minimize seams, it's useful for detailed and visible areas like faces to be one shell.

Automatic mapping is often a good starting point for laying out your UVs, but it can create many shells. Use Maya's new Unfold option when you want to preserve part of a surface as a single shell (**Figure 14.94**).

Unfold attempts to unwrap and flatten the UVs of an object, but it requires a bit of preparation in the form of strategically placed seams.

To use the unfold tool to map UVs:

1. Start with the unmapped phone from the previous tasks. You want the seams to be highlighted, so make sure the Highlight Texture Borders option is selected.

2. Choose Polygon UVs > Automatic Mapping, and press ⌷Enter⌷.

3. Select all the UVs, and click the Sew UVs button ⊞.
   This removes all the seams from your layout so you can insert your own.

4. Use the Select Edge Loop tool to select the edges along the edge of the front of the phone (**Figure 14.95**).

5. Click the ⊞ button to insert seams at these edges.

continues on next page

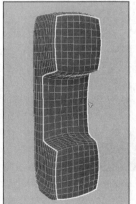

Figure 14.95 To split the phone into two sections (a front and a back), select all the edges around the front.

6. Choose Polygon UVs > Unfold UVs. The UVs are flattened and laid out, but one piece is distorted (**Figure 14.96**).

You may need to reposition and scale your UVs after an unfold.

7. Select the edges on the phone corners, and click ![icon] (**Figure 14.97**).

Now the shape can unfold like a piece of paper with tabs.

8. Choose Polygon UVs > Unfold UVs.

The UVs are now unfolded with less distortion, and they can be scaled and rotated into place (**Figure 14.98**).

✔ Tips

- Select Pin Selected in the Unfold option if you want to retain the layout of certain UVs. This prevents selected UVs from moving during the unfold operation.

- You can pin an object's corners or lines of symmetry to force the object to unfold a certain way. For example, aligning the center of a character's face and then pinning it, or pinning the corners of a flag in a square, forces the shape into a logical arrangement.

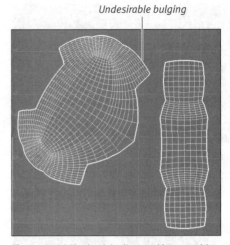

Undesirable bulging

Figure 14.96 The back is distorted because it's a concave shape with no seams to fold. It needs to be cut free to unfold properly.

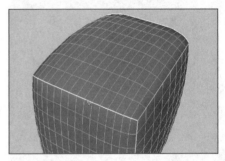

Figure 14.97 Select all four corners of the phone from front to back.

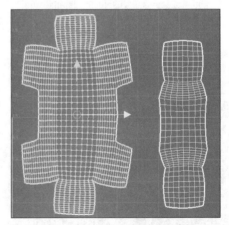

Figure 14.98 The phone now unfolds evenly, as one piece.

Using the UV Texture Editor toolbar

The UV Texture Editor toolbar holds shortcuts to many of the actions in the UV Texture Editor menus. The toolbar is divided into four main sections: UV Position buttons, Isolate Selection buttons, View buttons, and UV Edit buttons. They provide the following functions:

◆ **UV Position buttons**—This section holds shortcuts to many of the UV position tools, including flipping, rotating, sewing, and aligning UVs (**Figure 14.99**).

◆ **Isolate Selection buttons**—This section holds shortcuts to adding, removing, and toggling isolation tools (**Figure 14.100**).

◆ **View buttons**—This section holds snaps, toggles, and border menu shortcuts (**Figure 14.101**).

◆ **UV Edit buttons**—This section holds UV coordinate input fields as well as UV copying and pasting features (**Figure 14.102**).

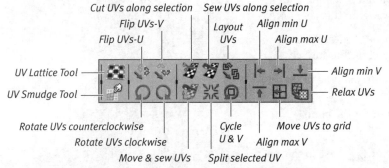

Figure 14.99 The UV Position buttons section of the UV Texture Editor toolbar.

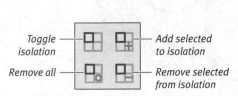

Figure 14.100 The Isolate Selection buttons section of the UV Texture Editor toolbar.

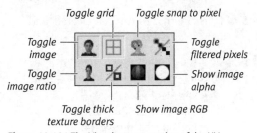

Figure 14.101 The View buttons section of the UV Texture Editor toolbar.

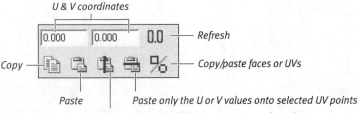

Figure 14.102 The UV Edit buttons section of the UV Texture Editor toolbar.

EDITING UVS

395

About projecting UV maps

Earlier in this chapter, you were shown how to project a texture; you can also project UV maps. One main difference is that a projected UV map sticks to the object even if it deforms, whereas a deforming object will "swim" through a projected texture.

To create a planar UV map for a polygon object:

1. Open the model of the polygon telephone you made in the first step of the task "To create automatic mapping for a polygon texture" earlier in this chapter.

2. Open the Hypershade, create a blinn material, and assign it to the surface.

3. Double-click the blinn material in the Hypershade.

   The Attribute Editor for the blinn material opens.

4. Click the Map button 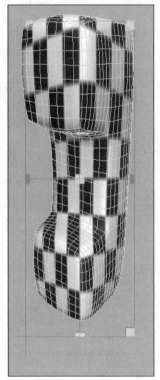 next to the Color slider.

   The Create Render Node window appears.

5. Make sure that Normal is selected, and then click Checker.

6. Select the phone surface, and, from the Polygon UVs menu, select the box next to Planar Mapping.

   The Polygon Planar Projection Options dialog box opens (**Figure 14.103**).

7. For Mapping Direction, click Camera, and click Apply.

   A projected mapping manipulator appears around the object (**Figure 14.104**).

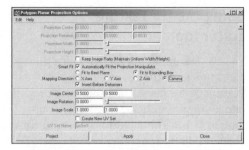

Figure 14.103 Use the Polygon Planar Projection Options dialog box to control how the object is mapped.

Figure 14.104 The projected mapping manipulator appears around the object.

EDITING UVs

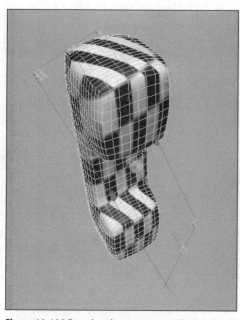

Figure 14.105 Rotating the camera reveals that the texture was projected from the camera's previous point of view (POV).

8. Rotate the camera by pressing ⓐ while you click and drag in the 3D view.

   The texture stretches across the object from the camera's previous position (**Figure 14.105**).

9. In the Polygon Planar Projection Options dialog box, click Apply again.

   The projected mapping manipulator changes position to match the camera's current direction (**Figure 14.106**).

   Using the camera option forces the projection to be created from the camera's current view.

10. In the Mapping Direction section of the Polygon Planar Projection Options dialog box, click Y Axis, and click Apply.

    The projected mapping manipulator changes position so that it projects directly down the *y* axis (**Figure 14.107**).

continues on next page

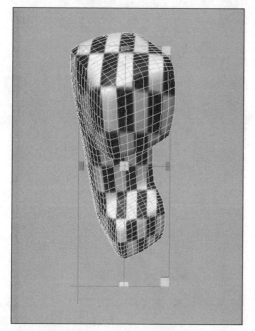

Figure 14.106 The projected mapping manipulator updates to match the current camera POV.

Figure 14.107 The projected mapping manipulator projects down the *y* axis.

EDITING UVS

11. Repeat step 10, but click the Z Axis button to project down the *z* axis (**Figure 14.108**) or click the X Axis button to project down the *x* axis (**Figure 14.109**).

12. Click and drag the green box on the texture projection manipulator.

This scales the manipulator and allows additional control over the placement of a UV projection (**Figure 14.110**).

13. Switch to selection-by-hierarchy mode ⌷, and select the phone.

14. Choose Deform > Create Nonlinear > Bend.

This applies a bend deformer to the object.

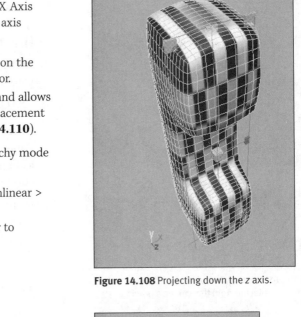

Figure 14.108 Projecting down the *z* axis.

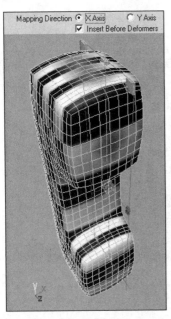

Figure 14.109 Projecting down the *x* axis.

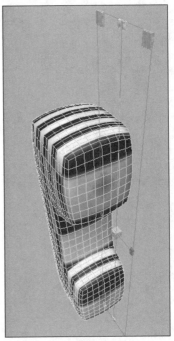

Figure 14.110 Drag the handles on the projected mapping manipulator to change its scale and position.

EDITING UVs

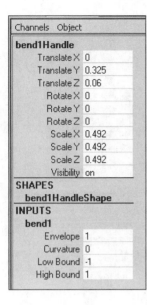

Channels Object

bend1Handle
Translate X	0
Translate Y	0.325
Translate Z	0.06
Rotate X	0
Rotate Y	0
Rotate Z	0
Scale X	0.492
Scale Y	0.492
Scale Z	0.492
Visibility	on

SHAPES
bend1HandleShape
INPUTS
bend1
Envelope	1
Curvature	0
Low Bound	-1
High Bound	1

Figure 14.111
Apply a bend deformer, and then expand the bend1 options under the Inputs section of the Channel Box.

15. In the Inputs section of the Channel Box, click bend1 to reveal the bend controls (**Figure 14.111**).

16. Using the middle mouse button, click and drag Curvature back and forth in the 3D view to set the value to .5.

    or

    In the numeric entry field, set Curvature to .5.

    The texture sticks to the object as the object deforms (**Figure 14.112**).

17. Deselect Insert Before Deformers, and click Apply again.

    The mapping changes to reflect the deformation of the object (**Figure 14.113**).

Figure 14.113 Deselect Insert Before Deformers to allow the mapping to be applied to the object in its current deformed shape.

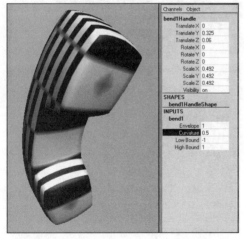

Figure 14.112 The object deforms, and the texture sticks to it.

To create a cylindrical UV map for a polygon object:

1. Repeat steps 1–5 from the previous task, "To create a planar UV map for a polygon object."

2. Select the phone surface, choose Edit Polygons > Texture, and select the box next to Cylindrical Mapping.

   The Polygon Cylindrical Projection Options dialog box opens (**Figure 14.114**).

3. Click Apply to accept the default values and update mapping on the surface (**Figure 14.115**).

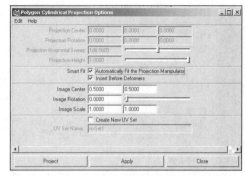

Figure 14.114 The Polygon Cylindrical Projection Options dialog box.

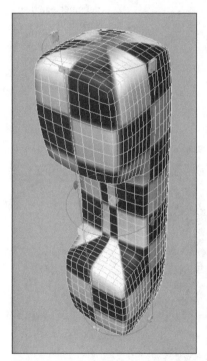

Figure 14.115 The mapping on the object updates, and the projected mapping manipulator appears.

EDITING UVs

Figure 14.116 Type a lower value into the Image Scale field to force the texture to be larger in relationship to the object.

Figure 14.117 Drag the handles on the projected mapping manipulator to control the position and scale of the projection in relationship to the object.

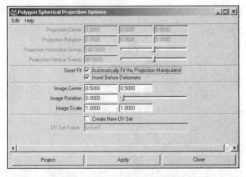

Figure 14.118 The Polygon Spherical Projection Options dialog box.

4. In the first numeric entry field, set Image Scale to .5; then, click Apply (**Figure 14.116**).

The mapping updates so that the texture around the object is larger.

5. Click and drag the red box on the texture projection manipulator to make the texture around the object larger or smaller (**Figure 14.117**).

To create a spherical UV map for a polygon object:

1. Repeat steps 1–5 from the task "To create a planar UV map for a polygon object," earlier in this chapter.

2. Select the phone surface, choose Edit Polygons > Texture, and select the box next to Spherical Mapping.

The Polygon Spherical Projection Options dialog box opens (**Figure 14.118**).

continues on next page

EDITING UVS

3. Click Apply to accept the default values and update mapping on the surface (**Figure 14.119**).

4. Click and drag the blue box on the texture projection manipulator to make the texture around the object smaller (**Figure 14.120**) or larger (**Figure 14.121**).

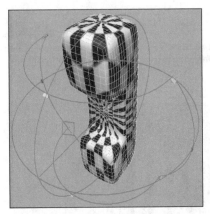

Figure 14.119 The mapping on the object updates, and the projected mapping manipulator appears.

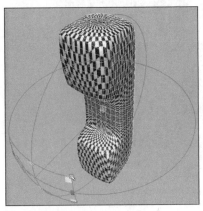

Figure 14.120 Drag the handles on the projected mapping manipulator to scale the projection and make it smaller...

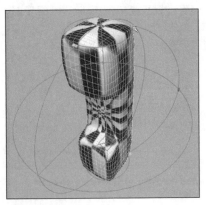

Figure 14.121 ...or larger.

Texturing Subdivs

Texturing subdiv surfaces is very similar to texturing polygons; and, under some circumstances, it can be done exactly the same way.

For instance, several of the UV commands can be found in the Subdiv Surfaces > Texture menu option, and these commands function like their poly equivalents.

However, in subdiv mode, the UVs correspond directly to the CVs—not the surface points. Additionally, you can't edit the UV mapping of a subdiv by switching to polygon mode. If you do, you'll lose any UV data adjusted in Subdiv mode. Instead, choose Modify > Convert > Convert to Subdiv Options to open the Convert to Subdiv Options dialog box. Then, select Proxy Object Subdivision Surface Mode. When you edit the UV mapping on the polygon cage, it will update UV mapping on the subdiv surface.

EDITING UVs

Swimming Textures

Swimming textures are an undesirable effect that can occur when you animate an object that has a 3D texture applied to it; the animated object moves, but the assigned texture stays in the same place. This happens because the 3D texture is assigned to the object based on the geometry's world position, not the UV coordinates. To avoid swimming textures, you can parent the placement node to the object or set the texture to local. If the object deforms, the only way to fix the problem is to convert the 3D texture to a file-based texture so that it uses UVs (which deform and move with the object).

To convert a 3D texture to a file texture:

1. Create a NURBS primitive sphere.

2. Open the Hypershade, create a new blinn material, and assign it to the sphere.

3. Double-click the blinn to open the Attribute Editor.

4. Click the Map button 🔲 for Color.

5. Select the 3D texture wood.

6. In the modeling window, select the sphere; in the Hypershade, (Shift)-select the blinn.

7. From the Edit menu in the Hypershade, select Convert to File Texture.

   An image file is generated, and the new blinn is assigned to the sphere.

Texturing Using Painting Tools

Simple image mapping isn't the only way to texture a surface. Maya provides options for painting directly on a surface and for importing a Photoshop document you've painted on. Both methods offer more interactive and artisan-based methods of texturing your models.

The 3D Paint tool lets you paint directly on a surface. You can create a new texture image from scratch with this method, and Maya creates a new image file.

It's important to make sure you've set your project (File > Project > Set) before you begin painting, because the current project determines where this image ends up. When you save the scene after painting, a folder named after your scene is created in the 3dPaintTextures folder of the project you're currently set to. Any images created by painting are put in that folder.

You can also paint on a surface that already has an image file textured on it—for example, you can add dirt or other details to an existing image.

To paint directly on a surface:

1. Open the Hypershade, create a lambert material, and assign it to a NURBS sphere.

2. With the sphere selected, from the Texturing menu, select the box next to 3D Paint Tool.

   The 3D Paint Tool Settings window opens (**Figure 14.122**).

3. Scroll down until you see the File Textures section (**Figure 14.123**).

   If necessary, you can change the image format that will be created.

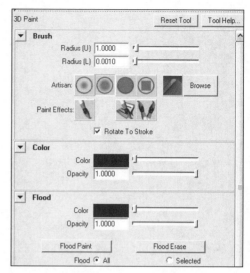

Figure 14.122 The 3D Paint Tool Settings window includes many controls that determine the look of your brush strokes.

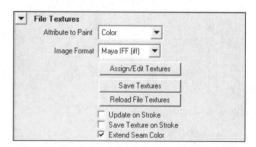

Figure 14.123 Under File Textures in the 3D Paint Tool Settings window, you can assign a texture to the material for a selected object. You can't paint on a surface that doesn't have a file mapped to its color.

Figure 14.124 Once you click Assign/Edit Textures, you can paint, because a file texture is connected to the material for the object you want to paint.

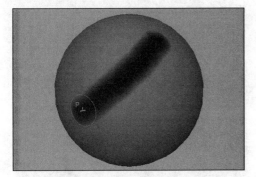

Figure 14.125 The paintbrush has been dragged across the sphere, producing this black mark.

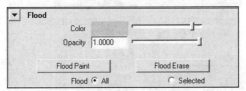

Figure 14.126 You can choose a color to flood the whole object by clicking the Color swatch.

Figure 14.127 A smiley face has been painted on the sphere with three brush strokes.

4. Click the Assign/Edit Textures button.

   The Assign/Edit File Textures window appears. You can increase the resolution of the texture here if you need a highly detailed texture. The default of 256 by 256 will suffice for now (**Figure 14.124**).

5. Click Assign/Edit Textures.

   A file texture is connected to the material so you can paint.

6. Click in the Perspective view, hold down b, and, using the middle mouse button, drag from right to left to get the brush down to size.

   The red circle, which represents brush size, shrinks.

7. Click and drag on the surface of the sphere to paint on it.

   A mark appears on the surface (**Figure 14.125**).

8. Click the swatch next to Color in the 3D Paint Tool Settings window under the Flood section (**Figure 14.126**).

   The Color Chooser appears.

9. Choose the yellow swatch at the top of the Color Chooser, and click Accept.

10. Click Flood Paint.

    The sphere turns yellow.

11. Paint a smiley face by clicking and dragging on the surface (**Figure 14.127**).

To use the 3D Paint tool:

1. Continue with the sphere from the previous task.

   If the paintbrush isn't visible or the tool options are no longer open, select the sphere; then, from the Texturing menu, select the box next to 3D Paint Tool.

2. Click the Get Brush button , which is to the right of Paint Effects in the 3D Paint Tool Options window.

   The Visor window opens.

3. Scroll down in the Visor, and click the Hair folder.

   Several hair types appear (**Figure 14.128**).

4. Click the hair of your choice.

5. Paint some hair on your smiley-face sphere (**Figure 14.129**).

6. Clear the surface texture by clicking the Flood Erase button under the Flood section.

   The texture is cleared, and the original gray surface is ready to be repainted.

✔ Tips

- After using a Paint Effects brush, you can return to a normal brush by clicking one of the Brush Profile buttons next to Artisan in the 3D Paint Tool Settings window (**Figure 14.130**).

- By decreasing the opacity in the 3D Paint Tool settings, you can paint on a surface but still see the color beneath your brush strokes—helpful if you're trying to make a surface appear dirty.

- You can use the 3D Paint Tool to paint areas roughly to mark the different parts of a surface. You can then open the image file (which is created once you save the scene) in Adobe Photoshop and paint the details there.

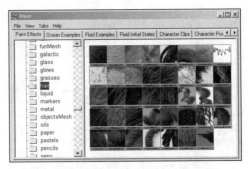

Figure 14.128 You can choose from a variety of brushes to use with the 3D Paint tool in the Visor. Here you see the brushes in the Hair folder.

Figure 14.129 Hair has been painted on the sphere by using one of the Paint Effects brushes.

Figure 14.130 To return to a normal brush, choose from one of the profiles of the Artisan brushes.

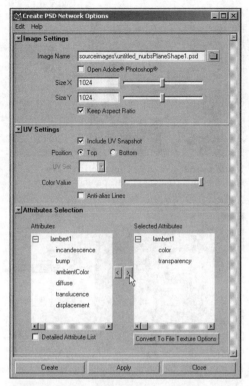

Figure 14.131 Select color and transparency, and click the right arrow (>) to add them to Selected Attributes.

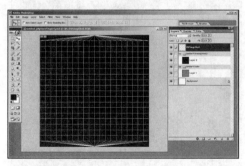

Figure 14.132 Open the PSD file that Maya created in Photoshop.

■ You can use the same steps for other attributes, such as transparency and displacement. Just select the desired attribute from the drop-down menu under File Textures.

Using Adobe Photoshop

In Maya, you can create layered PSD (Photoshop Document) files or use PSD image files with layers from Adobe Photoshop for textures. Being able to use layered files makes it simpler to manage complex textures that require individual image maps for one or more channels in a single shader.

To create layered PSD files in Maya:

1. Select an object, and choose Texturing > Create PSD Network.

   The Create PSD Network Options dialog box opens.

2. In the Attributes section, select color and transparency, and click the right arrow (>) to add them to Selected Attributes (**Figure 14.131**).

3. Click Create.

   The dialog box closes, and Maya saves the PSD file to the sourceimages folder in your current project directory.

4. Open the PSD file in Adobe Photoshop (**Figure 14.132**).

   The layered image file has a layer called UVSnapShot that you can use as a reference while painting in Photoshop (PS). The file also has layer sets named after the channels that were selected in the Create PSD Network Options.

continues on next page

5. Paint several strokes on the layer in the lambert1.transparency layer set (**Figure 14.133**).

   White is fully transparent, and black is fully opaque.

6. Click the eye icon 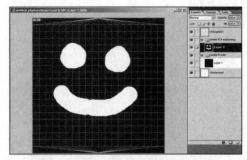 next to the lambert1.transparency layer set and the UVSnapShot layer so that they're hidden.

7. Paint some colorful strokes on the layer in the lambert1.color layer set (**Figure 14.134**).

8. Save the PSD file, and switch back to Maya.

9. In the active view, choose Shading > Hardware Texturing.

   The hardware shaded view can display texture maps assigned to surfaces.

10. Select the object for which the PSD texture was originally created, and choose Texturing > Update PSD Networks.

    The surface updates, displaying the color map that was created in Photoshop (**Figure 14.135**).

11. Choose Render > Render Current Frame.

    The Render View dialog box opens and renders the current view, showing the color channel and transparency channels that were painted (**Figure 14.136**).

Figure 14.133 Paint some strokes on the layer contained in the lambert1.transparency layer set.

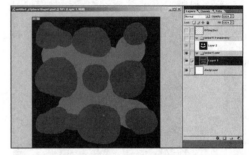

Figure 14.134 Paint some colors on the layer.

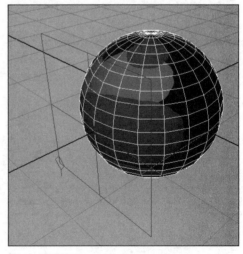

Figure 14.135 The surface displays the color map.

Figure 14.136. Render the view so that the transparency layer can be seen.

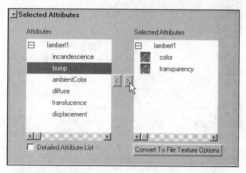

Figure 14.137 Any attribute that has been mapped has a corresponding icon that indicates whether it's currently controlled by a file, PSD, or texture.

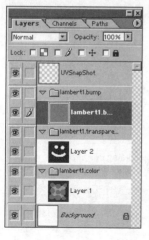

Figure 14.138
The new bump layer has been added to the PSD and can be edited in Photoshop.

To edit an existing PSD network:

1. Select the object from the last task.

2. Choose Texture > Edit PSD Network.

   The existing network appears, and the icons indicate which attributes have been linked to the PSD document (**Figure 14.137**).

3. Click bump, and then click the right arrow to assign a new attribute to the PSD file.

4. Click Apply.

5. Open your document in Photoshop; you can see a new layer has been added (**Figure 14.138**).

   or

   If your Photoshop document is already open, choose File > Revert to ensure the changes are reflected in your current document.

To use an existing layered PSD file in Maya:

1. Open the Hypershade, and, in the Create bar, expand 2D Textures.

2. Click Normal, and then click the PSD File icon (**Figure 14.139**).

   A PSD file node appears as psdFileTex1 in the Work Area (**Figure 14.140**).

3. Double-click the psdFileTex1 node to open its Attribute Editor.

4. Click the Folder icon ☐ next to Image Name.

   The Open dialog box appears (**Figure 14.141**).

Figure 14.139
The PSD file node is used to import a PSD document with layers instead of as a flat image (as the file node does).

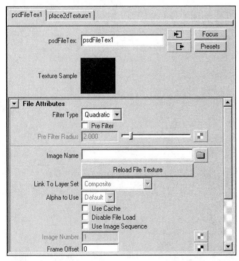

Figure 14.140 A PSD file node appears as psdFileTex1 in the Work Area.

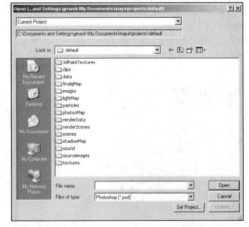

Figure 14.141 The Open dialog box appears and defaults to the current project directory.

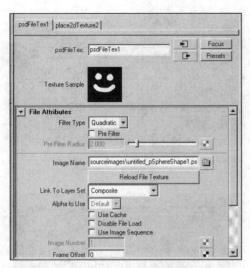

Figure 14.142 The texture sample updates with an image of the file that was selected.

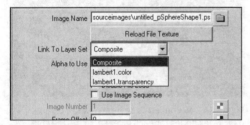

Figure 14.143 Choose Composite from the Link To Layer Set pull-down menu.

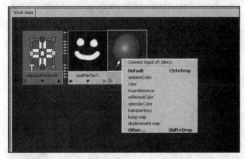

Figure 14.144 Middle-click and drag the psdFileTex1 node onto blinn1 to open the marking menu.

5. Select a PSD file from the hard drive, and click Open.

The Open dialog box closes, and the texture sample of psdFileTex1 updates with the PSD file that was selected (**Figure 14.142**).

6. From the pull-down menu next to Link To Layer Set, choose Composite (**Figure 14.143**).

This pull-down menu lists each layer set in the image. If the image has no layer sets, then Composite is the only item in the list. Composite is a flattened combination of all the visible layers in the PSD file.

7. In the Hypershade, create a blinn shader, and assign it to the surface.

The blinn shader appears in the Work Area next to the psdFileTex1 node.

8. With the middle mouse button, click and drag the psdFileTex1 node onto the blinn1 icon.

9. From the marking menu that appears, select Color (**Figure 14.144**).

The icon of the blinn1 shader updates with the new texture.

Maya provides a one-click method to convert a PSD file node into a layered texture. The Convert To Layered Texture command creates a separate PSD file node for each layer set and connects them to a layered texture node.

This command is also useful if you need to connect the layer sets to the channels of a shader. Convert to Layered Texture automatically creates additional PSD file nodes for each layer set and selects them in the Link To Layer Set section of the PSD file node attributes. Then you can use the middle mouse button to connect each PSD file node to the appropriate channel in the shader.

To create a layered texture from a PSD file node:

1. Follow steps 1–6 from the previous task.

2. Right-click the psdFileTex node, and select Convert To Layered Texture from the marking menu that appears (**Figure 14.145**).

   Several new nodes appear in the Work Area. For each layer set in the PSD file, a new psdFileTex node is created (**Figure 14.146**).

3. Click and drag the nodes so they don't overlap (**Figure 14.147**).

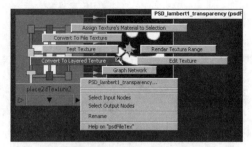

Figure 14.145 Right-click psdFileTex, and select Convert To Layered Texture from the marking menu.

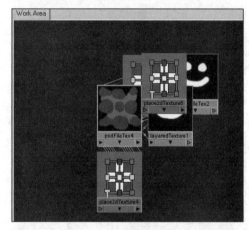

Figure 14.146 Convert To Layered Texture creates psdFileTex nodes for each layer set in the PSD file and connects them to a layeredTexture node.

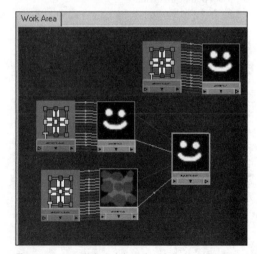

Figure 14.147 Click and drag the nodes to rearrange them.

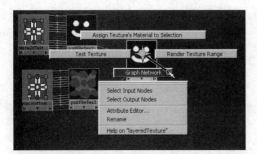

Figure 14.148 Right-click layeredTexture, and select Graph Network from the marking menu.

Figure 14.149
The graph of the psdFileTex nodes connected to the layeredTexture.

4. Right-click the layeredTexture node, and select Graph Network from the marking menu (**Figure 14.148**).

The Work Area updates, showing how the psdFileTex nodes are connected to the layeredTexture node (**Figure 14.149**).

5. With the middle mouse button, click and drag the layeredTexture node to any channel input of a shader.

6. Repeat step 5 with the individual psdFileTex nodes.

TEXTURING USING PAINTING TOOLS

413

CREATING LIGHTS

Figure 15.1 From dimly lit warehouses to bright fields, lighting controls the mood of your scene.

Figure 15.2 Use of heavily contrasting light in this shot highlights elements in a classic film noir look. Image by Raf Anzovin.

Lighting is an essential part of creating a scene. Whether it's photorealistic or heavily stylized, the light controls the look, warmth, mood, and visibility of the scene (**Figure 15.1**). Lighting in Maya holds many parallels to film lighting. The same techniques that aid painters and filmmakers will aid you in deciding how to illuminate your scene.

Lighting in Maya has advantages and disadvantages over lighting in the real world. Lights aren't visible in Maya, so they can be placed anywhere, even in plain view of the camera. Placing a light anywhere lets you highlight certain parts of a scene for dramatic effect (**Figure 15.2**). For instance, you can create a "negative" light to darken an area, which helps to create a moody scene by keeping areas obscured. Additionally, you can set lights to only illuminate specific objects, allowing you to bring a character or object away from its background.

Lighting comes with its own set of problems, however. Light in Maya doesn't perform like light in the real world. In the real world, light hits an object and is partially absorbed; then, having changed its properties slightly, it continues to bounce around almost infinitely. In Maya, light stops at the first thing it hits. This means your scenes are darker than a real world scene with the same lighting, because all the light is absorbed instead of scattered. Additionally, the lack of scattered light means your lights are more limited in effect, only illuminating things directly in their area of effect. To compensate for the dark and limited lights, you must use many more lights to fill in blanks.

Keep in mind, though, that the more lights you have in a scene, the longer the scene will take to render. The trick to lighting often comes from finding the right balance between appearance and render time.

In this chapter, we'll look at lights and lighting techniques, and the tradeoffs you must make to balance a realistic lighting setup with valuable render time.

Figure 15.3 Even with very bright light, the far side of the objects remains pitch black. This unnatural look must be addressed with additional lights.

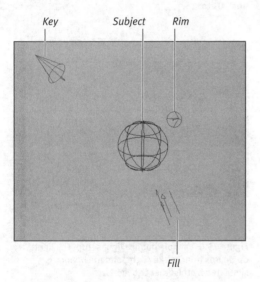

Figure 15.4 The three-point light rig has a Key light as a main source, a Fill light to illuminate the dark edges, and a Rim light for highlights. In the center is the object being illuminated.

About Lighting

As we mentioned, light in the real world bounces from object to object, changing subtly and moving on. This means any given area is receiving light that is varied in intensity, energy, and direction. In Maya, light moves from a light object until it hits model geometry, where it stops. Light in Maya can acquire color from transparent objects, but other than that, it's up to you to fill in the missing behavior.

As a result, most scenes include several different lights. In general, there is a light for every major visible source (bulbs, sun, moon, fires). Because the light from these sources doesn't illuminate the far side of the objects it hits, you need to create lights to fill in the dark areas (**Figure 15.3**). Usually, these lights are either ambient or dimmer lights pointing in the opposite direction from your primary lights. Your scene also may have areas that you simply want to be a bit brighter—those areas require their own lights, too.

Common rigs

As you can see, lighting in Maya can become fairly complicated. To help manage this, animators use a few general lighting strategies, commonly referred to as *light rigs*. Building one of these layouts of lights makes a good starting point for lighting your scene:

◆ **Three-point rig**—A basic setup suited for scenes with one major light source. The three-point rig consists of a Key light (the main source), a Fill light to illuminate the shadowed area, and a Rim light to highlight the edges of the object (**Figure 15.4**).

◆ **Dome lighting**—Refers to the technique of building a sphere (or hemisphere) of many fairly dim lights. Dome lighting produces smooth, diffuse, lighting and soft shadows, but due to the number of lights, it takes a very long time to render (**Figure 15.5**).

◆ **Bounce lighting**—Similar to a three-point rig but contains lights for the major sources. Additional dimmer lights are then set up to simulate the primary light bouncing off large surfaces. This is repeated until a satisfactory look is achieved. *Bounce light* is a common term for any light that is used in a similar fashion (**Figure 15.6**).

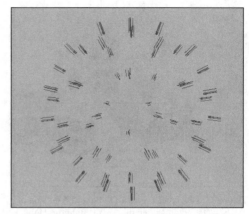

Figure 15.5 A dome light setup consisting of 60 directional lights. The lights here vary in intensity from .01 to .15.

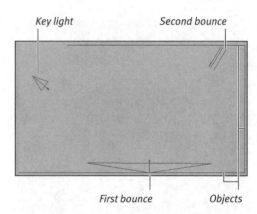

Figure 15.6 A simple bounce light setup. The light originates from the key light, and the bounce is simulated by the other two lights.

Light warmth

By default, all light in Maya is white. In the real world, light has a faint color (except, obviously, the colors in disco lights or stained glass and so forth). To approximate real life in Maya, you can assign a very faint color to your lights as well.

Cool lights are white or light blue, and come from very high-energy sources (like the noon sun). They are best used for well-lit or hard, uncomfortable scenes such as a brightly lit laboratory. *Warm* lights are yellow, usually from lower energy sources like incandescent bulbs, fires, or sunrise/sunsets. You'd use warm lights for cozy, dimly lit scenes like candlelit dining rooms and country kitchens. Counterintuitively, the brighter or hotter the light source, the cooler the light appears visually. Light source temperatures are typically measured in degrees Kelvin.

The following are common light temperatures:

◆ **1000 K**—Match flame or other small fires. The light is very red.

◆ **2000 K**—Sunrise or sunset. Light is golden orange and very warm looking.

◆ **3000–5000 K**—Incandescent lighting. The light is light yellow. Dimmer and older incandescent bulbs tend to have more color than new ones.

◆ **6000–7000 K**—Daylight. Like light at high noon, this is very close to white light. Fluorescents also tend to be close to this range.

◆ **8000–10,000 K**—Blue sky; sunlight not at noon. Sunlight is actually a light blue color. This light looks cool indoors and severe outdoors (such as in a desert).

ABOUT LIGHTING

Setting Up for Lighting

Setting up lighting is an inexact science. It's not unusual to spend hours adjusting the light attributes and positions. In this section, we'll go over some ways to streamline your workflow, starting with commonly used windows.

Four important windows are used to create an ideal lighting workflow: the Hypershade, the Render view, the Camera view, and the Attribute Editor. The Hypershade is used to create new lights (**Figure 15.7**) and adjust surfaces and advanced lighting options. The Render view lets you look at your Interactive Photorealistic Render (IPR) as you adjust your lights, or quickly do a non-IPR render. The Attribute Editor is useful for adjusting light properties quickly. It's also important to keep your Camera view open, because this is the view from which your scene needs to look good. If your scene contains multiple cameras, you may want to open multiple camera panels. You can tear off a camera panel by selecting Panels > Tear Off Copy (**Figure 15.8**).

Figure 15.7
The Create bar with an expanded Lights section.

Figure 15.8 If you have the screen space, you can tear off any view into a new window for a custom layout.

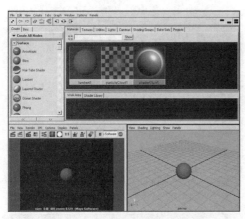

Figure 15.9 The Hypershade on top, the Render view pane at lower left, and the Perspective view in the lower-right pane.

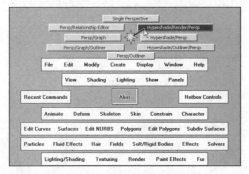

Figure 15.10 Streamline your setup with the Hypershade/Render/Persp option in the marking menu.

You can arrange your windows in whatever way works for you. Tasks in this chapter assume you have all four windows open. A Hypershade/Render/Persp preset (**Figure 15.9**) is available from the marking menu in the north quadrant of the Hotbox (**Figure 15.10**). Then you can open the Attribute Editor in a separate window and be ready to light.

Before you begin, though, you need something to light.

To create a practice scene:

1. Choose File > New Scene to create a new scene.

2. Create five or six primitives in the scene, and move them around randomly, with the bottom of each sitting on the grid (**Figure 15.11**).

3. Choose Create > NURBS Primitives > Plane to create a plane at the origin.

4. Scale the plane larger than the objects in your scene (**Figure 15.12**).

5. Save the practice scene as a file called practice.mb.

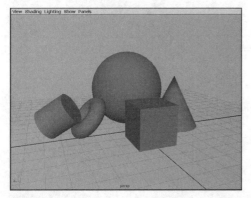

Figure 15.11 Create five or six primitives in the scene, and place them randomly.

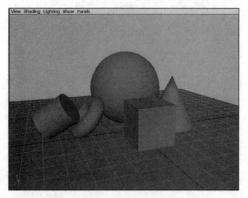

Figure 15.12 The plane is scaled larger than the objects in the scene.

SETTING UP FOR LIGHTING

The render settings for your scene affect the resolution of your rendered image and previews, as well as whether raytraced shadows will render. (More about rendering can be found in Chapter 16, "Cameras and Rendering.")

To adjust the render globals:

1. Click the Render Settings icon in the Render view.

   or

   Choose Window > Rendering Editors > Render Settings.

2. Expand the Image Size section of the Render Settings window; this section contains settings for the size and aspect of your output (**Figure 15.13**).

3. Choose 680x480 from the Presets drop-down list.

4. Under the Maya Software tab, expand the Raytracing Quality section (**Figure 15.14**).

5. Select the Raytracing check box.

   This option turns on raytracing in your scene. It will have no effect until you add elements to your scene that require raytracing.

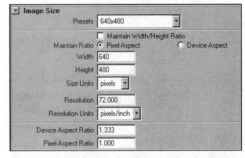

Figure 15.13 The Common tab contains attributes and settings shared by all renderers.

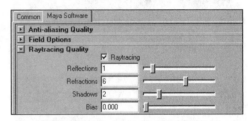

Figure 15.14 Turning on raytracing enables Shadows, Reflections, and Refractions. Without this checked, those features will not show up in a render.

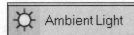

Figure 15.15 The Ambient Light icon.

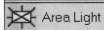

Figure 15.16 The Area Light icon.

Figure 15.17 The Directional Light icon.

About Lights

Maya uses six light types: *ambient, area, directional, point, spot,* and *volume.* You can combine these light types to produce just about any lighting scenario. A Maya scene must include at least one light, or objects will be in complete darkness. Most scenes use many different kinds of lights, because each is suited to different uses.

The following are the different light types and some of their common uses:

♦ **Ambient**—Produces a uniform, non-directional light throughout the scene (**Figure 15.15**). You should keep this type of light to a minimum, because the more you use it, the flatter and more devoid of contrast the scene will appear. Examples of ambient light include:

  ▲ Light that has no obvious source

  ▲ Light that has bounced off several surfaces since its source

♦ **Area**—Two-dimensional, rectangular light source that emits light from the entire rectangle in the direction of the normal (**Figure 15.16**). Examples of area light include the following:

  ▲ Illuminated ceiling panels and fluorescent lights

  ▲ Rectangular light bouncing off walls

♦ **Directional**—Parallel light rays that illuminate the whole scene evenly from one specific direction (**Figure 15.17**). Examples of directional light include:

  ▲ Sunlight and moonlight

  ▲ Any light source that is so far away that the angle at which the light hits an object will not change, even if the object moves

◆ **Point**—Radiates light out from its center in all directions. The farther an object is from this light, the less it's illuminated (**Figure 15.18**). Examples of point light include:

▲ Light bulbs

▲ LEDs

▲ Torches

◆ **Spot**—Lights an area within a variable cone shape. The light comes from the center point and travels in a specified direction (**Figure 15.19**). Examples of spot lights include:

▲ Flashlights

▲ Street lamps

▲ Headlights

▲ Spotlights

◆ **Volume**—Lights an area within a user-defined volume (**Figure 15.20**). Examples of volume light include:

▲ Areas around dim light sources like torches and fires

▲ Shafts of light coming through an area

All light types have the following common attributes. If you change the light type, only these attributes will be preserved (**Figure 15.21**):

◆ **Type** sets the kind of light: ambient, area, directional, point, spot, or volume. You can change this attribute at any time—for example, from a point to a spot.

Figure 15.18 The Point Light icon.

Figure 15.19 The Spot Light icon.

Figure 15.20 The Volume Light icon.

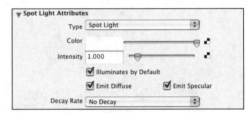

Figure 15.21 Common light attributes: Type, Color, Intensity, and Decay Rate.

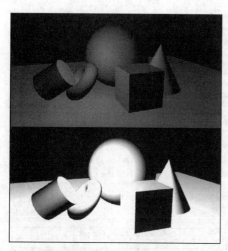

Figure 15.22 The top scene is lit with a light at low intensity; the bottom scene is lit with the same light at a high-intensity setting.

Spotlight   *Light direction*

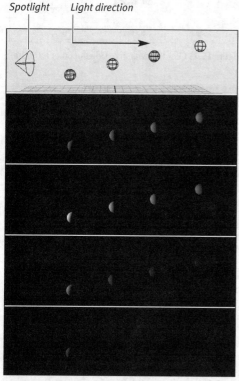

Figure 15.23 After the wireframe of the scene, the decay rates are shown top to bottom: no decay, linear, quadratic, and cubic.

◆ **Color** sets the color of the light and is usually very unsaturated. Low values make the light seem dimmer. Image maps may be added to vary the color of the light.

◆ **Intensity** sets the brightness of the light. If set to negative values, it sets the darkness of the light. For best results, start small and work your way up (**Figure 15.22**).

◆ **Decay Rate** controls how quickly the light's intensity decreases over distance. When you change this setting, you must also raise or lower the intensity of the light to make up for the decay-rate change. This isn't an attribute of the ambient, directional, or volume lights (**Figure 15.23**). Possible values are as follows:

▲ **No Decay**—Light has the same intensity regardless of distance.

▲ **Linear Decay**—The light's intensity diminishes with distance less abruptly than with Quadratic and Cubic decay.

▲ **Quadratic Decay**—The light's intensity diminishes at a rate between that of Linear and Cubic decay. This setting is closest to real-world light decay.

▲ **Cubic Decay**—The light's intensity diminishes most abruptly, substantially more abruptly than with Linear and Quadratic decay.

ABOUT LIGHTS

425

Ambient light

Ambient light is indirect light that is present without having an obvious source. Because it has bounced off several objects since leaving its original source, ambient light is usually fairly dim. This type of light illuminates the dark sides of objects and lets you see on a cloudy day.

In Maya, ambient lights illuminate all objects evenly, removing shadows. This behavior simulates the diffuse light in a room but also removes shadows and shading you may want. As such, you should use ambient light sparingly.

To create an ambient light:

1. Open the practice.mb file.

2. Choose Create > Lights > Ambient Light (**Figure 15.24**).

3. Select your Camera view, and click the IPR Render button ![IPR].

4. In the Render view, select an area of your image to update.

5. In the Attribute Editor, click the swatch beside the Color attribute (**Figure 15.25**). The color wheel opens.

6. Click in the color wheel to select a color for the light (**Figure 15.26**).

   Notice how much effect the light color has on the objects.

7. Click Apply to lock in the color.

✔ Tip

■ You shouldn't need more than one ambient light per scene. Ambient light can quickly flatten a scene's 3D effect.

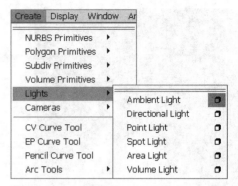

Figure 15.24 Select the box next to Ambient Light.

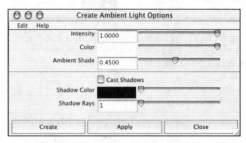

Figure 15.25 Click the swatch beside the Color attribute.

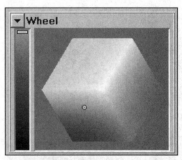

Figure 15.26 Select a color from the color wheel, which in Maya looks more like a color block.

Figure 15.27 The Ambient Shade attribute is set to 0, flattening the scene.

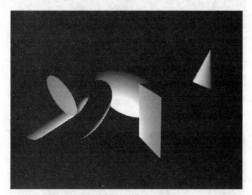

Figure 15.28 The Ambient Shade attribute is set to 1, making the light similar to a point light.

Figure 15.29 Set the Ambient Shade attribute to 0.

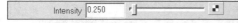

Figure 15.30 Set the intensity to .25.

The Ambient Shade attribute of the ambient light affects the direction of the light source. If Ambient Shade is set to 0, light comes from all directions (**Figure 15.27**). If it's set to 1, light comes from the source itself, acting similarly to a point light (**Figure 15.28**). You must be careful when adjusting this attribute because the lower the number, the flatter the image appears.

To change an ambient light's Ambient Shade attribute:

1. Start where the last task left off, with an ambient light selected and your IPR render refreshing a region.

2. Set the Ambient Shade attribute to 0 (**Figure 15.29**).

   The 0 value sends light evenly over the entire scene. Notice that the objects blend together flatly (Figure 15.27).

3. With the light still selected, go to the Attribute Editor and change the Ambient Shade attribute to .7.

   This value makes the ambient light act similarly to a point light, so that its intensity fades slightly as the distance from the light source increases.

4. In the Attribute Editor, set Intensity to .25 or less (**Figure 15.30**).

   This brings down the intensity of the ambient light and keeps the flattening of the scene to a minimum.

   The scene is very dark. Ambient lights are rarely used alone.

Area lights

Area lights produce light evenly from a rectangle. They're best for situations that call for lighting that is evenly bright throughout—for example, florescent lighting. Area lights can also be used for bounce lights. For instance, a very bright shaft of sunlight coming in through a window creates a hotspot on the wall. Setting up an area light on that wall simulates the reflection of the light from that specific spot. Area lights take longer to render than the other light types, and using them extensively in a scene can slow rendering.

To create an area light:

1. Open the practice.mb file.

2. In the Hypershade, select Area Light in the Lights section of the Create bar (**Figure 15.31**).

3. Scale the light to the size you want the area light to be.

   The position and direction of the area light indicate where it will illuminate.

4. Move and rotate the light around the scene until the surface normal points at the object or area you want to light (**Figure 15.32**).

5. Click the IPR Render icon 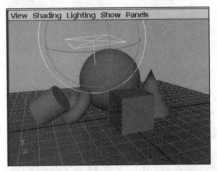.

   The scene is illuminated evenly in all areas directly under the light (**Figure 15.33**).

6. Scale the light to a different size, such as a very narrow strip.

   The light in the scene is reduced accordingly (**Figure 15.34**).

Figure 15.31 Select Area Light in the Lights section of the Create bar.

Figure 15.32 Point the surface normal at the area you want to light.

Figure 15.33 Objects under an area light are evenly illuminated. The brightness drops off after the edges of the light.

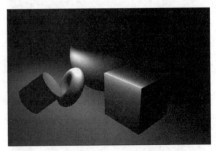

Figure 15.34 Scaling the area light to a strip produces a tube of light.

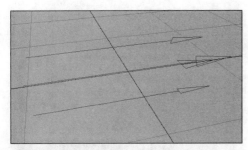

Figure 15.35 The default position of the directional light.

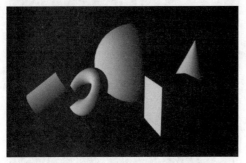

Figure 15.36 The perpendicular light rays of the directional light follow a horizontal direction by default.

Figure 15.37 Point the arrows in the direction you want the light to follow.

✔ Tip

- Translating a directional light has no effect on how it lights the scene; however, it could help you find or select that light later.

Directional lights

Directional lights are a lot like area lights, but they're infinitely large. They produce a wall of light in one direction, evenly illuminating the entire scene with light from that direction. The position of a directional light doesn't matter, because the light it sheds is entirely uniform and isn't obscured by objects.

Directional lights work great for representing sunlight and moonlight. They also work well when your objects are far from your light source. In these cases, the light rays coming from the source to your scene are nearly parallel. As a result, the characters aren't likely be struck by light from a different angle because they're moving. Directional lights also make good fill lights, because they evenly illuminate without the flattening effect of an ambient light.

To create a directional light:

1. Open the practice.mb file.

2. Choose Create > Lights > Directional Light.

   A directional light is created at the origin of the scene. The default direction points down the *z* axis in the negative direction (**Figure 15.35**). The perpendicular light rays follow a horizontal direction by default (**Figure 15.36**).

3. Create an IPR render of your scene, and select a region for tuning.

4. Select the directional light by clicking it. Rotate the light around the axes until the arrows point in the direction you want the light to follow (**Figure 15.37**).

   Notice the light illuminates all objects from the same direction, even objects that are behind it.

5. Position the light inside an object.

   All the objects are still illuminated. Directional light rays aren't obscured by objects.

Point lights

Point lights are great for bulbs and fires. They're also useful for adding a little light to a dark corner, removing light from an overlit area, or faking reflected light on an object.

Point lights illuminate in all directions and can be reasonable alternatives to area lights if you want to save render time. The falloff on point lighting makes smooth blending easier than with other light types, such as spot lights.

To create a point light:

1. Open the practice.mb file.

2. In the Hypershade, click the Point Light icon in the Lights section of the Create bar.

   The point light appears in the Work Area of the Hypershade window (**Figure 15.38**).

3. Double-click the Point Light icon in the Work Area to open the Attribute Editor.

4. Set the Color and Intensity attributes, and then close the Attribute Editor.

5. Click the light to select it, and move it above the ground plane to keep it from being obstructed by the plane (**Figure 15.39**).

6. Create an IPR render of your scene, and select an area for updating.

7. In the Attribute Editor, adjust the Decay Rate value to Quadratic (**Figure 15.40**).

   The light dims rapidly now. You can use the decay rate to limit the effect of a point light to a local area.

✔ Tip

■ Setting the Intensity attribute to a negative number subtracts light from the area around it.

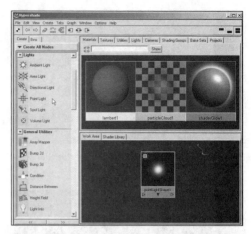

Figure 15.38 Click the Point Light icon to create a new light to work with in the Hypershade's Work Area panel.

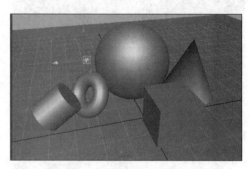

Figure 15.39 Move the light above the ground plane.

Figure 15.40 Decay rates increase exponentially. Quadratic makes the light bright nearby and dim for quite some distance away.

Figure 15.41 Set the Object Pick mask to select lights only.

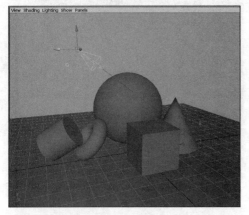

Figure 15.42 Pull up the *y*-axis translation manipulator on the spotlight to raise it above ground.

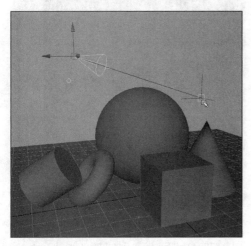

Figure 15.43 Move the end manipulator into a new position.

Spot lights

Spot lights are great for areas where you want to focus light. You can use them as stage or theater spotlights, headlights, or any cone-shaped light source. Very wide-angle spot lights are good alternatives to point lights or directional lights due to the increased control you have over light direction and falloff.

Spot lights generate light in a cone. You can adjust the angle of the cone as well as how focused it is. Most important, you can aim the light wherever you want.

To create a spot light:

1. Open the practice.mb file.

2. Click the Spot Light icon 🔲 in the Rendering shelf to create a spot light at the origin of the scene.

3. Set the Object Pick mask to Rendering objects only 🔲, and swipe across the Spot Light icon at the origin to select it (**Figure 15.41**).

   If the Object Pick mask is selected correctly, only the light will be selected.

4. Select the Show Manipulator tool by pressing ⌴ or selecting its icon 🔲 in the toolbar.

5. Pull up the *y* axis translation manipulator on the spot light to raise it above the ground (**Figure 15.42**).

   Notice when you're in the Show Manipulator tool that the end of the spot light stays in its original position, forcing the light to point at it.

6. Select the center square of the end manipulator, and move it to the position where you want the light to point (**Figure 15.43**).

7. Create an IPR render of your scene, and leave it open so you can adjust the light as you read about the attributes next.

A spot light has a number of attributes that you can change. Following are definitions of some of these attributes:

◆ **Cone Angle**—The larger the number you input here, the wider the cone (and thus the illuminated area) will be (**Figure 15.44**).

◆ **Penumbra Angle**—Adjusting the penumbra angle softens the edge of the spot light by blurring it. A negative number blurs inside the edge of the cone; a positive number blurs outside the edge of the cone (**Figure 15.45**).

◆ **Dropoff**—This attribute adjusts the intensity of the light from its center out to its edge. Raising the value results in a soft gradation from the center to the edge (**Figure 15.46**).

Figure 15.44 The default cone angle on top; the same light position but with a larger cone angle on the bottom.

Figure 15.45 Adjusting the penumbra angle blurs the edge of the spotlight. The top light has a setting of 0; the bottom light has a setting of 7.

Figure 15.46 Dropoff adjusts the intensity of the light from its center out to its edge. The light at the top has a default setting of 0; the light at the bottom has a setting of 8.

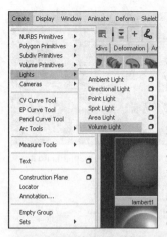

Figure 15.47
Select Lights ›
Volume Light
from the Create
menu to create
a volume light
at the scene's
origin.

Volume light

Volume lights fill an area with light. By default, they illuminate at full intensity at their center and fade off at the edge. Volume lights brighten areas with greater control than a point light, and they're also useful for creating shafts of light.

To create a volume light:

1. Open the practice.mb file.

2. Choose Create > Lights > Volume Light (**Figure 15.47**).

3. Scale the volume light until it surrounds the objects you want to illuminate (**Figure 15.48**).

4. Create an IPR render of your scene, and select an area for updating.

   The area is illuminated as if it were lit by a point light.

5. In the Attribute Editor, change the shape of the light to Box.

   The light now sheds light in a square area (**Figure 15.49**).

6. Scale the light down on one axis.

   Now there is a plane of light such as you might expect to come from under a door.

Figure 15.48 The volume light representation is similar to a sphere and should be placed around the objects you want to illuminate.

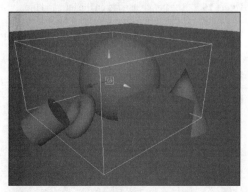

Figure 15.49 Changing the shape of the volume light can be useful in limiting the objects it illuminates.

ABOUT LIGHTS

Mapping Images to Lights

Many light attributes can have an image mapped to them, which gives you greater control over the light. You can use this technique to shape a light more precisely than the basic type allows, give it complicated coloration like concert lighting, or have it project images like a slide projector. For example, if you add an image into a light's Color attribute, the image is projected through it, which produces an effect similar to light coming through a stained-glass window (**Figure 15.50**).

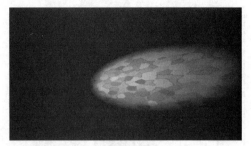

Figure 15.50 A light with an image mapped into it.

To add an image map to a light's Color attribute:

1. Click a spot light to select it.

2. In the Attribute Editor, select the map icon next to the Color slider ▦ to open the Create Render Node panel.

3. In the Create Render Node panel, select the Textures tab, and then click File in the 2D Textures section (**Figure 15.51**).

   This option creates a File node and also opens the Attribute Editor.

4. In the Attribute Editor, select the File icon ▣ next to the Image Name attribute.

   The Open dialog box appears.

5. Browse to the folder containing the image you want to use; select it, and click Open.

   The icon at the top of the Attribute Editor updates with the image you selected.

6. Render the Perspective view (**Figure 15.52**).

   The light displays the image, like a film projector.

Figure 15.51 From the Create Render Node panel, select the Textures tab; in the 2D Textures section, select File.

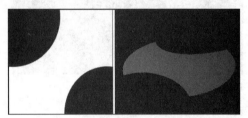

Figure 15.52 The image used is on the left, and the final render of the light with the image mapped into it is on the right.

✔ Tip

- You can map an image to the intensity of the light as well. This technique is useful for mimicking the shadows of objects that the light would pass through logically but that aren't actually in your scene (such as an out of view window, or a forest canopy).

Figure 15.53
Look Through Selected
can be chosen from
any pane menu or the
Hotbox.

Looking Through a Light

Pointing a light at just the right area of a scene can be difficult, but Maya makes it a little easier by allowing you to look through the light as you position it. As you look at the scene through the light, you can pan and dolly around until the light is pointing at the precise area of the scene you want to illuminate.

To look through a light:

1. Select the light through which you want to view the scene.

2. Inside a pane, select Panels > Look Through Selected (**Figure 15.53**).

   The view of the scene is now from the light's point of view (**Figure 15.54**).

✔ Tip

■ If you want to focus the light on an object, select the object and, from inside a pane, select View > Look at Selection.

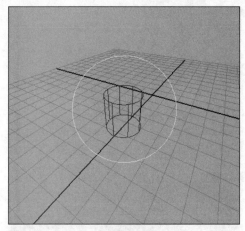

Figure 15.54 The cylinder is currently centered in the spotlight's view. The circle around the object defines the spotlight's view.

Light Linking

Light linking adds flexibility to lighting your scene. It lets you define a surface to be lit by only specific lights or define a light to hit only certain surfaces, both of which let you isolate and control the lighting of a specific area of your scene. Light linking can also save on render time, because you can limit the objects Maya considers when calculating the effects of a light.

Light linking is ideal for highlighting certain objects in your scene and making them stand out visually. This must be done carefully, because an object with vastly different lighting than that of its surroundings looks out of place.

To link a light to an object:

1. Start a new scene with two spot lights and three primitives aligned (**Figure 15.55**).

   Save this scene for later use.

2. Choose Lighting/Shading > Light Linking > Light-Centric (**Figure 15.56**). The Relationship Editor opens.

3. On the left side of the Relationship Editor, select the light for which you want to specify objects.

4. On the right side, select the objects you want the light to hit, and, if necessary, deselect any objects you don't want the light to hit (**Figure 15.57**).

5. Repeat steps 3 and 4 for each light to which you want to link objects.

6. Render the scene to see the results.

✔ Tip

■ You can click and drag across the object names in the Relationship Editor to select objects quickly.

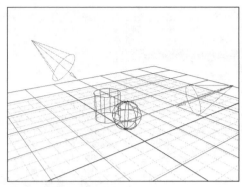

Figure 15.55 Create a simple scene to use for light linking.

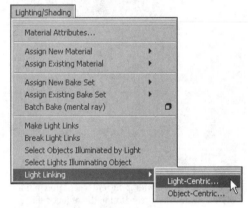

Figure 15.56 Choose Light-Centric to control the linking of one light to multiple objects.

Figure 15.57 SpotLight1 will illuminate only nurbsCylinder1.

LIGHT LINKING

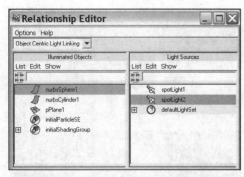

Figure 15.58 Select nurbsSphere1 on the left side and the lights you want to illuminate nurbsSphere1 on the right side. Here spotLight2 will be the only light hitting nurbsSphere1.

Figure 15.59 The lights in this scene are linked to specific objects, so no light hits the plane below.

To link an object to a light:

1. Open the scene created for the previous task, "To link a light to an object."

2. Choose Lighting/Shading > Light Linking > Object-Centric.
   The Relationship Editor opens.

3. On the left side of the Relationship Editor, select the object for which you want to define lighting (**Figure 15.58**).

4. On the right side, select the lights you want to hit the object, and, if necessary, deselect any lights you don't want to light the object.

5. Repeat steps 3 and 4 for each object to which you want to link lights.

6. Render the scene to see the results (**Figure 15.59**).

✔ Tip

■ For a glitzy effect, combine an extra light with light linking to create additional highlights. Doing so can add to the shiny look of these objects while saving on render time and preserving the normal finish of nearby surfaces.

About Shadows

Shadows are an important scene element because they secure an object's placement in a scene. Objects without shadows look free floating (**Figure 15.60**) and, by extension, unrealistic. Shadows are also important artistically. Most lights in Maya have the option to cast shadows, but you only want a few in each scene to cast them; the most dramatic effects are produced with a few bold shadows.

A real-world shadow is the complementary color of the light source: The sun is yellow; therefore, the shadows it casts are purple—in essence, there are no black shadows in the real world, only very dark representations of a particular color. Keep this in mind as you create both realistic and artistic shadows: If you apply this principle to your 3D work, you'll produce deeper, richer imagery.

A real shadow is darkest close to an object, fading and blurring as it gets farther away (**Figure 15.61**). The bounce of light and variations in light source illuminate a shadow and ensure it isn't pitch black (**Figure 15.62**). A shadow that is very precise or very dark will stand out and thus appear unrealistic.

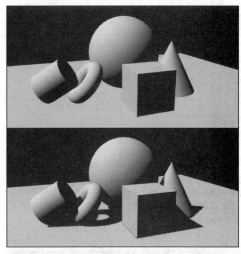

Figure 15.60 Shadows help to visually plant objects on the ground.

Figure 15.61 A real shadow's darkest area is slightly away from the object's edge, near the base of the shadow.

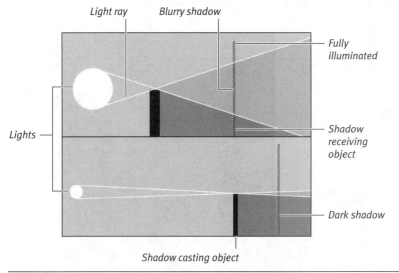

Light ray   Blurry shadow

Fully illuminated

Lights

Shadow receiving object

Dark shadow

Shadow casting object

Figure 15.62 Light from bright areas leaves from more than just one point. In the areas where light is partially blocked, a light, blurry shadow forms (Top). The closer a shadow is to the object that casts it, and the smaller the source, the sharper a shadow gets (Bottom).

Figure 15.63 Too many shadows make it hard to tell what is going on.

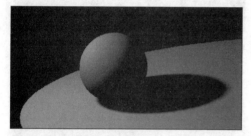

Figure 15.64 Depth-map shadow.

Figure 15.65 Raytraced shadow.

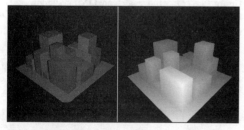

Figure 15.66 On the left is a render of the scene, on the right is the depth map used to determine which objects are closest to the light.

Creating shadows

Shadows are turned off on all lights by default. To see shadows in a render, you must turn them on. Because you will have many lights in most scenes, you should turn on shadows for only a few key lights. Always try to ensure that your shadows come from obvious light sources.

Another way to help your shadows look good is to be sure you don't have too many in your scene. Too many shadows can look as odd as none (**Figure 15.63**), and Maya gives you the ability to limit the shadows cast by objects. An individual object doesn't cast a shadow if shadow casting is turned off on the object. This applies even if the object is struck by a shadow-casting light.

Maya uses two types of shadows: *depth map* (**Figure 15.64**) and *raytraced* (**Figure 15.65**). Both methods can produce good-looking shadows, although raytracing often produces more realistic shadows with less effort and tweaking. However, raytraced shadows can take much longer to render than depth-map shadows, so the choice is a trade-off. It's a constant battle to produce good-looking shadows while keeping rendering time to a minimum for each scene.

Depth-map simulated shadows are usually much faster to render than raytraced shadows, but you pay for that speed with increased RAM use at render time. A *depth map* is an image file that contains a *depth channel* (a grayscale representation of how far objects are from the camera, the lights, and each other) rendered from a light's point of view (**Figure 15.66**). Maya uses the depth map to determine which surfaces have light hitting them and which surfaces are in shadow. Think of the depth map as a pre-drawn shadow brought into the scene just before it's rendered. This image is then projected from the light's point of view, like a texture,

439

darkening the areas where shadows should be. The image resolution and your object's distance from the light are key to ensuring a good-looking depth map. If you need to redo a render, these depth-map image files can be reused, saving even more rendering time.

In most scenarios, raytraced shadows produce great-looking, realistic images—results you wouldn't be able to achieve with depth-map shadows. One example is a transparent shadow cast from a partially transparent object (**Figure 15.67**).

However, raytraced shadows have some restrictions as well. For one, they don't show up if rendered with interactive photorealistic rendering because IPR doesn't allow raytracing. This represents an additional speed cost because you can use IPR to see depth-map shadows, making depth-map shadow adjustment much faster. You can also preview light placement and depth-map shadows using the shaded mode in any view.

Depth-map shadows

Depth-map shadows—which are available in all but ambient light—can simulate relatively realistic shadows without greatly affecting rendering time.

To create a depth-map shadow:

1. Select the light from which you want to produce a shadow.

2. In the Attribute Editor, click the arrow next to the Shadows heading to expand the shadow options.

3. Select the Use Depth Map Shadows check box under the Depth Map Shadow Attributes heading (**Figure 15.68**).

4. In the Shadows section, click the swatch next to the Shadow Color attribute (**Figure 15.69**).
   The Color Chooser opens.

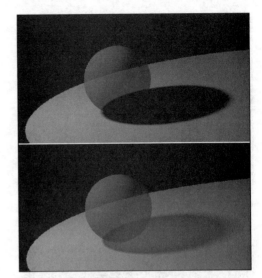

Figure 15.67 A depth-map shadow can't show an object's transparency within the shadow (top); a raytraced shadow can (bottom).

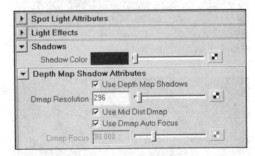

Figure 15.68 Select Use Depth Map Shadows.

Figure 15.69 Click the swatch next to the Shadow Color attribute to open the Color Chooser.

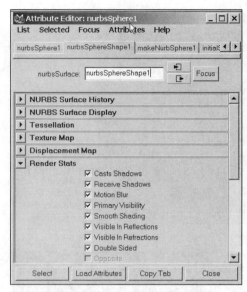

Figure 15.70 Select Casts Shadows in the Render Stats section of the Attribute Editor.

Figure 15.71 The final render with a depth-map shadow.

Figure 15.72 Select Lighting › Shadows to display depth-map shadows.

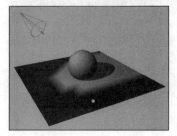

Figure 15.73 These depth-map shadows are a good approximation of the final rendering.

5. Select a shadow color from the color wheel.

6. Click Accept to lock in the color.

7. Select the surface you want to cast shadows.

8. In the Render Stats section of the surface's Attribute Editor, make sure that Casts Shadows (the default option) is selected (**Figure 15.70**).

9. Test-render the scene by selecting Render > Render > Persp in the Render view pane.

The render shows a depth-map shadow (**Figure 15.71**).

To preview depth-map shadows:

1. Continuing from the previous task, "To create a depth-map shadow," click in the Perspective pane.

A blue box around the Perspective view indicates that it's the active pane.

2. Press ⑤ to switch to shaded mode.

3. Press ⑦ to enable Use All Lights in the Perspective view.

4. Select Lighting > Shadows to display depth-map shadows (**Figure 15.72**).

You can now move the camera and play the animation with a good approximation of what the final lighting will look like (**Figure 15.73**). If the lights are set to raytraced shadows, then the shadows don't appear in the view.

continues on next page

ABOUT SHADOWS

5. Select Shading > High Quality Rendering (**Figure 15.74**).

The overall shading quality and especially the shadow edges should be greatly improved, giving an even more accurate preview of what the final shading will look like (**Figure 15.75**).

The following are common depth-map shadow attributes:

◆ **Dmap Resolution**—The resolution of the depth-map shadow file. Shadow edges appear pixilated if the resolution is too low (**Figure 15.76**). However, you should use the lowest possible setting that produces acceptable results, because this attribute is extremely memory intensive.

◆ **Dmap Filter Size**—Works in unison with Dmap Resolution to control the softness of the shadow's edges (**Figure 15.77**). Try to maintain a setting of 3 or less to avoid adding excessive render time.

Figure 15.74 Select Shading › High Quality Rendering to display depth-map shadows.

Figure 15.75 The overall shading quality is improved, especially the depth-map shadow edges.

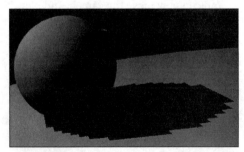

Figure 15.76 Shadow edges appear pixilated if the Dmap Resolution is too low.

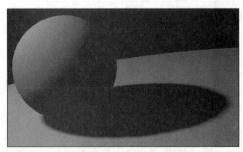

Figure 15.77 Dmap Filter Size controls the softness of the shadow's edges.

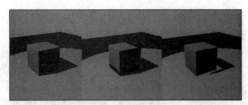

Figure 15.78 From left to right: Correct Dmap bias settings, bias set too high, bias set too low.

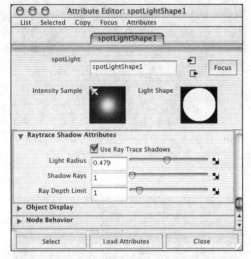

Figure 15.79 Select Use Ray Trace Shadows in the light's Attribute Editor.

◆ **Dmap Bias**—Moves the map closer to or further away from the light. You only need to use this attribute in the following circumstances:

▲ If a shadow appears detached from the shadow-casting surface, gradually decrease the Dmap Bias value until the shadow looks correct.

▲ If dark spots or streaks appear on illuminated surfaces, gradually increase the Dmap Bias value until the spots or streaks disappear (**Figure 15.78**).

Raytraced shadows

Raytraced shadows can create highly realistic shadows but also add expensive rendering time. To produce raytraced shadows, you must check three things:

◆ Raytracing must be selected in the Raytracing Quality section of the Render Settings window.

◆ Use Raytraced Shadows must be selected in the light's Attribute Editor.

◆ Casts Shadows must be selected in the Render Stats section of the Attribute Editor of each object you want to cast a shadow.

To create a raytraced shadow:

1. Select the light you want to produce a shadow.

2. In the Raytrace Shadow Attributes section of the light's Attribute Editor, select Use Ray Trace Shadows (**Figure 15.79**).

3. Above the Raytrace Shadows Attributes, open the Shadows section and click the swatch beside the Shadow Color attribute. The Color Chooser opens.

continues on next page

ABOUT SHADOWS

4. Click in the color wheel to select a shadow color.

5. Click Accept to lock in the color.

6. Test-render the scene by selecting Render > Render > Persp in the Render view window.

   IPR renders don't support raytraced shadows, so be careful not to perform one.

The following are common raytraced shadow attributes:

◆ **Light Radius**—Sets the softness of the shadow's edge relative to the size of the light, as we showed earlier in Figure 15.62. For example, smaller light values produce crisper shadows, and greater light values create softer shadows (**Figure 15.80**).

◆ **Shadow Rays**—Sets the number of sampling rays used to determine soft shadow edges (**Figure 15.81**). Increasing this attribute's value reduces grainy edges but increases rendering time, so keep it as low as possible.

◆ **Ray Depth Limit**—Determines whether a light casts a shadow if the light bounces off multiple mirrors before it hits your object.

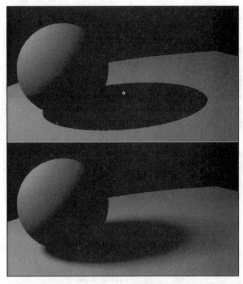

Figure 15.80 A default raytraced shadow (top), and a shadow with the Light Radius attribute turned up (bottom).

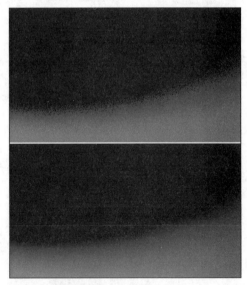

Figure 15.81 Changing the Shadow Rays attribute can cut down on grainy shadows.

CAMERAS AND RENDERING

Figure 16.1 Even these simple primitives look more like real objects when they're rendered.

Figure 16.2 Maya 7's new toon rendering features allow you to create the illusion of hand-drawn, cel-shaded images and animations.

Creating images in Maya, whether for print or video, depends on *rendering*. When you render a scene, you create a two-dimensional image based on a specified three-dimensional view of your scene. Maya does intensive mathematical calculations to realistically create lighting, shadows, reflections, and textures. You can take even a simple scene and make it look more realistic by rendering it (**Figure 16.1**). Alternately, you can use the toon features, new in Maya 7.0, to create a more stylized effect (**Figure 16.2**).

Maya comes with four different renderers: Maya Software, Maya Hardware, Maya Vector, and Mental Ray. Each of these renderers uses a different method to generate an image from a Maya scene. Because certain effects can only be created with a specific renderer, it's important to know the capabilities of each one. Each renderer has its own settings, which you can view and change in the Render Settings window, along with the common render settings.

About Cameras

An essential part of rendering is determining the point of view for your scene. Any time you view a scene in Maya, you're looking through a camera. The four views—Top, Front, Side, and Perspective—are actually four different cameras. You can render from any of these views, but in most cases you'll want to create a new camera specifically for rendering.

Cameras determine your view of the scene as well as the view that is rendered. When you tumble and track in the Perspective view, you're really just moving and rotating the persp camera. You can switch any view to a camera you've created, and then tumble, track, and dolly to reposition it.

In addition to creating a standard camera, Maya also lets you create a *camera and aim* or a *camera, aim, and up* (**Figure 16.3**). A camera and aim has an extra aim control. You can move the camera and aim independently, and the camera automatically rotates so that it always points at the aim. A camera, aim, and up has an additional up control, which allows you to adjust the tilt of the camera.

To create and adjust a camera:

1. Choose Create > Cameras > Camera.

   A new camera appears in the scene (**Figure 16.4**).

2. Use the Move and Rotate tools to adjust the camera's position and angle.

3. From the Panels menu in the Perspective view, select Look Through Selected.

   You're now looking through the camera that you just created. Note that the camera name at the bottom of the view has changed from persp to camera1 (**Figure 16.5**).

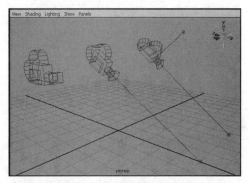

Figure 16.3 From left to right: a camera; camera and aim; and camera, aim, and up.

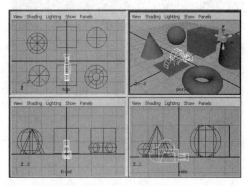

Figure 16.4 When a new camera is created, it appears at the origin.

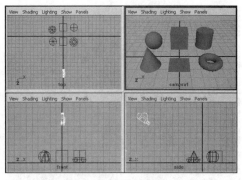

Figure 16.5 The camera has been moved and rotated, and the Perspective view has been switched to looking through the camera.

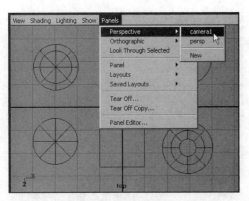

Figure 16.6 You can use the Panels › Perspective menu in any view to switch to a different camera.

Camera   Aim

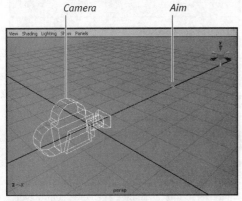

Figure 16.7 A camera and aim has been created. The aim is represented by a small circle with a dot in the middle.

Figure 16.8
Click to select the camera group in the Outliner.

4. Dolly, track, and tumble to further adjust the camera's placement.

✔ Tips

■ You can also change the camera you're looking through from the Panels › Perspective menu in the Perspective view (**Figure 16.6**).

■ Scaling a camera can make it easier to select, and doing so doesn't affect your view through it.

To create and adjust a camera and aim:

1. Choose Create > Cameras > Camera and Aim.

A new camera appears in the Perspective view. The dot in front of the camera is the aim (**Figure 16.7**).

2. Open the Outliner, either by selecting it from the Window menu or by switching to a layout that includes it in a panel.

3. In the Outliner, select the group node of the camera (**Figure 16.8**).

4. Move the camera group.

The aim and camera move together.

5. In the Perspective view, select and then move the aim.

The camera rotates to point at the aim.

continues on next page

ABOUT CAMERAS

6. In the Perspective view, select and then move the camera.

The camera moves, but it continues to point at the aim (**Figure 16.9**).

✔ Tip

■ You can change whether the camera has an aim or aim and up control after the camera has been created. Select the camera and open the Attribute Editor, and then expand the Camera Attributes section if necessary. You can choose among the three types of cameras from the Controls drop-down menu (**Figure 16.10**).

Animating the camera

By animating a camera, you can simulate the camera motion used in real-world film or create fly-throughs and other shots that would be impossible with a physical camera. You can also simulate camera cuts, where the view appears to switch to another camera at a different angle, simply by keyframing a camera using stepped tangents.

Animating a camera is, in essence, the same as animating anything else: You select it, keyframe it, change the current time, move it, and keyframe it again. It's often convenient to move a camera by tumbling, tracking, and dollying while using it to view your scene. Animation techniques like stepped tangents and motion paths can be very useful for animating cameras. Also, if your camera has an aim control, you can animate it independently, or even constrain it to another object.

One point you need to understand before you begin animating is that the selected camera isn't necessarily the one you're looking through. You can see the name of the camera you're looking through at the bottom of the view, and you can see the name of the currently selected camera in the Channel Box (**Figure 16.11**). One common

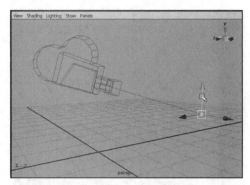

Figure 16.9 Wherever you move the aim, the camera rotates to point at it.

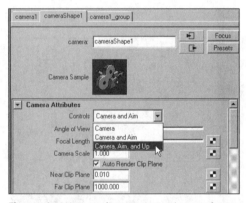

Figure 16.10 You can change a camera's control type in the Attribute Editor.

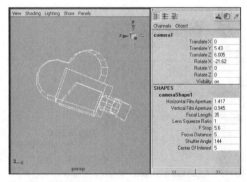

Figure 16.11 Here camera1 is selected, but the view is from the perspective camera, indicated by *persp* at the bottom of the view.

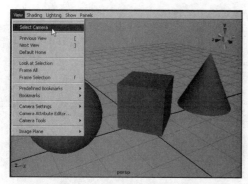

Figure 16.12 You can select a view's camera from its View menu.

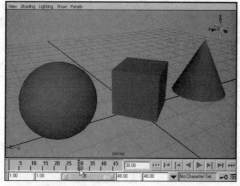

Figure 16.13 Click 30 in the Time Slider to move to frame 30.

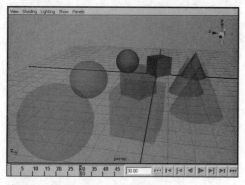

Figure 16.14 When you click play, the view changes over time, reflecting the camera's animation.

mistake is to move the view and then set keyframes without having the camera you're looking through selected. If you do this, the camera won't be keyframed.

To animate the camera using tumble, track, and dolly:

1. Create some objects, and arrange them in the scene so you have something to look at.

2. From the View menu in the Perspective view, choose Select Camera (**Figure 16.12**).

3. Press ⓢ to keyframe the camera.

4. In the Time Slider, change the current frame to 30 by clicking the number 30 (**Figure 16.13**).

5. Tumble, track, and dolly the camera to change the point of view.

   (See Chapter 2 for more on how to tumble, track, and dolly.)

6. Press ⓢ to keyframe the camera again.

7. Play the animation by clicking the play button in the timeline ▶.

   Because the camera's motion is animated, the view changes as you play the animation (**Figure 16.14**).

To make the aim of the camera follow an object:

1. Choose Create > NURBS Primitives > Sphere.

2. Choose Create > Cameras > Camera and Aim.

   A new camera with an aim control appears in the scene.

3. While the camera and aim are still selected, move them so that the aim control is at the center of the sphere (**Figure 16.15**).

4. Select the sphere, and then (Shift)-select the aim of the newly created camera.

5. From the Constrain menu in the Animation menu set, choose Point.

   The aim of the camera is point constrained to the sphere.

6. Select and move the sphere.

   The camera aims at the sphere (**Figure 16.16**). You can now animate the sphere, and the camera will automatically follow it.

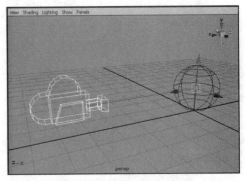

Figure 16.15 When a camera and aim is created, both the camera and its aim are selected, so you can move them together.

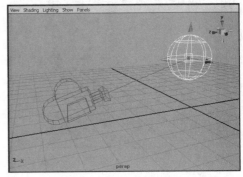

Figure 16.16 Once the camera's aim is point constrained to the sphere, the camera automatically aims at it.

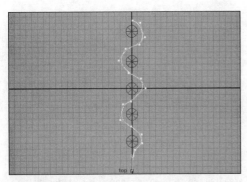

Figure 16.17 It's easiest to create this curve from the Top view.

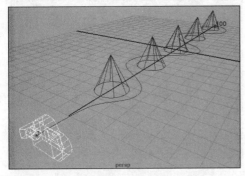

Figure 16.18 The camera is attached to this motion path, so it jumps to the beginning of the curve. However, it's facing the wrong way.

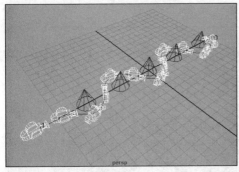

Figure 16.19 The camera, now oriented correctly, follows the curve as the animation is played back.

To animate a camera along a path:

1. Create a row of cones.

2. In the Top view, create a NURBS curve that weaves through the cones (**Figure 16.17**).

3. Choose Create > Cameras > Camera.

   A new camera appears in the scene.

4. With the camera still selected, [Shift]-select the curve.

5. Choose Animate > Motion Paths > Attach to Motion Path.

   The camera jumps to the beginning of the path, but it may not be pointing in the right direction (**Figure 16.18**).

6. With the camera still selected, click motionPath1 in the Inputs section of the Channel Box.

   Four attributes of the motion path appear.

7. Click Up Twist in the Channel Box, and then click and drag with the middle mouse button in the Perspective view until the camera is pointing down the path correctly.

8. Click the play button ▶ to play the animation.

   The camera travels down the path (**Figure 16.19**).

ABOUT CAMERAS

About the frustum

The *frustum* is the volume of space that can be viewed by a camera. Its cross-section is determined by the render resolution, and its depth is determined by the near and far *clipping planes* (**Figure 16.20**). The near clipping plane prevents objects that are too close to the camera from being displayed or rendered (**Figure 16.21**), and the far clipping plane does the same for distant objects. If this creates undesirable results for your scene, you can adjust the clipping planes in the Attribute Editor.

Depending on its aspect ratio (which is the ratio between width and height), a view may display a larger area than is encompassed by the camera's frustum. If you want to know what portion of a view will be visible when the scene is rendered, you can turn on the *resolution gate* for the camera. This displays a rectangular outline around the area that will be rendered.

To adjust the clipping planes:

1. Select the camera.

2. Press Ctrl/Control+a to display the Attribute Editor.

3. Under Camera Attributes, enter a new value for Near Clip Plane or Far Clip Plane.

To display the resolution gate:

◆ In the View menu of the camera's view, choose Camera Settings > Resolution Gate.

A rectangle frames the area that will be rendered (**Figure 16.22**).

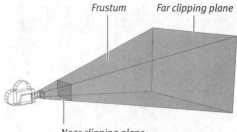

Figure 16.20 A camera's frustum encompasses the area that the camera can render; it's bounded by the near and far clipping planes.

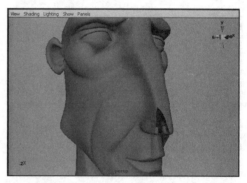

Figure 16.21 In this extreme close-up, the character's nose is intersected by the near clipping plane in the Perspective view, making part of it invisible.

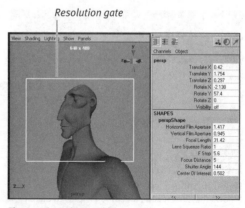

Figure 16.22 The resolution gate indicates the area of the view that will be rendered.

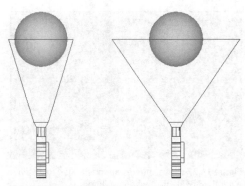

Figure 16.23 A wider angle of view (right) means objects will appear smaller, although the distance of the camera doesn't change.

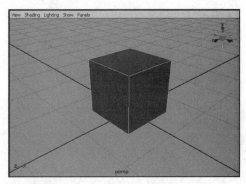

Figure 16.24 This cube appears as usual in the Perspective view, which has a default focal length of 35.

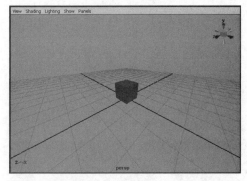

Figure 16.25 With the focal length set to 10, the cube seems much further away, even though the camera hasn't moved.

Focal length

Adjusting a camera's Focal Length attribute creates a zoom effect, making objects in the view appear larger or smaller. This is different from dollying in and out, because the camera doesn't actually move. Instead, the camera's angle of view gets wider or narrower (**Figure 16.23**). When the focal length is decreased, the angle gets wider, so more of the scene is visible in the view. Increasing the focal length makes the angle of view narrower so that less of the scene is displayed in the view. Decreasing the focal length also has the effect of exaggerating distances, whereas increasing it flattens them.

To adjust a camera's focal length:

1. Create a cube at the origin (**Figure 16.24**).

2. From the View menu in the Perspective view, choose Select Camera.

   The perspective camera becomes selected.

3. In the Channel Box, change Focal Length to 10.

   The cube seems farther away (**Figure 16.25**).

4. Dolly the camera in toward the object.

   The object appears to be distorted (**Figure 16.26**).

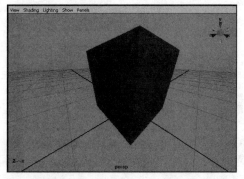

Figure 16.26 The camera has been moved close to the cube, with the focal length still set to 10. The effect is similar to that of a fisheye lens.

Depth of field

A real camera can only focus within a specific range, referred to as its *depth of field*. Objects that are in focus appear sharp. Objects that are out of focus, either because they're too close to the camera or too far away from it, are blurred. You can re-create this effect in Maya. Depth of field can be useful when you want your rendered image to look like a photograph, or when you're trying to focus the viewer's attention on a specific area of your scene.

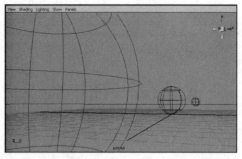

Figure 16.27 These spheres are positioned to display a depth of field effect when rendered.

To use depth of field:

1. Create a scene with three spheres and a plane. Move the spheres so that one is close to the camera, one is at the origin of the scene, and one is far away (**Figure 16.27**).

2. Assign a checkerboard material to the spheres. (See Chapter 14, "Shaders, Materials, and Mapping" for more information.)

   This will help you see the final depth of field effect.

3. From the View menu in the Perspective view, choose Select Camera.

   The perspective camera becomes selected.

4. Open the Channel Box.

   The camera's attributes are displayed.

5. Set FStop to 32.

   A larger FStop value will cause a larger portion of the scene to be in focus.

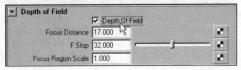

Figure 16.28
The Focus Distance setting allows you to determine where the depth of field effect is centered.

Figure 16.29 You must enable depth of field for a camera to use the effect.

Figure 16.30 Depth of field causes the sphere closest to the camera and the sphere farthest from the camera to be blurred.

6. Set Focus Distance to approximately the same value as Center Of Interest (**Figure 16.28**).

Focus Distance determines the midpoint of the area that is in focus. Center Of Interest is the distance from the camera to the origin, where the middle sphere is positioned. Setting Focus Distance to the same value as Center Of Interest ensures that the middle sphere is in focus.

7. Open the Attribute Editor. In the Depth of Field section, select the Depth Of Field check box (**Figure 16.29**).

This option enables depth of field for the camera.

8. Choose Render > Render Current Frame.

The scene is rendered. The depth of field causes the middle sphere to be in focus, while the other two are blurred and out-of-focus (**Figure 16.30**).

ABOUT CAMERAS

455

Image planes

An *image plane* is a component of the camera that remains in the background of the view regardless of how the camera is moved. An image plane can come in handy when you want to use an image as a template for modeling a character. Because image planes are rendered with the scene, you can also use an image plane as a backdrop.

To create an image plane:

1. From the View menu of the Perspective view, select Image Plane > Import Image.

   An Open dialog box appears.

2. Browse for your image, and click Open.

   The image plane now appears behind all the objects visible in the view (**Figure 16.31**).

To position an image plane:

1. Change the selection mask to Select by Component Type , and select the Miscellaneous icon .

2. Click the image plane to select it.

3. Open the Channel Box, and adjust the image plane's Offset X and Offset Y attributes (**Figure 16.32**).

   The image plane is now correctly positioned for your scene (**Figure 16.33**).

✔ Tips

- To delete an image plane, select it by following steps 1–2 above, and then press ⌈Backspace⌋/⌈Delete⌋.

- A quick way to hide an image plane is to uncheck Cameras on the view's Show menu. Because the image plane is a component of the camera, the image plane is also hidden.

Figure 16.31 A sky image has been added to the background of this scene. This image plane will stay in the same place relative to the camera even if you tumble, track, or dolly.

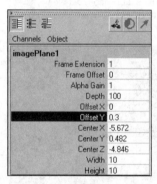

Figure 16.32 Increasing the image plane's Offset Y causes it to appear higher in the view.

Figure 16.33 The sky image is now positioned correctly.

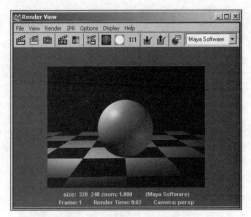

Figure 16.34 The Render View window allows you to view and save a rendered frame.

About Rendering

Rendering is how you create an image or series of images from your 3D scene. Maya allows you to quickly render the current frame to view or save, or to set up a *batch render* to automatically render and save any number of frames. The output of both of these rendering methods will vary depending on the options you select in the Render Settings window.

The Render Settings window includes a Common tab that allows you to set options common to all of Maya's renderers. It also includes a tab for the settings that are specific to the current renderer. At the top of the Render Settings window, you can switch to any of Maya's four renderers: Maya Hardware, Maya Software, Maya Vector, or Mental Ray.

Before you render your scene, you should save it and set your project. Doing so ensures that the rendered images will be saved in the correct folder. For more information on setting the project, see Chapter 1, "Maya Basics."

Maya's FCheck program allows you to view rendered images and image sequences. You can also use image-editing software like Photoshop to view and edit single images, or compositing software like After Effects for image sequences.

To render the current frame:

◆ Choose Render > Render Current Frame.

or

◆ In the Status Line, click the Render button 🎬.

The current frame is rendered and displayed in the Render View (**Figure 16.34**).

To batch render:

◆ Choose Render > Batch Render.

The status of the render is displayed in the command feedback line (**Figure 16.35**).

When the render is completed, you can find the rendered image(s) or animation file in the project's images folder (**Figure 16.36**).

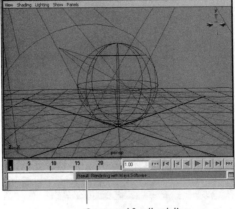

Command feedback line

Figure 16.35 You can see the status of a batch render in the command feedback line.

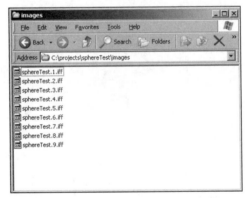

Figure 16.36 A batch render creates one or more files in the current project's images folder.

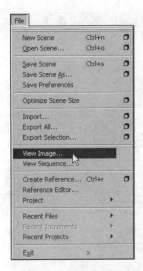

Figure 16.37
You can access
FCheck from Maya's
File menu.

Figure 16.38 FCheck allows you to view rendered images and image sequences.

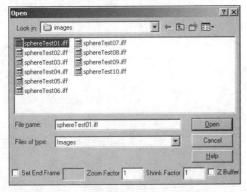

Figure 16.39 When you select and open the first image in a sequence, FCheck automatically finds the other images based on their name.

To view a rendered image in FCheck:

1. Choose File > View Image (**Figure 16.37**). An Open File dialog is displayed.

2. Navigate to the current project's images folder.

3. Select the image file, and click Open. FCheck opens to display the image (**Figure 16.38**).

To view a rendered image sequence in FCheck:

1. Choose File > View Sequence. An Open dialog is displayed.

2. Navigate to the current project's images folder.

3. Select the first image in the sequence, and click Open (**Figure 16.39**).

   FCheck loads the animation and then attempts to play it back at the current frame rate (FPS). If your animation appears too slow or too fast, you may need to adjust FCheck's FPS to match the intended frame rate of your animation.

   If the animation is still too slow, your computer's hardware may not be capable of displaying the animation at full speed. Try closing all other programs to free up memory, or press ⊤. This will play the animation in real time by skipping frames that can't be displayed quickly enough. Your animation may appear jerky, but it will play at the correct speed.

✔ Tips

■ You can click and drag in the FCheck window from left to right to scroll through an animation.

■ You can use FCheck to view a batch render in progress by choosing View Batch Render from Maya's Render menu.

ABOUT RENDERING

459

Common render settings

The Common tab of the Render Settings window allows you to view and set various render options (**Figure 16.40**). The upper portion of the tab displays the folder that files will be rendered to, the filename (and range, if rendering an image sequence), and the image size. Below this, you can adjust a number of render settings common to all renderers. For example, if you want to render from a camera you've created, you should select it from the Camera drop-down menu. To batch-render a sequence of frames, you need to set the first and last frames.

You can also use the Common settings to change the filename and file format that will be used for your rendered images. Image formats like Maya's IFF allow you to render single images or image sequences for compositing in another program, whereas animation formats like AVI let you create a single file that contains your entire animation.

You'll also need to choose a *resolution* at which to render. The resolution of an image is its size in pixels, usually given in the format [width] x [height]: for example: 640x480, which is read as 640 *by* 480. The higher the resolution, the longer the image will take to render. The resolution you should choose for your images depends on their final medium.

If you're creating a small image for a Web site, you might use the 320x240 preset. If you plan to put the images on NTSC video, you'll probably use 720 by 486. For printing, however, you're likely to need a much higher resolution. If you want to print an 8-by-10-inch image at 300 dpi (dots per inch), you'll need a resolution of 2,400 by 3,300 pixels—which will take a long time to render.

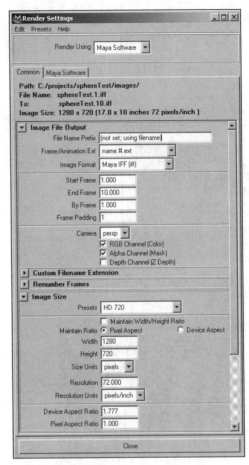

Figure 16.40 The top portion of the Common tab displays information about the file(s) that will be rendered, and the lower portion allows you to change various settings.

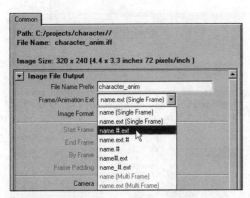

Figure 16.41 The pound sign (#) in the naming scheme you choose will be replaced by the frame number of each rendered image.

To open the Render Settings window:

◆ Choose Window > Render Editors > Render Settings.

or

◆ In the Status Line or the Render View toolbar, click the Render Settings button ▦.

The Render Settings window opens.

To change the Common settings:

1. Open the Render Settings window.

   The Common tab is displayed by default.

2. In the File Name Prefix field, type a file name to use for the rendered images.

3. Click the Frame/Animation Ext drop-down menu, and select name.#.ext (**Figure 16.41**).

   This option allows you to render a sequence of images. The pound sign (#) will be replaced with the frame number of each image.

4. Select a format from the Image Format drop-down menu.

   Maya IFF is the default, but not all programs can read this format. You may want to choose something more common, like Tiff or Targa.

5. Set the start and end frames, as determined by the duration of your animation.

continues on next page

ABOUT RENDERING

6. Change Frame Padding to 4.

This will put zeros in front of the number in each image name, so that each number is four digits long. Without frame padding, your images may be listed in the wrong order when sorted by name.

7. Choose the camera view from which you want to render (**Figure 16.42**).

Even if you've created new cameras, perspective is still the default camera in the Render Settings window. It's a common mistake to overlook this option and render the wrong camera view.

8. From the Presets menu in the Image Size section, choose CCIR 601/Quantel NTSC (**Figure 16.43**).

This is a good choice if your image is going to end up on NTSC video.

9. Close the Render Settings window, and choose Batch Render from the Rendering menu to render with the new settings.

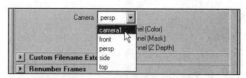

Figure 16.42 If you want to render your scene from a camera you've created, you need to select it from the Camera drop-down menu.

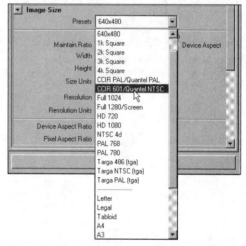

Figure 16.43 Maya provides a wide variety of Image Size presets. You can also adjust the image size settings manually.

Figure 16.44 This software rendered frame of an animation has a depth-mapped shadow, and motion blur on the wolf's moving tail.

Figure 16.45 This software rendered image of a glass of water includes both reflection and refraction effects.

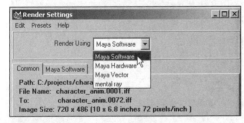

Figure 16.46 Software rendering is the default in Maya, but if the renderer has been changed, you can set it from the Render Using drop-down menu.

About the Maya Software Renderer

The Maya Software renderer can create high-quality images with lighting, shadows, texture, and motion blur (**Figure 16.44**). For added realism, you may also need reflections and refractions (**Figure 16.45**), which can be enabled by turning on *raytracing* in the Maya Software renderer settings. Raytracing can also be used to create more accurate and realistic-looking shadows for your objects. Because raytracing requires additional calculation, raytraced images take longer to render.

The Maya Software renderer has a number of important settings, including those for raytracing, anti-aliasing, and motion blur. It's also the only one of Maya's renderers to support toon shading, which is controlled through the Toon menu rather than the Render Settings.

To render a scene using the Maya Software renderer:

1. Open or create a scene to render.

2. Choose Window > Rendering Editors > Render Settings.
   The Render Settings window opens.

3. If it isn't already selected, use the Render Using drop-down menu to set the renderer to Maya Software (**Figure 16.46**).

4. If necessary, adjust the Common render settings as you did in the task "To change the Common settings."

5. Click the Maya Software tab.
   You can change any of the Maya Software settings here. For more information on these settings, see the sections "Anti-Aliasing," "Motion Blur," and "Raytracing," later in this chapter.

6. Choose Render > Render Current Frame for a single image or Batch Render for an image sequence.

Anti-aliasing

The display of a computer monitor is based on pixels, each of which is a tiny square of a single color. Pixels are very small, but they're still discretely visible. The fact that you can see individual pixels sometimes leads to unwanted visual effects, or *artifacts*, in images displayed on a monitor. Anti-aliasing can be used to reduce these artifacts (**Figure 16.47**).

Maya includes a number of anti-aliasing methods as well as various settings to fine-tune their results. However, in most cases, you can use one of the Quality presets to get the result you're looking for. As with many rendering options, there's a tradeoff with anti-aliasing: the higher the quality, the longer your render will take.

To use anti-aliasing:

1. Open or create a scene to render.

2. Choose Window > Rendering Editors > Render Settings.
   The Render Settings window opens.

3. If it isn't already selected, set the renderer to Maya Software.

4. Click the Maya Software tab.

5. If the Anti-aliasing Quality settings aren't already displayed, click the arrow next to Anti-aliasing Quality (**Figure 16.48**).

6. Use the Quality drop-down menu to select the Intermediate Quality preset (**Figure 16.49**).

   This setting is a good compromise between the fast but poorly anti-aliased Preview Quality setting and the high-quality but slow-to-render Production Quality setting.

7. Select Render Current Frame from the Render menu, or click the Render button in the Status Line [icon].
   Your scene is rendered with the new anti-aliasing settings.

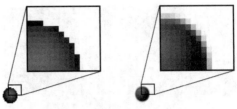

Figure 16.47 Edge anti-aliasing has been used to smooth out the jagged edge of the sphere on the right.

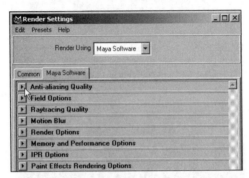

Figure 16.48 Each group of render settings can be shown and hidden independently.

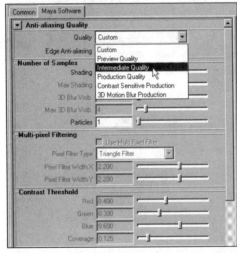

Figure 16.49 Selecting a preset from the Quality menu automatically changes the individual anti-aliasing settings.

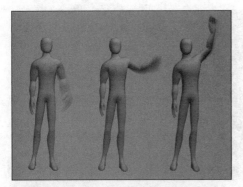

Figure 16.50 When rendered with motion blur, each frame of animation is selectively blurred in the area where there is movement.

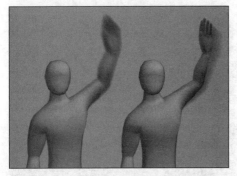

Figure 16.51 3D motion blur (right) is slower to calculate but more realistic-looking than 2D motion blur (left).

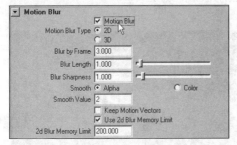

Figure 16.52 Motion blur is off by default; to turn it on, select its check box.

✔ Tip

■ Increasing the Blur by Frame value causes more frames to be used when the motion blur is calculated, resulting in a more extensive blur.

Motion blur

When moving objects are recorded on film by a real camera, they may be blurred, depending on the speed of their motion and the camera's shutter speed. Rendering an animation with motion blur simulates this effect (**Figure 16.50**). This technique can make your animation look smoother, especially for fast movement.

Maya provides two types of motion blur: 2D and 3D. 2D motion blur is faster to render than 3D, but it may not look as good. 3D motion blur is calculated more accurately, so it generally looks more realistic (**Figure 16.51**).

To use motion blur:

1. Open or create a scene with an animated object. (For more on animation, see Chapter 12, "Animation.")

2. Choose Window > Rendering Editors > Render Settings.
   The Render Settings window opens.

3. In the Common tab, set the Frame/ Animation Ext to render multiple frames, and then set the frame range to render.

4. If it isn't already selected, set the renderer to Maya Software.

5. In the Maya Software tab, set the anti-aliasing quality to Intermediate Quality or higher.
   3D motion blur won't render correctly using Preview Quality.

6. Click the arrow next to Motion Blur to display the motion blur settings.

7. Click the Motion Blur check box to turn on Motion Blur (**Figure 16.52**).

8. Select 2D or 3D for Motion Blur Type.

9. Choose Render > Batch Render.
   Your scene is rendered with motion blur.

Raytracing

Using raytracing allows you to render reflections and refractions as well as more realistic-looking shadows. Although these effects can significantly increase the time a scene takes to render, they also make the scene look much more realistic.

Reflections are created when light rays bounce off one surface, then another, and then into your eyes or a camera lens. Because the real world is full of surfaces, reflective objects always reflect something, but in a Maya scene, this may not be true (**Figure 16.53**).

Without additional objects in a scene, reflective objects won't look very reflective. You can change this by connecting an environment map to the *reflective color* attribute of a surface. Doing so causes the surface to reflect an image that's been mapped to a virtual sphere or cube surrounding the scene (**Figure 16.54**). This technique makes it look like the surface is reflecting a larger environment, which can appear more realistic even though it isn't an accurate simulation of the scene.

Refraction is the bending of light as it travels through a dense, transparent material such as glass or liquid. Without it, glass doesn't look real. You can set a *refraction index*, which determines how much the light bends as it passes through the surface (**Figure 16.55**).

Raytraced shadows can create effects that the standard depth map shadows can't. These effects include blurring and lightening as the shadow's distance from the object increases (when using area lights), as well as colored shadows from transparent colored surfaces. Like the other raytracing options, raytraced shadows take longer to render.

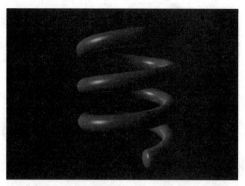

Figure 16.53 This coil has a highly reflective surface, but there are no other objects in the scene for it to reflect.

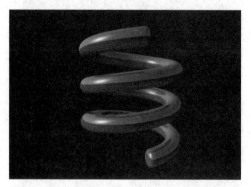

Figure 16.54 With an environment map, the coil seems more reflective.

Figure 16.55 Each transparent sphere has a different refractive index: left 1.0, middle 1.2, right 2.0.

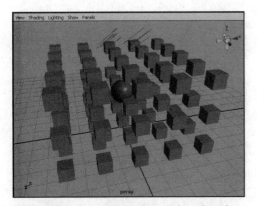

Figure 16.56 When raytracing is turned on, the sphere will be able to reflect the cubes when the scene is rendered.

Figure 16.57 By default, a phong material has a Reflectivity value of 0.5. Increasing this value makes the material more reflective.

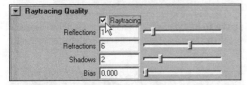

Figure 16.58 Raytracing is off by default and must be turned on for reflections to render.

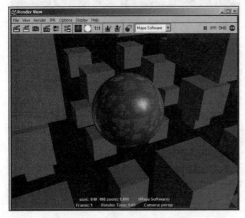

Figure 16.59 When the scene is rendered, you can see the cubes reflected in the sphere.

To create reflections:

1. Create a scene with a sphere surrounded by a number of cubes (**Figure 16.56**).

2. Using the Hypershade, create a phong material, and assign it to the sphere. (For more information on materials, see Chapter 14, "Shaders, Materials, and Mapping.")

3. Double-click the phong material to bring up the Attribute Editor.

4. Under Specular Shading, increase the reflectivity to 0.8 (**Figure 16.57**).

5. Open the Render Settings window.

6. In the Maya Software tab, click the triangle next to Raytracing Quality.

7. Click the Raytracing check box to activate raytracing (**Figure 16.58**).

8. Frame the sphere in the Perspective view, and then click the Render button 🎬. The image is rendered with reflections (**Figure 16.59**).

✔ Tips

- Objects can be visible or invisible in reflections. To change an object's reflection state, select the object and open the Attribute Editor, expand the Render Stats section, and uncheck Visible in Reflections to make the object not visible in reflections.

- In the real world, two properly positioned mirrors will create reflections within reflections within reflections. In Maya, the default is for reflections to be calculated only once; but you can increase the Reflections setting under Raytracing Quality in the Render Settings window to allow surfaces to reflect other reflective surfaces more accurately.

ABOUT THE MAYA SOFTWARE RENDERER

To create refraction:

1. Create a scene with a sphere on top of a plane (**Figure 16.60**).

2. Using the Hypershade, apply a checkered material to the plane and a phong material to the sphere.

3. Double-click the phong material to bring up the Attribute Editor.

4. Under Common Material Attributes, drag the Transparency slider to the right. The color field next to Transparency becomes white (**Figure 16.61**).

5. Scroll down in the Attribute Editor, and click the arrow next to Raytrace Options. The Raytrace Options are expanded.

6. Click the Refractions check box to enable refractions for this material (**Figure 16.62**).

7. Change Refractive Index to 1.5.

8. In the Render Settings window, click the Raytracing check box under Raytracing Quality.

9. Click the Render button. The scene is rendered with refractions (**Figure 16.63**).

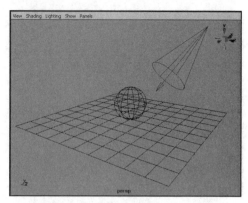

Figure 16.60 This simple scene will be used to demonstrate refraction.

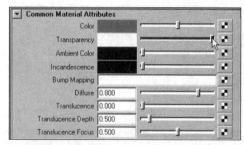

Figure 16.61 Moving the Transparency slider all the way to the right makes the material completely transparent.

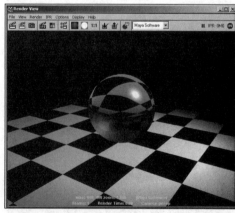

Figure 16.63 The sphere refracts the light that passes through it, which causes the checkered pattern of the plane to appear warped.

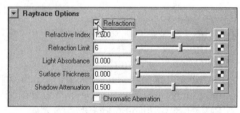

Figure 16.62 Unlike reflections and transparency, refractions must be specifically enabled for a surface to be refractive.

Figure 16.64 Top row, from left to right: Solid Color, Shaded Brightness Two Tone, and Shaded Brightness Three Tone. Bottom row, from left to right: Dark Profile, Rim Light, and Circle Highlight.

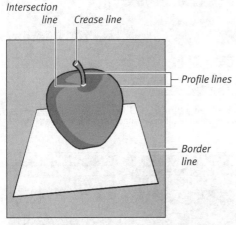

Figure 16.65 For clarity, the intersection and crease lines have been rendered white in this image. By default, they're black.

Figure 16.66 From left to right: Charcoal Thin Brush, Neon Blue Brush, and Yellow Yarn Brush used as toon lines.

Toon shading

By using Maya 7's new toon shading features, you can create renders that resemble 2D cel animation. Toon shading mimics the appearance of this traditional ink and paint look through *fill shaders* and *outlines*, which can be created from the new Toon menu.

Fill shaders, also referred to as *toon shaders*, render the 3D objects of your scene using flat areas of a single color—the paint of ink and paint. The Toon menu provides a number of default shaders to allow you to create the look you want quickly and easily (**Figure 16.64**), but you can also fine-tune the settings of any of these shaders.

There are four different types of toon lines, which you can create by adding an outline to an object (**Figure 16.65**):

◆ **Profile lines** are drawn around the outside of an object, outlining it relative to the camera.

◆ **Crease lines** appear on an object's surface when it bends sharply.

◆ **Intersection lines** are created when two surfaces intersect.

◆ **Border lines** highlight single-polygon edges.

You need only one outline to create all four types of lines, and you can control the settings for each type of line independently.

An object can only have one toon shader, but it can have multiple outline nodes if necessary. Each node has its own settings. You can also assign a single outline node to multiple objects, which can make it easier to adjust the overall appearance of the toon lines in your scene.

By default, toon lines are just simple lines, but you can add a Paint Effects brush to them to create a wide variety of different effects (**Figure 16.66**).

To add a toon shader to an object:

1. Create a scene with a primitive sphere and a light (**Figure 16.67**).

2. With the sphere selected, go to the Toon > Assign Fill Shader menu and choose the Shaded Brightness Three Tone shader (**Figure 16.68**).

3. Open the Render Settings window, and make sure the Maya Software renderer is selected.

   Or

   Choose Maya Software from the Render > Render Using menu.

4. Click the Render button.

   The sphere is rendered with its new toon shader (**Figure 16.69**).

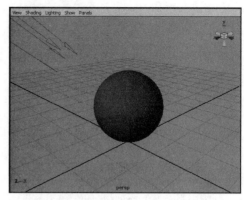

Figure 16.67 This simple scene consists of a NURBS primitive sphere and a directional light.

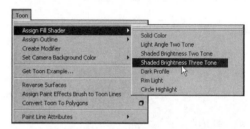

Figure 16.68 You can use the Toon menu to assign one of a number of different shaders to the selected object.

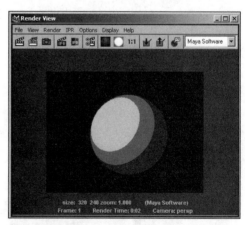

Figure 16.69 Here the sphere has been rendered using the Shaded Brightness Three Tone shader.

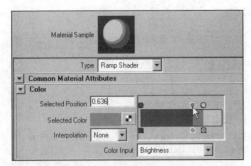

Figure 16.70 When you slide one of the toon shader's color handles, the Material Sample thumbnail updates automatically to display your changes.

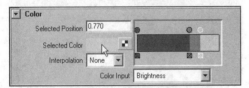

Figure 16.71 You can click the Selected Color chip to modify the selected color.

Figure 16.72 Setting the Specularity value to 0.5 adds a specular highlight to the shader.

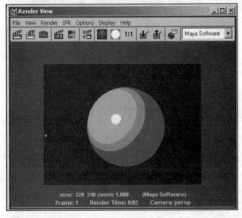

Figure 16.73 Here the sphere has been rendered to display the modified toon shader settings.

To adjust a toon shader's attributes:

1. Select the sphere you created in the previous task.

2. Press ⌃Ctrl+ⓐ to display the Attribute Editor, and then select the Three Tone Brightness Shader tab.

   This displays the attributes for the sphere's toon shader.

3. In the box to the right in the Color section, click the central circular color handle, and then drag it to adjust the relative sizes of the shader's color bands.

   You can see the effect in the Material Sample thumbnail above the color section (**Figure 16.70**).

   You can also click within the gradient to add another color, or click the square color handles below the gradient to delete colors.

4. Click the right circular color handle to select it, and then click the Selected Color chip (**Figure 16.71**).

   A standard Color Chooser window opens, which you can use to modify the color for that band of the toon shader.

5. Scroll down, expand the Specular Shading section, and then set the Specularity value to 0.5 (**Figure 16.72**).

   A specular highlight is added to the shader.

6. Click the Render button 🖼.

   The sphere is rendered with the modified toon shader settings (**Figure 16.73**).

ABOUT THE MAYA SOFTWARE RENDERER

To add toon lines to an object:

1. In the scene created in the previous task, select the sphere.

2. Choose Toon > Assign Outline > Add New Toon outline (**Figure 16.74**).

   A toon outline is added to your object. Geometry is created in your scene to represent the toon lines (**Figure 16.75**).

3. Choose Toon > Set Camera Background Color > persp.

   A standard Color Chooser window is displayed, allowing you to select a color for the background of your scene. By choosing a color other than black, you'll be able to see the black outline around the sphere when it's rendered.

4. Click the Render button 🎬.

   The sphere is rendered with an outline (**Figure 16.76**).

✔ Tip

- By default, toon lines add geometry to your scene to provide a preview of how they will render. The additional calculations required for this geometry may slow down interaction with your scene. If so, you can turn it off. Click to select the toon lines, and then set Draw as Mesh to Off in the Channel Box. This option won't affect the way the toon lines render, only how they are displayed in the view.

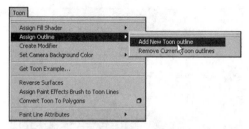

Figure 16.74 You can use the Toon menu to add toon lines to the selected object.

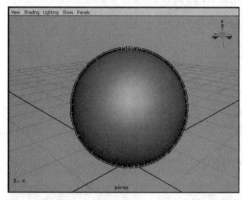

Figure 16.75 The highlighted toon line geometry is used to display a preview of the toon lines. When rendered, the lines are created using Paint Effects strokes.

Figure 16.76 Here the sphere has been rendered against a gray background to display its new toon outline.

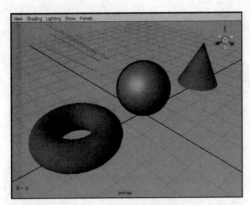

Figure 16.77 A torus and a cone have been added to the scene with the toon-shaded sphere.

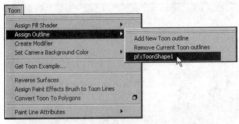

Figure 16.78 By assigning the same toon outline to multiple objects, you can quickly adjust the overall appearance of toon lines in your scene.

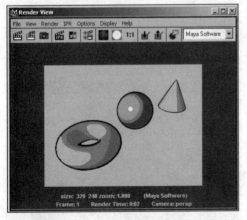

Figure 16.79 When rendered, the objects have identical toon lines.

To add an existing toon outline node to a new object:

1. In the scene created in the previous task, add a torus and a cone (**Figure 16.77**).

2. Select the new objects, and assign a toon shader to them using the Toon > Assign Fill Shader menu.

3. With the objects still selected, go to the Toon > Assign Outline menu. It will include a new menu item called pfxToonShape1 for the toon outline you created previously. Select this outline to add it to the new objects (**Figure 16.78**).

4. Click the Render button 🖼.

   All three objects are rendered with toon lines (**Figure 16.79**).

To adjust a toon outline's attributes:

1. In the scene created in the previous task, click to select one of the toon outlines in the view, or select the pfxToon1 entry in the Outliner.

   The toon outline geometry for all three objects is highlighted in the view (**Figure 16.80**).

2. Press Ctrl + a to display the Attribute Editor.

   The toon outline attributes are displayed.

3. Under Common Toon Attributes, change the Line Width to 0.05 (**Figure 16.81**).

   The toon line geometry displayed in the view becomes narrower to reflect the change.

4. Click the Render button 🎬.

   The scene is rendered with the modified settings (**Figure 16.82**).

✔ Tip

■ Changes made in the Common Toon Attributes section affect all four toon line types. Each individual line type also has its own attributes in its own section.

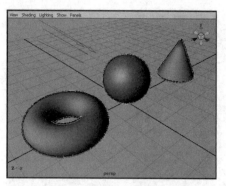

Figure 16.80 Because the same toon outline node has been assigned to all three objects, clicking to select any of their outlines selects all of their outlines.

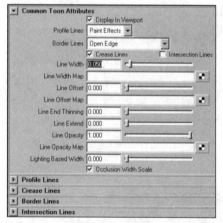

Figure 16.81 Changes made in the Common Toon Attributes section affect all the toon lines.

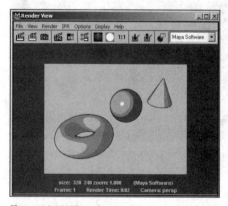

Figure 16.82 When the scene is re-rendered, the toon lines of all three objects are narrower.

Figure 16.83 The Paint Effects tab in the Shelf holds buttons for Paint Effects commands and brushes.

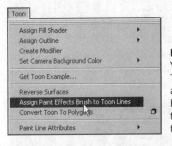

Figure 16.84
You can use the Toon menu to assign a Paint Effects brush to the selected toon lines.

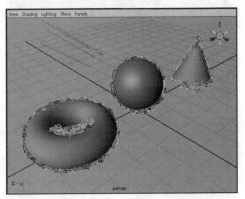

Figure 16.85 By default, Paint Effects brushes add geometry to your scene to provide a preview of their final effect. You can turn off this option to improve scene interaction speed.

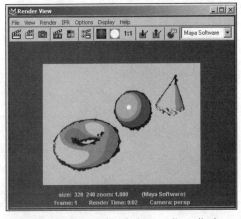

Figure 16.86 When rendered, the toon lines display the effects of the Ink Splash brush.

To add a Paint Effects brush to a toon outline:

1. In the scene created in the previous task, select the toon outline, either in the view or from the Outliner.

2. In the Shelf, click the Paint Effects tab (**Figure 16.83**).

3. Click the Ink Splash Brush button 🔘.

4. Choose Toon > Assign Paint Effects Brush to Toon Lines (**Figure 16.84**).

   The toon line geometry changes to reflect the Paint Effects brush (**Figure 16.85**).

5. Click the Render button 🔘.

   The scene is rendered with the modified toon lines (**Figure 16.86**).

✔ Tips

■ Once you've applied a Paint Effects brush to your toon outline, you can adjust the settings for the brush as well as the toon line attributes. To access these settings, select the toon outline, open the Attribute Editor, and select the Paint Effect's brush tab: for example, InkSplash1 for the Ink Splash brush.

■ The preview geometry generated for Paint Effects strokes can slow scene interaction significantly. If you're using Paint Effects with your toon lines, you may want to turn off their display in the view. You can do this by unchecking Display in Viewport in the Common Toon Attributes section of the Attribute Editor. The toon lines will no longer be visible in the view, but they will render as normal.

ABOUT THE MAYA SOFTWARE RENDERER

About the Maya Hardware Renderer

Maya Software rendering can take a long time. If you want to make a preview of your animation without having to software render it, you can hardware render it instead. The quality of the result will be somewhere between a Playblast and a software render, depending on the features and processing power of your graphics card. The most powerful cards can provide results similar to software rendering, but many cards lack the capacity to display reflections, bump maps, and shadows.

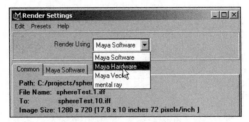

Figure 16.87 The Render Using drop-down menu allows you to switch to any of Maya's four renderers.

To render an image using the Maya Hardware renderer:

1. Open or create a scene to render.

2. Open the Render Settings window, and set Render Using to Maya Hardware (**Figure 16.87**).

3. Set the Common settings by following the steps in the "To change the Common settings" task earlier in this chapter.

4. On the Maya Hardware tab, click the triangle next to Quality to expand the options.

5. From the Presets drop-down menu, choose Preview Quality (**Figure 16.88**).

   This preset automatically sets several of the options and is a good choice for quick render tests. For high-quality renders, choose Production Quality.

6. Choose Render > Batch Render.

   The scene is rendered. You can view its progress in the Command Feedback line.

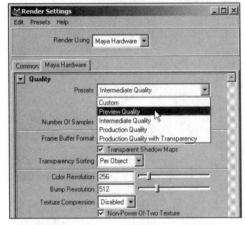

Figure 16.88 The Preview Quality preset provides the fastest possible render.

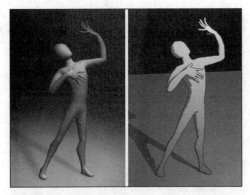

Figure 16.89 The image on the left is a bitmap created using the Maya Software renderer, and the vector image on the right was rendered with the Maya Vector renderer.

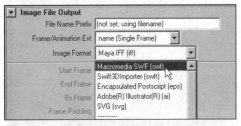

Figure 16.90 The SWF format and other vector formats are only available when the Maya Vector renderer is set as the current renderer.

About the Maya Vector Renderer

The Maya Vector renderer allows you to render your scene to a vector-based format, as opposed to Maya's other renderers, which render each image as a bitmap. Bitmaps and vectors are two very different ways of storing images, each with their own advantages and disadvantages.

A bitmap is a grid of pixels, each of which can be a different color. However, if you scale up a bitmap, these pixels become visibly blocky. A vector-based image, on the other hand, is constructed from lines and areas of color or color gradients that are calculated mathematically. Vector-based images can be scaled up easily without loss of image quality. However, because these blocks of color are much larger than a single pixel, vector images are generally less detailed and more stylized than bitmaps (**Figure 16.89**).

The Maya Vector renderer can be used to render the most common vector file formats, including SWF files for Macromedia Flash, AI files for Adobe Illustrator, Encapsulated Postscript (EPS) files, and Scalable Vector Graphics (SVG).

To render an image as vectors:

1. Open or create a scene to render as vectors. Use a point light to light the scene, because the Maya Vector renderer doesn't calculate other types of lights.

2. Open the Render Settings window, and set Render Using to Maya Vector.

3. From the Common tab, select Macromedia SWF (swf) for the Image Format (**Figure 16.90**).

continues on next page

4. Set the frame range for your animation, or change the Frame/Animation Ext option to name.ext (Single Frame).

5. Select the Vector Renderer tab.

6. In the Fill Options area, make sure Fill Objects is checked, and select the Single Color radio button (**Figure 16.91**).

This option fills each object with a single flat color. You can select Two or Four Color for a more 3D effect, similar to a toon shader, or select Area Gradient to create a smooth gradient across each object.

7. In the Edge Options area, check Include Edges to add outlines to your objects (**Figure 16.92**).

8. Select Render > Batch Render.

The scene is rendered as a SWF. If you don't have Macromedia's Flash Player plug-in, you'll need to download and install it to view the SWF in your browser (**Figure 16.93**).

✔ Tips

- You can use Render Current Frame with the Maya Vector renderer to preview rendered images in Maya, but you can't save these preview images to a vector format. To create your final images, you'll need to batch render.

- When using the Two Color or Four Color option, your objects' shading is likely to appear blocky. You may be able to improve your results by increasing the resolution of your objects.

- The Full Color and Mesh Gradient settings, found under Fill Options, render your scene in more detail than the other settings. However, they tend to give surfaces a faceted appearance, which is generally undesirable.

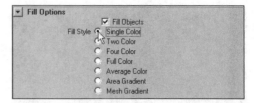

Figure 16.91 Single Color is the simplest of the Fill Options, shading each object with a flat color.

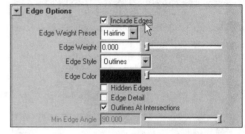

Figure 16.92 Outlines are off by default, but you can turn them on to add definition to your vector images.

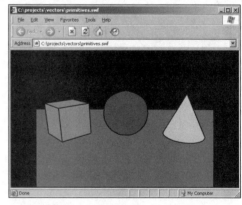

Figure 16.93 Using the Flash Player plug-in, you can view SWF files in your browser.

Figure 16.94 This scene has been lit with a single light. The image on the left was rendered using the Maya Software renderer, and the image on the right was rendered using global illumination in Mental Ray.

Figure 16.95 Reflective caustics cause light to reflect from the ring onto the plane.

Figure 16.96 The light pattern on the checkered plane is caused by refractive caustics.

About Mental Ray

Mental Ray is similar in functionality to the Maya Software renderer, but it's generally faster when rendering the same scene using equivalent settings. It also provides advanced rendering features such as caustics and global illumination, which can simulate realistic light effects. However, as with raytracing, the calculations required to create this level of realism result in longer render times. In addition, Mental Ray can't be used to render Paint Effects or any of the new toon effects.

Global illumination is a method of calculating lighting that is more realistic but slower than Maya's default method. When you use global illumination, virtual light rays can bounce off objects and illuminate other objects. Without global illumination, objects can only be lit directly by lights. Because global illumination is closer to how light works in the real world, using it can result in more realistic-looking renders (**Figure 16.94**).

Caustics have an effect similar to that of global illumination, but the indirect lighting comes only from the specular highlights of objects, not their diffuse or overall lighting. This often creates more distinct patterns of light cast onto other objects, rather than the more general effect of global illumination. Caustics can be reflective (**Figure 16.95**) or refractive (**Figure 16.96**).

Mental Ray can produce very photorealistic renders, but this realism requires a long rendering time. Be aware that although using global illumination and/or caustics can yield fantastic results, it's often more efficient to find a way to approximate your desired effect. For example, rather than using global illumination to simulate light bouncing off the ground and then illuminating your object, you could create a low-intensity directional bounce light, aimed upward from the ground.

To create caustics:

1. Create a refractive sphere on a plane by following the instructions described in "To create refraction," earlier in this chapter.

2. Open the Render Settings window, and set Render Using to Mental Ray.

3. In the Mental Ray tab, select PreviewCaustics from the Quality Presets drop-down menu (**Figure 16.97**).

   This option automatically turns on raytracing and caustics and sets various other Mental Ray settings to provide a preview-quality render for scenes with caustics.

4. Select the scene's light, and press (Ctrl)+(a) to display the Attribute Editor.

   Be sure your scene is lit using a spot light or a point light rather than a directional light. You should avoid using directional lights for caustics or global illumination.

5. In the Attribute Editor, expand the Mental Ray > Caustic and Global Illumination section, and check the Emit Photons check box (**Figure 16.98**).

   The light will now emit photons, which will be used to calculate the caustic effects. The more photons a light emits, the more accurate the final image will be—and the longer it will take to render. Here you'll use the default of 10,000 photons.

6. Click the Render button .

   The scene is rendered in the Render View (**Figure 16.99**).

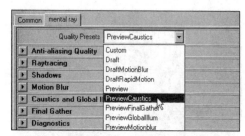

Figure 16.97 The PreviewCaustics preset automatically sets a number of Mental Ray's settings.

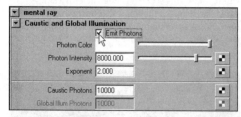

Figure 16.98 To render caustics, you must have at least one light that emits photons.

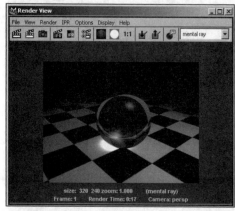

Figure 16.99 The bright spot cast on the plane at the base of the sphere is caused by caustics.

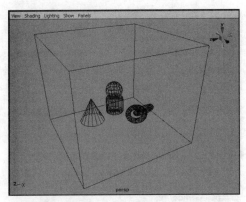

Figure 16.100 Create a scene similar to the one shown.

Figure 16.101 Be sure to do a test render without global illumination to make sure the scene looks the way it should.

Figure 16.102 Global illumination is very blotchy when rendered with a preview quality preset.

To add global illumination:

1. Create a test scene consisting of a primitive cube "room" that contains several other primitives (**Figure 16.100**).

2. Add a point light within the cube.

3. With the point light selected, open the Attribute Editor, and expand the Shadows > Raytraced Shadow Attributes section.

4. Select Use Ray Trace Shadows.

   Although it isn't necessary to use shadows with global illumination, they help demonstrate its effects.

5. To soften shadow edges, set Light Radius to 0.3 and Shadow Rays to 50.

6. Open the Render Settings window, and set the renderer to Mental Ray, if necessary.

7. Click the Render button 🖼 to do a test render of the scene (**Figure 16.101**).

   The lighting should be fairly dark, because the scene will get significantly brighter when the reflected light from global illumination is calculated.

8. In the Render Settings window, set the Quality setting to PreviewGlobalIllum.

   This option automatically turns on global illumination and specifies various settings for a preview-quality render.

9. In the Attribute Editor for the point light, expand the Mental Ray > Caustic and Global Illumination section, and check the Emit Photons check box.

10. Click the Render button 🖼.

    The scene is rendered with global illumination at preview quality. The result is blotchy, but it gives a general sense of how the scene is lit (**Figure 16.102**). To improve the quality of the render, you'll need to adjust several settings.

ABOUT MENTAL RAY

481

To adjust global illumination settings:

1. Create a scene with global illumination by following the steps of the previous task, "To add global illumination."

2. Open the Attribute Editor for the scene's light. In the Mental Ray > Caustic and Global Illumination section, increase the number of global illumination photons to 20,000.

3. In the Render Settings window, expand the Caustics and Global Illumination section. Set Global Illum Accuracy to 600 and Global Illum Radius to 3.0 (**Figure 16.103**).

4. Click the Render button 🎬.

   The scene is rendered with the new global illumination settings. This takes some time, but the final result is a much cleaner example of global illumination (**Figure 16.104**).

✔ Tip

■ Mental Ray has many options and rendering capabilities. For more advanced information about Mental Ray, see the Maya Help files.

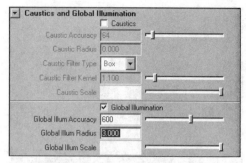

Figure 16.103 Higher values for Global Illum Accuracy and Radius improve the final result at the cost of increased render time.

Figure 16.104 Here the scene has been rendered with the new global illumination settings.

Figure 16.105 Here the snow particles are on their own layer, allowing them to be rendered using the Maya Hardware renderer while the wolf is rendered with the Maya Software renderer.

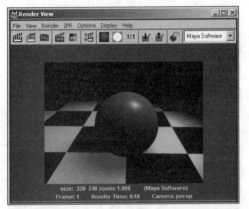

Figure 16.106 The test scene displayed as a single rendered image.

About Render Layers

Maya's render layers allow you to render different parts of your scene independently, either to different files or to different layers of an Adobe Photoshop PSD file. For example, if you're rendering an animation from a stationary camera, you can render a single frame of the background, and then render a character alone, to be composited onto the background later. Render layers can also let you access the functionality of more than one renderer for a scene—for example, hardware-rendered particles on top of a software-rendered background (**Figure 16.105**).

You can also use render layers to separate the visual components of an object: for example, the diffuse, specular, and shadow. By rendering these components to separate images, you can make quick changes in a compositing program rather than having to re-render the entire 3D scene.

To use render layers:

1. Create a scene with a sphere resting on a plane and a spot light aimed at the sphere.

2. Add a checkered material to the plane and a phong material to the sphere.

3. Select the light, and open the Attribute Editor. Under Shadows > Raytrace Shadow Attributes, check Use Raytraced Shadows, and then increase Light Radius to 0.3 and Shadow Rays to 20.

   These options create a soft-edged shadow to render in a separate shadow layer.

4. Click the Render button 🖼 to preview the scene (**Figure 16.106**).

continues on next page

5. Choose Window > Rendering Editors > Render Layer Editor.

The Render Layer Editor opens on the right side of the Maya interface (**Figure 16.107**).

6. Select the plane and the light in the view, and then choose Create Layer from Selected from the Layer Editor's Layers menu.

A new layer is created in the Layer Editor, along with the masterLayer for the entire scene (**Figure 16.108**).

7. Double-click layer1 in the Layer Editor, and enter the name Background in the Edit Layer dialog box (**Figure 16.109**).

8. Click the masterLayer to display the other objects in the view again.

9. Select the sphere and the light, and then choose Create Layer from Selected from the Layers menu. Rename this layer Diffuse.

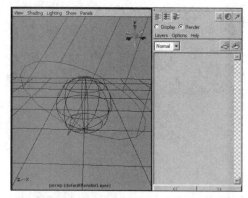

Figure 16.107 The Layer Editor appears where the Channel Box would be. You can restore the Channel Box by selecting the Show Channel Box button in the upper-left corner of the Layer Editor.

Figure 16.108 When you create a layer, the masterLayer for the scene is also displayed in the Layer Editor.

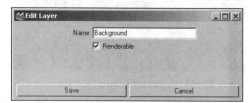

Figure 16.109 Naming your layers descriptively makes them easier to keep track of.

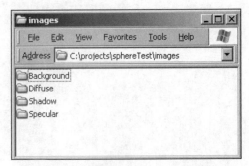

Figure 16.110 The Diffuse preset automatically sets the layer to render diffuse only.

Figure 16.111 From left to right and top to bottom: the Background, Diffuse, Specular, and Shadow layers.

10. Right-click the Diffuse layer, and select Presets > Diffuse (**Figure 16.110**).

    The Diffuse preset automatically sets the layer to render diffuse only.

11. Repeat steps 9–10 to create Specular and Shadow layers for the sphere.

12. In the masterLayer, select the plane, and then right-click the Shadow layer and choose Add Selected Objects.

    Without the plane, the sphere would have nothing to cast shadows on.

13. Choose Render > Batch Render to render the scene.

    When the render is complete, the images folder of your project directory contains a separate folder of images for each render layer. Combined, these images include all the visual information that existed in the non-layered render (**Figure 16.111**).

✔ Tips

- To adjust the Render Settings for any render layer, click the small Render Settings icon to the left of the layer's name. For each attribute you want to change independently of the other layers, right-click the name of the attribute and select Create Layer Override from the context menu.

- You can select a layer and render it in the Render View window, or render the masterLayer to see the entire scene.

MEL AND

EXPRESSIONS

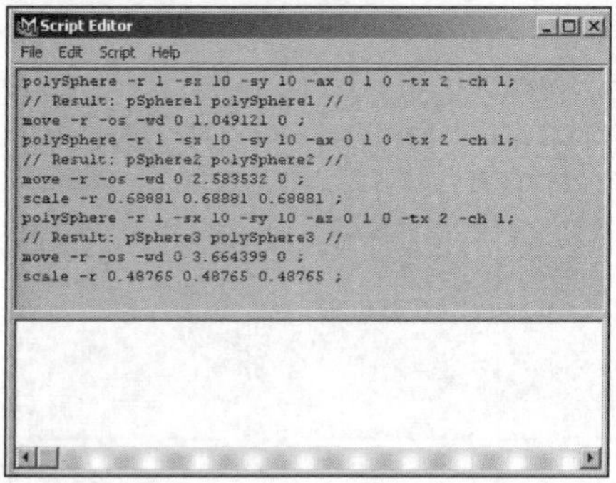

Figure 17.1 The Script Editor displays the MEL commands for the tasks you perform in Maya.

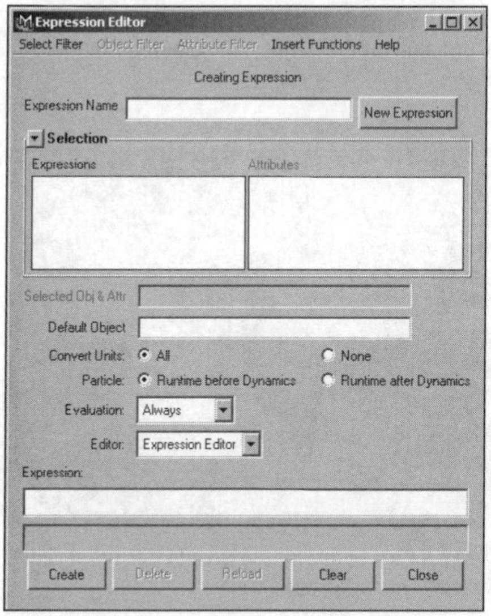

Figure 17.2 The Expression Editor allows you to create and edit expressions.

In Maya, many repetitive tasks can be made easier with Maya Embedded Language (MEL) or expressions. MEL is a scripting language that uses *commands* to cause Maya to do different things. In fact, most of the tools you use in Maya create their effects by executing MEL commands. You can view these commands in the Script Editor, which makes it easy to learn the MEL commands for specific tasks (**Figure 17.1**). You can also use the Script Editor to write and execute MEL scripts, which are simply multiple commands executed in sequence.

Expressions are another form of scripting used to control keyable attributes. Rather than being executed once, like a MEL script, expressions are *evaluated* at every frame. The result of this evaluation becomes the new value for the attribute the expression controls. You can use MEL commands or mathematical equations in expressions. You can create and edit expressions in the Expression Editor (**Figure 17.2**).

About the Script Editor

The Script Editor is where you edit and execute MEL scripts. You can also use it to view the MEL commands that are generated and executed as you do various things in Maya.

The Script Editor is divided into two areas: the top pane, which displays a list of all executed commands, and the bottom pane, where you type in and execute your scripts.

To open the Script Editor:

◆ Click the Script Editor icon [img] in the lower-right area of the Maya interface, or choose General Editors > Script Editor from the Window menu.

The Script Editor opens.

To execute a MEL script in the Script Editor:

1. In the bottom pane of the Script Editor, type in the MEL command or commands you want to execute. For example, type sphere; to create a NURBS sphere (**Figure 17.3**).

2. Press [Ctrl]/[Control]+[Enter], or [Enter] on the numeric keypad.

   The MEL script you entered is executed and disappears from the bottom pane. It's displayed, along with its result, in the top pane (**Figure 17.4**).

3. Close or minimize the Script Editor to see the effect of the script on your scene (**Figure 17.5**).

To view a MEL command in the Script Editor:

◆ Use the Maya interface to perform a task. For example, select Create > Polygon Primitives > Sphere to make a sphere.

   The MEL command executed by Maya to perform the task appears in the top pane of the Script Editor.

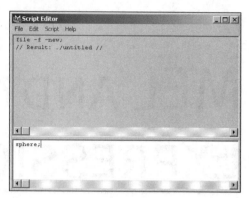

Figure 17.3 The sphere command creates a NURBS sphere.

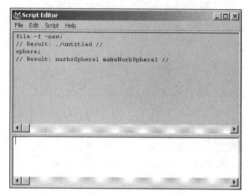

Figure 17.4 When executed, MEL commands appear in the top pane of the Script Editor, along with their result.

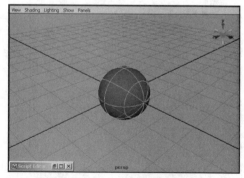

Figure 17.5 By minimizing the Script Editor, you can see that a sphere has appeared in the view.

About MEL Commands

Most MEL commands follow a similar format. The command name is always entered first; it may be followed by a list of optional *flags*, which can be applied in any order. Next come the names of the object(s) the command will be applied to, if necessary, and/or the value(s) the command will use. For example, you could use the command `sphere -r 3` to create a sphere with a radius of three, or `parent sphere1 sphereGroup` to parent an object named sphere1 to sphereGroup.

Flags are used to change the effect of the command in specific ways. Each flag has a name, which may be abbreviated to its equivalent *short name*. This name is always preceded by a dash: `-n` or `-name`, for example. The name of each flag is followed by the value for that flag: for example, `-name "mySphere"`. If you execute a command without including some or all of its flags, Maya will use the default values for those flags.

You can find a complete list of MEL commands in the MEL Command Reference included with Maya. You can browse the list alphabetically or by category, or use the filter to find a specific command more quickly. Each command is linked to an entry that describes its effect, the syntax you need to use, and a list of flags, if any.

To view the MEL Command Reference:

◆ From the main Help menu or the Script Editor's Help menu, select MEL Command Reference (**Figure 17.6**).

The MEL Command Reference opens in a new browser window (**Figure 17.7**).

To find a specific command in the MEL Command Reference:

◆ In the "By substring(s)" field of the MEL Command Reference, enter the name or part of the name of the command.

The list of commands is automatically filtered to display only the names that match your text (**Figure 17.8**).

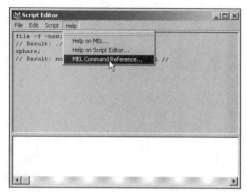

Figure 17.6 You can quickly access the MEL Command Reference from the Script Editor's Help menu.

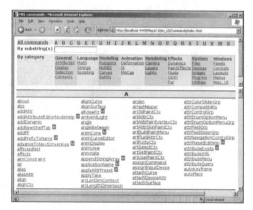

Figure 17.7 The MEL Command Reference displays commands alphabetically by default, but you can also browse by category.

Figure 17.8 Entering text in the "By substring(s)" field causes the MEL Command Reference to display only the commands that match that text.

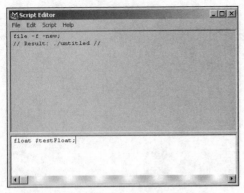

Figure 17.9 A line of MEL script should always be followed by a semicolon. This line declares the variable $testFloat as a float.

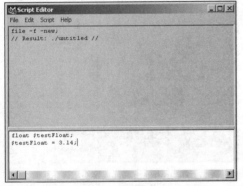

Figure 17.10 The second line sets the value of $testFloat to be 3.14.

About Variables

MEL uses *variables* to store information. Each variable must have a name that begins with a dollar sign, like $newValue or $random_float.

There are several kinds of variables, each of which holds a specific kind of data. An *int* stores integers, such as 1, 5, or 47. A *float* can be used to store a number with a decimal point, such as 1.001. A *string* stores text, like "hello world." By *declaring* a variable, you can tell Maya what type you want that variable to be.

You can also define an *array* for any variable type. An array contains a list of values of its type. For example, an array of strings could contain the text "red", "green", and "blue".

To declare a variable and set its value:

1. In the Script Editor, enter the variable's type—for example, float.

2. After the variable type, enter a name for the variable, followed by a semicolon (;). For example: $testFloat; (**Figure 17.9**).

3. Press ⏎Enter to start a new line.

4. Type in the variable name, followed by an equal sign, the value you want the variable to have, and a semicolon. For example: $testFloat = 3.14; (**Figure 17.10**).

continues on next page

5. Press (Enter) on the numeric keypad to execute the script.

The value 3.14 is assigned to the variable $testFloat (**Figure 17.11**).

✔ Tips

■ If you use a variable without declaring it, Maya will determine its type automatically, which may lead to unexpected results. For example, $x = 1 defines $x as an int, because 1 is an integer. If you then enter $x = 1.3, the result will still be 1, because an int can't store fractional values.

■ You can combine declaring a variable and setting its value in a single line. For example: float $x = 1;.

To use a variable:

1. Declare a variable, and set its value using the steps in the previous task.

2. In any MEL command, enter the variable's name where you would otherwise use a value of the same type. For example: sphere -radius $testFloat;.

When the command is executed, the variable's current value is used (**Figure 17.12**).

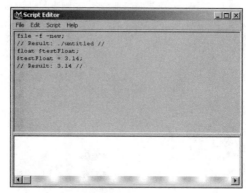

Figure 17.11 When the script is executed from the Script Editor, it disappears from the bottom pane and reappears in the top pane, along with its result.

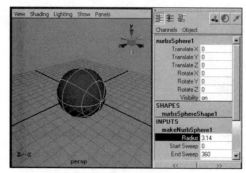

Figure 17.12 Because the value of $testFloat is 3.14, the newly created NURBS sphere has a radius of 3.14.

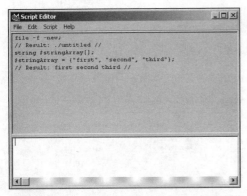

Figure 17.13 An array containing the strings "first", "second", and "third" has been created.

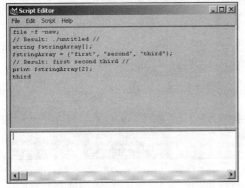

Figure 17.14 The print command displays a string.

To declare an array and assign values to it:

1. In the Script Editor, enter the type that the array will hold—for example, string.

2. After the array type, enter a name for the array, followed by a set of square brackets and a semicolon. For example: $stringArray[ ];.

   The square brackets indicate to Maya that you're declaring an array of strings, not just a single string variable.

3. Press (Enter) to start a new line.

4. Type in the array's name, followed by an equal sign and a list of values separated by commas and surrounded by curly braces. For example: $stringArray = {"first", "second", "third"};.

   The items are stored in the array in the order in which you list them.

5. Press (Enter) on the numeric keypad to execute the script.

   The array $stringArray is created, and the values you entered are assigned to it (**Figure 17.13**).

To access an element of an array:

1. Declare an array, and set its values using the steps in the previous task.

2. In any MEL command, use the array name followed by the element's index in square brackets to access the value at that position in the array. For example: print $stringArray[2]; (**Figure 17.14**).

✔ Tip

- Array indexes start at zero, not one. So, if you have an array called $array with five elements, the first element is at $array[0] and the last element is at $array[4], not $array[5].

About Loops and If Statements

A simple MEL script may perform a set of specific tasks once and perform them in the same way every time it's run, but you can also create more complex scripts using *loops* and *if statements*. Loops allow you to execute a group or *block* of commands repeatedly, and if statements allow you to execute a block of commands only under specified conditions. Blocks of commands are contained within curly braces, and each command should be followed by a semicolon as usual.

To use a `for-in` loop:

1. Declare an array, and set its values: `string $array[] = {"firstSphere", "secondSphere", "thirdSphere"};`.

2. Declare a variable of the same type as the array: `string $sphere;`.

   This variable will be used to hold the current element of the array.

3. Add the `for-in` statement that will control the loop: `for($sphere in $array){`.

   The code after the opening brace ({) and before the closing brace (}) will repeat as many times as there are elements in `$array`, and `$sphere` can be used to access the current element of the array within this block.

4. Add the commands that you want to be executed within the loop.

5. Type the closing brace (}) at the end of the script to close the `for-in` loop.

   The script should look like **Figure 17.15**.

6. Press (Enter) on the numeric keypad to execute the script.

   Each of the spheres in the array is translated one unit on the *y* axis, moving them up to rest on the grid (**Figure 17.16**).

Figure 17.15 The for-in script should look like this.

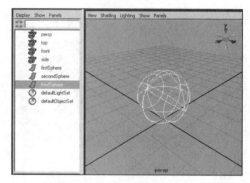

Figure 17.16 When the script is executed, it creates three spheres, all of which are placed at the origin. They're named using the strings in $array, as seen in the Outliner panel on the left.

✔ Tip

■ You can loop through all selected objects by using a `for-in` loop with the MEL command `` `ls -sl` `` instead of an array name. For example: `for($object in `ls -sl`)`.

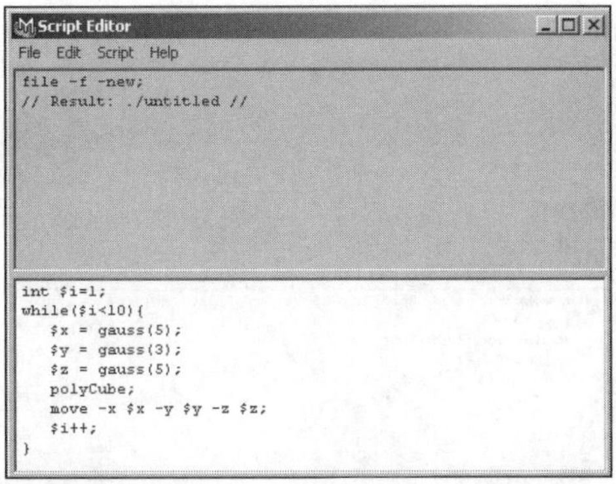

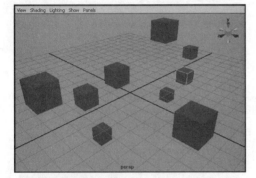

Figure 17.17 The while script should look like this.

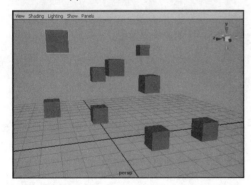

Figure 17.18 When the script is executed, it creates nine randomly placed cubes.

Figure 17.19 With the if statement, all the cubes are placed at positive *y* values, above the grid.

✔ Tip

- To edit and reuse a script you've already executed, select it in the upper pane of the Script Editor and then drag it into the lower pane.

To use a while loop:

1. Declare a new integer variable, and set its value to one: `int $i=1;`.

   This variable is used to count how many times the loop has been executed.

2. Add the while statement that will control the loop: `while($i<10){`.

   As long as $i is less than (<) the value 10, the code after the opening brace ({) and before the closing brace (}) will repeat. When $i reaches 10, the loop will end, and any code after it will be executed.

3. Add the commands that you want to be executed within the loop. Be sure to put a semicolon after each command.

4. Type `$i++;` after the other commands. This *increments* $i, adding 1 to its value.

   Because the loop will continue to repeat until $i is equal to 10, it's important to increase the value of $i within the loop. Otherwise, the script will loop infinitely, and Maya will stop responding.

5. Type the closing brace (}) at the end of the script to close the while loop.

   The script should look like **Figure 17.17**.

6. Press (Enter) on the numeric keypad to execute the script.

   Nine cubes are placed randomly in the view (**Figure 17.18**).

To use an if statement:

1. Using the script you created in the previous task, "To use a while loop," add the following before the move statement:

   `if ($y < 0) { $y = -$y; }`

   If $y contains a negative value, it will be set to the positive equivalent instead.

2. Press (Enter) on the numeric keypad to execute the script.

   The new randomly placed cubes are all positioned at or above the grid (**Figure 17.19**).

About Procedures

Procedures provide a method of reusing blocks of code. At minimum, a procedure consists of a name and a block of code, or *body*, that is executed when the procedure is *called*. You must define a procedure before you use it, similar to the way you define a variable. A procedure's definition begins with the keyword proc, followed by the procedure's name and then a bracketed code block.

Procedures may also have one or more *arguments*. Arguments are variables that must be defined in parentheses after the procedure's name. You can then use these variables within the body of the procedure, without assigning values to them. Their values are determined when you call the procedure.

To call a procedure you've defined, simply use its name in a script, followed by the values for its arguments (if any) in parentheses.

Procedures are local by default. Local procedures can only be accessed from the same script they're defined in. You can also define a procedure as being *global* by adding the global keyword before its proc definition. This allows it to be accessed from any script.

To define a procedure:

1. In the Script Editor, enter proc followed by the name of the procedure. For example: proc cubeStack.

2. If you want the procedure to have arguments, declare their variables in a list separated by commas and enclosed in parentheses. For example: (int $height, float $x, float $z). Otherwise, enter a pair of parentheses: ( ).

3. Add a brace ({) to begin the procedure's body, and then press (Enter) and enter the commands to be executed by the procedure. When you're done, add a closing brace (}) to end the procedure's body.

The script should look like **Figure 17.20**.

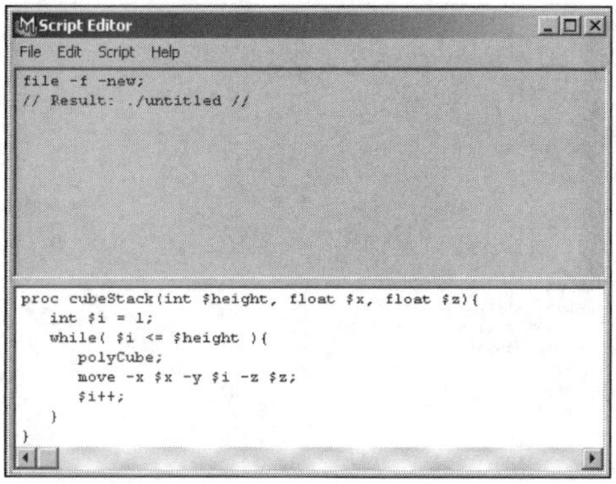

Figure 17.20 The procedure should look like this.

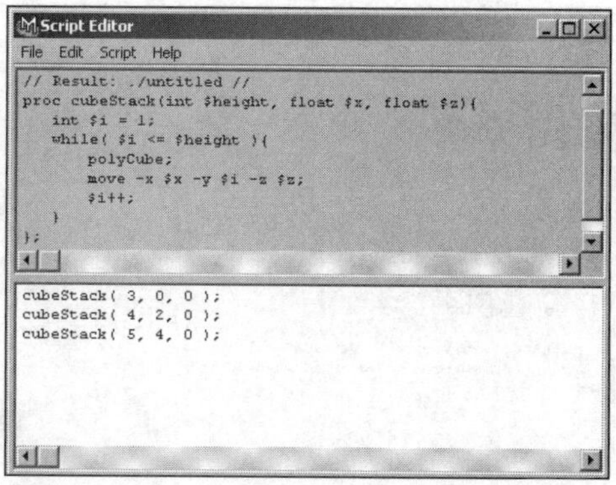

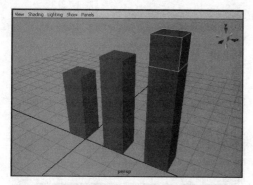

```
// Result: ./untitled //
proc cubeStack(int $height, float $x, float $z){
    int $i = 1;
    while( $i <= $height ){
        polyCube;
        move -x $x -y $i -z $z;
        $i++;
    }
};
```

```
cubeStack( 3, 0, 0 );
cubeStack( 4, 2, 0 );
cubeStack( 5, 4, 0 );
```

Figure 17.21 You can call a procedure with different arguments to get different results.

Figure 17.22 Here the cubeStack procedure has been called three times, with different values for $height and $x.

To call a procedure:

1. Define a procedure by following the steps in the previous task.

2. After the procedure's definition, enter the name of the procedure followed by parentheses enclosing its arguments, if any, and then a semicolon. For example: cubeStack(3, 0, 0);.

3. Repeat step 2 as many times as you want to call the procedure. If the procedure has arguments, you can use different values for them with every call (**Figure 17.21**).

4. Press [Enter] on the numeric keypad to execute the script.

   Three stacks of cubes are created, each with a different position and height (**Figure 17.22**).

Using MEL Scripts

Once you've created a MEL script in the Script Editor, there are several ways to save it for future use. You can add it to the Shelf, save it as a .mel file in your Maya scripts folder, or even embed it in a specific scene using a script node. Script nodes can be useful because they execute in response to certain events, such as opening the scene file or rendering a frame. For example, you might use a script node to create and open a custom interface window whenever the scene file is opened.

In addition to creating your own scripts, you can find a wealth of free MEL scripts at Web sites like www.highend3d.com. Most of these scripts provide installation and use instructions at the beginning or are packaged with a *readme* file. Reading the scripts can also be useful for learning more about MEL.

To add a MEL script to the Shelf:

1. Enter your script in the bottom pane of the Script Editor (**Figure 17.23**).

2. Select the text of the script.

3. Click and drag the selected text to the Shelf.

   A new MEL icon appears on the Shelf (**Figure 17.24**).

✔ Tip

■ If you add multiple MEL scripts to the Shelf, it can be difficult to tell them apart. You can use the Shelf Editor to add a short name to the icon and to change its tooltip to something more descriptive.

To change a Shelf icon's name and tooltip:

1. Click the arrow to the left of the Shelf, and select Shelf Editor from the pull-down menu that appears.

   The Shelves dialog box opens with the current shelf automatically selected.

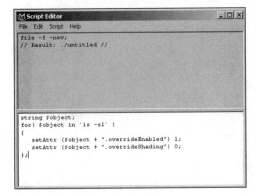

Figure 17.23 This script will cause the selected objects to be displayed as wireframes.

Figure 17.24 When you drag a script to the Shelf, a new MEL icon is created for the script.

Figure 17.25 From the Shelf Contents tab, select the script that you would like to edit.

Figure 17.26 The icon name is displayed by the script's icon.

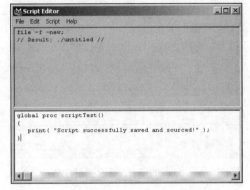

Figure 17.27 This simple procedure displays the text "Script successfully saved and sourced!" when it's called.

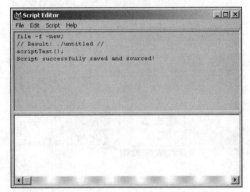

Figure 17.28 Once the script has been saved and sourced, entering scriptTest( ) in the Script Editor displays this message.

2. Click the script whose icon you'd like to edit (**Figure 17.25**).

3. In the Icon Name field, enter a name for the icon, and press [Enter]. Names longer than four characters may be truncated when displayed.

4. In the Label & Tooltips field, add a comment, and press [Enter].

5. Click Save All Shelves.

   The icon in the Shelf now has a name (**Figure 17.26**), and when you hold the cursor over the icon, its new tooltip is displayed.

To save and source a MEL script:

1. Enter your script in the bottom pane of the Script Editor. To enable you to call the script from Maya later, it should be defined as a global procedure (**Figure 17.27**).

2. Select the text of the script.

3. From the Script Editor's File menu, choose Save Selected.

   A Save dialog box opens for the Maya scripts directory.

4. Enter a name for the script, and click Save.

5. From the Script Editor's File menu, choose Source Script.

6. Navigate to the scripts folder, if necessary, and select the script you just created; then, click Open.

   The script is *sourced*, meaning that you can now access the procedure defined in it as a MEL command from Maya.

7. Enter the name of the script's global proc in the Script Editor, and press [Enter] on the numeric keypad.

   The procedure defined in the saved and sourced script is executed (**Figure 17.28**).

USING MEL SCRIPTS

To create a script node:

1. From the Window menu, select Animation Editors > Expression Editor. The Expression Editor opens.

2. From the Expression Editor's Select Filter menu, select By Script Node Name.

3. In the Script Node Name field, type HelloWorld.

4. In the Script field, enter the following script: confirmDialog -message "Hello World" -button "OK"; (**Figure 17.29**).

5. Click Create.

   The HelloWorld script appears in the Script Nodes section of the Expression Editor.

6. From the Execute On menu, select Time Changed (**Figure 17.30**).

7. Move to a new frame in the timeline.

   When the current frame is changed, it triggers the HelloWorld script, and the dialog box appears (**Figure 17.31**).

To delete a script node:

1. Open the Expression Editor.

2. From the Select Filter menu, select By Script Node Name.

3. In the Script Nodes section, click the name of the script node you would like to delete.

4. Click Delete.

   The name of the script node disappears from the Script Nodes section.

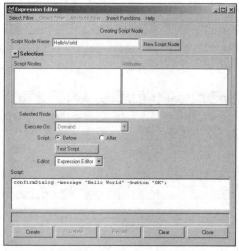

Figure 17.29 Script nodes need to be created in the Expression Editor using the By Script Node Name filter.

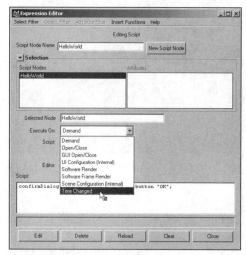

Figure 17.30 Changing the Execute On property of the script node to Time Changed makes the script run whenever the time slider is moved.

Figure 17.31 When you move to a new frame in the timeline, this dialog box appears.

Figure 17.32 Entering an expression in an attribute's field turns the field purple.

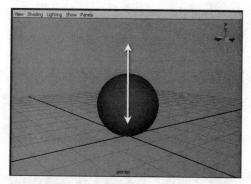

Figure 17.33 When you click Play, the sphere moves up and down.

✔ Tip

- The time keyword used in this task is a variable that's only accessible from an expression, not in ordinary MEL scripts. It provides the current time in seconds and fractions of a second. You can also use the frame keyword in an expression to get the current frame number.

Using Expressions

Expressions are MEL scripts that control keyable attributes and are executed at every frame. They're used in animation to set attribute values, based either on the current time or on other attributes that are animated directly.

You can create, view, and edit expressions in the Expression Editor. It displays a list of expressions in the Selection area, and selecting one of these expressions displays it in the Expression text box for editing. When no expression is selected, you can use the Expression text box to create a new one.

You can also create an expression for an attribute in the Attribute Editor.

To create an expression:

1. Select an object, and press
   Ctrl / Control + a to open the
   Attribute Editor.

2. In the Transform Attributes section, in the field for the attribute that you want the expression to control, type an equal sign (=) followed by the MEL script that will determine the attribute's value. For example, enter =sin(time) in the middle Translate field.

   The field turns purple, indicating that it is controlled by an expression (**Figure 17.32**).

3. Click Play ▶ to see the effect of the expression.

   The sphere moves up and down as determined by the value of the sin(time) function, which is based on a sine wave (**Figure 17.33**).

To edit an expression:

1. Create an expression by following the steps in the previous task.

2. Right-click the purple field, and select Edit Expression from the pull-down menu that appears (**Figure 17.34**).

   The Expression Editor opens with the object and attribute selected (**Figure 17.35**).

3. Edit the MEL script in the Expression text box. For example, replace sin(time) with sin(time*10).

4. Click Edit to save the changes.

5. Click Play ▶ to view the modified effect of the expression.

   The object now moves much faster.

Figure 17.34 You can right-click a field that's controlled by an attribute to access a pull-down menu of relevant options.

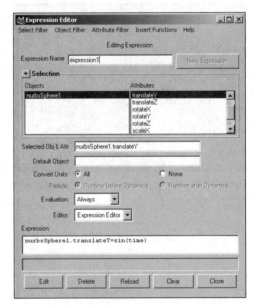

Figure 17.35 Choosing Edit Expression from the attribute's pull-down menu opens the Expression Editor.

DYNAMICS

Figure 18.1 Rocket trails created using particle effects.

As you build your scenes in Maya, you'll likely encounter effects that would be difficult to create using basic shaders (**Figure 18.1**), or situations that would be nearly impossible to animate using traditional keyframing. Leaves blowing across the landscape, for example, or a glass shattering as it hits the ground can take hours to animate by hand—and the scene still may not end up looking realistic.

Maya's Dynamics tools simulate real-world physics. Using these tools, you can create objects that bounce off each other, that have mass and momentum, and that deform in a realistic way. Dynamics can simulate complicated scenarios, like a truck full of marbles tipping over, as well as simpler things, like a pencil falling off a desk. For example, with just a few mouse clicks (and without setting a single keyframe), you can make a leaf appear to be pushed along by the wind as it simultaneously collides with and rolls along the ground.

While using the Dynamics menu set can be fun, it can also be frustrating. Using Dynamics requires assigning many objects in your scenes a large number of new attributes by hand. In addition, hundreds of options are available for most dynamic simulations. In this chapter, we'll concentrate on the basics so that you can get up and running quickly.

Particles

Particles have a myriad of uses. Alone, they can populate a scene with objects, create fireworks, or generate clouds. Combined with dynamics, they can simulate sandstorms, fire, explosions, or even swarms of bugs.

A particle is a point in 3D space that can be affected by simulated physical forces. Particles can be displayed as a number of items, including spheres, clouds, images, and blobby surfaces—even specific objects like leaves or bugs.

You can draw particles in a scene by using the Particle tool, or you can create them with an emitter, which emits particles automatically. Depending on the effect desired, emitters can do this in a variety of ways, even from the surface of objects.

Let's begin by creating a simple particle object and changing the size in the Attribute Editor.

To create a particle object:

1. Switch to the Dynamics menus by pressing F4 or by choosing Dynamics from the pop-up menu in the top-left corner of the Maya interface.

2. From the Particles menu, select Particle Tool (**Figure 18.2**).

3. Click in the Top view to place particles in the scene. Each click creates one particle (**Figure 18.3**).

   You can use any view you want, and the particles will be placed on the grid. As you place the particles, they're displayed as crosshairs.

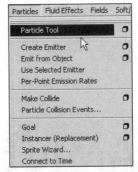

Figure 18.2 From the Particles menu, select Particle Tool.

Figure 18.3 Create particles by clicking in the Top view.

PARTICLES

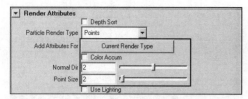

Figure 18.4 Use the Render Attributes section to change the look of the particle.

4. Place as many particles as you like. When you have finished, press [Enter] to complete the particle object.

A particle object is a group of individual particles. Each individual particle is a component of the particle object.

5. With the particle object selected, open the Attribute Editor by pressing [Ctrl]/[Control]+[a].

6. Scroll down to the Render Attributes section of the Attribute Editor.

7. Click Add Attributes For Current Render Type.

Additional attributes are now available for you to adjust (**Figure 18.4**).

8. Change the value of Point Size to make the particles bigger or smaller.

This changes the size in the display as well as in the hardware render.

✔ Tip

■ By default, you create particles by clicking in the View pane. In the options for the Particle tool, you can turn on the Sketch option to draw particles on the grid.

PARTICLES

Emitters

Particles can also be produced by an emitter, which generates particles in a particular speed and direction. There are three main types of emitters:

- **Omni**—Emits particles in all directions (**Figure 18.5**)

- **Directional**—Emits particles in one user-specified direction (**Figure 18.6**)

- **Volume**—Emits particles from a primitive shape such as a cube, cone, or cylinder (**Figure 18.7**)

You can select the type of emitter that you want to use when you create the object (in its Options window), or you can change the emitter type in the Attribute Editor.

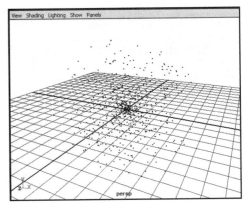

Figure 18.5 An Omni emitter.

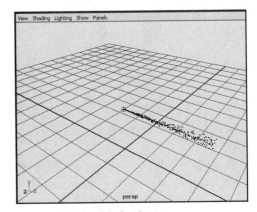

Figure 18.6 A Directional emitter.

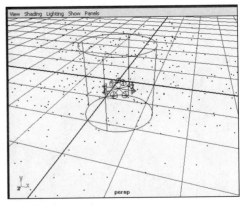

Figure 18.7 A cylindrical Volume emitter.

EMITTERS

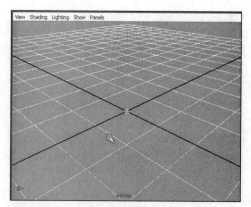

Figure 18.8 An emitter is created at the center of the grid.

Figure 18.9 Particles emit in all directions from an Omni emitter.

To create an emitter:

1. From the Particles menu, select Create Emitter.

   By default, an Omni emitter is created, and its icon appears at the center of the grid. This is where the particles will be emitted (**Figure 18.8**).

2. Click Play ▶ in the playback controls.

   You'll see particles emitting from the center of the emitter (**Figure 18.9**).

3. With the particles selected, open the Attribute Editor by pressing Ctrl / Control + a.

4. In the Attribute Editor, select the particleShape1 tab.

5. Scroll down, and open the Lifespan Attributes section.

6. From the pop-up menu, select Constant.

   You can now change the duration of the particles once they've been emitted. (Particle duration is the length of time that the particle is visible.) With a Constant value of 1, they last for just one second and then disappear.

7. Click Play again to see the results.

   The emitter now emits particles from the center of the grid, and the particles' lifespan is one second.

EMITTERS

There are a large number of settings for each emitter and particle object. By altering these settings, you can customize the look of an emitter to suit your task.

To change emitter settings:

1. From the Particles menu, select Create Emitter.

2. In the Channel Box, change the Emitter Type to Directional (**Figure 18.10**).

   The emitter now emits a stream of particles in the positive *x* direction.

3. Press ⓣ to select the Show Manipulator tool.

4. Set the Rate to about 200 by dragging the yellow square (**Figure 18.11**).

   Now the emitter emits particles twice as fast.

5. Click the input node ring to bring up the Direction manipulator.

6. Adjust the manipulator to where you want the emitter to aim (**Figure 18.12**).

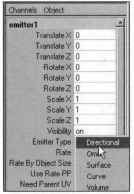

Figure 18.10 You can change the emitter type at any time from the Channel Box or Attribute Editor.

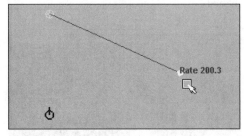

Figure 18.11 The Rate controls the number of particles emitted per second.

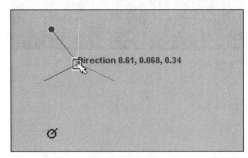

Figure 18.12 The aim of the emitter adjusts like a spotlight.

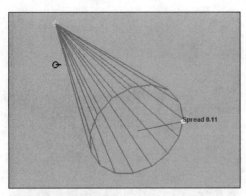

Figure 18.13 Particles are randomly emitted within the angle of the cone. A spread of 1 is 180 degrees. A spread of .5 is 90 degrees.

Figure 18.14 With the changes made, the particles now emit rapidly in a cone-shaped pattern.

7. Click the input node ring again, and adjust the spread of the emitter by clicking and dragging the yellow square (**Figure 18.13**).

   The spread of the emitter determines the initial direction of any particles it emits.

8. Click ▶, and watch the particles in their new shape (**Figure 18.14**).

✔ Tips

- You can also use the Attribute Editor to adjust these inputs. Each emitter type has its own attributes dealing with controls specific to that type of emitter.

- Attributes with a random input vary their source attribute by that amount. For instance, with Speed set to 1 and Speed Random set to .4, the Speed of any particle will be a random number from .8 to 1.2. This approach is great for adding organic variation to an emitter, because it adds irregularity and detail.

Unlike standard emitters, which emit from a few simple forms, emitting particles from an object allows you to precisely control the direction and shape of an emitter. The object can be hidden at render time or kept as a background. Emitting particles from an object can be useful when used in combination with instancing of particles. You might use these two functions to populate a field with flowers, for instance.

EMITTERS

To emit particles from an object:

1. Make a simple ground plane (**Figure 18.15**).

   The plane in this example was made by first creating a NURBS plane with 10 subdivisions and then pulling some CVs to make gentle slopes.

2. From the Particles menu, select the box next to Emit from Object (**Figure 18.16**).

3. Set the Emitter Type to Surface (**Figure 18.17**).

   This option causes the particles to be emitted in the direction of the surface normal.

4. Click Apply, and play your scene 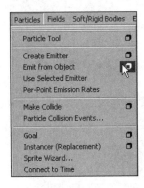.

   The particles emit evenly from the plane (**Figure 18.18**). Some particles are sent out at an angle because they emit from the slope of the hills.

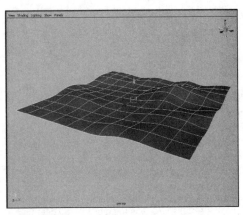

Figure 18.15 Create a simple ground plane. Be sure to add some hills so the effects of the emitter will be visible later.

Figure 18.16 Select the option box for Emit from Object.

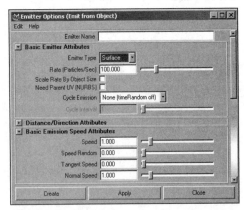

Figure 18.17 Surface emitters are a great way to specify a precise area from which particles should originate.

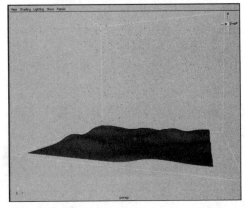

Figure 18.18 Particles flow from the plane. The rate can be controlled on a per-square-centimeter basis for a surface emitter.

EMITTERS

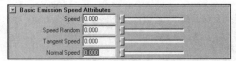

Figure 18.19 Set the Speed and Normal Speed to 0.

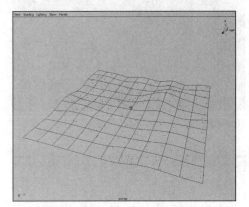

Figure 18.20 Speckled dots appear on your surface as the scene plays.

Figure 18.21 The Instancer places instanced geometry instead of basic particles.

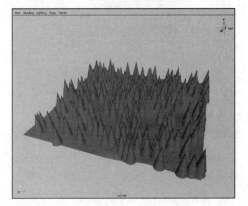

Figure 18.22 With just a few clicks, you now have a forest!

To instance particles:

1. Start with the scene from the previous task.

2. Select the emitter, and press [Ctrl] / [Control] + [a] to open the Attribute Editor.

3. Under the emitter1 tab, set the Basic Emission Speed Attributes as shown (**Figure 18.19**).

   Tangent Speed and Normal Speed are relative to the surface of the object. Setting all the speeds to 0 means the particles won't move once created.

4. Press [▶] to see the effects.

   Small dots appear on the surface but don't move (**Figure 18.20**).

5. Create a simple NURBS cone.

6. Select the cone and then particle1.

   When using the Instancer, the last object selected must be the particle system that will be used to place the instances.

7. From the Particles menu, choose Instancer (Replacement) (**Figure 18.21**).

8. The dots on your surface are now cones, and the scene looks like a forest (**Figure 18.22**).

✔ Tip

- When you're happy with the number of "trees," you can stop the particle emitter from producing new instances by keyframing the Rate at which new particles are emitted to 0.

Render Types

You determine the appearance of your particles by assigning to each a render type: Points, MultiPoint, Streak, MultiStreak, Sprites, Spheres, Tube [s/w], Blobby Surface [s/w], Cloud [s/w], or Numeric. Most of these types are rendered through the Hardware Render Buffer. The types whose names include [s/w] are rendered through software. (See Chapter 16, "Cameras and Rendering," for more information on hardware and software rendering.)

To change a particle's render type:

1. Select a particle object (**Figure 18.23**).

2. Open the Attribute Editor by pressing Ctrl / Control + a.

3. On the particleShape1 tab, open the Render Attributes section, and select the pop-up menu for Particle Render Type.

4. Select Cloud [s/w] from the list.

    The particles now look like circles in the Perspective view (**Figure 18.24**).

5. Click Add Attributes For Current Render Type (**Figure 18.25**).

    This places new attributes specific to the render type. To save space, Maya by default doesn't include all the attributes.

6. Change Radius from 1 to 3 by adjusting the slider.

    This option allows you to interactively change the size of the cloud particle for the display as well as the render.

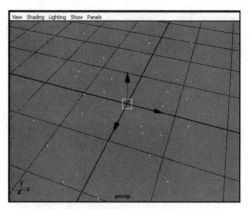

Figure 18.23 A selected particle object.

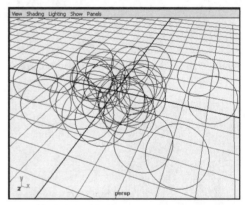

Figure 18.24 Cloud particles appear as circles in the Perspective view.

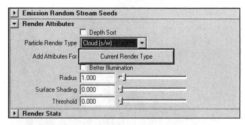

Figure 18.25 Each render type has a number of different attributes to adjust.

RENDER TYPES

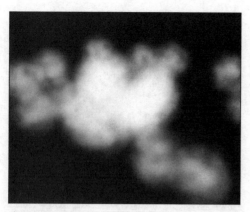

Figure 18.26 The rendered particles appear in a cloud-like shape, making for a fuller looking set of particles.

Figure 18.27 Points render as dots.

Figure 18.28 MultiPoints render as clusters of dots.

7. To render the cloud particle, click the Render Current Frame button .

or

Choose Window > Rendering Editors > Render View.

Now the particles look like clouds (**Figure 18.26**).

Hardware render types

Maya offers the following hardware render types for particles:

◆ **Points**—Points render as dots on the screen (**Figure 18.27**). The radius is adjustable, but the dots remain two-dimensional.

◆ **MultiPoint**—MultiPoints render as clusters of dots on the screen (**Figure 18.28**). Additional attributes include MultiRadius, which controls the size of each cluster, and MultiCount, which controls the number of dots in each cluster.

◆ **Streak**—Streaks render as lines on the screen (**Figure 18.29**). Additional attributes include Size, Line Width, Tail Size, and Tail Fade.

continues on next page

Figure 18.29 Streaks render as straight lines.

RENDER TYPES

- **MultiStreak**—Like Streaks, MultiStreaks render as lines on the screen (**Figure 18.30**). MultiStreaks have the same attributes as Streaks, plus MultiCount and MultiRadius.

- **Sprites**—Sprites have an image file attached to them (**Figure 18.31**). From the Particles menu, select Sprite Wizard to choose the image file you want to use.

- **Spheres**—Spheres render as opaque spheres (**Figure 18.32**). You can assign any shader you want to a Sphere particle. Transparency is not supported.

- **Numeric**—Numeric particles have a number value associated with them (**Figure 18.33**). These number values can represent static, dynamic, or per-particle attributes. This allows you to have single numeric values on particles that don't move and multiple number values on fully moving particles.

Figure 18.30 MultiStreaks render as clusters of lines.

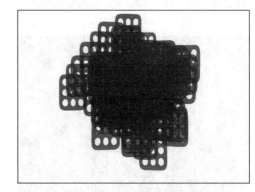

Figure 18.31 Sprites appear as images and support opacity and alpha channels.

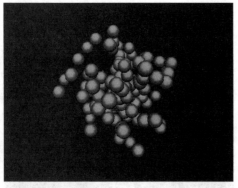

Figure 18.32 Spheres render as polygonal spheres that can be textured.

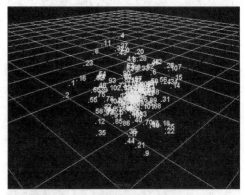

Figure 18.33 Numeric particles appear with specified information pertaining to the particle. Numeric particles render as dots.

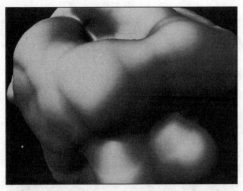

Figure 18.34 Blobby Surfaces render as spheres but look as though they're melting or blending together.

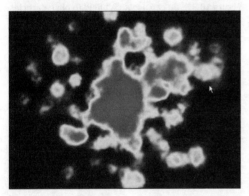

Figure 18.35 Clouds render as foggy or cloudy surfaces that are partially transparent.

Figure 18.36 Tubes render as cylindrical surfaces and look a bit like Streak particles; the difference is that you can render them via the Software Render window.

Software render types

Maya offers the following software render types for particles:

- **Blobby Surface**—Blobby Surface particles render as spheres that can appear to melt into one surface (**Figure 18.34**). Attributes include Radius and Threshold:
  - ▲ **Radius**—Determines the initial size of the particle.
  - ▲ **Threshold**—Determines how much the particles blend together. As the Threshold attribute increases, the radius of the particle diminishes, and the particle begins to blend with other particles.

- **Cloud**—Clouds render as spheres that grow more transparent as you move farther from the center (**Figure 18.35**). Clouds behave like Blobby Surfaces but render with a Particle Cloud shader. You can adjust the shader's density, color, and other attributes in the Hypershade. (See Chapter 13 for more information on shaders.)

- **Tube**—Tubes render as cylinders that grow as the animation progresses (**Figure 18.36**). You can specify where the cylinder begins and stops expanding with the Radius0 and Radius1 attributes. Tail Size determines the length of the tube.

RENDER TYPES

Fields

Fields are used in conjunction with particle objects to give them a specific behavior. Maya has nine types of fields: Air, Drag, Gravity, Newton, Radial, Turbulence, Uniform, Vortex, and Volume Axis. You can use more than one field on any particle object to achieve the desired motion for your animation.

The following is a list of field types and their effect on particle objects:

- **Air**—The Air field produces the effect of a moving volume of air (**Figure 18.37**). The three default Air field types are Wind, Wake, and Fan:

  ▲ **Wind**—This type of Air field blows particles in a specified direction until they catch up to the speed of the Air field.

  ▲ **Wake**—As the Air field moves through a particle object, it disturbs the particles and drags them along, creating a wake effect.

  ▲ **Fan**—This type of Air field pushes particles in a 45-degree spread, simulating a fan.

- **Drag**—The Drag field helps slow down, or add friction to, a moving particle.

- **Gravity**—The Gravity field simulates a real-world gravity effect on the selected particle; you can apply it in any direction you specify.

- **Newton**—A Newton field attracts particles.

- **Radial**—A Radial field attracts or repels particles in a spherical manner.

- **Turbulence**—A Turbulence field disrupts the position of the particles. You can use this field type to randomize the movement slightly for your particle animation.

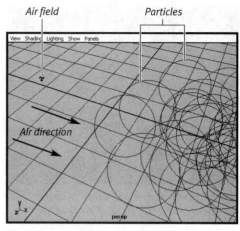

Figure 18.37 You can use an Air field to push particles in a specific direction.

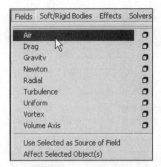

Figure 18.38 Choose Fields > Air.

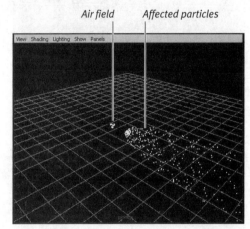

Air field   Affected particles

Figure 18.39 The Air field blows the particles in the
x direction.

♦ **Uniform**—This field's effect is similar to
that of the Air field: It pushes the particles in a specified direction.

♦ **Vortex**—A Vortex field exerts a spiraling
force on the particles. You can use it to
create a tornado effect.

♦ **Volume Axis**—A Volume Axis field is
defined by a volume shape. This lets you
affect particles with a shape, such as a
sphere or cube.

Common attributes

The following attributes are common to
all fields:

♦ **Magnitude**—Sets the amount of force
exerted from the field.

♦ **Attenuation**—Sets the degree to which
the force drops off as the affected object
moves away from the field. 0 means the
force is constant throughout the scene.

♦ **Direction**—Determines the direction of
the force, usually as an X, Y, Z value.

♦ **Use Max Distance**—Allows you to set
a maximum distance to define the area
of effect.

♦ **Max Distance**—Sets the value, in units,
that the field affects.

To attach a field to a particle object:

1. Create an emitter.

2. Click Play ▶ once to emit the particles;
click it again to halt playback.

3. Select the particles.

4. Choose Fields > Air (**Figure 18.38**).
This option attaches the field to the
selected object.

5. Play back the animation (**Figure 18.39**).

continues on next page

FIELDS

6. Select the Air field.

If you have trouble selecting the Air field, try selecting Window > Hypergraph and then clicking the Air field.

7. Open the Attribute Editor by pressing [Ctrl] / [Control] + [a].

8. On the Air Field Attributes tab, change Magnitude to 20 (**Figure 18.40**).

9. Play back the animation again to see the effect of the magnitude change.

The Air field pushes with more force as the magnitude increases.

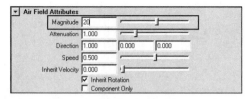

Figure 18.40 Increasing the Magnitude attribute of an Air field makes the particles blow away from it faster.

✔ Tip

■ You can animate Air field attributes. Try setting keyframes on the Magnitude attribute to make its value change over time.

Unless impacted by a new force, particles keep moving with the same rate of energy throughout a scene. The Drag field simulates a dampening effect on the particles, as if they were affected by friction in a real environment, such as air or water. The Drag field also has interesting effects when combined with other fields.

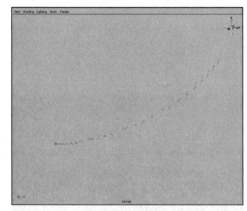

Figure 18.41 The gravitational force of a Newton field is similar to that of a planet and draws the particles to it.

To use a Drag field for effect:

1. Create a directional emitter with the settings Rate 200 and Spread .05.

2. Select particle1, and choose Fields > Newton.

3. Position the Newton field above and to the right of the emitter—in this case, at (1.25, .75, -.75).

The particles are drawn up into the field (**Figure 18.41**).

FIELDS

newtonField1	
Translate X	1.25
Translate Y	0.75
Translate Z	-0.75
Rotate X	0
Rotate Y	0
Rotate Z	0
Scale X	1
Scale Y	1
Scale Z	1
Visibility	on
Magnitude	10
Attenuation	1
Max Distance	-1

Figure 18.42 Set the Magnitude of the field to 10 to make it draw the particles into a rigid orbit.

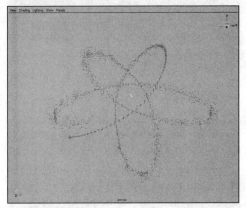

Figure 18.43 The particles enter into an elliptical orbit like electrons around a nucleus.

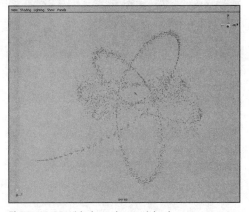

Figure 18.44 With drag, the particles lose energy on each pass and are gradually drawn into the center.

4. In the Channel Box, set the Magnitude of the field to 10 (**Figure 18.42**).

5. Press ▶ to see the effect of the field. You may need to set the length of your scene to around 300 frames to see the full effect.

The particles enter into orbit around the Newton field (**Figure 18.43**).

6. Select particle1, and choose Fields > Drag.

7. In the Channel Box, set the Magnitude of the Drag field to .1 and the Speed Attenuation to .2.

Speed Attenuation is a new feature in Maya 7.0 that lessens the effect of the field on slower moving particles.

8. Press ▶ to see the effect of the field.

The particles are now slowly drawn down to a steady orbit of the Newton field (**Figure 18.44**).

Collisions

If you had added a Gravity field to any of your particle objects, the particles would have fallen out of view because there was nothing in the scene to stop them. You can use the Make Collide command to tell Maya to make the particles collide with certain geometry.

For example, for a scene in which you want fog to roll along the ground, you can create a particle object, attach Air and Gravity fields, and have the particles collide with the ground. The particles then will fall to the ground and be pushed along by the Air field.

To create a particle collision:

1. Create a particle object and attach an Air field, following the steps in the task "To attach a field to a particle object."

2. Select the particle, and, from the Fields menu, select Gravity.

3. From the Create menu, select the box beside NURBS Primitives > Plane.

4. In the Options dialog box that opens, give the plane 10 patches in U and V.

5. Click Create.

6. Scale the plane so that it's large enough to represent the ground. Select a few CVs around the center of the plane, and translate them in the positive *y* direction to create a hill (**Figure 18.45**).

7. In object mode, translate the plane in the negative *y* direction so that the plane is below the particles.

8. Select the particle object and the ground plane (**Figure 18.46**).

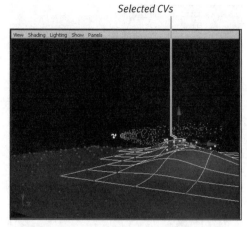

Selected CVs

Figure 18.45 Create a small hill for the particles to collide with.

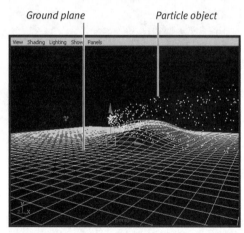

Ground plane   *Particle object*

Figure 18.46 Select the ground plane and the particle object to make them collide.

COLLISIONS

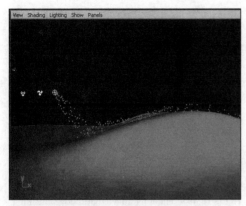

Figure 18.47 Particles collide with the ground geometry and flow over the hill.

9. From the Particles menu, select Make Collide.

10. Rewind the animation by clicking the Rewind button ⏮, and then click Play ▶ to see the effect.

    The particles now fall to the ground and are pushed along the surface by the Air field (**Figure 18.47**).

✔ Tip

- So you can more easily see and select the particles, select the particle, open the Attribute Editor by pressing Ctrl/Control+a, and change the render type to Cloud.

Rigid-Body Dynamics

Body dynamics are used to simulate the effect of forces and collisions on actual geometry. Maya contains two kinds of body dynamics: soft and rigid. Rigid bodies don't flex or bend, unlike soft bodies, which are elastic and pliable. By using Maya's rigid-body dynamics, you can simulate what occurs when one or more hard objects collide.

Imagine trying to animate a bowling ball crashing into 10 pins at the end of the alley—it would take a lot of time and talent to make that action appear realistic. Maya solves this problem by letting you define objects that you want to interact with (or hit) each other; Maya can then simulate what happens when they make contact (**Figure 18.48**).

You can create active rigid bodies, which react to collisions and fields (Gravity, Air, and so on), or you can create passive rigid bodies, which are unaffected by collisions or fields. You use passive rigid bodies for things like floors and walls—basically, any unmovable object that an active body will collide with.

To create a rigid-body simulation:

1. Create a NURBS sphere.

2. Translate the sphere in the positive *y* direction.

3. Create a NURBS plane, and scale it up to create the floor. Rotate it -5 degrees on the *z* axis (**Figure 18.49**).

4. Select the sphere.

5. From the Soft/Rigid Bodies menu, select Create Active Rigid Body (**Figure 18.50**).

Figure 18.48 A rendering from a rigid-body simulation. The ball collides with the pins, which in turn collide with the back wall, the floor, and each other.

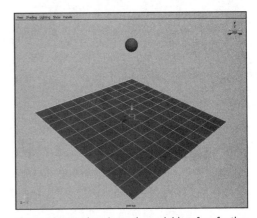

Figure 18.49 A plane is used as a rigid surface for the ball to bounce off.

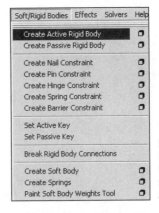

Figure 18.50 From the Soft/Rigid Bodies menu, select Create Active Rigid Body.

Figure 18.51 The more severe the rotation of the plane, the faster the sphere bounces off it.

Visibility	on
Magnitude	20
Attenuation	1
Max Distance	20
Apply Per Vertex	off
Use Max Distance	on
Volume Shape	None
Volume Exclusion	off
Volume Offset X	0
Volume Offset Y	0
Volume Offset Z	0
Section Radius	0.5
Volume Sweep	360
Direction X	-1
Direction Y	0
Direction Z	0

Figure 18.52 The Air field will create a strong wind in the –x direction.

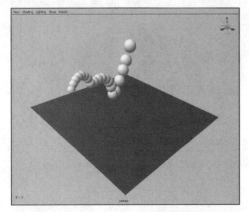

Figure 18.53 The wind blows the light sphere clear off the plane, despite the slope.

6. Select the plane.

7. From the Soft/Rigid Bodies menu, select Create Passive Rigid Body.

8. Select the sphere.

9. Choose Fields > Gravity.

    This attaches a Gravity field to the sphere to make it fall to the ground.

10. Play back the animation to see the result (**Figure 18.51**).

Bodies have additional properties for specifying simulated behavior. By changing these properties, you can make the geometry behave more like the objects it's supposed to represent. For example, you can assign a large mass to your bowling ball so that it doesn't merely bounce off the pins but rather plows through them.

To assign properties to a body:

1. Start with the scene from the previous task.

2. Select the sphere, and choose Fields > Air.

3. Set the Air field's magnitude to 20 and the direction to -1,0,0 (**Figure 18.52**).

4. Press ▶ to see the effects of the field.

    The sphere is blown right back off the slope because it's very light, like a beach ball (**Figure 18.53**).

continues on next page

5. Select the sphere, and press
[Ctrl]/[Control]+[a] to open the Attribute
Editor.

6. In the rigidBody2 tab, set the Mass to 30
and the Bounciness to .2 (**Figure 18.54**).

7. Press ▶ to see the effects of the changes.
The Sphere bounces minimally and continues rolling (**Figure 18.55**).

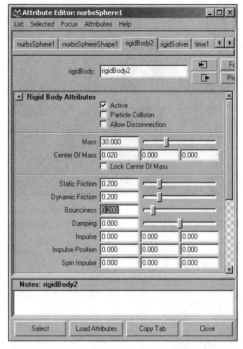

Figure 18.54 Set the ball to be heavy and less bouncy,
like a bowling ball.

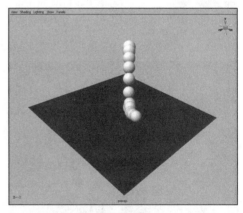

Figure 18.55 The heavy ball takes more energy to
move, so the wind affects it less.

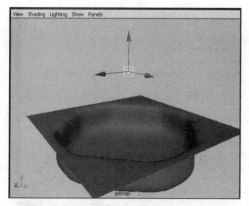

Figure 18.56 An Air field pushing part of a soft-body plane down in the negative *y* direction.

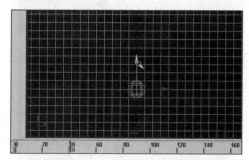

Figure 18.57 Setting a keyframe at frame 40 in the timeline.

Soft-Body Dynamics

Unlike rigid bodies, Maya's soft bodies have elasticity. Each CV, or vertex, has an associated particle, which can be affected by other dynamics (such as fields) or by particle collisions, thereby deforming the object (**Figure 18.56**).

With particles affecting the surface, you can make flags wave in the wind, gelatin cubes wiggle when they hit the ground, or a belly jiggle as a character walks.

Soft bodies can also use non-soft objects as goal shapes. A goal shape represents a target shape for the soft body to settle into. The particles affecting the soft body are attracted to the CVs, or vertices, of the goal object—almost as if they were attached by springs. This means that you can animate the original geometry, and the soft body will lag behind it, overshooting the original geometry before finally settling into that shape. An overweight man with a double chin that jiggles and lags behind the chin bone's movement is one example of this.

To create a soft body:

1. Create a NURBS sphere.

   In the timeline at frame 1, set a keyframe on the sphere by pressing ⓢ.

2. Move to frame 40 in the timeline.

3. Translate the sphere 10 units in the negative *y* direction (**Figure 18.57**). Set another keyframe by pressing ⓢ.

4. Move back to frame 1, and select the sphere.

5. From the Soft/Rigid Bodies menu, select the box next to Create Soft Body to open the options.

6. From the pop-up menu, select Duplicate, Make Copy Soft.

continues on next page

7. Check the boxes next to Hide Non-Soft Object and Make Non-Soft a Goal (**Figure 18.58**).

   These options duplicate and hide the original geometry and make the duplicate a soft body. The goal then will be the original animated geometry that is hidden.

8. Click Create.

   If you play back the animation now, the soft body jiggles slightly as a whole at the end of the motion. This is because the goal weights on the soft body are all even.

Goal weights can be adjusted, even painted, on a soft body so that you can get just the right amount of movement from your object. In the next task, you'll make the top of the sphere lag behind and wiggle as the sphere stops.

To adjust goal weights for a soft body:

1. Select the soft-body sphere.

2. From the Soft/Rigid Bodies menu, select the box beside Paint Soft Body Weights Tool.

   The Paint Attributes tool window opens, and your soft body turns white (**Figure 18.59**).

3. In the Tool Settings window for the Paint Attributes tool (which looks like the Attribute Editor), click the Reset Tool button at the top right.

4. In the Paint Attributes section, change Value to 0.5.

5. Paint the top of the sphere by clicking and dragging.

   The color on the top should turn gray (**Figure 18.60**).

6. Play back the animation.

   You should see the top jiggle as the sphere stops at frame 40 (**Figure 18.61**).

Figure 18.58 The options for creating a soft body.

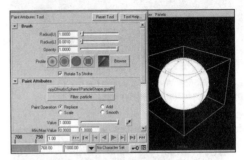

Figure 18.59 You use the Paint Attributes tool to paint soft-body goal weights.

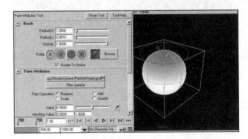

Figure 18.60 The Paint Attributes tool lets you interactively paint weight values on your objects.

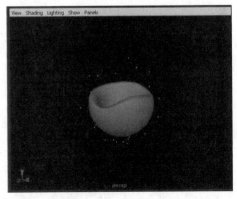

Figure 18.61 As the original sphere stops at frame 40, the soft body jiggles on the top until it comes to rest in its original shape.

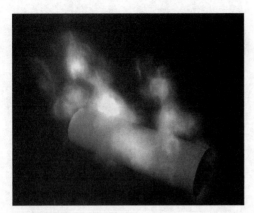

Figure 18.62 The Fire effect.

Effects

Maya provides all sorts of premade particle effects to set objects on fire, emit smoke, produce lightning, even make a river flow through a valley. You can produce all of these effects with particles on your own, but the presets provide a quick and easy way to get started on common effects. None of these look ideal by default, so you'll need to adjust them to get a more polished effect.

When you choose an effect from the menu, Maya creates a whole new network of particles and shaders automatically. In some cases, it also adds its own attributes and expressions to make adjusting the effect easy. When you make fire using the Create Fire effect, for example, Maya automatically connects Turbulence, Gravity, and Drag fields to the particles, as well as a premade shader and special expressions to give you added control.

Here is a brief description of each of the seven premade effects:

◆ **Create Fire**—Produces an emitter that has Gravity, Drag, and Turbulence fields attached to a Cloud particle. You can set Density, Radius, Direction, and Intensity using the Options menu. Fire can be emitted from a surface, curve, or directional point. A directional point emits fire particles in a specified direction from any point in space (**Figure 18.62**).

continues on next page

EFFECTS

◆ **Create Smoke**—Produces an emitter that uses Sprite images instead of Clouds or Points (**Figure 18.63**). To use a particular set of images, select Sprite Wizard from the Particles menu. A default set of images and directions are included with the program. You can set Lifespan, Opacity, Direction, Spread, and Speed in the Options menu.

◆ **Create Fireworks**—Produces a cluster of rockets and explosions according to the options you set (**Figure 18.64**).

◆ **Create Lightning**—Creates an animated electric bolt between two or more objects (**Figure 18.65**). You can adjust Thickness, Spread, Jagged Sections, Glow, and Light Intensity in the Options menu.

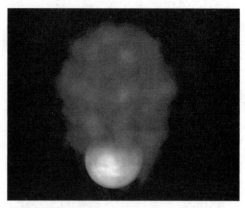

Figure 18.63 The Smoke effect.

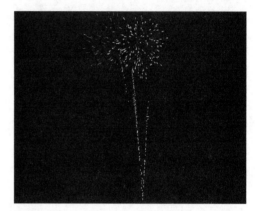

Figure 18.64 The Fireworks effect.

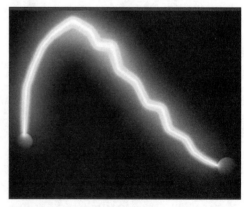

Figure 18.65 The Lightning effect.

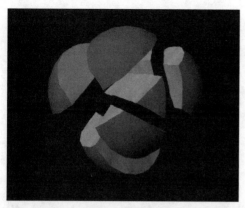

Figure 18.66 The Shatter effect.

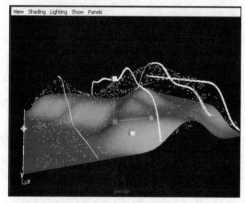

Figure 18.67 The Surface Flow effect.

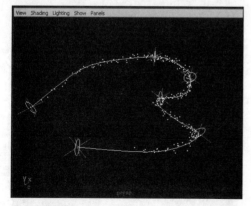

Figure 18.68 The Curve Flow effect.

◆ **Create Shatter**—Lets you break apart an object into a specified number of pieces (**Figure 18.66**). There are three types of Shatter: Surface, Solid, and Crack.

◆ **Create Surface Flow**—Creates manipulators that direct particles to flow along a NURBS surface (**Figure 18.67**).

◆ **Create Curve Flow**—Produces manipulators to control the flow of particles along a curve's path (**Figure 18.68**).

To make an object emit fire:

1. Create a polygon cylinder. Rotate and scale it to represent a log (**Figure 18.69**).

2. Select the cylinder, and, from the Effects menu, select Create Fire.

3. Click Play ▷ to start the fire simulation (**Figure 18.70**).

4. Click Stop ◼ at any point in the timeline, and render the Perspective view to see the results.

5. Select the particles, and open the Attribute Editor. Go to the particleShape1tab.

6. Under Extra Attributes, change Fire Density to 20, Fire Lifespan to 0.2, and Fire Speed to 10; then play back the animation to see the effect (**Figure 18.71**).

   Try changing these and other attributes to get a different type of fire effect.

7. Make your changes. Rewind, play, stop, and render to see the results.

✔ Tip

- To create realistic fire, you may wish to place several different fire systems on the same object and tune each one separately. That way, you can get different effects in the same fire, such as small flickering flames around the edge, big roaring flames in the middle, and sparks coming off the whole thing.

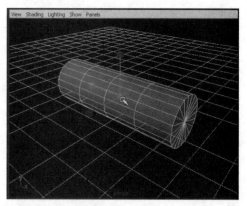

Figure 18.69 A cylinder used to represent a log.

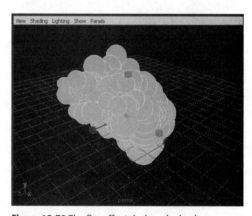

Figure 18.70 The fire effect during playback.

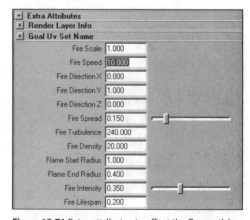

Figure 18.71 Extra attributes to affect the fire particles.

Figure 18.72 Two spheres used to create a lightning effect.

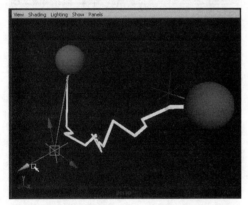

Figure 18.73 Select the locator, and move it to put an arc in the lightning bolt.

Selection handle

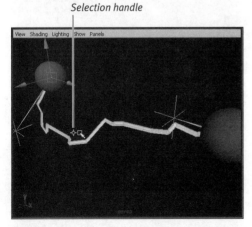

Figure 18.74 The selection handle for the lightning effect.

To create lightning:

1. Create two spheres, and translate them so that they aren't overlapping (**Figure 18.72**).

2. Select both spheres.

3. From the Effects menu, select Create Lightning.

   A zigzag appears between the two spheres. Also created are two locators, a light, and a selection handle.

4. Select one of the locators, and translate it away from the objects.

   The lightning now has a curve in its trajectory (**Figure 18.73**).

5. Select the selection handle in the middle of the lightning object (**Figure 18.74**).

6. In the Channel Box, adjust the attributes for Thickness, Start and End, and Color to get the desired effect.

   You can also find these attributes in the Attribute Editor on the Lightning1 tab in the Extra Attributes section.

✔ Tip

■ Lightning often travels from one location to another. The Lightning Start and Lightning End controls dictate where the end points of the bolt are. Animating these attributes can make the bolt appear to travel from one object to the other.

EFFECTS

531

The Dynamic Relationships Editor

Sometimes you'll want to attach a particle object or a rigid or soft body to an existing field or collision object. The Dynamic Relationships Editor lets you see a list of a scene's nodes as well as the existing fields, collisions, and emitters—all of which you can then connect.

To connect a field to a particle using the Dynamic Relationships Editor:

1. From the Particles menu, select Create Emitter.

2. Choose Fields > Gravity.

   If you play the animation at this point, the particles won't fall because the particle object wasn't selected when you created the Gravity field—which means the two aren't connected.

3. Choose Window > Relationship Editors > Dynamic Relationships.

   On the left side of the editor is a list of the scene's nodes. You should see emitter1, particle1, and gravityField1 in this column (**Figure 18.75**).

4. Select particle1 from the left column.

   Now, on the right side of the editor, gravityField1 appears in the list. It's not highlighted at this point because the two nodes have not been connected.

5. Click gravityField1 on the right side of the editor (**Figure 18.76**).

   Particle1 is now connected to gravityField1.

6. Play back the animation to make sure the Gravity field has caused the particles to fall.

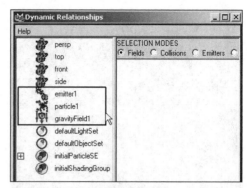

Figure 18.75 The Dynamic Relationships Editor.

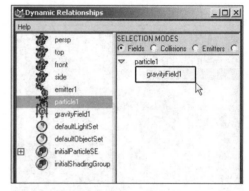

Figure 18.76 Connecting a particle object to a gravity field in the Dynamic Relationships Editor.

INDEX

P.S.
when things are the other way around its just my fault. and I'm a bad boyfriend.

my prediction-
elain will yell at me because if i never asked her to come over then she would've never had dropped my ds addon. yes, this day cannot be her fault nor her attitude's fault. it is somehow my fault for wanting our relationship to be fair. yes, i'm brainwashed for thinking that its not ok for me to visit her once a week and be intimate with her. i'm brainwashed into thinking this relationship is one way.